REPAIRING THE REGIME

REPAIRING
—THE—
REGIME

PREVENTING THE SPREAD
OF WEAPONS
OF MASS DESTRUCTION

EDITED BY

JOSEPH
CIRINCIONE

ROUTLEDGE
NEW YORK   LONDON

Published in 2000 by
Routledge
29 West 35th Street
NewYork, NY 10001

Published in Great Britain by
Routledge
11 New Fetter Lane
London EC4P 4EE

Printed in the United States of America
on acid-free paper. Designed and typeset by
The Whole Works®, New York

10 9 8 7 6 5 4 3 2 1

Library of Congress Cataloging-in-Publication Data

Repairing the regime : preventing the spread of weapons of mass
destruction/ edited by Joseph Cirincione.
p. cm.
Includes bibliographical references.
ISBN 0-415-92595-9 (hc) — ISBN 0-415-92596-7 (pb)
1. Nuclear arms control. 2. Nuclear nonproliferation.
3. Chemical arms control. 4. Biological arms control.
5. Weapons of mass destruction.
I. Cirincione, Joseph

JZ5665 .R47 2000
327.1'745 — dc21
99-056509

CONTENTS

ACKNOWLEDGMENTS

In January 1999, over 450 experts, officials, academics, and journalists gathered in Washington, D.C., for the Carnegie International Non-Proliferation Conference. The stimulating and insightful discussions of the conference participants became the catalyst for this writing project. I am grateful for their permission to adapt several of their presentations and panel debates as chapters for this book. I appreciate the scholarship and diligence of David Albright, Mathew Bunn, Camille Grand, Neil Joeck, Richard Speier, Alexander Pikayev, Dan Morrow, and Michael Carrier, all of whom prepared papers specifically commissioned for this volume.

Repairing the Regime has been prepared under the auspices of the Carnegie Endowment for International Peace and is supported by generous grants to the Non-Proliferation Project from the Carnegie Corporation of New York, the W. Alton Jones Foundation, the Ford Foundation, the John Merck Fund, the Ploughshares Fund, and Prospect Hill Foundation. I am especially grateful to Carnegie Endowment president Jessica Mathews and vice president Tom Carothers for their support, inspiration, and valuable suggestions throughout the conference planning and editing process.

This book would not have been possible without the dedicated work of the Carnegie Non-Proliferation Project staff. Jon Wolfsthal and Toby Dalton did a superb job at all levels: assisting in all the editing, editing several chapters in their entirety, organizing the process, keeping the editor calm, and supervising the production of the detailed appendixes and charts that help make this volume a valuable research tool. Matt Rice, a junior fellow with the project, helped immensely: first with the conference, then with the original book proposal and (before departing for law school) with the initial editing. Researchers Denis Dragovic and Janice Sung got more than they bargained for in their summer jobs, with each providing critical facts, charts, and tables (Janice on chemical and biological weapons, Denis on nuclear and missile stockpiles) and fine-tuning the chapters. Junior fellow Todd Sechser assisted with the final stages of production and fact-checking and with designing the website that complements this printed product. Project interns Bonnie Burset and Joshua Hanson provided valuable fact-checking and research assistance during the completion of the manuscript. My warm thanks also to Toni Elam, who helped plan and execute the conference, transcribe the sessions, and administer the book's production.

We could not have staged the conference without the professional services of co-ordinator Kim Sescoe from Special ProjX. Special thanks go to Eric Nelson and Amy Shipper from Routledge who are responsible for bringing this book to press. I would also like to thank Carnegie librarians Jennifer Little, Kathleen Daly, and Christopher Henley for their kind, precise, and incredibly rapid help in obtaining obscure research materials with a moment's notice.

Finally, I would like to thank my wife, Priscilla, and my growing children, Amy and Peter, for allowing me to put in long hours at work, have a great time doing it, and always come home to a warm and loving family.

Joseph Cirincione
Director, Non-Proliferation Project
Carnegie Endowment for International Peace

FOREWORD

For over fifteen years, scholars at the Carnegie Endowment for International Peace have tracked the spread of weapons of mass destruction around the globe. During that time, the Carnegie Non-Proliferation Project has produced a steady stream of insightful analysis and reliable reports from its offices in Washington and—for the past six years—Moscow. A vital element of this research effort has been the regular Carnegie International Non-Proliferation Conferences.

Begun in 1989, the annual conference has detailed the challenges of preventing proliferation and has grown into the premier event of its type in the foreign policy field. United Nations Undersecretary-General Jayantha Dhanapala notes later in this volume, "The annual Carnegie conferences have become somewhat of an institution in themselves. . . . They have helped both to forge a global community of informed citizens that are equipped to address these challenges and to sensitize that community to the perils and pitfalls in our work to achieve these solemn goals."

Over 450 experts, officials, and journalists from seventeen nations attended the Carnegie conference in Washington on January 11 and 12, 1999. This volume emerged from their energetic discussions and debates. Editor Joseph Cirincione, who also serves as project director, commissioned many of the following chapters from the conference participants especially for this collection. In other cases, he has artfully edited some of the more intriguing panel discussions and presentations to capture in print the dynamic exchanges that took place when, for example, representatives from the United States, Israel, and Russia sat down to discuss Russia's assistance to Iran's missile program. Also captured are the hopes, plans, and proposals advanced at the conference by senior government officials, including U.S. National Security Adviser Sandy Berger and Secretary of Energy Bill Richardson, China's director general of arms control and disarmament, Sha Zukang, and Russia's first deputy minister of atomic energy, Lev Ryabev. Thus, the reader will have the opportunity to judge how well the nations implemented their respective agendas. But critics should take care not to judge too harshly from the comfort of their armchairs. These have been tough times for the global regime.

OVERVIEW

The last two years of the twentieth century have been critical years for nonproliferation and for global efforts to control weapons of mass destruction. Of the many significant events in these years, four stand out: the nuclear tests in May 1998 by India and Pakistan; the August 1998 political and economic crisis in Russia; in Iraq, the first-ever war in the name of non-proliferation; and the failure of the U.S. Senate to ratify the Comprehensive Test Ban Treaty (CTBT).

There is of course much more beyond just those headlines. There has been the on-again, off-again prospect of ratifying the second Strategic Arms Reduction Treaty. Missile tests in North Korea have seriously threatened the 1994 Agreed Framework Agreement. U.S. relations with China deteriorated over congressional charges of nuclear espionage, while missile tests in Iran placed deep strains on U.S.-Russia relations. These tensions were further exacerbated by the war in Kosovo and by U.S. plans to deploy anti-missile defense systems. There were also the bombing of Osama Bin Laden's alleged chemical weapons facility and a general lack of progress on both the Biological Weapons Convention (BWC) and the CTBT ratification.

On the positive side, there has been some real progress on the fissile material production agreement. Brazil's ratification of both the CTBT and the Nuclear Non-Proliferation Treaty (NPT) put a cap on seven years of remarkable progress in South America. What was a very serious proliferation standoff between Argentina and Brazil now stands with both countries having turned away from that route and joining the regime.

What can we make of this mixed bag of events? We can draw a few observations. First, it's too soon for history to judge most of these developments. Clearly, there's very little that's unequivocally positive in this list, and it's fair to say that the apparent negatives well outweigh the positives. But it is still too early for conclusions. For example, in South Asia, if, through economic and diplomatic pressure, India and Pakistan join the CTBT and Fissile Material Cut-Off Treaty, and if there is agreement not to deploy missiles, then it's possible that history will judge the tests quite differently than we may see them today.

We don't know yet whether 1998 and 1999 will turn out to be just a delay or a permanent turning point in the wrong direction on the CTBT and on the BWC. We don't know whether the Agreed Framework in North Korea will hold. We don't know whether START II will ultimately be ratified or sidestepped on the way to START III or some other more positive path. We can't tell yet what path Russia will ultimately follow and what will be the long-term consequences of its political and economic crisis on national security and weapons of mass destruction (WMD) policy.

Probably the clearest negative of the past two years has been the unraveling of what seemed to be, just one year ago, a major success for international cooperation, namely, the United Nations Special Commission on Iraq, or UNSCOM. At the beginning of 1998, we were looking at an international operation sustained through extraordinary difficulties and unceasing resistance, operating with enormous delicacy and difficulty in collaboration and operational intelligence sharing. To a much larger extent than military operations during the Gulf War, UNSCOM ferreted out, uncovered, and stymied Iraq's WMD plans. By the beginning of 1999, it looked very different, as UNSCOM inspections ground to a complete halt.

The second conclusion has to do with whether we're looking at the whole or its parts. For as long as we have had a non-proliferation community, there has been tension between those who look at the big picture—the importance of maintaining a global regime underpinned by universal norms—and believe that each individual state's security lies in the integrity of that regime and those who say non-proliferation has to begin with the particular, with the individual security needs of each country or group of countries. The proponents of the latter view argue that norms are fine, but a military threat across the border is something quite else: that a country will always make its decisions based on concrete realities rather than a universal norm. In this view, a successful non-proliferation approach can only be built by dealing with security needs case by case and putting the global agreements very much in the background. Otherwise, in this view, there is the possibility that we would have the satisfaction of casting a very broad net only to see the very few fish that really matter swim away from it.

This long-persisting tension was brought to the fore by the South Asian tests. We were forced to confront very directly whether the global norm or the security needs of the region should take precedence in deciding how to respond. While it's too soon for judgments, it appears that the right answer is a delicately blended mix of the two.

A third observation recalls a now famous American political conclusion, "It's the economy, stupid." That slogan was posted in the Clinton presidential campaign head-quarters in 1992, and it meant: "This is the only issue in this election, everything comes back to the economy." That is not literally true on the international scale, but to a degree we've never seen before, security issues have been supplanted by eco-nomic ones as both the driving force of non-proliferation and as one of the tools for dealing with crises. In Russia, for example, the need for economic security drives government policy on exports and international assistance, while international con-cerns for the security of the existing Russian stockpiles of fissile materials and nuclear weapons stem from the government's inability to pay for those who guard and maintain them.

On the positive side, it would appear that in both Russia and the United States, economic forces provide perhaps the strongest momentum for continued progress in strategic weapons reduction. Economic forces have also been both a major motiva-tion behind North Korea's missile program (for export earnings) and a potentially powerful tool for constraining the program. Following the tests in South Asia, we have seen how strongly economic sanctions can work when their effect is multiplied by the judgments of the private marketplace.

These issues, trends, and dilemmas are carefully examined in the volume before you. It provides strong arguments for both marshaling international resources to repair and sustain the global non-proliferation regime and for dealing concretely with the particular security concerns of the nations and regions most affected by the new proliferation threats. True to his mandate to keep the endowment on the cutting edge of these debates, the editor has also uploaded to the Internet an extensive supplement to this book with updates to all the tables, charts, and chapters, allowing the reader to get the latest information by simply clicking on: www.ceip.org.

Jessica Mathews
President, Carnegie Endowment for International Peace
August 1999

I ask you to stop and think for a moment what
it would mean to have nuclear weapons in
so many hands, in the hands of countries large
and small, stable and unstable, responsible and
irresponsible, scattered throughout the world.
There would be no rest for anyone then, no
stability, no real security, and no chance of effective
disarmament. There would only be the increased
chance of accidental war, and an increased necessity
for the great powers to involve themselves in what
otherwise would be local conflicts.

John F. Kennedy
—July 26, 1963

—GLOBAL—
ASSESSMENT

—1—

Historical Overview and Introduction

Joseph Cirincione

The first post Cold War decade was in many ways a period of progress and global growth. The world's population grew 10 percent to six billion people. The American economy enjoyed its longest peacetime expansion ever, with the Dow Jones industrial average rocketing from 2,600 to almost 12,000. Many other economies also prospered, as Asian countries expanded, crashed, and rebounded. Not coincidentally, the world's nations now spend 30 to 40 percent less on defense than they did during the Cold War, despite several major regional conflicts. Computers increased exponentially in speed, cell phones multiplied even faster, and the Internet grew from a backup system for nuclear war to an indispensable global network linking students, experts, and nations. It was a remarkable decade for the sciences, particularly astronomy, as space- and ground-based instruments extended our vision closer to the far edges of the universe and the beginning of time.

In one crucial area, though, the past decade failed to live up to expectations. The threat of the mass destruction of human beings by the most heinous weapons ever invented still haunts world capitals and vexes military and political leaderships. During the 1990s, fears that some group or nation would use internationally banned biological or chemical weapons actually increased. United Nations inspectors after the 1991 Persian Gulf War discovered that Iraq had assembled hundreds of weapons filled with VX and sarin nerve gas and two dozen others with biological agents, including anthrax, botulinum toxin, and aflatoxin (see tables in chapter 11). The 1995 sarin gas attack on the Tokyo subway by the Japanese cult Aum Shinrikyo led some experts to warn of future "superterrorism" battles. U.S. Secretary of Defense William Cohen calls it "a grave new world of terrorism—a world in which traditional notions of deterrence and counter-response no longer apply."[1]

Other experts caution that the media and fictional novels have exaggerated the chemical and biological weapon threats. Few can ignore, however, the brooding presence of the mountain of nuclear weapons and nuclear materials that still fill global arsenals. As the new millennium begins, eight nations possess a total of almost 32,000 nuclear bombs containing 5,000 megatons of destructive energy. The equivalent of about 416,000 Hiroshima-size bombs, a global arsenal more than sufficient to destroy the world.[2]

With the collapse of the Soviet Union, the danger is no longer a global thermonuclear war. Americans do not fear thousands of Soviet warheads screaming over the Pole; nor do Russians worry about volleys of American warheads pulverizing their nation. However, there remains a very real danger that nuclear, biological, or chemical weapons will be used in smaller—but still horrifically deadly—numbers. Whether delivered in the cargo hold of a ship, the belly of an airplane, or the tip of a missile, the use of just one thermonuclear weapon would be the most catastrophic event in recorded history. A 1-megaton bomb would destroy fifty square miles of an urban area, killing or seriously injuring one million to two million people.[3] Even a smaller, more portable device of 100 kilotons (eight times larger than the Hiroshima bomb but small by today's standards) would result in a radiation zone twenty to forty miles long and two to three miles wide in which all exposed persons would receive a lethal dose of radiation within six hours.[4]

It is not difficult to find official expressions of concern about the mounting proliferation problems.

- President Clinton on several occasions has cited "the unusual and extraordinary threat to the national security, foreign policy, and economy of the United States posed by the proliferation of nuclear, biological, and chemical weapons and the means of delivering such weapons."[5]
- Secretary of Defense William Cohen said, "Of the challenges facing the Department of Defense in the future, none is greater or more complex than the threat posed by weapons of mass destruction."[6]
- Secretary of State Madeleine Albright noted, "The proliferation of weapons of mass destruction is the single most pressing threat to our security."[7] She and then Russian foreign minister Yevgeny Primakov agreed at the 1998 ASEAN summit that non-proliferation was the "premier security issue of the post–Cold War period."
- Lieutenant General Patrick Hughes, director of the Defense Intelligence Agency, concluded bluntly in his annual testimony to Congress, "The proliferation of nuclear, chemical, and biological weapons, missiles, and other key technologies remains the greatest direct threat to U.S. interests worldwide."[8]
- In January 1992, the member states of the United Nations Security Council declared that the spread of weapons of mass destruction constituted a "threat to international peace and security." Chapter VII of the UN Charter authorizes the Security Council to impose economic sanctions or to use military force to counter such threats.

One might expect that the response would be to redouble efforts to stop the spread of these deadly weapons, including the ratification of treaties and agreements to prevent and reduce the threats. In fact, the reverse is occurring.

THE NON-PROLIFERATION REGIME

The first and strongest line of defense against the spread or use of weapons of mass destruction remains the non-proliferation regime—an interlocking network of treaties, agreements, and organizations. Centered on a series of treaties including the nuclear Non-Proliferation Treaty (NPT), the Chemical Weapons Convention, and the Biological Weapons Convention, the regime is buttressed by numerous multilateral and bilateral agreements, norms, and arrangements.[9]

The non-proliferation regime has been built over the past fifty years by many nations, but almost always with the leadership of the United States. It has grown most quickly and most surely when both major U.S. political parties shared in the construction. The initiatives of one president or Congress would often be fulfilled by the next, regardless of party affiliation. Over these decades, Republican presidents have often led the efforts, as described below.

Now, a series of crises has shaken confidence in the regime. It urgently needs repair and revitalization but suffers from inattention and the mutual mistrust of many of its members. As we enter the new century, concerns with missile and nuclear programs in North Korea, Iran, and Iraq remain unresolved; the slow-motion arms race in South Asia keeps both nations intent on deploying nuclear weapons; Russia—the world's largest warehouse of nuclear weapons, materials, and expertise—spirals in economic decline; China modernizes its nuclear arsenal, Japan partners with the United States in missile defense, and the three nations link with the Koreas, Taiwan, India, and Pakistan to form an Asian nuclear reaction chain that vibrates dangerously with each nation's defense deployments. Meanwhile, international negotiations at the Conference on Disarmament and the Non-Proliferation Treaty review sessions drift inconclusively; the Republican-dominated U.S. Senate delivered a stunning rejection of the Comprehensive Test Ban Treaty three years after it was signed; and it appears that President Clinton may complete his eight years in office without signing a single strategic nuclear reductions treaty, as compared with the two his predecessor signed during his four-year term.

This volume is dedicated to a detailed discussion of the problems confronting the regime—and the potential solutions—in the hope that greater knowledge will inspire greater actions. The writings concentrate on nuclear proliferation, but increasingly the once distinct areas of nuclear, chemical, and biological weapons proliferation form an integrated whole. Developments in one area—good or bad—inevitably reverberate throughout the system. The authors also tackle one of the central issues confronting a regime under assault by hard-line conservatives in the United States: Is it military might or "pieces of paper" that best ensure national security?

THE REGIME WORKS

The need for military counters to the proliferation of weapons of mass destruction remains a necessary condition of international affairs. Certainly, the threat of devastating retaliation helps deter the use of these weapons. Today, conventional forces alone threaten national destruction on a scale that few leaders would risk. Nations also have a variety of counterforce options deployed and in development to strike mass destruction weapons, launchers, and facilities before they can be used. Finally, should all else fail, a third line of active missile defenses might provide some protection. Missile defenses, however, have a dual nature. While they promise an alluring technological solution to one type of mass destruction delivery system, mere talk of their introduction stimulates the very arsenals they hope to deter.

Historically the non-proliferation regime has one great factor in its favor: It works. Not even the most fervent advocate would claim the regime works perfectly, and there exists a long line of experts (as this volume demonstrates) ready to discuss in detail the flaws in the regime.

Nonetheless, since its birth the non-proliferation regime has, if not prevented, at least greatly restricted, the spread of mass destruction weapons. President John F. Kennedy worried in the early 1960s that while only the United States, the Soviet Union, the United Kingdom, and France then possessed nuclear weapons, fifteen or twenty nations could obtain them by the end of the decade. However, with determined bipartisan presidential efforts and global cooperation, only China had joined the ranks of the five recognized nuclear weapon states by 1970.

Fifteen years ago, experts and governments warily eyed the nuclear proliferation risks posed by the top ten states of concern: India, Israel, South Africa, Pakistan, Argentina, Brazil, Iraq, Libya, South Korea, and Taiwan.[10] Today, three of these (South Africa, Argentina,and Brazil) have abandoned their nuclear weapon programs, two (South Korea and Taiwan) would be a risk only if their regional situation sharply deteriorates, one (Libya) is of moderate concern, one (Iraq) remains of high concern, and three (India, Pakistan, and Israel) now have nuclear weapons. There are other states that bear watching, but over the past fifteen years only two other nations of high concern must be added to the list: North Korea and Iran, for a total of seven countries remaining on the active nuclear proliferation "watch list."

At the same time, the governments have used the instruments of the regime on a number of fronts with impressive results. Perhaps the most historically significant is the successful denuclearization of Ukraine, Belarus, and Kazakhstan (after those new nations had inherited thousands of nuclear weapons from the dissolution of the Soviet Union in 1991) and the implementation of the Nunn-Lugar-Domenici Cooperative Threat Reduction programs in the states of the former Soviet Union. These programs provide, for example, financial and technical assistance to help the states of the former Soviet Union fulfill their obligations under the first Strategic Arms Reduction Treaty (START I). For the cost of one B-2 bomber ($2.5 billion over the last seven years) these programs have funded the deactivation of 4,838 nuclear warheads and the elimination of 387 nuclear ballistic missiles, 343 ballistic missile silos, 136 nuclear submarine launch tubes, and 49 long-range nuclear bombers in the former Soviet Union.

On other diplomatic fronts, the Intermediate Nuclear Forces Treaty eliminated an entire class of missiles from the arsenals of the United States and the Soviet Union (846 U.S. and 1,846 Soviet missiles, including the modern Pershing II and SS-20 systems). UNSCOM inspectors in Iraq uncovered and verified the destruction of far more biological and chemical weapons and facilities than were destroyed in the massive bombing and ground assaults of the 1991 Persian Gulf War. The Agreed Framework with North Korea, for all its problems, is successfully containing and perhaps reversing a nuclear weapons program that threatened to plunge the Korean peninsula into war in 1994. A Council on Foreign Relations Task Force concluded, "The Agreed Framework stands as the major bulwark against a return to the kind of calamitous military steps the United States was forced to consider in 1994 to stop North Korea's nuclear program."[11]

Meanwhile, South Africa dismantled its arsenal of six clandestine nuclear devices in the early 1990s and joined the NPT and the African Nuclear Free Zone. Algeria flirted with a secret nuclear program but renounced such ambitions and joined the NPT in 1995. Argentina and Brazil formalized the end of their nuclear programs by acceding to the NPT in 1995 and 1998, respectively.

The regime has sustained serious setbacks and defeats; there may very well be more in the near future; and there remains a distinct possibility of a catastrophic collapse of the regime. Overall, however, the treaty regime has done a remarkable job of checking the unrestricted global proliferation Kennedy feared.

A GLOBAL LEADERSHIP, NOW DIVIDED

The regime is a true international effort. Large states and small have all played crucial roles. Ireland, for example, introduced the United Nations resolution in 1961 that began the negotiations for the Non-Proliferation Treaty. South Africa played a key role in the extension and strengthening of the NPT in 1995, and Australia was instrumental in securing the successful negotiation of the Comprehensive Test Ban Treaty in 1996. As the discussion in chapter 18 details, states capable of making nuclear weapons but who have eschewed their development, such as Canada, Sweden, South Africa, and Brazil, are critical to efforts to forge a new agenda for the regime.

The United States, however, plays a unique role. While some demonize it as the source of many of the regime's problems, the United States remains the one nation in the world with the resources, status, and potential leadership capable of galvanizing international non-proliferation efforts. That leadership role has always been strongest when it has enjoyed the support of both major political parties. The relative inability of the United States to lead now can be traced in large part to the fierce partisan divide that characterizes American politics at the turn of the century.

The proliferation policy debates of the past few years have been dominated by calls from influential members of the U.S. Congress and their allies for increases in military spending, for more resolute opposition to arms control treaties, and for the rapid deployment of new weapons systems, particularly missile defenses.

Numerous senators took to the Senate floor in the days after the India tests, citing the "India threat" as justification for a crash program to field a national missile defense system. Although the legislation was blocked (twice) by Democrats, Senate Majority Leader Trent Lott said in support of the bill, "Only effective missile defense, not unenforceable arms control treaties, will break the offensive arms race in Asia and provide incentives to address security concerns without a nuclear response."

Hundreds of articles and speeches by conservatives have used the South Asian tests and the Korean and Iranian missile launches as proof that future threats are inherently unpredictable, intelligence estimates are consistently unreliable, the proliferation of weapons of mass destruction is fundamentally unstoppable, and, thus, the only truly effective response is reliance on American defense technology. Conservatives have skillfully deployed expert commissions and congressional investigations to endorse this view.

The reports of the Rumsfeld Commission on the Ballistic Missile Threat to the United States in 1998 and the Cox Committee on U.S. National Security and the People's Republic of China in 1999 were particularly influential in shaping media and political elite opinion. The Clinton administration's response has been to cede ground, embracing increased defense budgets and missile defense (the Republican bill cited above has been passed and signed into law) while husbanding the political and personal capital that could be devoted to threat reduction. With the most conservative elements of the Republican Party in control of congressional committees, treaty ratifications and diplomatic appointments have been delayed for years. The Senate's rejection of the Comprehensive Test Ban Treaty (an agreement supported by every U.S. ally and friend) on October 13, 1999, capped a dismal congressional record of disdain for multilateral solutions. The impact is global. A regime in need of repair and revitalization remains in a state of suspended anticipation.

A REPUBLICAN-BUILT REGIME

It was not always this way. The non-proliferation regime has enjoyed bipartisan support in the United States for most of the past fifty years. In fact, a quick historical review indicates that many may have overlooked the important role Republican presidents played in creating and nurturing the regime.

Efforts to contain the spread of weapons of mass destruction began immediately after World War II, spurred by the initiatives of Presidents Truman, Eisenhower, and Kennedy.[12] As part of his efforts, President Dwight D. Eisenhower proposed the creation of the International Atomic Energy Agency (IAEA) to promote the peaceful uses of atomic energy while the world's nuclear powers "began to diminish the potential destructive power of the world's atomic stockpiles."[13]

President Kennedy presented a "Program for General and Complete Disarmament" to the United Nations on September 25, 1961. His ambitious plan included all the elements that negotiators still pursue today: a comprehensive nuclear test ban; a ban on the production of fissile materials for use in weapons (plutonium and highly enriched uranium); the placement of all weapons materials under international safeguards; a ban on the transfer of nuclear weapons, their materials, or their technology; and deep reductions in existing nuclear weapons and their delivery vehicles, with the goal of eventually eliminating them. In his short tenure, President Kennedy was able only to secure the Limited Test Ban Treaty, ending nuclear tests in the atmosphere, under water, and in outer space.

In 1968, President Lyndon Johnson successfully completed negotiations for the Treaty on the Non-Proliferation of Nuclear Weapons. President Richard Nixon signed the treaty, bringing it into force, at a Rose Garden ceremony on March 5, 1970. "Let us trust that we will look back," he said, "and say that this was one of the first and major steps in that process in which the nations of the world moved from a period of confrontation to a period of negotiation and a period of lasting peace."

President Nixon followed his treaty signing with efforts that successfully established in the early 1970s the Non-Proliferation Treaty Exporters Committee (known as the Zangger Committee) to control the export of nuclear weapons-related materials and equipment. He negotiated and implemented the Anti-Ballistic Missile (ABM) Treaty limiting defensive armaments and the companion Strategic Arms Limitation Treaty (SALT) limiting offensive arms, both signed in May 1972.

President Nixon also dramatically announced in November 1969 that the United States would unilaterally and unconditionally renounce biological weapons. He ordered the destruction of all U.S. weapons stockpiles and the conversion of all production facilities for peaceful purposes.[14] At the same time he announced that after forty-four years of U.S. reluctance, he would seek ratification of the 1925 Geneva Protocol prohibiting the use in war of biological and chemical weapons (subsequently ratified under President Gerald Ford on January 22, 1975). The president renounced the first use of lethal or incapacitating chemical agents and weapons, unconditionally renounced all methods of biological warfare, and threw the resources of the United States behind the effort to negotiate a Biological Weapons Convention. The treaty, signed by President Nixon on April 10, 1972, and ratified by the Senate in December 1974, prohibits the development, production, stockpiling, acquisition, and transfer of biological weapons.

Presidential candidate Ronald Reagan opposed the SALT II treaty negotiated by President Jimmy Carter, but, as President, Reagan observed the treaty's limits for years after assuming office. In his second term, President Reagan negotiated and signed on December 8, 1987, the landmark Intermediate-Range Nuclear Forces Treaty, a process begun by President Jimmy Carter's two-track policy of deployment and negotiation. The treaty required the destruction of all U.S. and Soviet missiles and their launchers with ranges between 500 and 5,500 kilometers (a treaty that some argue should be globalized to prohibit all missiles of this range anywhere in the world). As Richard Speier details in chapter 14, President Reagan also began the first effort to control the spread of ballistic missile technology—the Missile Technology Control Regime—in 1987, and he negotiated the first strategic treaty that actually reduced (rather than limited) deployed strategic nuclear forces.

President George Bush signed the Strategic Arms Reduction Treaty (START) in 1991 and kept the momentum going by negotiating and signing in January 1993 START II, the most sweeping arms reduction pact in history. That same month President Bush also signed the treaty he had negotiated, the Chemical Weapons Convention, prohibiting the development, production, acquisition, stockpiling, transfer, or use of chemical weapons. In a move that had particular significance in this time of negotiations deadlock, President Bush on September 27, 1991, announced that the United States would unilaterally withdraw all of its land- and sea-launched tactical nuclear weapons and would dismantle all of its land- and many of its sea-based systems. The president also announced the unilateral end to the twenty-four-hour alert status of the U.S. bomber force and the de-alerting of a substantial portion of the land-based missile force. (On October 5, 1991, President Mikhail Gorbachev reciprocated with similar tactical withdrawals and ordered the de-alerting of 503 Soviet intercontinental ballistic missiles.)

In his first term, President Clinton seemed to be continuing the momentum established by his predecessors. Secretary of Defense William Perry and Secretary of Energy Hazel O'Leary firmly established and expanded cooperative threat reduction programs with the states of the former Soviet Union and helped convince Ukraine, Belarus, and Kazakhstan to abandon their inherited nuclear weapons and join the NPT regime. President Clinton successfully managed the indefinite extension and strengthening of the NPT in 1995; led efforts to conclude and sign the Comprehensive Test Ban Treaty in 1996; failed in 1996 but came back in 1997 to win Senate ratification of the Chemical Weapons Convention; and resisted repeated efforts to repeal the Anti-Ballistic Missile Treaty.

Today, thousands of dedicated civil servants in the United States and around the world toil to implement and strengthen the institutions Republicans and Democrats have built for pragmatic security needs and as a legacy for future generations.

THE BOOK AHEAD

This volume seeks to provide a comprehensive assessment of the global non-proliferation regime as it currently exists, to identify weakened areas, and to offer positive suggestions for repair.[15]

United Nations Undersecretary-General Jayantha Dhanapala provides his informed view of the overall health of the regime in chapter 2. He details the threats from outside the regime, noting, "If countries are perceived to derive certain benefits from ignoring such fundamental global norms, the risk could grow that others will either follow suit or seek various forms of compensation for continued participation." He recalls his closing remarks as president of the 1995 NPT conference to underscore the serious threats that arise from inside the regime: "Permanence of the Treaty does not represent a permanence of unbalanced obligations . . . non-proliferation and disarmament can be pursued only jointly, not at each other's expense." We are fortunate to have this seasoned and senior diplomat provide his insights in this volume.

Secretary of Energy Bill Richardson and National Security Adviser Sandy Berger give us the U.S. administration's agenda in chapters 3 and 4. Secretary Richardson reminds us that the futures of the United States and Russia "remain inexorably linked." It is essential, he argues, that as Russia navigates perilous economic conditions, "we take steps to help the scientists and engineers behind the Russian nuclear complex find other ways of supporting themselves." We must also help to secure Russian nuclear materials and install modern security and accounting systems in their nuclear complexes, he says. Mr. Berger discusses the mounting challenges to international security and outlines America's policy initiatives for preventing and addressing proliferation in the new century. He warns in particular, "If the Senate rejected or failed to act on the Test Ban Treaty, we would throw open the door to regional nuclear arms races and a much more dangerous world."

In chapter 5, three officials and experts discuss the crisis in Russia's "nuclear cities" cited by Secretary Richardson. Russia's first deputy minister of atomic energy, Lev Ryabev, reveals that government plans call for "a deep reduction of those working in the weapons complex from 75,000 to 40,000 by the year 2005. This is one of the most serious issues today." Assistant Secretary of Energy Rose Gottemoeller cites the new Nuclear Cities Initiative as "an ideal model of how the NGO community can work together with government to develop a concept and make it happen." Former Energy Department official Ken Luongo describes his efforts, now as the director of the Russian-American Nuclear Security Advisory Council, to bring the key people in both nations together first to generate this concept and then to shepherd it through both administrations. Matthew Bunn suggests some alternative employment solutions for Russia's former nuclear scientists.

U.S.-Russian negotiations to reduce global nuclear arsenals have always been a critical part of the non-proliferation regime. In chapter 6, Alexander Pikayev describes the deadlock in this process from his unique vantage point as a former staff member of the Russian Duma and now as a scholar in residence at the Carnegie Endowment Moscow Center. He marshals an impressive historical analysis to support his unfortunately pessimistic view: "This deadlock has jeopardized the future of negotiated, bilateral strategic arms control. Prospects for future talks on tactical nuclear weapons and warhead transparency measures, which could be conducted parallel to negotiations on a START III agreement, are dim."

By far, the greatest security challenge facing the United States and the world today is the continued danger of nuclear proliferation resulting from the collapse of the Soviet Union and the current state of Russian security over nuclear materials and technology. Chapter 7 provides the most comprehensive assessment to date of the risks posed by the collapse of Russia's nuclear infrastructure. Harvard scholar Matthew Bunn offers a masterful account of the dire state of the nuclear complex and the formidable challenges posed by the massive stockpiles of often poorly secured fissile material. Bunn outlines a series of provocative recommendations for how to marry political will with effective technical solutions to the problems.

In chapter 8, China's highest-ranking arms control official, Ambassador Sha Zukang, presents his nation's views on the regime and proposals for expansion and improvement. He notes that "missile non-proliferation is the most underdeveloped part of the entire international non-proliferation regime" and proposes serious consideration of ideas to globalize the ABM treaty. He warns, "If a country, in addition to its offensive power, seeks to develop advanced TMD or even NMD in an attempt to attain absolute security and unilateral strategic advantage for itself, other countries will be forced to develop more advanced offensive missiles."

The implications of India and Pakistan's nuclear tests for each country and for the region are examined by Neil Joeck of Lawrence Livermore National Laboratory in chapter 9. Issues such as strategic planning, weaponization, deployment, and command and control, "which," he says, "heretofore were relegated to the back burner, may no longer be deferred." In a nuclear accounting supplement to the chapter, David Albright of the Institute for Science and International Security provides new estimates of the fissile material and nuclear weapons in South Asia.

Daniel Morrow and Michael Carriere provide in chapter 10 the first concrete analysis of the actual impact of the sanctions on India and Pakistan following those nations' nuclear tests. With details on the direct and indirect financial consequences of the sanctions, Morrow and Carriere find the impact may well have been understated at the time. They note, for example, that while the direct impact of the sanctions on India was modest, "foreign investment in India fell sharply in May 1998 and remained well below the levels of 1997. . . . Receipts from external commercial borrowing were also significantly lower after May 1998."

The participants in the Carnegie conference were honored to have Ambassador Richard Butler address the assembly. Then the chairman of the United Nations Special Commission on Iraq, Butler waged an heroic effort in the face of determined Iraqi obstructionism to hold that nation to its pledge to disclose and destroy its chemical and biological weapons of mass destruction and missile systems. He modestly recounts these efforts in chapter 11, which is enriched by the addition of charts prepared by the Non-Proliferation Project staff and special background material prepared by Toby Dalton and Mathew Rice on the ability of Iraq to reconstitute its weapons of mass destruction capabilities.

One of the more illuminating sessions of the conference was the fascinating debate on Russian assistance to Iran by three officials intimately involved in the dialogue. Reproduced in chapter 12, the discussion features Ambassador Robert Gallucci, a skilled diplomat and now dean of the Georgetown University School of Foreign Service, who presents his personal observations as he engaged the Russians as a special envoy of the United States government on these issues. Dr. Viktor Mizin of the Russian Foreign Ministry responds with, understandably, quite a different view of the situation. Israel's deputy director for arms control and disarmament, Robbie Sabel, rings the alarm about Iran's intentions with a detailed description of that nation's nuclear and missile programs.

Chapter 13 closes out the treatment of the Near and Middle East with another exchange of views among U.S., Israeli, and Iraqi experts. While the Arab-Israeli conflict in the Middle East has been the principal focus of international attention to the region, attention is turning to the development of weapons of mass destruction capabilities by Iraq and Iran. Soon, these nations may challenge Israel's strategic monopoly in the region. Ariel Levite, director of the Israeli Bureau of International Security and Arms Control, former Iraqi nuclear official Khidhir Hamza, Benjamin Frankel, editor of *Security Studies*, and Bruce Jentleson of the United States Institute for Peace provide a dynamic examination of the key issues.

Chapter 14 tackles the thorny issue of missile proliferation. Richard Speier, who helped construct the Missile Technology Control Regime while an official in the Reagan and Bush administrations, argues that a "false dichotomy" has emerged. Many believe that missile non-proliferation and missile defense excluded each other. In fact, he argues, "from the earliest days of the MTCR, many advocates of each had seen the other as substantially complementary." He presents an historic guide to demonstrate his point, in the process helping readers understand this part of the regime and reach their own conclusions on whether missile non-proliferation has failed.

Jonathan Tucker of the Monterey Institute for International Studies reminds us in chapter 15 of the serious risks represented by biological warfare materials and expertise that were once part of the Soviet Union's offensive biological warfare program. Brad Roberts of the Institute for Defense Analysis joins in with an examination of the potential threat and the corresponding implications for the use of biological weapons in warfare, noting that many existing constraints may be gradually disappearing. Finally, Elisa Harris, a CBW expert on the staff of the National Security Council, presents an alternative view: that the risk of chemical and biological weapons use may actually be waning.

In chapter 16, French analyst Camille Grand takes us to the core of the issue as he looks at efforts to negotiate a treaty ending the production of fissile material (plutonium and highly enriched uranium). The treaty, he believes, "is not so much a Cold War arms control measure finally signed, as it is a key event defining the future of nuclear weapons in the next decades: an end to nuclear arms races, tighter limits on existing weaponry, and enhanced transparency of the nuclear complexes."

The lack of progress in U.S. and Russian strategic negotiations, dissected in chapter 17, poses a serious threat to the non-proliferation regime, which is conditioned in large part on the pledge made by the nuclear powers to reduce and eventually eliminate their nuclear arsenals. Michael Krepon, president of the Henry L. Stimson Center, summarizes the recommendations of leading experts for jumpstarting the strategic reduction process. Bruce Blair of the Brookings Institution describes in elegant detail his proposals for supplementing this process by duplicating the Bush-Gorbachev actions that took large parts of the respective arsenals off hairtrigger alert without time-consuming negotiations. The former special representative of the president for non-proliferation Thomas Graham summarizes the case for improving U.S. and global security by embracing a doctrine of pledging never to be the first to use nuclear weapons. Robert Bell of the National Security Council staff, a chief architect of the Clinton administration arms control policies, defends the approaches he helped craft during the 1990s.

Progress in building the non-proliferation regime has historically depended on the agreement of the nuclear-weapon states. But progress does not necessarily begin with these states. As chapter 18 demonstrates, the historical tradition of small and medium-size states serving as catalysts for global change is alive and well. Darach MacFhionnbhairr from Ireland (one of the key architects of the New Agenda Coalition) and Luiz Machado from Brazil discuss the New Agenda Coalition proposals. Marina Laker from Canada discusses her nation's Human Security Agenda, and Patricia Lewis, director of the United Nations Institute for Disarmament Research, provides an overview of these new initiatives and the role of nongovernmental organizations.

Finally, the appendixes provide rich detail and a valuable research resource for students and scholars on the specifics of the non-proliferation regime, the characteristics of the various weapons of mass destruction commonly deployed, and the facts and figures on who has what where.

THE CRITICAL ROLE OF NONGOVERNMENTAL ORGANIZATIONS

It is fitting that this first chapter ends by citing the founder of the Carnegie Non-Proliferation Project and the Carnegie International Non-Proliferation Conferences. For thirteen years, Leonard "Sandy" Spector guided this project and its work. He established an international reputation for scholarship, dependability, and cordiality. He addressed the Carnegie conference from his current position as director of the Office of Non-Proliferation and Arms Control at the Department of Energy. For those outside government who may despair that their words and work fall on fallow fields, we close this introductory chapter with these words of solace:

> The contribution that the non-proliferation community, this astonishing community of experts, makes to the United States Government, is very singular, indeed. If you look at the government programs in the field of arms control and non-proliferation, you'll see the great importance of this group. For example, the Pentagon's Cooperative Threat Reduction program was initiated by a group at Harvard University prior to their joining the Clinton Administration. The HEU purchase agreement, which is purchasing highly-enriched uranium from Russia and blending it down so it can no longer be used for weapons, is the brainchild of Thomas Neff. At DOE, the program for material protection, control, and accounting was spurred by a number of outsiders, including Thomas Cochran of the Natural Resources Defense Council, and steered and guided by other experts, such as William Potter of the Monterey Institute, Todd Perry of the Union of Concerned Scientists, and others.
>
> The Pentagon's programs go into the billions of dollars, the HEU purchase agreement is hundreds of millions of dollars, and the Reduced Enrichment for Research and Test Reactors program at DOE is a multimillion-dollar program launched with the thoughts and efforts of Paul Leventhal at the Nuclear Control Institute. Most recently, the Department of Energy launched the Nuclear Cities Initiative, stimulated by the work of Ken Luongo and Frank von Hippel of Princeton University.
>
> There is also the enormous benefit that is provided by the training that goes on in the organization represented at the Carnegie conference. From the Arms Control Association, the Monterey Institute for International Studies, the Carnegie Endowment, of course, and others, we have seen some of the best and brightest people throughout the government cut their teeth and then join us on the other side. It is an enormous contribution. Finally, there are the support efforts that non-governmental groups mount on behalf of the number of important arms control initiatives sponsored by this administration.
>
> I hope I have reinforced the judgment that the work you do is very important and a tremendous help to all of us inside government. We welcome your continued involvement and depend on it a great deal more than many of you may realize.
>
> Thank you.

NOTES

1. "Prepare for a Grave New World," *Washington Post,* July 26, 1999, A19.

2. The Royal Swedish Academy of Science in 1982 concluded that a thermonuclear war using approximately 5,000 megatons would destroy all major cities of 500,000 population or greater in the United States, Canada, Europe, the USSR, Japan, China, India, Pakistan, Korea, Vietnam, Australia, South Africa, and Cuba. Theoretically, in 1985 the United States and the Soviet Union had the ability to destroy the world three times over with their strategic nuclear weapons and could still do so at least once today. Carl Sagan and others warned that a war involving as low as 100 megatons could trigger a nuclear winter. This would involve, say, hitting one hundred cities with 1-megaton warheads. This would induce such a drop in global temperatures and reduction of light that the resulting starvation and weather extremes would conceivably reduce the population of the planet to prehistoric levels. By this measure, we had then the ability to destroy the world 148 times in 1985 and 50 times over today.

3. "The Effects of Nuclear War," Office of Technology Assessment, Congress of the United States (Washington, D.C., 1979). The Public Broadcasting Service has constructed a website that allows users to plot the effects of a nuclear detonation on their city: (http://www.pbs.org/wgbh/pages/-amex/bomb/sfeature/mapablast.html).

4. Lachlan Forrow, Bruce G. Blair, Ira Helfand, George Lewis, Theodore Postol, Victor Sidel, Barry S. Levy, Herbert Abrams, Christine Cassel, "Accidental Nuclear War—A Post–Cold War Assessment," *New England Journal of Medicine*, April 30, 1998. The authors conclude: "U.S. and Russian nuclear-weapons systems remain on high alert. This fact, combined with the aging of Russian technical systems, has recently increased the risk of an accidental nuclear attack. As a conservative estimate, an accidental intermediate-sized launch of weapons from a single Russian submarine would result in the deaths of 6,838,000 persons from firestorms in eight U.S. cities. Millions of other people would probably be exposed to potentially lethal radiation from fallout. An agreement to remove all nuclear missiles from high-level alert status and eliminate the capability of a rapid launch would put an end to this threat." See: (http://www.nejm.org/content/1998/0338/0018/-132.asp) or (http://www.psr.org/consequences.htm).

5. National Emergency declared by Executive Order 12938 on November 14, 1994, reissued on November 12, 1998, and Letter to the Speaker of the House and President of the Senate, November 12, 1998.

6. *Defense Reform Initiative Report* (Washington, D.C.: Department of Defense, November 1997), 19.

7. Remarks to the NATO-Russia Permanent Joint Council, May 28, 1998.

8. Lieutenant General Patrick M. Hughes (USA), Statement for the Record, Senate Select Committee on Intelligence, January 28, 1998.

9. For a detailed description of the regime, see Appendix I, "The International Non-Proliferation Regime."

10. See, for example, Roger Molander and Robbie Nichols, *Who Will Stop the Bomb?* (New York: Facts on File Publications, 1985); Council on Foreign Relations, *Blocking the Spread of Nuclear Weapons, American and European Perspectives* (New York: Council on Foreign Relations, 1986); Leonard S. Spector, *Going Nuclear* (Cambridge, Mass.: Ballinger, 1987).

11. *U.S. Policy toward North Korea: A Second Look*, Report of an Independent Task Force Sponsored by the Council on Foreign Relations (Washington, D.C.: Council on Foreign Relations, July 27, 1999).

12. For a more complete history, see Joseph Cirincione, "The Non-Proliferation Treaty and the Nuclear Balance," *Current History*, May 1995, available at (http://www.stimson.org/campaign/curr-hst.htm).

13. President Eisenhower warned in a speech to the United Nations on December 8, 1953, "First, the knowledge now possessed by several nations will eventually be shared by others—possibly all others. Second, even a vast superiority in numbers of weapons . . . is no prevention, of itself, against

the fearful material damage and toll of human lives that would be inflicted by surprise aggression." Nations naturally had begun building warning and defensive systems against nuclear air attacks. But, he cautioned, "Let no one think that the expenditure of vast sums for weapons and systems of defense can guarantee absolute safety for the cities and citizens of any nation. The awful arithmetic of the atomic bomb does not permit of any such easy solution."

14. At the time the United States had a formidable biological weapons capability. The weapon thought most likely to be used was the E133 cluster bomb, holding 536 biological bomblets, each containing 35 milliliters of a liquid suspension of anthrax spores. A small explosive charge would, upon impact, turn the liquid into aerosol to be inhaled by the intended victims. At the time the program was dismantled, the United States held in storage some 40,000 liters of antipersonnel biological warfare agents and some 5,000 kilograms of antiagriculture agents. All were destroyed. The Soviet Union had a similar, if not larger, program. Former first deputy director of Biopreparat Kenneth Alibek testified before the U.S. Senate that the Soviet program employed over 60,000 people and stockpiled hundreds of anthrax weapon formulations and dozens of tons of smallpox and plague. See (http://www.fas.org/irp/congress/1998_hr/alibek.htm).

15. Complete transcripts and audio and video files of the conference proceedings are available on the Internet (http://www.ceip.org/npp). The analysis provided in this book was current as of September 1999.

2

The State of the Regime[1]

Jayantha Dhanapala

As we draw closer to the next Non-Proliferation Treaty (NPT) Review Conference in the year 2000, nongovernmental organizations (NGOs) will play an important role in ensuring a higher standard of accountability by the state parties throughout the treaty's newly strengthened review and evaluation process. Nongovernmental organizations played important roles in helping to achieve an indefinite extension of the NPT in 1995. I expect they will now continue their efforts to ensure the full implementation of the package of decisions that led to that historic achievement. Theirs is a moral responsibility on behalf of civil society.

The Carnegie Endowment has played such a role over so many years on behalf of the NPT's worthy goals of nuclear disarmament and non-proliferation. The annual Carnegie conferences have become somewhat of an institution in themselves and have traditionally begun the annual calendar of events in this important field. They have helped both to forge a global community of informed citizens who are equipped to address these challenges and to sensitize that community to the perils and pitfalls in our work to achieve these solemn goals.

The results of the preparatory committee meetings for this important review conference were, I am afraid, inauspicious. Deep differences continue to divide the non-nuclear weapon state parties from the nuclear weapon state parties, especially over the implementation of article VI of the treaty relating to nuclear disarmament.

It was particularly discouraging that there were considerable differences in the interpretation of the package of decisions that was adopted at the 1995 NPT review and extension conference. The delay in finalizing the officeholders of the conference is also disconcerting. And 1998's nuclear tests have led many observers to express concerns over the future of the treaty and the stability of its associated regime.

It is important to recall that with the decision in May 1995 to strengthen the review process for the NPT, state parties had underlined their willingness to accept greater accountability for their actions and to ensure that the undertakings contained in the treaty and in the decisions adopted at the review and extension conference will have greater prospects of being achieved. The success of the conference will ultimately depend on the evolution of fresh consensual approaches transcending political divisions and the abandonment of rigid postures or complacent attitudes over the "done deal" of the treaty's indefinite extension.

THE STATE OF THE REGIME

The theme of 1998's Carnegie conference was "Repairing the Regime." It implies that the NPT regime is broken—for as the American adage goes, "If it ain't broke, don't fix it." Much of the recent public discussion about the NPT has been focused on the threats arising from outside the treaty—or what might be called "external threats." As a result, threats arising from within that regime itself—some of them coming from certain birth defects of the NPT—have been glossed over.

So let me now address the general state of the nuclear regime. Given the slings and arrows that some commentators and public officials have aimed at the regime in the wake of the eleven declared nuclear detonations in South Asia in May 1998, I will attempt to address the impact of these tests on the regime and to discuss in a somewhat broader perspective the challenges and new possibilities that lie ahead.

In the immediate aftermath of the South Asia tests, some observers drew the hasty and erroneous conclusion that the regime has been crippled by these tests. The truth, however, is that the regime has in many respects fared quite well, even under these trying circumstances.

First, I believe the regime is continuing to demonstrate its vitality in the world community today. The nuclear tests have not inspired parties to abandon the NPT and its associated regime. The tests surely did not interfere with Brazil's decision to join the treaty in 1998. The treaty is about as close to full universal membership as is possible: Its norms represent global norms. Neither the NPT nor the safeguards system of the International Atomic Energy Agency (IAEA) can be blamed for the decisions by two nonparties to test nuclear weapons.

Inherent weaknesses in the NPT—such as the asymmetry of obligations between nuclear weapon states and non-nuclear weapon states—are a legitimate grievance of those within the treaty but not of those outside it. As for past weaknesses in safeguards, they have also been addressed by a strengthened safeguards protocol, one that has already been signed by thirty-five countries, including all of the European Union, the United States, and, most recently, China.

Viewed globally, compliance with the NPT has been commendable, despite certain significant instances where various state parties have engaged in—or are still engaging in—activities that are inconsistent with their treaty obligations. The general norms of the regime—including those with respect to export controls and the basic requirement for full-scope IAEA safeguards as a condition for nuclear commerce—are increasingly being integrated into the domestic laws and regulations of NPT parties, which now number 187.

As for the norm against testing, it is noteworthy that last year's tests have been condemned by diverse multilateral institutions on no less than twenty-five occasions—

institutions that together represent virtually all inhabited regions on Earth. Prospects also remain good for obtaining the necessary signatures on the Comprehensive Test Ban Treaty: I hope this will happen this year and that the treaty will enter into force as soon as possible thereafter. There is widespread support indeed throughout the world for the norm against nuclear testing.

As for the objective of complete nuclear disarmament, this too has been endorsed by virtually all countries—including not just the five nuclear weapon states but also the three non-NPT states that have either tested nuclear devices or have nuclear weapons capability. That objective is certainly not achieved by more states crossing the nuclear threshold.

This brings me to my second point about the overall health of the regime—namely, that one has to acknowledge that there are threats from within the regime as well as from outside it. This might seem somewhat paradoxical, given all the public attention that has been devoted to the recent nuclear tests by nonmembers of the regime.

THREATS FROM OUTSIDE THE REGIME

After all, these external threats to the regime are real. The tests in South Asia do indeed pose threats to the global norms of both non-proliferation and disarmament, primarily through their potential demonstration effect. If countries are perceived to derive certain benefits from ignoring such fundamental global norms, the risk could grow that others will either follow suit or seek various forms of compensation for continued participation in the regime. This is admittedly a hypothetical danger but one that nevertheless deserves to be taken seriously. It is a danger, incidentally, that applies to the goals of both non-proliferation and nuclear disarmament.

Other such external threats include criticisms of the NPT by nonparties that are preventing the treaty from achieving full universality. Moreover, the fact that certain NPT parties are engaging in civil nuclear cooperation in South Asia without any requirement for full-scope IAEA safeguards may—over time—unleash commercial pressures to abandon that responsible global standard. It is also worth noting that this is not the only region in which nuclear weapons have been acquired or detonated in the name of disarmament and world peace.

Consider for a moment some of the official statements made after past nuclear detonations over the last fifty-four years. U.S. Secretary of War Henry Stimson issued a statement on August 6, 1945—the day of the Hiroshima bombing—indicating that "Every effort is being bent toward assuring that this weapon and the new field of science that stands behind it will be employed wisely *in the interests of the security of peace-loving nations and the well-being of the world*."

I also recall the official statement by President Charles de Gaulle after the first French nuclear test on February 13, 1960, in which he declared that the event would place France in—and I am now quoting—"an even better position to further its action toward the conclusion of agreements among the atomic powers *with a view to achieving nuclear disarmament*."

On October 16, 1964, the Chinese government—whose leaders had long condemned nuclear weapons as a "paper tiger"—issued a statement following its first nuclear test stressing that "China is developing nuclear weapons not because we believe in the omnipotence of nuclear weapons . . . [but] to break the nuclear monopoly of the nuclear powers and to *eliminate nuclear weapons*."

We have all heard similar statements coming from South Asia about the value of nuclear weapons for purposes of both deterrence and disarmament, about how each new nuclear nation can be trusted, about how all the new weapons are products of native genius, and other such remarks that echo these voices of the past.

Yet the recent nuclear tests are indeed, as Secretary-General Kofi Annan stated to the Security Council last June, "unquestionably disturbing developments with far-reaching consequences for the region and for the international community." They amount to eleven steps backward in history—they symbolize a retreat by the rulers of a significant fraction of humanity from a collective global effort to devalue and delegitimize nuclear weapons, and they come at a time when so many compelling human needs in this region remain unfulfilled.

The possession of nuclear weapons does not level North/South disparities. Only economic development and reform of the international economic system can do that. The prospect of nuclear war also does little to inspire investor confidence in any region of the globe. Nor do such weapons automatically confer great-power status, enhanced national security, or electoral popularity. Nuclear weapons are not the proverbial "great equalizer"—they are instead the "great destabilizer." That is the lesson for all nuclear weapon states—real, putative, or potential.

Neither the continued possession of nuclear weapons by those within the NPT nor these acquisitions by states outside the NPT serve the cause of international peace and security. Yet despite my concerns over these external threats to the regime, I am equally if not more concerned about certain trends and tendencies that may be emerging from inside the regime.

THREATS FROM WITHIN THE REGIME

The key threats arising from within the regime are in part conceptual and in part based on divergent perspectives on material interests.

TROUBLESOME CONCEPTS

First and foremost, the nuclear weapon states under the NPT have a long way to go in fulfilling their commitments to the goal of nuclear disarmament. Making matters worse, there are voices within these states that favor a complete separation of the goals of non-proliferation from disarmament, a trend more noticeable since the 1995 indefinite extension of the NPT. In my opinion, the official adoption by the nuclear weapon states of such an approach would truly cripple the regime—substantial progress in achieving the disarmament objective is absolutely crucial to the future of the nuclear regime.

In my closing remarks as president of the NPT review and extension conference in 1995, I cautioned that the "permanence of the Treaty does not represent a permanence of unbalanced obligations, nor does it represent the permanence of nuclear apartheid between nuclear haves and have-nots." I also noted that "non-proliferation and disarmament can be pursued only jointly, not at each other's expense."

A senior official in the U.S. delegation to that conference, Ambassador Thomas Graham—who has since retired—echoed these views in New Delhi last September. In his words, "the objective of the NPT is the elimination of nuclear weapons." He added that the NPT "is the only legally binding international commitment undertaken by the nuclear weapon states to pursue nuclear disarmament; if the NPT dissolves, this commitment will no longer exist."

Ultimately, I believe that the indefinite perpetuation of this deadlock on nuclear disarmament will jeopardize the regime far more than even last year's nuclear detonations. One cannot, of course, exclude the possibility that some additional country might follow this long and unfortunate tradition I noted above of acquiring the bomb on the basis of tributes to global nuclear disarmament and deterrence theory. Devaluing nuclear weapons as a currency of power can only be achieved by their total elimination, not by a logic that would lead to their total proliferation.

Indeed, the doctrine of nuclear deterrence continues to captivate strategic thinkers across the globe, even though—as CNN says—the Cold War is now history. It is a strategic concept that has now evidently found fertile ground in South Asia. Elsewhere, first-use nuclear doctrines are still being espoused by certain countries. The greater the reliance that is placed on such postures, the harder it will be to discourage the possession or proliferation of such weapons globally. Progress in reviewing and abandoning such doctrines would surely brighten prospects for progress this year in the ad hoc committee on negative security assurances in the conference on disarmament and, thereby, correspondingly strengthen the nuclear non-proliferation regime.

Another internal threat arises less from the tests than from the various concepts that have been given new life in response to these tests, in particular, suggestions that proliferation is simply "inevitable," that "managed proliferation" should replace "non-proliferation" as a policy objective, and, in certain cases, that the nuclear weapon states should even provide technical assistance to make various types of improvements in nuclear weapons design or deployment practices by other countries. I regard such recommendations as profoundly contrary to the "not in any way to assist" taboo in article I of the NPT, a norm that has served the world community well for over a quarter of this century. We cannot have any new doctrine of "proliferation for peace."

Still other commentators see proliferation as a military problem best solved exclusively by military means. Yet if effectiveness still counts—as it must—as a criterion for pursuing non-proliferation and disarmament strategies, then surely we should not ignore the limitations of military force as an exclusive means of achieving such goals. Nor should we shortchange the value of international cooperative approaches, including such worthy initiatives as the Cooperative Threat Reduction program to improve controls over nuclear materials of the former Soviet Union.

And with specific regard to Iraq, it is important to recognize that agencies acting under UN auspices have destroyed far more weapons of mass destruction capacity than were destroyed during the Gulf War. Multilateral agreements—supported by effective verification regimes, the prospect of severe consequences for violations, and ample mechanisms for pursuing the peaceful settlement of disputes—will ultimately be a more valuable means of achieving the world community's solemn nuclear non-proliferation and disarmament goals than reliance on military force alone.

Another of my concerns relates to the rising calls from certain commentators for a more explicitly discriminatory regime—one that treats proliferation by friendly countries as a benign counterpoint to proliferation by so-called rogue regimes. Some of these critics ridicule the very notion of what they call a "one-size-fits-all" regime. Such formulations are not only unhelpful, but if they achieve the status of policy, they may well lead to a complete unraveling of that regime. They in essence stand for a policy of "discrimination for peace," a stance that will only add to the risks of a nuclear-armed world.

Not only does such a policy compromise on the principle of nuclear non-proliferation—and serve to perpetuate the possession of nuclear weapons—but it also opens the question that Lord Palmerston once settled when he said, "We have no eternal allies and we have no perpetual enemies. Our interests are eternal and perpetual, and those interests it is our duty to follow." Under the new formulation, it appears that we would end up with perpetual enemies, ephemeral interests, and eternal proliferation.

Perhaps the least popular internal threat arises from occasional calls—most notably from certain sections of the academic community—for additional nuclear weapons proliferation in the name of strategic stability. To the best of my knowledge—and to my great relief—none of their recommendations has yet been incorporated into national policy. Signs of pending increases in military budgets around the world, however, coupled with lingering dangers of a new arms race in strategic ballistic missile defense systems, could together be the thin end of the wedge leading both to more proliferation and dimmer prospects for disarmament.

COMPETING INTERESTS

There are of course other potential threats arising from within the regime—threats emanating less from concepts than from certain competing material *interests*, like the pressure to relax non-proliferation standards to pursue export opportunities, or to debase a disarmament standard in order to provide business to local industries, or to use the proliferation of conventional arms as a diplomatic instrument to pursue symbolic nuclear non-proliferation concessions. These threats are as many as they are deceptive—since they come clothed in the seductive garb of national interest and realism.

- There will be persisting efforts inside governments to sacrifice both non-proliferation and disarmament for other tactical diplomatic objectives.
- There will be calls for the selective enforcement of non-proliferation laws.
- There will be new risks of nuclear terrorism not just from illicit nuclear trafficking around the world—this is truly a global problem not limited to

any one country or region. Other such threats may arise from the potential loss or theft of weapons-usable nuclear materials that continue to be produced, stockpiled, and transported in many countries for commercial uses.

- There will be substantial obstacles to overcome in achieving a global ban on the production of fissile nuclear materials for weapons, given the concerns by many countries over the asymmetrical distribution of such materials both inside and outside the nuclear regime.
- There will be continued bureaucratic resistance to greater transparency in the implementation of non-proliferation policy, particularly in these areas of export controls and sanctions.
- There will be continued efforts within the regime—whether driven by budgetary or policy considerations—to curtail funding of non-proliferation activities by international organizations.
- And there will no doubt continue to be weaknesses in the coordination of multilateral responses to proliferation after it occurs, particularly responses designed to raise the costs of proliferation.

SOME KEY CHALLENGES AHEAD IN MEETING THESE THREATS

One of the biggest challenges ahead relates to the old tradition of national sovereignty—not sovereignty per se, just extreme variants of it. A key challenge ahead will be to resist the tendency of many countries to apply maximalist definitions of national sovereignty in interpreting their non-proliferation and disarmament commitments. A good regime requires verification, enforcement, transparency, and reciprocity.

Verification means right of access. Enforcement means predictable and effective responses to behavior that violates global norms. Transparency means greater public scrutiny of the progress and setbacks of non-proliferation and disarmament. And reciprocity means a national will to engage in consensus building even in the face of political conflict.

Maximalist interpretations of sovereignty will hinder the achievement of all of these qualities of stable and effective regimes. And such interpretations will only contribute to the triumph of minimalist expectations about the nuclear regime.

Of equal importance will be overcoming complacency and ignorance, and here is a specific area where NGOs can make significant contributions by helping to educate the public and by providing constructive ideas and proposals for national officials to deliberate.

The NGOs can also help in broadening the political base of the nuclear regime. They can help to develop tactics and strategies to ensure that disarmament and non-proliferation are widely understood as serving the interests and ideals of all the countries that make up the regime.

I would like in conclusion to urge all who care about non-proliferation and disarmament to hold firm on global standards, to spread the word about the diverse benefits for all countries from disarmament and non-proliferation, and to continue your instinctive opposition to proposals that would only spread the diseases that the regime is designed to prevent.

The building of societal resistance to nuclear weapons and their proliferation will be, in the final analysis, the ultimate bulwark protecting the international community from nuclear anarchy.

NOTE

1. UN Undersecretary General Dhanapala delivered the luncheon address to the participants at the Carnegie International Non-Proliferation Conference on January 11, 1998. This chapter is adapted from his remarks with his permission.

—3—

Post–Cold War Nuclear Challenges

Bill Richardson[1]

President Clinton has frequently stated that no greater threat than the proliferation of weapons of mass destruction confronts us as we enter the next millennium. As a government and a nation, we recognize that as these weapons spread, the risk rises that they may one day be used. President John F. Kennedy alluded to this desperate prospect when he announced the Limited Test Ban Treaty, warning of a potential time when none could rest, when danger would lurk in every corner of the world.

America bears a unique responsibility in tempering this threat and defusing its dangers. Our nation's history and our unique geostrategic and economic standing lead the world's eye to America as we cross the threshold of the millennium.

We must renew our national commitment to peace. We must redouble our efforts to preserve and strengthen the existing non-proliferation regime, while also pursuing new and innovative approaches to ensure our collective security and prosperity.

The role of the Department of Energy is indeed unique, at the leading edge of our national commitment. From our headquarters on Independence Avenue to the department's national labs to our dozens of field offices, the Energy Department serves as one of America's central providers of safety and security against the threat of weapons of mass destruction.

From our work supporting global arms control agreements and the non-proliferation regime, to our extensive activities in the former Soviet Union, the Energy Department is working to deliver security for our country.

ENDING NUCLEAR TESTS

Ratification of the Comprehensive Test Ban Treaty (CTBT) in 1999 is essential. Without this treaty, we will lose one of the most important tools available to us for constraining the development of more advanced nuclear weapons and limiting the spread of nuclear weapons to new states. Failure to ratify also seriously erodes our ability as a nation to lead in non-proliferation matters. Without ratification, we undercut our credibility in persuading India and Pakistan to join us in this important regime.

Without ratification, we are not eligible to join with other nations later this year to discuss ways to facilitate the treaty's entry into force, if necessary. Moreover, it would run counter to the desires of most Americans, who want this treaty to enter into force. The Senate's failure to act this year would reduce, not increase, our national security.

In 1995, when President Clinton announced his decision to pursue a true, zero-yield CTBT, he stated that U.S. entry into this treaty would be conditioned upon the conduct of six specific CTBT "safeguards," including a Science Based Stockpile Stewardship Program. This program is necessary to ensure a high level of confidence in the safety and reliability of U.S. nuclear weapons.

At the Department of Energy, we have worked hard to put the Stockpile Stewardship Program in place. We have come a long way since the inception of this program in 1993. Today, in our laboratories, we use computers to answer questions about the condition of our weapons that are one thousand times more powerful than those we used only six years ago.

We have also put in place new processes and equipment at our labs, and will acquire even greater scientific tools over the next five years to help ensure the safety and reliability of our deterrent. In short, the Department of Energy has created a vibrant and robust Stockpile Stewardship Program, and it is working today.

Because this program has enabled us to maintain confidence in our nuclear deterrent, Secretary Cohen and I were able to sign the third annual certification to the president that the stockpile is safe and reliable and that nuclear testing is not required at this time. This certification process, which we conduct each year, consists of a rigorous review by our nation's best nuclear experts. The process itself allows us to revalidate our confidence in the stockpile and our continued adherence to the treaty on an annual basis.

This program has fueled debate in national security circles. Some who oppose the treaty's ratification argue that we cannot guarantee the credibility of our nuclear deterrent without testing. Others argue we should wait for the stewardship program to mature fully before ratification. Still others argue we have too robust a Stockpile Stewardship Program.

In response to these points, let me be perfectly clear: Without a credible Stockpile Stewardship Program, we would not have a CTBT. Maintenance of a safe and reliable nuclear deterrent is a cornerstone of our national security strategy. At the Energy Department, we have worked very hard to make this program a reality and I am pleased to report that our success to date will enable us to adhere to a Comprehensive Test Ban Treaty, should the U.S. Senate give its advice and consent to ratification.

Now we must look beyond the department, to the Senate, to take the next step in advancing our national security through approval of the CTBT.

DISMANTLING COLD WAR ARSENALS

Working to free the world of nuclear testing is just one way that Energy Department resources reinforce and advance the global arms control regime. As the guardians of America's nuclear deterrent, we are also carrying out nuclear reductions of historic proportions, while paving the way for deeper, more secure reductions in cooperation with our Russian partners. We have already dismantled over thirteen thousand nuclear weapons. If we meet the president's goal of further reductions under the START III framework, we will have reduced our deployed arsenal by 80 percent from its Cold War peak.

The goal of strategic arms control thus far has been to limit the systems that delivered nuclear weapons. In this new era, we will pursue a new stage in strategic reductions where warheads themselves will be eliminated.

The Energy Department is at the center of this new mission. At the president's direction, we have developed a framework for potential warhead dismantlement monitoring regimes. We look forward to both Russian ratification of START II and a START III agreement that will enable further deep reductions in our nuclear arsenal.

As many of you know, the challenge will not end once these weapons are taken apart. In fact, in achieving our warhead elimination goals, we generate the new work of disposing of the excess nuclear material harvested from that process.

SECURING NUCLEAR MATERIALS

It is proverbial wisdom that one shall reap what one has sown, and we are now facing a daunting harvest. The nuclear investment made by the United States and Russia during the Cold War resulted in a massive legacy of nuclear waste and excess materials.

In the United States, we enjoy a robust domestic security system that is the international standard in physical protection. Moreover, we have taken broad steps to provide transparency over our excess nuclear materials and have in conjunction with Russia developed plans for material disposal.

A far different scenario is unfolding in Russia. There the historic system of controls over nuclear facilities and materials has weakened, and resources are simply not available to maintain it. We have also discovered that Russia's system of accounting was not consistent with modern systems of control and accounting.

Today, the Department of Energy and our national laboratories are working at over fifty Russian sites to secure nuclear materials and install modern security and accounting systems. This work is being carried out by the department's Materials Protection, Control, and Accounting Task Force, in partnership with Russian scientists. Dozens of men and women are at work in Russia to install basic safeguard systems and standards and procedures that can help provide for the long-term protection of these weapons-usable materials.

The extraordinary goodwill and cooperation that have developed between the department and our Russian counterparts have fueled our optimism for this program.

As a result, we are now cooperating at virtually every single site in Russia that stores or uses plutonium or highly enriched uranium.

Still, we recognize the changing complexity of the problems in Russia. The current economic crisis brings new urgency to our efforts particularly during a winter predicted to be the harshest in forty years. We have moved quickly to address special problems such as providing basics like winter clothing and space heaters to guards at facilities. This modest investment will keep our broader security work intact through this volatile period.

And while securing materials in place boosts global security, it is not an end in itself. Excess materials in the United States and Russia present a proliferation problem if these materials are not disposed of. The United States is beginning to blend down its surplus highly enriched uranium (HEU) for peaceful use in commercial reactor fuel, and we are working very hard to facilitate our agreement with Russia for the purchase of 500 metric tons of HEU. We hope to soon bring closure to the recent issues that have dogged our progress on implementing this important agreement.[2]

Already, this agreement has seen over 36 tons of Russian HEU blended down and delivered to America for use as reactor fuel. Think about it: Enough nuclear material for over fourteen hundred nuclear weapons has been transferred from one former intractable foe to another. Who among us would have predicted this possibility even ten years ago?

Plutonium disposition is a much more complicated issue, but we continue to make progress. While both countries have identified 50 tons of plutonium as no longer required for weapons, we still have a long road ahead of us before we successfully convert our first ton of weapons plutonium to the spent-fuel standard.

Many have hotly debated the option of disposing of plutonium by burning it as MOX fuel. The technical challenges presented by plutonium disposal led us to adopt the spent-fuel standard. This will make surplus plutonium as inaccessible and unattractive for retrieval and weapons use as the plutonium remaining in spent fuel from commercial reactors.

We remain firmly committed to a policy of no commercial reprocessing of spent nuclear fuel in the United States. The use of plutonium in reactors does not make economic sense, and the United States remains firm in its commitment to the once-through fuel cycle. But we are planning to burn plutonium in reactors to gain the non-proliferation benefits of a joint disposition program with our Russian partners.

At the same time, we recognize that Russia does not have the resources to address this problem on its own. We continue to work with the G-8 countries and others to develop a broad-based and realistic formula to fund the Russian plutonium disposition effort.

THE RUSSIAN NUCLEAR COMPLEX

The United States remains firmly committed to working with Russia as it develops democracy and finds a new place in the community of nations. Our futures remain inexorably linked.

Since the end of the Cold War, the United States has been engaged in a major downsizing and restructuring of our nuclear weapons complex. We have produced no new nuclear weapons since 1991, and we have cut our workforce by more than half from our 1990 levels. Russia, too, must now join in rightsizing its nuclear weapons complex, and we are prepared to work with Russia in facing this challenge together.

As Russia faces perilous economic conditions, it is essential that we take steps to help the scientists and engineers behind the Russian nuclear complex find other ways of supporting themselves. While with the president in Russia last September, we saw the difficult conditions that many Russian nuclear workers face each day. As their nuclear complex is reconfigured, tens of thousands of nuclear experts living in or near the nuclear cities are going to be underemployed or unemployed. Ways must be found for these people to channel their energy and expertise into new civil economic opportunities, to remove incentives for these scientists to sell their services to would-be proliferators.

To do just that, the department has launched the Nuclear Cities Initiative, designed to develop, in cooperation with private industry, alternative commercial enterprises in the ten Russian nuclear cities. Last September, I was pleased to sign the Nuclear Cities Agreement with Russian minister of atomic energy Adamov. Under this initiative, some of the near-term projects we are considering include:

- Establishing commercial software enterprises in the formerly secret cities of Sarov and Snezhinsk.
- Extending telecom linkages into the municipal centers of these cities and into Zheleznogorsk, our third focus city during FY1999.
- Opening business centers in all three cities to facilitate commercial development.

As these cities reorient themselves toward commercial activities, great opportunities for business development will be created.

SPECIAL CHALLENGES

Our progress cannot, however, diminish the truth that we face serious challenges in our relationship with Russia. And no challenge is as great as that created by Russian institutes' and labs' cooperation with the Islamic Republic of Iran. On this issue, we have grave concerns. The flow of information, technology, and equipment to Iranian programs threatens to worsen the situation in the Middle East, undermine critical non-proliferation and export control norms, and undercut support for our cooperative programs in Russia.

The president and his cabinet have worked tirelessly to help the Russian government understand our concerns. Our message to them is simple: money made in business dealings with Iran may cost Russia far greater benefits, financial or otherwise, associated with U.S. business and assistance.

It is important that a message to Russian officials and scientists comes through loud and clear: Continued contacts and commerce with Iran on nuclear weapon and missile technology is a threat to the United States, to Russia, and to the world. We welcome recent steps by Russia to tighten their export controls, but more needs to be done. We extend our hand of cooperation to further improve these controls. Russia would be wise to take it.

In undertaking all these activities the Clinton administration is driven by one basic assumption: that the proliferation of weapons of mass destruction fundamentally threatens our global system of peace and security, a system built with sweat and labor over five decades. We must continue to do all we can to convince states that acquiring such weapons does not improve their security but threatens it and that helping others to acquire such weapons does not improve international status but lowers it.

The thaw of the Cold War has revealed many opportunities for the advancement of global peace and prosperity, a goal we all strive to one day find. But this new season reveals as many challenges to this same goal. There is much work to be done. Another proverb that comes to mind when I consider the nuclear legacy that remains before us is "those that sow the wind may reap the whirlwind." We should heed this warning. It is our job to ensure our harvests are ones of a peaceful bounty.

NOTES

1. Secretary of Energy Bill Richardson delivered this keynote address to the Carnegie International Non-Proliferation Conference on January 12, 1999. With his permission, the speech is presented here with some of the numbers cited by the secretary updated to reflect the situation as of mid-1999.

2. *Editor's Note*: The U.S.-Russia highly enriched uranium purchase agreement—or HEU deal, as it is commonly referred to—was signed in 1993. Under this agreement the United States Enrichment Corporation (USEC) will purchase 500 metric tons of HEU from dismantled Russian nuclear weapons for $12 billion over a twenty-year period. The HEU is blended with natural uranium in Russia to create low enriched uranium (LEU), which is then sold by USEC for use in commercial nuclear power reactors. The first delivery of LEU took place in 1995, and as of mid-1999, 60 metric tons of blended-down HEU had been delivered to USEC, and that total was expected to reach 81 metric tons by the end of 1999. Russian concerns over payment for the natural uranium used in the downblending (an estimated $4 billion of the $12 billion deal), coupled with a falling market for uranium, nearly derailed the agreement in 1998. In a late-1998 congressional emergency supplemental funding bill, however, Senator Pete Domenici added $325 million to purchase the natural uranium from Russia that had been used in the LEU received in 1996 and 1997. In March 1999, Russia and the United States finalized an agreement for this payment at the same time that Russia signed a fifteen-year deal with the Western uranium suppliers for future natural uranium purchases, putting the HEU deal back on track.

4

Proliferation Challenges[1]

Samuel R. Berger

Nineteen ninety-eight was a troubling year—a year of living dangerously. There was some significant progress, but several problems took a turn for the worse, and perilous new trends have emerged. The key developments were:

In May, India, and then Pakistan, conducted nuclear tests that blew the lid off South Asia's long-simmering nuclear rivalry. These explosions threaten to trigger a full-fledged nuclear and missile race in the region. Also ominous was some of the early rhetoric surrounding the blasts—suggesting that many politicians and citizens in India and Pakistan believed that a nuclear weapons capability provided instant great-power status.

In July, Iran's test of the Shahab-3 missile—its version of the North Korean No Dong—extended Tehran's capability to target U.S. friends and allies in the Middle East, as well as our forces in the region. Combined with Iran's continued pursuit of nuclear weapons, this missile development threatens the stability of the region—as if the stability of that region needed any further threatening.

In August, North Korea tested its Taepo Dong missile over Japan. This test, with the revelation that North Korea is constructing a suspicious underground site, has raised questions about North Korean compliance with the 1994 Agreed Framework, which aimed at creating stability and discouraging proliferation on the Korean peninsula. If the agreement unravels, we could quickly return to an environment like the 1993–94 crisis, with increased risk of war and North Korean resumption of plutonium production.

By August, Russia's economic crisis heightened the challenge for Russia to control the leakage of sensitive weapons-related materials and technology beyond its borders. Weapons scientists and institutes face increased financial pressures to sell their wares to whoever is in the market, including rogue states.

Finally, in December, Saddam Hussein once again broke his commitments to cooperate with UN inspectors, ignoring our warnings. The United States, together

with our British allies, responded with military force. We attacked Iraq's program
to develop and deliver weapons of mass destruction (WMD) and its capacity to
threaten its neighbors. But we have not eliminated the danger, and our resolve to
curb the threat Saddam poses will not diminish.

In addition to these specific developments, two broad and dangerous trends have
emerged. First, as the president has repeatedly warned, the risk is increasing that
terrorists will acquire and seek to use chemical or biological weapons as weapons
of terror. Second, ballistic missile proliferation has intensified, as demonstrated by
the Iranian and North Korean missile tests and advances in the missile programs of
India and Pakistan. While the technology to develop intercontinental range missiles
remains out of reach for a large number of countries, shorter-range missile capabilities "based on liquid-fueled SCUD technology" are widely available. The Missile Technology Control Regime (MTCR) helps to limit the spread of missile
technology, but several key suppliers, such as North Korea, are outside the MTCR.
Unfortunately, in regions like the Middle East and South Asia, ballistic missiles are
increasingly seen as essential to national status and security, and political dynam-
ics weigh against agreements to limit these missiles.

Not all the news on non-proliferation was bad last year. There were several encouraging developments. Brazil ratified the Comprehensive Nuclear Test Ban
(CTBT) Treaty—as did seventeen other nations—and joined the Non-Proliferation
Treaty, completing a remarkable process that has almost eliminated the threat of
nuclear proliferation in Latin America. The multinational Conference on Disarmament, based in Geneva, agreed to arrangements to begin negotiations on a global
Fissile Material Cut-Off Treaty, which would halt the production of additional
material for nuclear weapons. China agreed in June to seriously study joining the
MTCR. At home, our Congress passed critical legislation to implement the Chemical Weapons Convention, which the Senate ratified in 1997.

Also encouraging was the global reaction to the nuclear tests by India and Pakistan: They were condemned in nearly every corner of the world. Here was an issue
where the United States, China, and Russia found a common voice, where nuclear
powers agreed with many nations of the developing world. Far from demonstrating
the death of international norms against proliferation, the international reaction to
the tests showed the resilience of these norms.

But these positive signs were overshadowed by the mounting challenges. We
need your commitment, the public's commitment, our Congress's commitment, the
commitment of responsible nations more than ever to build a safer future. Let me
outline America's policy initiatives for preventing and addressing proliferation as
we reach a new century.

STRENGTHENING THE REGIME

The United States will redouble existing efforts and seek new approaches and solutions—this year and beyond—on multiple fronts.

First, we will move aggressively to strengthen the non-proliferation regime, by which I mean international consensus and the international agreements and structures aimed at curbing weapons of mass destruction and ballistic missiles. Bolstering this regime is critical if we are to give nations greater confidence that they can forgo or limit weapons of mass destruction and ballistic missiles without finding themselves at a disadvantage against rivals brandishing such weapons. The regime is also essential for isolating nations outside the regime and pressuring them to restrain their programs and eventually to join.

With respect to strengthening the regime, let me say that President Clinton will make one of his top priorities for 1999 obtaining advice and consent to the CTBT in the United States Senate.

The president has called the CTBT the "longest-sought, hardest-fought prize in the history of arms control." It bans all nuclear explosive tests. We should pause and contemplate this development: 151 nations have signed an accord to never, or never again, test a nuclear device. We must not let this extraordinary opportunity slip away.

By its terms, the CTBT cannot enter into force until the United States and other key designated nations ratify it. If we fail to ratify, we will undercut our own efforts to curb further nuclear arms development, particularly in South Asia, where India and Pakistan each have announced an intention to adhere to the CTBT by this coming September. That is the right choice for those countries, one we have been urging for some time. Senate action on the CTBT before September will greatly strengthen our hand in persuading India and Pakistan to fulfill their pledges.

The treaty is in America's national interest. Four former chairmen of the Joint Chiefs of Staff—Shalikashvili, Powell, Crowe, and Jones—plus all six current members of the JCS agree on that. The directors of our three national nuclear weapons labs and numerous outside experts have said we can maintain a reliable deterrent without nuclear explosive testing. Polls show that 75 to 80 percent of all Americans support the treaty. Indeed, public support has been strong for more than forty years, ever since President Eisenhower first proposed a test ban treaty.

The treaty will constrain the development of more advanced nuclear weapons by the nuclear powers—and limit the possibilities for other states to acquire such weapons. It will also enhance our ability to detect and deter suspicious activities by other nations. As the experts assembled here well know, with or without a CTBT, we must monitor such activities. The treaty gives us new tools to pursue this vital mission: a global network of sensors to supplement our national intelligence capabilities and the right to request short-notice, on-site inspections in other countries.

If the Senate rejected or failed to act on the CTBT, we would throw open the door to regional nuclear arms races and a much more dangerous world. Ratification will take a serious effort from all of us. But it would be a terrible tragedy if our Senate failed to ratify the CTBT this year.

In addition to the CTBT, we want to make rapid progress on the treaty I mentioned earlier to ban further production of fissile materials. Last fall, we called on all countries that have tested nuclear devices to adhere to a voluntary production moratorium. In fact, the United States, the United Kingdom, France, Russia, and

China have all stopped producing fissile material, and we hope they, along with India and Pakistan, will formally join this moratorium while we seek a treaty through the Conference on Disarmament.

We will also work to strengthen other components of the nuclear non-proliferation regime, including the safeguards applied by the International Atomic Energy Agency. And we will implement the initiative Presidents Clinton and Yeltsin announced in Russia to dispose safely of 50 tons of plutonium each that is no longer needed by our military programs—enough to make literally thousands of nuclear weapons.

Another strong catalyst for convincing nations to forgo nuclear weapons would be continued progress in the START process—the effort by the United States and Russia to reduce our nuclear arsenals. We hope the Russian Duma will promptly ratify START II, which will clearly benefit Russia's security, as well as ours. And we remain committed to concluding a START III for even deeper cuts based on the agreement reached by Presidents Clinton and Yeltsin at Helsinki in 1997.

Our commitment to strengthening the global non-proliferation regime extends, of course, beyond nuclear weapons. I am proud that this administration obtained ratification of the Chemical Weapons Convention. This year, we will continue to pursue aggressively another key priority, announced by the president in last year's State of the Union address: strengthening our ability to determine whether nations are complying with the Biological Weapons Convention. We will push to obtain international agreement this year on compliance and inspection measures, making it much more difficult for nations to cheat and thereby increasing our safety from the threat of biological weapons. Undersecretary of State John Holum, who is leading our diplomatic efforts, will be in Geneva next week to explore ideas for pushing the negotiations to a successful conclusion.

The chemical and biological conventions are vital not only to preventing states from acquiring weapons of mass destruction but also, in combination with law enforcement and intelligence, to keeping these weapons away from terrorists. Yes, the conventions are focused on the obligations of states, not substate actors. But virtually every state on our State Department's list of terrorism sponsors has weapons of mass destruction programs. As potential suppliers of such weapons to terrorists, there is no more worrisome source than these state sponsors. Under a strong non-proliferation regime, states that fail to join or comply with the conventions will be isolated, cut off from weapons materials, and thus hindered from assisting terrorists with WMD activities.

REGIONAL INITIATIVES

Our second set of priorities focuses on the most pressing regional proliferation challenges.

With respect to South Asia, we have pressed for a strong international response to deter India and Pakistan from additional testing. Secretary Albright and Deputy Secretary Talbott have engaged in intense diplomatic efforts to move India and Pakistan away from nuclear confrontation. In 1999, we will further intensify our diplomacy and encourage Indo-Pakistani dialogue in pursuit of concrete results: adherence to the CTBT, establishment of strong export controls, and restraint on fissile materials production and ballistic missile development and deployment. I hope that by the end of the year sufficient progress will have been made to enable the president to travel to the subcontinent to hail a more stable and secure South Asia.

Dealing with North Korea—the most isolated nation in the world—is a delicate balancing act that requires a judicious mix of deterrence, diplomacy, and aggressive non-proliferation efforts. To preserve the Agreed Framework, we must work toward arrangements with the North to resolve our concerns about the underground activity. We must intensify our efforts to dissuade and deter the North from conducting additional long-range missile tests and continuing its missile technology exports. We are working closely with our allies the Republic of Korea and Japan, and with China, to achieve these goals. We are also conducting an overall review of U.S. policy, with the help of former defense secretary Bill Perry, to develop a sustainable long-term strategy toward North Korea beyond the Agreed Framework.

As we work with China on common non-proliferation goals, we will continue to express our hope that it will join the Missile Technology Control Regime—and do so this year.

On Iraq, the administration will use all means—including, if necessary, additional military force—to obtain Saddam's compliance with Iraq's commitments regarding weapons of mass destruction and with the relevant Security Council resolutions. We will adhere to our position that disarmament under these resolutions is the only pathway to sanctions relief. And we continue to believe that UNSCOM is the appropriate entity to verify and monitor Iraq's disarmament. It is up to Saddam to decide whether he wants sanctions relief by giving up his weapons of mass destruction. In the meantime, we will be ready to act again if we see Iraq rebuilding a WMD capability.

We will also continue to offer humanitarian assistance to the Iraqi people and, most important, work toward the day when Iraq has a government that respects its people and lives in peace with its neighbors. It is clear that real disarmament in Iraq will come only when there is a new government in Baghdad.

As to Russia, we will continue to work aggressively with the Russian leadership to halt Russian entities' cooperation with Iran's missile and nuclear weapons programs. This issue has been at the top of our agenda with the Russian government. We continue to urge Russia to enforce and strengthen its export controls and take actions against Russian entities that violate those controls, selling out Russia's own non-proliferation and security interests for their own financial gain.

We will continue to take action against these entities ourselves. In that regard, I want to announce that today the United States is imposing economic penalties against three additional Russian entities—the Moscow Aviation Institute, Mendeleyev University, and NIKIET, or the Scientific Research and Design Institute of Power Technology—for providing sensitive missile or nuclear assistance to Iran. Last July we took action against seven others. Let me be very clear: The administration has authority to act against entities that violate international non-proliferation standards, and we will use this authority to protect our security.

In the end, though, the most effective shield against proliferation from Russia is not U.S. penalties but a Russian export control system that is designed to work and does so. Only Russia can police its own borders, factories, and technology institutes. That is why President Clinton and President Yeltsin agreed at last year's Moscow summit to create seven export control working groups to improve Russia's capacity to stop the flow of sensitive technology and equipment. It is also why we are funding the International Science and Technology Center in Moscow and other initiatives to help thousands of weapons scientists apply their skills to civilian purposes. It is why we are funding the Nuclear Cities Initiative, announced by Energy Secretary Richardson last September, to help Russia convert its nuclear weapons production facilities to peaceful uses.

We currently are considering enhancement of existing threat reduction programs—to work together with Russia to secure and dispose of dangerous materials, convert WMD resources to peaceful use, tighten export controls, and help ensure that Russian scientists are engaged in work other than proliferation activity. We hope to be able to say more on this in the near future.

Our third set of priorities recognizes that despite our efforts to strengthen the international regime and resolve regional issues, we cannot prevent all forms of proliferation in all cases—and that weapons of mass destruction already are out there, in the hands of dangerous actors. So we must devote sufficient resources to develop defensive capabilities to protect the United States and our allies in the event these weapons are used.

To deal with the spread of ballistic missile technology in key regions, we have stepped up our theater missile defense programs, including those with Israel and Japan. We are also committed to the development of a limited national missile defense system that could, if we decide, be deployed to counter the emerging ballistic missile threat from rogue nations. In the next budget we present to Congress, we will propose to include funds—approximately $7 billion over the next six years—that would be necessary if we later decide to deploy a limited national missile defense system.

Let me be clear: We remain strongly committed to the 1972 Anti-Ballistic Missile Treaty—a cornerstone of our security—and we would seek agreement with the other treaty parties if any missile defense activities necessitated modifying the ABM Treaty.

To be ready to protect our citizens from the threat of terrorist use of chemical and biological weapons, we have launched a robust program under our new national coordinator for security, infrastructure protection and counterterrorism. We have created a National Office of Domestic Preparedness to train and equip fire, police, and medical personnel across the country to deal with chemical, biological, and nuclear emergencies. We are readying National Guard units in every region to meet this challenge. We have begun the work necessary to improve our public health surveillance system—so that if a biological weapon is released, we can detect it and save lives. We have begun the effort to create the first-ever civilian stockpile of needed medicines. We have increased funding for research and development on medications. And I am confident that in the budget the president will submit next month, we will deepen our efforts on the public health front. We also hope to make progress at the NATO summit here in April to better equip our alliance to deal with this growing threat.

All of these efforts—strengthening the non-proliferation regime, addressing regional threats, and bolstering defenses—are absolutely essential. And the Clinton administration is committed to making 1999 a year of progress and achievement on each front.

The president's continuing focus on these matters—in talks with world leaders, meetings with experts, policy sessions with his national security team, and speeches to the public—makes plain that the United States will not shrink from the fight against weapons of mass destruction. By your presence here, you show that you have not given up on this most important of causes. Together, let us do all we can so that the next time we assemble we can find renewed cause for hope—hope for a safer future for all peoples.

NOTE

1. On January 12, 1999, National Security Adviser Samuel Berger delivered the keynote speech to the Carnegie International Non-Proliferation Conference. His speech is presented here in full with his permission.

—RUSSIA—

5

The Crisis in Russia's Nuclear Cities

Ken Luongo, Matthew Bunn, Rose Gottemoeller, Lev Ryabev

The Russian nuclear complex is the largest in the world, encompassing ten dedicated "closed" cities and dozens of other facilities and employing hundreds of thousands of employees across the Russian Federation. Formerly dedicated to the production of plutonium and highly enriched uranium and of nuclear weapons, these cities now face serious economic and social problems brought on by the end of the Cold War, the collapse of the Soviet system, and the reduced demand for nuclear weapon–related activities in Russia. The Russian Ministry of Atomic Energy has, after several years, finally acknowledged that the size of the nuclear complex must be reduced to reflect current economic and security requirements. The United States and Russia have launched the Nuclear Cities Initiative (NCI) to facilitate commercial development in these closed cities, thereby providing alternative, peaceful employment for scientists and technicians that might otherwise be forced to sell their nuclear related skills to the highest bidder. The nuclear cities' current situation and Russian and U.S. efforts to address those situations are discussed below.

TAKING THE INITIATIVE
By Ken Luongo

It has been very difficult to focus the attention of the public or of policymakers on the serious problems that currently exist in Russia's closed nuclear cities. While some attention has been given to various pieces of the problem, the underlying economic issues and the need to redirect scientific activities in the cities remain largely ignored. These issues need to be addressed in a comprehensive manner if the proliferation problems emanating from the Russian nuclear complex are to be adequately addressed and ultimately solved. The risk of nuclear materials and technology leaking out of the nuclear cities to rogue regimes or terrorist groups is a clear example of how economics is affecting proliferation. There are ten closed nuclear cities in Russia. During the Cold War, these cities were dedicated to nuclear weapon design, weapon assembly and disassembly, and the production of fissile materials. For the last ten years, these cities have been struggling to diversify some of their activities to non-defense-related work. While these efforts have shown mixed results, Russia is taking internal steps, in cooperation with international programs, to address this issue.

FIGURE 5.1

RUSSIA'S NUCLEAR CITIES

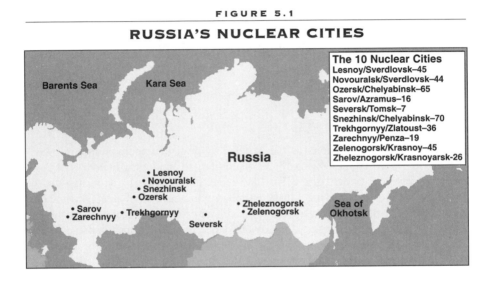

The 10 Nuclear Cities
Lesnoy/Sverdlovsk–45
Novouralsk/Sverdlovsk–44
Ozersk/Chelyabinsk–65
Sarov/Azramus–16
Seversk/Tomsk–7
Snezhinsk/Chelyabinsk–70
Trekhgornyy/Zlatoust–36
Zarechnyy/Penza–19
Zelenogorsk/Krasnoy–45
Zheleznogorsk/Krasnoyarsk-26

The list of Russian accomplishments in reorienting the cities is pretty short, and much more remains to be done. We estimate that thirty thousand to fifty thousand jobs need to be created or alternative employment needs to be found. Such levels are required in order for the Russian complex to be reduced to a more manageable size consistent with post–Cold War realities. These two missions—creating non-weapons employment opportunities and downsizing the nuclear complex in Russia—are the two major goals of the Nuclear Cities Initiative (NCI).

The Nuclear Cities Initiative is a good example of how nongovernmental organizations can help facilitate policy. There existed an underlying desire in both governments to work cooperatively on the nuclear cities problem. The U.S. and Russian national laboratories had discussions on this issue, and there were also some basic discussions taking place at the governmental level. But government officials tend to be too diversified and too frantic with their current priorities to really think comprehensively about what should be done. With no dedicated project in place, and no concrete plan from which to begin, little progress was made.

As one of its first acts, the nongovernmental Russian-American Nuclear Security Advisory Council (RANSAC) organized a roundtable in Moscow designed to identify steps the United States and Russia could take to address the economic and employment issues plaguing the Russian complex. This meeting was attended by, among others, Dr. Lev Ryabev from MINATOM, who was accompanied by Dr. Evgeny Avrorin, then the director of the nuclear weapon design laboratory at Chelyabinsk-70. Dr. Avrorin has proved to be instrumental in the development of the NCI. Other key Russian participants included the directors of Arzamas-16 and Tomsk-7 and the chief engineer from Krasnoyarsk-26. The meeting discussed a variety of topics, including what types of projects might interest Russian participants and what the American government might be willing and able to do. All the participants left with a feeling of accomplishment and enthusiasm for the number of new ideas that had emerged from their cooperative efforts.

On the basis of the results of the meeting and subsequent analysis, RANSAC drew up a proposal for expanded action between the U.S. and Russian governments in this area and recommended that an initial budget of $60 million be established. The proposal recommended that activities be initiated in three major areas: product commercialization and business training, non-proliferation analysis and collaboration, and environmental restoration.

The proposal was released in early September 1997 in advance of the ninth session of the Gore-Chernomyrdin Commission, with the goal of the United States and Russia's accepting this proposal as part of the Gore-Chernomyrdin process. A statement of support was made at this meeting, and in March 1998 Vice President Gore and Prime Minister Chernomyrdin approved the initiation of the Nuclear Cities Initiative. In summer 1998, Senators Joseph Biden and Pete Domenici sponsored an amendment to fund the new NCI effort at $30 million (subsequently reduced to $15 million in the final legislation). An intergovernmental agreement on NCI was finalized in September 1998, and the program was under way.

The birth of the Nuclear Cities Initiative is a very successful example of how nongovernmental organizations can work collaboratively with the U.S. and Russian governments in support of an important policy initiative. RANSAC did not try to pressure either government into action but instead created a process for mutually respectful collaboration, provided a balanced analysis of the problem, and presented both governments with a road map of recommendations. This facilitated an understanding of what each government could and could not live with, brought key officials and experts together, allowed people on the ground at the individual Russian nuclear facilities to provide their perspective and needs, and created a policy framework that the U.S. and Russian governments could endorse. This process certainly is not a strict recipe for future action but rather a description of one method that led to a successful conclusion.

A big debt of gratitude is owed to Dr. Ryabev, who has been extremely open to suggestions and very good at explaining his complex, and also to Rose Gottemoeller, who really carried the ball inside the U.S. government, leading to the creation of the Nuclear Cities Initiative.

ALTERNATIVE EMPLOYMENT OPPORTUNITIES
By Matthew Bunn

In order to achieve its objectives of downsizing the Russian nuclear complex and providing sustainable employment for displaced nuclear employees, the new Nuclear Cities Initiative should focus on four critical areas:

PRIVATE-SECTOR JOB GROWTH

Neither the U.S. government nor the Russian government has the money to forever employ nuclear workers who are no longer needed, so in the long run private job growth in the nuclear cities is the only answer. Given the current economic collapse in Russia, however, fostering private-sector growth and attracting foreign investment in Russia's nuclear cities will not be easy. These cities face a huge number of obstacles to private-sector growth. In addition to the political risks and structural problems that plague private-sector activities in Russia in general, the nuclear cities are physically isolated and their closed status makes access difficult (forty-five days' advance permission is typically required for a foreign visit). Moreover, their populations have virtually no experience with private businesses or a market economy, and they have virtually no business infrastructure (not having needed it in the past). But the cities offer potential opportunities as well, principally a large number of highly skilled scientists and engineers, willing to work at wage rates far below those that prevail in Western countries. To overcome these obstacles and seize these opportunities, the approach of most past U.S. efforts related to defense conversion, focused on funding high-tech R&D and providing some business training, will be helpful but will not be enough. The full spectrum of tools that have been used to promote private-sector growth in other areas (in Russia and elsewhere)—business centers, loan guarantees, political risk insurance, start-up capital for new enterprises, tax incentives, and the like—are likely to be necessary.

While the Department of Energy (DOE), which is managing the Nuclear Cities Initiative, is not well suited to employ all of these tools, other U.S. and international agencies are, and it will be essential to draw in their experience and resources. The Regional Investment Initiative established under the Gore-Chernomyrdin Commission has been designed to target a broad range of assistance to particular regions; a similar approach can and should be taken with the nuclear cities (though their economic prospects are much more problematic than those of the regions chosen for the Regional Investment Initiative). It will be critical for the U.S. government to work closely with the private sector—particularly those large firms that have already been involved in the nuclear cities or have explored involvement, such as Microsoft, Intel, and Sun Microsystems, among others—to find out what forms of support will be needed to leverage larger private-sector commitments. Working with other governments to target similar efforts in these cities is also likely to be key to success. It appears likely that the areas with the most promise for a small amount of government investment to lead to substantial private growth and job creation are (a) low-tech small and medium-size enterprises within the cities, largely providing products and services needed within Russia and (b) approaches in which Western firms hire nuclear city experts as knowledge workers (mathematicians, computer programmers, etc.) so that access to secret production lines, transportation of goods, and the like are not major issues. With the shortage of software experts and other engineers in the United States, U.S. firms are increasingly putting together global teams including engineers around the globe, in which experts from the nuclear cities would be prime candidates for participation.[1]

NON-PROLIFERATION AND ARMS CONTROL

Shifting some former nuclear weapons scientists to non-proliferation and arms control activities should also be a fundamental part of the Nuclear Cities Initiative. This approach would provide jobs for nuclear scientists while at the same time accomplishing objectives that the United States would want accomplished in any case. While there is no prospect for employing tens of thousands of workers on non-proliferation, for the small cadre of top scientists this can be an important avenue of employment. To date, there are significantly more former weapons scientists in the United States who have successfully "converted" to work on non-proliferation and environmental analysis and R&D than have been employed by commercial high-tech firms spun off from the labs. If initial U.S. funding helps establish non-proliferation centers of excellence at the Russian weapons labs, and the centers succeed in demonstrating the value and importance of their work, it is possible that the Russian government itself will ultimately pick up the tab for their continued operation if and when the economic situation improves. There are dozens of examples of non-proliferation and arms control issues crying out for the application of additional expertise of the kind nuclear weapons scientists could bring to bear—from developing databases of key technologies on which to base nuclear export control decisions, to developing means to verify deep reductions in nuclear warhead and fissile material stockpiles. Recently, a collaboration between U.S. nongovernmental organizations and foundations and the U.S. government has provided start-up funding for new non-proliferation and arms control analysis centers at Sarov (formerly Arzamas-16), Snezhinsk (formerly Chelyabinsk-70), the Kurchatov Institute in Moscow, and the Institute of Physics and Power Engineering at Obninsk, but there is far more that could be done.[2]

NUCLEAR REMEDIATION, ENERGY, AND ENVIRONMENTAL TECHNOLOGIES

The United States certainly does not have the funds to pay for cleanup of the Russian nuclear complex or for deployment of new energy and environmental technologies in Russia. But these are all areas where the U.S. government funds hundreds of millions of dollars annually developing new technologies—a small portion of which might be done by experts from Russia's nuclear cities. This would be a win-win-win approach: The United States would get the work done for less (given the low wage rates in Russia), Russian nuclear experts would get challenging and interesting work making use of their skills, and both sides would be able to make use of the resulting technologies. Development of nuclear cleanup technology, in particular, is a "natural" for NCI: both the United States and Russia face massive nuclear cleanup problems in their nuclear complexes, and Russian experts can bring a range of fresh ideas to the U.S. cleanup R&D program at low cost—as well as to heavily contaminated sites where the technologies they develop could be tested. More broadly, it would make sense for the secretary of energy to direct all the leaders of DOE programs that sponsor substantial R&D programs to pull together lists of projects in their areas that could be accomplished cost-effectively by contracting efforts to experts from the Russian nuclear cities. By this means, tens of millions of dollars in near-term funding for real jobs in the Russian nuclear cities could be arranged in a manner that would contribute to, rather than detracting from, the other priorities of the U.S. government.[3] While a "Contract Research Initiative" along these lines is being discussed within DOE, the outcome, if and when a decision is made, seems likely to be substantially more limited than the tens of millions of dollars per year proposed here (which would be drawn from, and contribute to, existing DOE R&D budgets, rather than requiring new funding).

SHRINKING THE RUSSIAN NUCLEAR WEAPONS COMPLEX

Today, Russia still maintains a massive nuclear weapons infrastructure, capable—if Russia had the funds—of producing thousands of nuclear weapons components and nuclear weapons a year. The United States, by contrast, has downsized its complex to the point that it no longer has the capability to produce more than a few hundred nuclear weapons or components annually. With the end of the Cold War, Russia has no need for a nuclear weapons complex of this scale, and cannot afford it in its current economic circumstances. Thus, it is in both the U.S. interest and the Russian interest to substantially reduce the capacity of the remaining weapons production infrastructure in Russia. Russia has already announced that it will close two of its four nuclear weapons assembly and disassembly facilities in the next few years (the two smallest: the Avangard plant at Sarov and the plant at the closed city of Penza-19). The NCI should work with Russia to help facilitate the permanent closure of these plants (along with other excess facilities for producing plutonium and HEU weapons components, for example) and the reemployment of their workers. More broadly, the United States should encourage Russia to develop a coherent plan for the transition to a greatly downsized nuclear complex, working on a less formal lab-to-lab basis to provide information on the U.S. experience of planning the downsizing (which Russia has requested) and perhaps even working together to sketch out plans for a minimum sustainable complex for the future.

While the future of Russia's closed nuclear cities is critically important, there are also many nuclear facilities with potentially vulnerable nuclear material that are *not* in the closed cities, whose future must also be addressed. Russia's civilian nuclear complex, like its nuclear weapons complex, is not economically sustainable over the long haul. Yet the managers of each facility would, of course, like to keep their facility open, and little high-level planning has gone into thinking about what facilities should stay on their present course, what facilities should be redirected to other missions, and what facilities should be closed. Wherever there are facilities with weapons-usable material or weapons-related information, there are U.S. interests at stake, and the United States should work with Russia to initiate a sustainable transition to a smaller complex, with appropriate alternative employment for the excess nuclear experts.

THE NUCLEAR CITIES INITIATIVE:
A GOOD START DOWN A LONG ROAD
By Rose Gottemoeller

The Nuclear Cities Initiative is an ideal model of how the nongovernmental community can work with government officials in both the United States and Russia to develop and help implement important initiatives. The NCI is entering the tough stage, going from concept to implementation, and the help of nongovernmental organizations (NGOs) will be needed in the coming years if NCI is to be successful in its goals. The NCI is a complicated effort and will require a lot of fine-tuning as time goes on. But the program is moving in the right direction, and with the combined efforts of the U.S. and Russian governments and the help of the NGO community, the initiative will be able to make quick progress in establishing itself.

Unlike the traditional focus of our efforts in the Russian nuclear weapons complex, the NCI is not just concerned about individuals at the very top levels of the scientific establishment. A growing focus on the insider threat has emerged from the economic hardship affecting technical workers at all levels. This insider threat is becoming a great concern and is helping to motivate U.S. effort to establish this program.

Beyond its direct impact, the initiative itself is helping define the future direction of U.S.-Russian nuclear cooperation. The initiative builds on several principles that were not present or highly developed when nuclear threat reduction work began in Russia six years ago. The three principles are realism, partnership, and complementarity.

REALISM

In today's context, realism is the recognition that the economic problems of Russia in general, and the nuclear cities in particular, are much more persistent than had been expected in the mid- and early 1990s. As late as last spring, U.S. and Russian specialists alike had believed that in 1998, the Russian economy would turn around and begin to grow. Now it is widely understood that this is going to take a long time to accomplish.

For our work in the nuclear cities, this reality calls for projects that will produce fast results in terms of job creation. We know that hard results will be needed in order to gain greater U.S. and Russian acceptance of the NCI concept. For example, software development and engineering consulting are two areas that are receiving heavy attention, since they require relatively little capital improvement and can tap directly into the brain power of the Russian complex. Successes here will help establish positive short-term momentum.

At the same time, however, it is critical to focus on the long-term problem of consistent economic development. This requires consistent work on the infrastructure problems of the cities, such as the communications infrastructure, and also on training the workforce in business practices and management. Realism in the Nuclear Cities Initiative context means working toward both short-term results and long-term potential in a very difficult economic environment.

PARTNERSHIP

Partnership is a somewhat tarnished word after six years of post-Soviet cooperation between Russia and the United States. Nevertheless, this term captures the notion that each side is capable of working on an equal footing with the other, with each bringing its own resources and expertise to the table.

This kind of partnership is the essence of the Nuclear Cities Initiative. The Russians initially approached the U.S. government with the NCI concept, after they had already begun to plan for the conversion and transformation of their nuclear complex. The necessity of focusing on nonweapon economic development and job creation in the nuclear cities was an idea that moved from East to West.

But Russia approached the United States with the hope of learning from the U.S. experience in downsizing its own nuclear weapons complex, where there are both successes and failures to discuss. This is one reason why the initiative is focusing on the establishment of city-to-city relationships. Such activities were exemplified by a successful trip by the mayor of Livermore to Snezhinsk (Chelyabinsk-70) in November 1998. And it is that kind of city-to-city communication that the NCI is seeking to encourage, because it is one important conduit by which the experience of the U.S. nuclear weapons complex can feed directly into the Russian nuclear weapons complex.

The Russians have been clear throughout that their own resources will go into the effort to transform the nuclear cities. They are not expecting the United States to foot the entire bill, although U.S. resources will certainly be part of the mix and will be important during this period of economic crisis in Russia.

COMPLEMENTARITY

In addition to the targeted resources of the Nuclear Cities Initiative, the United States will also be taking advantage of other existing programs and resources both in and out of government. A prime example of this is the Initiatives for Proliferation Prevention (IPP) program, which has already been working in the nuclear weapons establishment for five years.

IPP will continue to provide funds to scientists in the nuclear cities, working in the laboratories and stressing the development of commercialization of the technologies that come out of those laboratories. The Nuclear Cities Initiative will focus on job creation in the cities themselves, not necessarily dependent on commercialization of technologies emerging from the weapons labs. So the two programs are complementary but by no means identical in their goals or in their purposes.

A good example here is that of software development where there has already been some encouragement from U.S. software firms in their interest in the cities. This does not involve the development and commercialization of technologies but really uses the brainpower and expertise of the people in the institutes to go into software projects. The stress here, once again, is on developing viable and long-term non-weapons-related jobs.

It is important to underscore that the NCI does not seek or intend to replicate work that is being done in other agencies. For example, the Commerce Department already has an extensive program for business training and the initiative need only serve as a conduit to get that training to the nuclear cities.

The NCI is focused on complementarity because there is no desire to reinvent the wheel. People in Congress and the larger policy community have already expressed some concern that NCI may try to repeat current activities. It's important to underscore, therefore, that NCI is aware of the many resources that are already in existence and the experience that has emerged over the last six years. And while NCI will seek to take advantage of that and build on it, there is no intent to re-create those programs.

The transformation of the nuclear cities of Russia is a path that the Russians stepped onto first and then invited the United States to join. There is valuable experience to share that should enable Russia to avoid some of the pitfalls that were encountered over the last thirty years of downsizing the U.S. nuclear weapons complex.

Despite the economic crisis in Russia, the NCI expects to quickly gain momentum in 1999 in a few key areas in each of the three target cities in which we are working, that is, Sarov, Snezhinsk, and Zheleznogorsk. The NCI is establishing the basis for long-term expertise and infrastructure creation, and while this is a daunting task, it is one that has been embraced because of the success of the established working relationship with our Russian colleagues.

THE NUCLEAR CITIES INITIATIVE:
A RUSSIAN PERSPECTIVE
By Lev Ryabev

During the last few years, there has been much discussion and speculation, including stories in the mass media, about the situation in Russia's nuclear weapons complex. Some have called for the demolition of the nuclear weapons complex. Others have suggested that Russia's weak economy might lead to the possibility of nuclear weapons from Russia's stockpiles being sold to some third countries, although this concern was not expressed during the conference on global management of nuclear materials.

There are problems, but they are under strict control, and in order to avoid any dangerous accidents or incidents, further government efforts are required. As far as the theft of nuclear materials is concerned, there were two attempts in 1992, but the last attempt dates back to 1994. Since then the situation has dramatically improved, to a great extent due to cooperation with the United States in the area of nuclear materials accounting, control, and physical protection.

Russia's nuclear weapons complex comprises seventeen industrial enterprises and scientific research institutes, which are mostly located in the ten closed cities. The total population of these ten closed cities is 756,000, while the typical population is somewhere between 21,000 and 100,000 people.

TABLE 5.1

CLOSED CITIES OF RUSSIA'S MINATOM
Total Population, 756,000

City	Population	Main Defense Production
Sarov (Arzamas-16)	83,000	Nuclear weapon design, assembly
Zarechnyy (Penza-9)	64,000	Nuclear weapon assembly
Novoural'sk (Sverdlovsk-44)	96,000	Uranium enrichment
Lesnoy (Sverdlovk-45)	58,000	Nuclear weapon assembly
Ozersk (Chelyabinsk-65)	88,000	Pu production reactors, reprocessing, waste, MOX fuel
Snezhinsk (Chelyabinsk-70)	48,000	Nuclear weapon design
Trekhgornyy (Zlatoust-36)	33,000	Nuclear weapon assembly
Seversk (Tomsk-7)	119,000	Pu production reactors, U-enrichment, reprocessing
Zhelenznogorsk (Krasnoyarsk-26)	100,000	Pu production reactors, reprocessing
Zelenogorsk (Krasnoyarsk-45)	67,000	Uranium enrichment

During the last few years there have been significant changes in the activities of Russia's nuclear weapons complex. The manufacturing of uranium and plutonium for weapons has ceased. The nuclear weapon stockpiles, which were considerable, have been dramatically reduced, and government defense orders have also been reduced by seven times since 1990.

Nuclear disarmament should be a well-organized and not spontaneous process. This is a process that is closely associated with radioactive hazardous materials. It deals with the safety and security of the nuclear weapon stockpiles. It is closely linked with nuclear materials accounting, control, and physical protection. And there is a close association with proper weapons dismantlement and disposal and with retraining of personnel for peaceful activities. From this viewpoint, the Nuclear Cities Initiative is a good opportunity for Russia.

There are three stages of the Russian nuclear dismantlement process that should be highlighted. First is the reduction of nuclear weapon delivery vehicles, but unfortunately this does not cover the issue of irreversibility of nuclear reductions. Next is stopping nuclear weapon tests, and therefore the ability to qualitatively improve the next generation of nuclear weapons. And last is the dismantlement of nuclear warheads, which is the next issue for negotiations between Russia and the United States.

Together with the United States, Russia has started a huge and far-reaching program of dismantlement of nuclear weapons. The problem of highly enriched uranium is being resolved, and the problem of plutonium is on the agenda. Just recently an agreement that deals with the retraining of scientific personnel for peaceful activities and the military denuclearization of the enterprises in some of the nuclear cities was signed. Right now this process is just beginning.

In association with the measures in the area of nuclear disarmament and the radical changes in the nuclear weapons complex of Russia, a targeted program for restructuring and conversion of nuclear industry has been developed. The program will begin with ceasing the assembly of nuclear warheads at a number of enterprises. In addition, this program foresees the restructuring of each complex and enterprise.

TABLE 5.2

TARGETED PROGRAM "RESTRUCTURING AND CONVERSION OF NUCLEAR INDUSTRY (NUCLEAR WEAPONS COMPLEX) ENTERPRISES"

Beginning in 2000: cease assembly of nuclear warheads at two of four facilities
Beginning in 2003: cease dismantlement of warheads at two of four facilities
Consolidate manufacturing of fissile material components for warheads at one of two facilities
Core conversion of three plutonium production reactors
Consolidate defense procurement activities to increase capacity for civil production
Establish production capacities for manufacturing nuclear power fuel from former-weapon uranium and plutonium
Differentiate nuclear weapons activities and civil activities
In 2005: reduction of defense procurement order employees in nuclear weapons complex from 75,000 persons to 40,000 persons

Further disarmament should be taken in the area of defense activities. This program foresees a deep reduction of those working in the weapons complex from seventy-five thousand to forty thousand by the year 2005. This is one of the most serious issues today. It is difficult to speak about the irreversibility of the nuclear disarmament process while the scientists are still thinking in terms of nuclear weapons. At the present time, however, competition for government purchase orders will continue because the well-being of the scientific and technical staff depends on it.

On the other hand, there is a definite risk of losing the ability to properly manage the high-tech experts in this area. Naturally, this risk should be minimized. This problem is complicated by the unemployment problem. In these ten cities there are some eighteen thousand unemployed workers who are not registered. The program will also try to resolve this issue by means of creating new employment at the level of about fifteen thousand jobs.

Like the national labs in the United States, these closed cities are a large part of the nation's wealth. These nuclear cities have a concentration of knowledge in high technologies, but in many cases, these cities face problems resulting from the nature of their work, including radioactive contamination at the enterprises and in their vicinity. In addition, the nuclear weapons complex enterprises are the only industry in these cities. They are located far from any large industrial and cultural centers. These matters should be taken into consideration in our joint activities.

Russia believes that the closed cities can play a very important role in resolving proliferation problems. One of the provisions of the Non-Proliferation Treaty is the development of safe nuclear power technologies. The Nuclear Cities Initiative should play an important role in this process. The possibility of cooperation in this area was discussed during the tenth session of the Gore-Chernomyrdin dialogue in March 1998. The secretary of energy has initiated the development of an agreement in this area. Our ministry has supported this initiative, and, in September 1998, the agreement was signed by the secretary of energy of the United States and by the minister of the Russian Federation for Atomic Energy. Both sides have a lot of work to do in converting the nuclear weapons complex. Issues ranging from scientific conversion to conversion of plutonium-producing reactors to nuclear power plants need to be dealt with. Generally speaking, the implementation of this agreement will considerably help the scientists from these closed cities to enter the world community and will provide an opportunity to resolve a number of social problems as well.

Actually, the mutual trust between Russia and the United States in this sensitive area is growing. From this mutual trust comes more openness. The mutual management of the conversion of the nuclear weapons complex will further improve relations between Russia and the United States, and this agreement will serve the noble goals and well-being of all peoples.

NOTES

1. See, for example, Zachary G. Pascal, "The Rage for Global Teams," *Technology Review*, July–August 1998.

2. These centers were established at the initiative of RANSAC, particularly Kenneth N. Luongo and Frank von Hippel. For further discussion of non-proliferation and arms control programs that could be pursued, see, for example, Matthew Bunn, Oleg Bukharin, Jill Cetina, Kenneth Luongo, and Frank von Hippel, "Retooling Russia's Nuclear Cities," *Bulletin of the Atomic Scientists*, September–October 1998.

3. The author is grateful to Siegfried Hecker for suggesting this concept. Hecker and others at the Los Alamos, Livermore, Sandia, and Pacific Northwest laboratories have elaborated this idea in the "Contract Research Initiative" proposal now being considered by the Department of Energy.

6

Deadlock in the Strategic Reductions Process: A Russian Perspective

Alexander A. Pikayev

At a historic meeting in the Kremlin on January 3, 1993, Presidents George Bush of the United States and Boris Yeltsin of the Russian Federation signed the Treaty on Further Strategic Nuclear Arms Limitations and Reductions (START II), which followed START I, concluded in July 1991. The treaty promised to be the grandest achievement of the negotiated bilateral strategic arms control process between Moscow and Washington. That process, initiated in the early 1970s by U.S. president Richard Nixon and Soviet general secretary Leonid Brezhnev, had been the centerpiece of U.S.-Soviet relations for more than twenty years. The importance of strategic reductions to both sides was witnessed by the fact that the process continued despite deep declines in the bilateral relationship following the Soviet invasion of Afghanistan in 1979, as well as sharp disagreements on the future of the Anti-Ballistic Missile (ABM) Treaty, triggered by President Ronald Reagan's 1983 Strategic Defense Initiative and by instances of Soviet noncompliance with the treaty.

In the late 1980s, Mikhail Gorbachev's *perestroika* and new thinking policy led to a radical change in bilateral relations and significant progress in strategic arms control talks. In July 1991, Presidents Bush and Gorbachev signed START I, which, for the first time, obliged the two nuclear superpowers to reduce, rather than merely limit, their deployed strategic arsenal to 6,000 warheads.[1] The treaty also established a stringent verification and monitoring regime.

START II not only stipulated reducing U.S. and Russian strategic nuclear capabilities to 3,500 deployed warheads, but it also provided an opportunity to limit the most destabilizing weapons by requiring the elimination of all intercontinental ballistic missiles with multiple independently targeted reentry vehicles (MIRVed ICBMs). The "MIRV ban" covered all Russian SS-18 "Satan" missiles, which, with the ability to carry ten warheads each, were of greatest concern to the United States. As a result, START II would require the United States, and Russia especially, to reconfigure their strategic triads into a more stable composition of mobile and silo-based single-warhead ICBMs, as well as submarine-launched ballistic missiles (SLBMs). For the first time, Moscow also agreed to give up its long-held insistence on strategic nuclear parity with the United States. President Yeltsin stated that under certain circumstances Russia might agree to deploy not more than three thousand strategic warheads, five hundred below the treaty limit.

The end of the Cold War, the collapse of the Soviet Union, and democratic reform in Russia all created high hopes for strategic nuclear disarmament. Most policymakers expected START II to be the second in a series of relatively rapid steps toward further radical bilateral reductions, which might eventually incorporate the other three declared nuclear powers—United Kingdom, France, and China. However, history has witnessed completely opposite developments. For more than six years START II has been awaiting ratification by the State Duma, the lower house of the Russian Parliament. Bilateral dialogue on further reductions has not moved beyond a few rounds of consultations. By summer 1999, it seemed certain that START II had been finally shelved in the Duma without any realistic prospects for entry into force, at least until presidential elections in Russia and the United States are held in 2000.

This deadlock has jeopardized the future of negotiated, bilateral strategic arms control. Prospects for future talks on tactical nuclear weapons and warhead transparency measures, which could be conducted parallel to negotiations on a START III, are dim. Furthermore, this strategic reduction malaise has eroded another important strategic weapons limitation agreement, the ABM Treaty. Finally, the inability of the two largest nuclear powers to demonstrate progress toward their long-standing commitment to nuclear disarmament, embodied in article VI of the nuclear Non-Proliferation Treaty, might severely weaken the entire international nuclear non-proliferation regime.

This deadlock did not arrive overnight, however. Several factors in the 1990s contributed to the decline of strategic arms control:

- A rise in U.S.-Russian cooperation at the end of the Cold War removed traditional arms control from the center of the bilateral relationship. Both Moscow and Washington became much less concerned with each others' missiles and preferred to focus on more pressing topics instead (e.g., safety of nuclear materials, leakage of sensitive technologies, promoting Russia's democratic and market reforms).

- The decline of the Russian economy made it difficult for Moscow to maintain even the relatively low START II force levels. It is widely acknowledged that irrespective of the treaty's future, the number of strategic warheads Russia can deploy will drop by at least several thousand. This realization significantly reduced Washington's incentive to gain Russia's disarmament through formal arms control agreements, which require concessions from both sides.

- Nuclear and missile proliferation in the developing world provided new incentives for the United States to deploy an antiballistic missile system and gradually eroded its interest in maintaining the ABM Treaty, which is historically, strategically, and militarily interconnected with the strategic arms control process.
- The end of the honeymoon in the U.S.-Russian bilateral relationship, marked by growing disagreements over NATO enlargement, colliding interests in the post-Soviet space, and opposite approaches to conflict resolution in Bosnia, Iraq, and Kosovo considerably spoiled the Russian domestic political prospects for START II ratification. As a result, provisions like numerical disparity, asymmetry in breakout capabilities, and different methods of achieving reductions, which seemed irrelevant when the treaty was negotiated in 1992–1993, gained higher profile and attention.
- Ironically, Russia's nascent democracy quickly learned several lessons from the U.S. model. On the domestic political stage, START II became hostage to a tense relationship between the executive branch and the opposition-dominated legislature. In the United States, controversies between the White House and the Congress, together with a desire to promote Russian ratification, prevented the launching of START III talks before START II was ratified.

MOVING SECURITY PRIORITIES

The dissolution of the Soviet Union and end to confrontation with Moscow led the United States to significantly rethink its national security priorities. The primary U.S. task during the Cold War of deterring the USSR by a combination of military and arms control measures was replaced by a much less concrete mission: to retain the necessary capabilities to deter a Russia that sometime in the future might reemerge as an assertive power threatening the United States and its allies.

By the late 1990s, the remarkable unilateral decline in Russia's military power reached a point at which Moscow was unable to sustain the conventional force levels necessary to conduct large-scale offensive operations in Europe. By 1999, the Russian armed forces had been reduced to just 1.2 million personnel, down from 2.8 million in May 1992. During the Soviet period, annual defense spending exceeded $100 billion, whereas Russia's FY99 defense budget would not exceed $4 billion.[2] In 1989, the Soviet first line of defense was located in the center of present-day Germany, 2,000 kilometers west of Moscow. Now that line has receded to merely 400 kilometers from Moscow.

Given the longer life of nuclear weapons, however, there has not been a corresponding decline in the nuclear forces. During the 1990s, Moscow did not face serious difficulties in maintaining the force levels required by START I. The exception lies in the strategic nuclear submarine (SSBN) fleet, which, due to lack of financing, has been decommissioned ahead of the START I schedule. Since 1990, the number of operational SSBNs has been reduced 2.5 times, affecting even relatively modern Delta III and Typhoon subs.[3]

More important, nuclear procurement has been drastically curtailed. During the height of the Cold War the Soviet Union produced more than one hundred nuclear missiles annually. In modern Russia the production rate has never exceeded ten ICBMs per year. Not one new strategic nuclear submarine has been completed. (Construction of a new SSBN started in 1996, with initial plans for completion in 2002, but it has been delayed until 2007.[4]) Production of SLBMs[5] and heavy bombers was halted (with many difficulties and delays in completing the assembly of the Tu-160 aircraft started before 1992).[6]

In the 1990s Russia set its strategic nuclear modernization programs according to the START II provisions. It successfully completed development and testing of the new Topol M (SS-27) single-warhead ICBM, which can be deployed in both silo and road-mobile versions. The system was first deployed in late 1997, but just ten missiles were deployed by the end of 1998. Ideally, Moscow hopes to increase the production of Topol Ms to thirty to forty ICBMs per year, but financial constraints will make achieving even this relatively modest task quite problematic.[7] In July 1998, the Russian Security Council decided to develop a new SLBM based on Topol M technology.[8] If the program is successful, the future sea leg of Russia's strategic triad will be based on light SLBMs carrying a small number of MIRVs per missile.

The combination of these three factors—early decommissioning of some strategic systems, very low procurement rates, and transition to light ballistic missiles with single or a few warheads—will most certainly lead to a radical decline in Russian strategic force levels around 2010, when Russia will start withdrawing its MIRVed ICBMs from service. Unless new programs to develop MIRVed ICBMs and accelerate production of new SSBNs are adopted in the next few years, Russia's strategic nuclear deterrent force could fall below one thousand deployed warheads sometime in the next two decades.[9] Some Russian officials are predicting an even lower number of perhaps several hundred deployed warheads.

With radical changes in political relations between Moscow and Washington, and Russian reductions almost guaranteed despite the absence of new arms limitations, the Cold War task of guaranteeing Russia's strategic nuclear disarmament through negotiated arms control treaties lost a significant part of its rationale for the United States. The lack of adequate resources and political will effectively prevent Moscow from maintaining numerical strategic parity with the United States, which the Soviet Union had reached by the 1970s, even at the level of START II.

Moreover, the decay of Russia's nuclear force has resulted in a situation unthinkable just ten years ago. Now there is a growing perception that U.S. national security is threatened not by Moscow's nuclear strength but by its weakness. The disintegration of the Soviet Union, Russia's uneasy and chaotic transition to democracy and a market economy, financial shortfalls, and continuing social and economic degradation have elevated concerns about the insecurity of the country's huge nuclear complex. At worst, unauthorized access to Russia's huge stockpiles of nuclear warheads and materials might greatly increase global nuclear proliferation and bring nuclear weapons into the hands of regimes and terrorist groups hostile to the United States (for more details, see chapter 7).

According to U.S. estimates, Russia possesses about fourteen hundred tons of weapons-usable nuclear material—separated plutonium and highly enriched uranium (HEU). The material is stored at more than fifty sites throughout Russia.[10] Due to the collapse of the old Soviet system of administrative control, which had protected these materials from unauthorized access, they are more accessible now than at any other time in history.[11] Three cases of diversion of significant HEU quantities in Russia have been the subject of criminal prosecution,[12] and a report by a U.S. congressional commission documents four other instances of fissile material theft since 1992.[13]

In the mid-1990s, it was believed that the protection of nonweaponized fissile materials was the biggest problem in Russia. However, two incidents in 1998 involving troops responsible for nuclear weapons were reported. In the first case, a nineteen-year-old sailor on an Akula-class nuclear attack submarine killed seven other servicemen and blocked himself in a torpedo compartment for twenty hours, threatening to blow up the submarine. In the end he either committed suicide or was killed by counterterrorism commandos. Although authorities denied the presence of nuclear warheads on board, the case significantly increased concerns about the discipline of Russian troops protecting nuclear weapons. These concerns were heightened as a result of a second case, when five soldiers from the elite Twelfth Main Directorate forces, the principal guardians of Russia's nuclear weapons, killed another soldier and took hostages at Russia's nuclear test range at Novaya Zemlya. They then asked for a plane to fly to their home in the Republic of Dagestan, located in the turbulent North Caucasus region of Russia. The hostages were eventually freed and the hijackers detained by the Federal Security Service.[14]

These pressing events have diverted U.S. attention away from the strategic nuclear arms control agenda. This was quite natural; the end of the Cold War established an excellent political environment in which the United States and Russia possessed unique chances to build a radically new, nondeterrent bilateral nuclear relationship. Had this relationship been formed, the relevance of both deterrence and strategic nuclear arms control would have been further reduced. Although Washington has launched a set of cooperative initiatives aimed at addressing Moscow's concerns, these efforts were insufficient to make a real breakthrough in moving beyond the traditional deterrence paradigm. Moscow demonstrated a lack of creative thinking, too. Thus, new nondeterrent nuclear relations were not established, and both deterrence and strategic nuclear arms control continue to be important issues, albeit now stagnant. In light of these developments, inadequate attention to strategic arms control over the past decade was a mistake that has led to the revival of traditional thinking in Russia.

DEBATES IN RUSSIA:
ARGUMENTS PRO ET CONTRA

From the very beginning, START II faced bitter criticism in Russia. Initially, the most vocal critics could be found in the Supreme Soviet, the opposition-dominated, retrograde parliament, which was dissolved by President Yeltsin in September 1993.

Later, mainstream politicians began to criticize the treaty, although a significant number of them continued to advocate conditional treaty ratification. These politicians believed that treaty deficiencies could be corrected during negotiations on a follow-up agreement, START III. They thought that since the treaty had already been signed, it would be better to ratify it with conditions. A simple nonratification—although it could not be excluded—might trigger severe negative consequences:

- Bilateral relations with the United States could be dramatically damaged; Moscow's attempts to integrate into the world economy and to join the club of privileged, developed nations might be significantly complicated.
- The overall strategic arms control process would be disrupted without START II. Russia's strategic force levels would go lower than the START I and START II ceilings. Russia could maintain approximate numerical strategic parity with the United States only by involving Washington in arms control agreements. The weaker Russia became, the more it was interested in arms control.
- The United States might withdraw from other agreements, such as the ABM Treaty, which Moscow wants to preserve.
- START II inaction and withdrawal from some other agreements could provoke a nuclear buildup by other nuclear powers (e.g., China). It could also undermine the international non-proliferation regime. (This especially should concern Russia, given that it is literally surrounded by current and potential proliferators).
- Strategic arms control is an important tool that permits Moscow to capitalize on its huge nuclear arsenal to gain a high-profile role in formulating global policy. In other words, the country's international prestige cannot be maintained just by possession of nuclear weapons. Russia needs an instrument that allows it to leverage its nuclear arsenal.[15]

At the same time, critics and advocates generally agreed that the treaty contained considerable deficiencies. First, for Russia, it was not a disarmament, but rather a rearmament, agreement. After dismantling all MIRVed missiles, as the treaty stipulates, Moscow would be able to keep only approximately 350 deployed SS-25 Topol ICBMs—and, for a limited time—105 older SS-19 missiles downloaded to one warhead each. Thus, in order to maintain forces at the START II ceilings, Russia would have to produce more than a thousand new single-warhead ICBMs. This task was unattainable within the initial START II implementation period of 2003. In practical terms, it required an increase in the annual production rate to more than two hundred missiles—comparable to or even higher than the production rate the Soviet Union achieved during the Cold War. In addition to wasting modest available resources, such a task would be highly controversial in the post–Cold War period.

The following example illustrates this point. In order to maintain START II levels after dismantling those systems banned by START II, Russia would have to produce about fifteen hundred new single-warhead ICBMs and MIRVed SLBMs.

The vast majority of the new missiles would have to be built by 2003 (the initial deadline for treaty implementation). This huge burden would coincide with the most difficult period of Russia's struggle for economic recovery. Conversely, to maintain the START I sublimit of 4,900 accountable warheads deployed on strategic ballistic missiles, Moscow would have to produce just 490 new MIRVed ICBMs and SLBMs, assuming that every missile carries ten warheads. These missiles could be produced within a more comfortable period of time (ten to fifteen years) that matched the rate of natural decommissioning of deployed systems. And prolonging the life of existing missiles could also postpone the new production for several years. Thus, it has been argued by some in the Duma, by keeping the higher START I ceiling, Russia would ultimately spend three times less money for new missile production compared with the costs necessary to meet the START II conditions.[16]

Certainly this argument was too simplistic. It does not account for problems with developing and testing a new MIRVed ICBM. In reality, such a program would duplicate spending, rather than save money. It would require either halting the Topol M program, thereby wasting significant funding already spent for implementation, or producing both the Topol M and a new MIRVed ICBM. However, the simple arithmetic above seemed to affect the thinking of Duma members much more than sophisticated counterarguments.

Second, for the United States START II was much easier to implement than for Russia. While Russia had to destroy the vast majority of systems slated for dismantlement, the United States was free to make its reductions through downloading (i.e., removing extra warheads from the missiles and storing them nearby). This asymmetry was not just more costly to Russia but also provided Washington with significant breakout advantages. Should the treaty fail, the United States could relatively quickly return downloaded warheads to their Minuteman III and Trident II missiles, thereby reconstituting its forces to levels in excess of START I. The reconstitution capability for Moscow is much lower, as only 500 warheads could be returned to SS-19 ICBMs. But even that opportunity would be available only for a short period of time, as the SS-19s likely would have to be decommissioned by 2010 anyway.

Third, Russia's strategic deterrent would change from its traditional reliance on silo-based MIRVed ICBMs to SLBMs and mobile ICBMs. More reliance on submarines raises vulnerability concerns due to U.S. naval predominance, especially in the area of antisubmarine warfare. Fewer Soviet submarines were on constant patrol as compared with U.S. subs, and since the Soviet collapse, the submarine situation has deteriorated further with most Russian subs now rusting in their berths.[17] These subs, which carry up to two hundred warheads each and are concentrated in bases, represent a very cost-effective and attractive target. With one or two warheads, a potential adversary could destroy several hundred Russian warheads in one attack. Thus, submarines clustered in bases, rather than on patrol, invite a disarming attack that makes the nuclear balance much less stable.

This increased reliance on mobile ICBMs and SLBMs would also undermine the survivability and redundancy of both positive and negative control of Russia's nuclear forces.[18] Communication with strategic submarines on patrol was always considered an Achilles heel of the Soviet deterrent. Contrary to the U.S. command and control system, Russian SLBMs, reportedly, cannot be launched from SSBNs on patrol without receiving deblocking codes from the National Command Authority (NCA). However, such a transmission might become impossible if relevant communications facilities were destroyed by a surprise conventional or nuclear attack or if communications failed as a result of electronic warfare. Recently, with the overall degradation of Russia's military capabilities and its new geostrategic vulnerabilities, concerns over the redundancy of positive control of the sea-based leg of the triad are quite legitimate.

Similar to Russia's submarines, its mobile ICBMs are routinely kept in lightly protected hangars where they are vulnerable to nuclear and highly accurate conventional attacks. On patrol, they are unprotected targets and could be destroyed by a high-yield nuclear blast or even from a bullet shot from a high-powered gun. This would mean that Russia's missiles are potentially exposed to special force operations in wartime and to terrorist attacks in peacetime.

Concerns also exist with respect to the degradation of Russia's ballistic missile early-warning system. Five of the eight phased-array early-warning radar stations, the centerpiece of the Soviet Union's system, are stranded outside Russian borders. One of the stations has been decommissioned, and Moscow's access to those located in Azerbaijan and Ukraine has not been completely secured legally and operationally. Due to insufficient financing, space-based early-warning components have also been significantly degraded. According to some estimates, up to 70 percent of Russia's early-warning satellites have either exceeded their life expectancy or face other serious problems. As a result, Russia's missile early-warning system most likely cannot provide reliable coverage of the 60,000-kilometer national border. The North Korean missile test conducted in August 1998 reportedly went undetected by Russian early-warning systems.[19]

Problems with early warning are considered especially dangerous because a significant portion of Russia's land-based ballistic missiles remain on a "hair trigger" alert. This increases the risk of launch due to, for example, a mistaken assessment of a flying object. In January 1995, President Yeltsin activated his nuclear briefcase for the first time after the Russian early-warning system detected what turned out to be a scientific rocket launched by Norway. Russia had been previously notified of the rocket launch, although word did not reach the early warning command structure. This identification failure indicates that the system, though it detected the launch successfully, was unable to assess accurately and quickly the nature of the launch, and distinguish it from a hostile missile attack.[20]

The debate on nuclear survivability has gained new momentum as a result of NATO's eastward expansion. With new NATO conventional deployments in Poland and, possibly in the future, the Baltic states, the NCA in Moscow would be vulnerable to a surprise attack with very little notice. For instance, a supersonic fighter could reach Moscow in fifteen minutes if it was deployed in Latvia. In such an event, the NCA might not have sufficient time to transmit deblocking codes to the submarines on patrol. In addition, some Strategic Rocket Force bases situated in

European Russia could be reached by NATO tactical aircraft. Mobile missiles would not have time to leave their hangars, and missiles on patrol might be detected and destroyed by aircraft or cruise missiles.

As a result of the NATO expansion debate, the redundancy of negative control might become more of an issue. Radical decreases in warning time could force Russia to reconsider launch procedures for strategic submarines by delegating more responsibility to the crew in peacetime. Silo-based ICBMs are considered the most redundant weapon in terms of negative control (i.e., they are the most protected from unauthorized launch). Negative control over mobile and sea-based systems may not be equally effective. In a crisis, submarine or mobile missile commanders might enjoy more freedom of action than their colleagues in ICBM silos. From that viewpoint, the transition of Russian strategic forces to sea-based and mobile launchers might further degrade negative control and increase the likelihood of an accidental or unauthorized launch.

Finally, treaty critics do not dispute the argument that irrespective of START II, Russia's strategic forces will go below the treaty levels anyway. They argue, however, that in the absence of START II the difference in numbers between Russia and the United States would be much lower than if the treaty was implemented. By some calculations, under START II the ratio could be as high as six to one in the U.S. favor if the breakout advantages were taken into account. In the absence of the treaty, the gap would be approximately three or four to one. While this ratio is still a significant disadvantage, Russia would preserve its most reliable strategic component, land-based MIRVed ICBMs. If needed, Moscow could also keep its options open for future buildup. This would also make it easier to maintain a hedge against the rise of other nuclear powers, especially China.

THE 1997 COMPROMISE

During the March 1997 Helsinki summit between Presidents Clinton and Yeltsin, the two leaders elaborated areas for future compromise on START III and the ABM Treaty. The following September in New York, Foreign Minister Primakov and Secretary of State Albright formalized one portion of the Helsinki agreements by signing the START II Extension Protocol and several ABM demarcation statements. Those documents would enter into force after their ratification in both countries. In a parallel move in May 1997, the leaders of the NATO countries were joined by President Yeltsin in Paris to sign the NATO-Russia Founding Act. This act established a mechanism for consultations and interactions between Moscow and NATO and provided Russia with nonbinding assurances that NATO would not authorize nuclear and large-scale conventional deployments on the territory of its new members.

The decisions made in Helsinki, Paris, and New York partially—but only temporarily—alleviated Moscow's concerns on NATO, START, and ABM issues. In the NATO case, through the establishment of a Permanent Joint Council, Russia received a consultative voice in NATO decision making.[21] During the 1997 Madrid summit, NATO leaders also avoided making any explicit commitment to the accession of the Baltic states—the question of concern to Moscow. Together with the

NATO assurances on nondeployment and promises to adapt the Convention Forces in Europe Treaty to the new security situation in Europe, the decision on the Baltic states moved Russia's debates on the matter in a more positive direction: how and to what extent to interact with the Alliance.

In the ABM area, though, the United States refused to agree to imposing clear quantitative limits on high-speed missile interceptors. The New York demarcation statements, in fact, gave a green light for the implementation of all planned U.S. theater missile defense programs for the foreseeable future. However, Russia received binding assurances that the U.S. theater missile defense programs would not be directed against its nuclear deterrent and that future concerns would be solved through bilateral consultation. Moreover, Moscow's concessions on the ABM would be considered as part of a broader package that included certain START-related gains.

The Helsinki START package could be the greatest achievement of Russian diplomacy on strategic arms control since the Soviet collapse. The United States agreed to prolong the START II implementation period by five years, to December 31, 2007. This delay permits Russia, by prolonging the life of some of its MIRVed ICBMs, to synchronize their natural decommissioning rate with the treaty requirements.[22] It would also help to avoid a dramatic decline in strategic force levels shortly after START II implementation. If the treaty had to be fulfilled by the original date of 2003, that year the Strategic Rocket Forces, after dismantling all MIRVed ICBMs, would control about 550 single-warhead and downloaded systems, and more than two-thirds of them would be road-mobile. After the expiration of the new implementation period, force levels would be higher, especially if a better economic situation permits an increase in the production rate of new ICBMs.

More important, the two sides reached an agreement to conclude a new follow-on START III, under which Russian concerns with START II would be met. It was decided that the new treaty would further reduce the strategic arsenals of each party to a level of two thousand to twenty-five hundred deployed strategic nuclear warheads. This lower level will help Russia avoid either a massive missile buildup in order to maintain the high START II ceilings. The presidents also agreed that the new treaty should solve the issue of rapid breakout capabilities. In practical terms, this might mean that for the first time in history a strategic arms control agreement would cover not only delivery vehicles but nuclear warheads as well (by extending verification measures to warheads removed from downloaded carriers, or even by dismantling those warheads). And in accordance with the philosophy of correcting START II mistakes, the implementation of START III should be completed by the same extended deadline of December 31, 2007.

Also for the first time, both sides indicated the possibility of initiating talks, to be held in parallel START III, on tactical nuclear arms control. Such negotiations could address U.S. concerns on the opaqueness of Russia's presumably large arsenal of tactical nuclear weapons. In return Moscow might expect to conclude limits on long-range sea-launched cruise missiles, which it has sought for several decades.

The compromises reached with the United States and NATO in 1997 received a mixed review in Russia. The majority of lawmakers considered the Founding Act a merely symbolic document, devoid of any explicit security guarantees. NATO's refusal to make a binding commitment not to deploy nuclear and large-scale conventional weapons on the territory of the alliance's new member states produced concerns that such a deployment might actually take place in the foreseeable future. The ABM demarcation agreements were also negatively met by Strategic Rocket Force officials, since they, in fact, did not restrict tests of high-speed theater missile defense interceptors.

The START package received a more positive response. The major point of concern centered on the provision of the Helsinki Bilateral Statement that indicated START III negotiations could begin only after START II entered into force. Treaty critics pointed out that while the end date for treaty implementation was agreed upon, no specific date for starting the negotiations was determined. In fact, the schedule for the future strategic reductions agenda determined in Helsinki did not seem very reliable. First, Russia needed to ratify START II, the Extension Protocol, and the ABM demarcation agreements.[23] By the time of the Helsinki summit, START II had already languished for more than four years, and completing the ratification process might take more time yet. Once Russia ratified these agreements, the U.S. Senate would have to approve the Extension Protocol and demarcation agreements, an action far from certain. Only then, if neither the Duma nor the Senate amended the ratification resolution with provisions linking START II entry-into-force with other issues, could START III negotiations begin. The negotiations would face significant difficulties, especially in the area of warhead transparency, and, thus, their early conclusion is also far from certain. Then the new treaty would likely be shelved for a few more years by both Russian and U.S. lawmakers. Thus, START III might enter into force too late for it to be implemented by December 31, 2007. This complicated schedule questioned the validity of the provision that supposedly synchronized the implementation deadline for both treaties.

Sensing this timing controversy, the Clinton administration initiated in the fall of 1997 informal consultations on START III. Several rounds of consultations took place, and lower ceilings of fifteen hundred warheads have been discussed. Reportedly, the two sides informally agreed to complete START III negotiations by 2003.[24] However, despite the importance of that move, no evidence of the progress reached during the consultations has been made public.

DEMOCRACY VERSUS RATIFICATION: 1997–99

Although the 1997 compromises alleviated some Russian concerns related to START II, the Duma still did not ratify the treaty. Instead, ratification was held up by several factors, both domestic and international. Domestically, the treaty was held hostage to the tense relationship between the Yeltsin administration and the opposition-dominated Duma. Internationally, ratification was negatively affected by the continuing deterioration of the U.S.-Russian relationship, particularly by disagreements over conflicts in Iraq and Kosovo, as well as over the NATO out-of-area operations concept. And in January 1999, the situation was further aggravated by a

Clinton administration decision to seek modification of the ABM Treaty to allow for deployment of a national missile defense.

Domestic disagreements, together with mistakes made by the Kremlin in the winter and early spring of 1998, prevented Yeltsin from obtaining ratification of START by the Duma in its spring 1998 session. Initially, with no explanation, the Kremlin delayed sending the New York agreements, concluded on September 26, 1997, to the parliament. Thus, Yeltsin lost a critical window of opportunity, opened by the 1997 compromises and Duma ratification of the Chemical Weapons Convention in late October 1997. In winter 1997–98, relations between the lawmakers and the Kremlin remained relatively calm, and against that background the ratification process had good chances for moving forward smoothly and quickly.

The New York agreements were not officially submitted for ratification until April 13, 1998, and by then the domestic political environment had soured significantly. In late March President Yeltsin suddenly fired the cabinet led by Viktor Chernomyrdin and asked the Duma to approve Sergei Kiriyenko as the new prime minister.[25] Although Chernomyrdin was not very popular among the Duma opposition, he had established a certain modus vivendi with the leftist Duma fractions during his more than five years as prime minister. Kiriyenko, on the other hand, had served as minister for fuel and energy in the Chernomyrdin cabinet and was a close associate of then first vice prime ministers Boris Nemtsov and Anatoly Chubais, both of whom were highly unpopular in the Duma. Not surprisingly, the Duma received the Kiriyenko nomination very negatively. However, in order to prevent dissolution of the Duma, the lawmakers approved Kiriyenko's nomination after several stormy debates.

The Kiriyenko debacle put the Communists, the largest Duma fraction, under strong pressure from their radical wing. The radicals heavily criticized the moderate leadership of the party for its opportunistic approach toward the Kremlin and threatened to split the party unless this collaboration was halted. Moreover, Duma members from all parties felt extremely humiliated by the way President Yeltsin had treated them. Yeltsin completely ignored the members' opinion in his decisions to sack Chernomyrdin and to nominate a relatively unknown and unpopular candidate. Consequently, after the Kiriyenko confirmation debate, the Duma sought revenge and used every opportunity to let the Kremlin know that it would pay for its behavior.

Despite this highly negative environment the Yeltsin administration made unprecedented efforts aimed at promoting the treaty from April to June 1998. Earlier, in 1997, Washington had linked the prospect of another Clinton-Yeltsin summit with Russia's START II ratification. Given President Yeltsin's personal penchant for high-visibility events, this was a reasonable strategy that played a positive role in stimulating the Kremlin to make more energetic efforts to market the treaty. However, the strategy had the opposite effect on the Duma: The lawmakers complained that Yeltsin paid more attention to recommendations from Washington than from his own parliament.[26]

In this context, while the Yeltsin administration energetically promoted treaty ratification as never before, the Duma did its best to postpone it. After a month-long procedural delay, treaty opponents led by General Albert Makashov urged the Committee on Defense to postpone ratification until autumn. On May 19 the Duma Council agreed to that proposal. In response, the Kremlin put very strong pressure on the lawmakers in an attempt to convince them to abandon this decision. President Yeltsin, Prime Minister Kiriyenko, the foreign and defense ministers, the General Staff, and even the heads of the Atomic Energy Ministry and Foreign Intelligence Service actively participated in the proratification campaign. However, the Duma majority firmly resisted the attack. Some hope remained as Duma liberals pushed for treaty hearings for the end of the spring session, but a week later the Duma formally voted to postpone the ratification process until fall.

Though its efforts failed, the Kremlin's active promotion of START II had some positive results. In late May, Yuri Maslyukov, then chairman of the Duma Committee on Economic Policy, distributed a letter urging members of the Communist fraction to support treaty ratification. This was the first endorsement of the treaty publicly expressed by one of the top Communist leaders.

In August 1998, Russia suffered a severe financial crisis, which forced President Yeltsin to fire the Kiriyenko cabinet and, for the first time since the Soviet collapse, incorporate representatives of the Duma left into a new cabinet led by Yevgeny Primakov. After the financial situation stabilized, a period of relative domestic calm ensued in fall 1998 and spring 1999. From the domestic standpoint START II ratification looked favorable.

In October 1998 the Duma reconvened after its summer recess. Soon, the new Primakov government launched an active lobbying campaign aimed at revitalizing START II ratification prospects. In response to these efforts, on November 6 the Duma Council decided to hold an extraordinary closed plenary meeting devoted to, among other items, START II. The decision to discuss ratification at the extraordinary session—in a much more representative forum than hearings the Duma had refused to arrange in June—clearly signaled that the ratification process was no longer blocked. The special session took place on November 10 and was reportedly attended by the prime minister, first deputy prime minister, and ministers of foreign affairs, defense, economics, and finance.[27] Again, in sharp contrast to its behavior the previous spring, the Duma Council gathered later the same day and tasked the relevant committees to prepare the draft ratification bill within ten days.

Despite strong support from the Duma leadership, preparation of the ratification bill faced significant difficulties, and an agreed text was not finished until early December.[28] The draft contained ten articles, eight of which stipulated conditions for START II implementation. The ninth article delayed the exchange of the instruments of ratification until the United States ratified the 1997 New York ABM demarcation agreements. Other conditions linked treaty implementation with concluding START III by the end of 2003, ABM Treaty compliance, and military activities of the United States, NATO, and other nuclear powers.[29]

Completion of the draft text was followed by painful debates inside the Communist Party. While its moderate leadership was ready to ratify the treaty, the hardliners aggressively denounced the idea. Due to this disagreement, on December 8 and, again, on December 15 the Duma Council failed to adopt a procedural decision asking the president to formally submit the agreed draft text of the ratification bill.[30] The debates inside the Communist Party continued until December 16, when, reportedly, they came very close to permitting free voting on START II. The agreement was expected to be settled in the morning of December 17. Thus it was widely predicted that on December 17 the Duma Council would call on the president to submit the bill and assuming no delays from the presidential side, the Duma would ratify the treaty on December 25, the last day prior to the New Year recess.

However, several hours before the scheduled meeting of the Duma Council, the United States and Britain launched air strikes against Iraq. The Communist fraction immediately linked the air strikes with START II ratification and delayed treaty consideration for the indefinite future. After attending the meeting, then first vice prime minister Yuri Maslyukov, who two days before had energetically supported ratification, said: "I am not an idiot enough to insist on START II ratification while air strikes are being made on Iraq."[31] As a result, the Duma Council failed again to consider START II. The environment in the legislature became so unfavorable that Alexander Kotenkov, the presidential representative in the Duma, predicted that the current Duma would not ratify the treaty at all.[32] As treaty proponent Vladimir Lukin pointed out, the ratification "was postponed not by the State Duma, but by the American government and President [Clinton]."[33]

Nevertheless, Russia's urgent debt service needed support from "the American government and the president." After the New Year, the cabinet launched a new attack on the Duma. This new offensive made good progress, despite the strenuous objections of hard-liners in the Communist fraction and the January 1999 announcement by the Clinton administration that the United States would seek modification of the ABM Treaty. In fact the Yeltsin administration used the U.S. National Missile Defense (NMD) debates as an argument in favor of START II ratification. Primakov personally stressed that ratification would prevent Washington from withdrawing from the ABM Treaty.

The domestic political environment for START II remained favorable. Similar to fall 1998, the left continued to provide political support to the Primakov cabinet, paving the way for the conclusion of the START II ratification bill.

On March 16, the Duma Council formally asked the president to submit the agreed ratification bill, a motion it had failed to agree on three months before. The council decision was followed by the unusual appearance of Primakov, Maslyukov, and top military officials on Russian national TV, where they defended treaty ratification.[34] On March 18, Primakov met for three hours with leaders of the left Duma fraction. The next day during a plenary meeting, the Duma included START II ratification on the agenda for the nearest "ratification day"—Friday, April 2.[35] On March 22, the president formally resubmitted the START II ratification bill to the Duma.

Prime Minister Primakov left for the United States on March 24 for a scheduled meeting with Vice President Al Gore. In the course of his flight it became clear that NATO air strikes against Yugoslavia were imminent. In protest, the prime minister turned his plane around over the Atlantic and returned to Moscow.

The air strikes had a shocking effect in Russia. Spontaneous anti-NATO rallies broke out in Moscow's streets. The Duma interrupted its recess and held an extra-ordinary plenary meeting on March 27 devoted to the situation in Yugoslavia. In a resolution approved at the meeting the legislature requested that the president recall the START II ratification bill. The majority of deputies believed that as a result of the NATO out-of-area action, which was not supported by any UN Security Council or Organization of Security and Cooperation in Europe resolution, a new security situation had emerged that might require a reassessment of some of previously concluded arms control agreements.[36] Prospects for START II were essentially killed and the outlook for U.S.-Russian relations was poor.

WHAT NEXT?

The end of the Cold War did not result in radical changes in U.S. and Russian attitudes toward strategic nuclear reductions. Washington and Moscow remained preoccupied by traditional strategic arms control and failed to seize the new opportunities for deep reductions opened by an end to the East-West confrontation. This preoccupation prevented them from breaking out of their Cold War–type deterrence relationship. Moreover, traditional strategic arms control, itself based on many Cold War paradigms, ensured the continued elevation of those paradigms in U.S.-Russian relations. This not only created a serious obstacle to building new bilateral post–Cold War cooperation, but also affected the overall relationship and became one of the factors in that relationship's evident regress since 1993. This regress was so painful to Moscow that it negatively influenced strategic arms control itself and created challenges to Russia's commitment to other parts of the nonproliferation regime.

Although formal strategic arms control has less importance in the post–Cold War environment, and preoccupation with it could even produce a negative reverse effect, turning away from it would be detrimental. Politically, such a halt could further undermine the U.S.-Russian relationship and the two sides would become more suspicious of each other's intentions in the nuclear area. Leaving START II unratified without negotiating a new agreement might also add to the disappointment of non-nuclear weapon states at the inability of the leading nuclear powers to fulfill their obligations under article VI of the NPT. In broader terms, the continuing deadlock in strategic arms control could produce a chain reaction by triggering the erosion and even collapse of other regimes, such as the 1987 Intermediate-Range Nuclear Forces Treaty and the 1996 Comprehensive Test Ban Treaty. Furthermore, formal agreements provide an opportunity to transform ad hoc commitments into formal obligations, making it more difficult to abandon them. And unlike informal arrangements, formal agreements create higher predictability and certainty; they guarantee transparency on a stabler and longer-term basis.

Today the United States and Russia face very different choices than in 1991–93. In the early 1990s, they had a chance to gain momentum from the nuclear reductions established by START I and the 1991 Bush-Gorbachev initiatives and to move forward quickly toward an extradeterrence relationship. By 2000, however, the bilateral relationship had deteriorated to the point that repair of the strategic arms control process became a *necessary* condition for maintaining relations between the two countries and preventing further erosion of other bilateral and multilateral non-proliferation regimes, where Russia's participation remains crucial. But progress in only the U.S.-Russian strategic arms control area would be *insufficient* to guarantee a breakthrough in relations between Moscow and Washington beyond the logic of the Cold War. In its turn, such a breakthrough would greatly contribute to efforts to sustain and consolidate other non-proliferation regimes.

To achieve this breakthrough, strategic arms control should be accompanied by other cooperative measures that might help Russia and the United States rely more on extradeterrence elements in their nuclear interaction. At the end of the Cold War, Washington and Moscow demonstrated certain progress in capitalizing on cooperative aspects of their nuclear relations, which better responded to postconfrontational security realities. Not surprisingly, despite a deadlock in the formal arms control process, these "nontraditional" steps permitted ad hoc commitments in areas that would not be covered by formal agreements for several more years at least. These achievements include:

- Reciprocal parallel withdrawing of tactical nuclear warheads from military units to storage sites, resulting from the October 1991 initiatives made by Presidents Bush and Gorbachev.
- Unilateral, partially verified large-scale disassembling of nuclear warheads as a result of the U.S.-Russian uranium purchase agreement and other bilateral cooperative projects.
- Halting fissile material production for weapons use, an outcome of the U.S.-Russian agreement on converting three Russian plutonium production reactors.
- Restricting use of available fissile material stockpiles for military purposes.
- Eliminating of strategic nuclear delivery vehicles beyond the START I limits through bilateral cooperation, particularly in the area of submarine and solid rocket fuel dismantlement and disposal.
- Reducing Russia's industrial base for producing ballistic missiles by engaging some enterprises, including the Khrunichev SS-19 production plant, in bilateral space cooperation projects.
- Establishing transparency measures on segments of the nuclear weapons and fissile material production cycle.
- Detargeting of U.S. and Russian ballistic missiles from each other's territories by an arrangement concluded in 1994.
- Commencing cooperation on ballistic missile early warning in September 1998.
- Cooperating on missile defense projects like the Russian-American observation satellite (RAMOS) project, joint simulation of a tactical intercept missile, and experiments with a plasma generator.

The experience of the 1990s demonstrates that a creative double-track strategy—a combination of informal commitments with formal strategic arms control negotiations and treaties—is the most promising route for an exit from the recent deadlock.

In the START/ABM area, the final compromise should contain provisions that meet the basic security concerns of the United States and Russia:

- The ABM Treaty could be modified to provide the United States with sufficient flexibility in ABM testing and deployment, enabling it to respond effectively to perceived threats from missile proliferators. At the same time, the modifications should not affect the viability of the treaty.
- In exchange, Russia could receive adequate assurances that potential U.S. ABM deployments would not affect the credibility of its strategic deterrent. This could be done through restrictions on ABM deployments and alleviating certain START II limitations, especially on MIRVed ICBMs. The United States might be interested in keeping intact key elements of START II, such as the ban on heavy ICBMs and de-MIRVing of ballistic missiles.
- The two should find a solution on the irreversibility of deep reductions. In order to reach an agreement relatively quickly, irreversibility should be provided by modest technical measures, like establishing subceilings on certain types of delivery vehicles or modifying the platforms of downloaded carriers.
- To meet the wishes of non-nuclear states, START III should contain overall ceilings much lower than in START II, and ideally even lower than were agreed to in Helsinki.

While negotiating future ABM/START agreements, the United States and Russia need to make coordinated efforts aimed at formal or informal multilateralization of some existing arms control agreements or their separate provisions. Special attention should be paid to Chinese concerns on missile defense deployments. For its part, Beijing could be more attentive to others' sensitivities about its potential buildup of strategic and intermediate-range nuclear forces, possibly including MIRVs.

Upon concluding a new ABM/START agreement, both sides should proceed with negotiations on tactical nuclear arms control. Their agreement on further strategic reductions could be conditional on greater involvement of other nuclear powers in the nuclear arms reductions and limitation process.

On the informal track, the United States and Russia should take measures toward the following goals:

- Transparency and monitoring of all nuclear-weapons-usable material and warheads from cradle to grave.
- Verifiable de-alerting of each other's ballistic missiles by establishing a transparency and inspection regime at missile bases and command posts.
- Gradual transition from arms control to arms cooperation and joint development of new strategic offensive and defensive technologies and hardware.[37]

When and if these gains are achieved, Moscow and Washington could finally abandon Cold War paradigms in their nuclear relations. In the end, nuclear deterrence and strategic arms control would give way to strategic nuclear partnership and cooperation.

NOTES

1. The figure of 6,000 accountable warheads uses specific accounting rules agreed to under the START treaty.

2. *The Russia Journal,* May 10, 1999, "Petr Romashkin. Voyenny byudzhet Rossiyskoy Federatsii" (Military Budget of the Russian Federation); *Yadernoye Rasprostraneniye* (Periodic Compilation of Documents and Materials), Carnegie Moscow Center, Issue 26 (November 1998): 23–28 (in Russian).

3. START I Memorandum of Understanding, September 1990 and January 1999; Rady Zubkov, "Neopredelyonnoye buduschee podvodnykh raketonostsev" (Vague Future of Missile Submarines), *Nezavisimoye voyennoue obozreniye,* no. 47 (1998): 6 (in Russian).

4. Yuri Maslyukov, "Dogovor SNV-2 i buduschee strategicheskikh yadernykh sil Rossii" (START II Treaty and Future of Russia's Strategic Nuclear Forces), *Izvestiya,* December 16, 1998, 6 (in Russian); "First Typhoon May Be Decommissioned Next Year," Bellona Foundation (http:/www.bellona.no/e/russua/nfl/news/981208.html).

5. Viktor Litovkin, "Yuri Dolgoruky budet peredelan esche na stapele" (Yuri Dolgoruky Will Be Reconstructed While in the Dock), *Izvestiya,* September 9, 1998, 4 (in Russian).

6. Yuri Maslyukov, "Dogovor SNV-2," 6; Nikolai Sokov, "Modernization of Strategic Nuclear Weapons in Russia: The Emerging New Posture," Davis Center for Russian Studies, Harvard University, 1998.

7. Yuri Maslyukov, ibid.

8. Mikhail Petrov, "Strategicheskim raketam net alternativy" (There Is No Alternative to Strategic Missiles), interview with Yuri Solomonov, general designer, Moscow Institute of Thermal Technology, *Nezavisimoye voyennoe obozreniye NG,* no. 5 (1999): 1, 6 (in Russian).

9. Vladimir Berezko, Mikhail Sidelnikov, "Strategicheskaya stabilnost' na povestke dnya" (Strategic Stability on Agenda), interview with Sergei Rogov, director of the Institute for USA and Canada Studies, *Krasnaya Zvezda,* March 11, 1999, 1, 2.

10. *MPC&A Program Strategic Plan,* U.S. Department of Energy, January 1998, 2.

11. John Deutch, "The Threat of Nuclear Diversion," testimony before the U.S. Senate, Committee on Governmental Affairs, Permanent Subcommittee on Investigations, in *Global Proliferation of Weapons of Mass Destruction,* Part 2, 104th Cong., 2d sess., 104–422, March 20, 1996.

12. Highlights of Significant Fissile Material Smuggling Cases, *Nuclear Successor States of the Soviet Union: Status Report on Nuclear Weapons, Fissile Material, and Export Controls,* Carnegie Endowment for International Peace and Monterey Institute of International Studies, no. 5 (March 1998): 105–12.

13. "Combating Proliferation of Weapons of Mass Destruction," report of the Commission to Assess the Organization of the Federal Government to Combat the Proliferation of Weapons of Mass Destruction, July 1999, 2.

14. Vladimir Georgiev, "Underlying Reason: Crime in the Russian Army Has Rolled Up to Nuclear Munitions Unit, but the Ministry of Defense Believes Russia Is Capable of Controlling Weapons of Mass Destruction without Foreign Intervention," *Nezarivisimoye Voyennoye Obozreniye,* no. 34 (September 11–17, 1998): 1.

15. "Russian Premier, His Deputy and Military Discuss Ratification of START-2 Treaty," Program *Zdes' I seichas* (Here and Now), *Russian ORT Channel,* 18:45 msk, March 16, 1999 (in Russian), English transcript in *BBC Worldwide Monitoring,* British Broadcasting Corporation, March 16, 1999. See also Interview with Defense Minister Igor Sergeyev, *Slovo,* May 21–25, 1999, 1–3 (in Russian).

16. See Pavel Felgengauer, "Time to Abandon START II," *Moscow Times,* December 31, 1998. See also interview with Colonel General Vladimir Yakovlev, commander in chief of Strategic Rocket Forces, *Vek,* no. 48 (December 1998): 7.

17. Nikolai Sokov, "Modernization of Strategic Nuclear Weapons in Russia."

18. Positive control guarantees authorized missile launch; negative control prevents an unauthorized launch.

19. Talk with Russian missile expert, Moscow, September 1998; Viktor Litovkin, "Treschina na schite Rossii" (Crack on Russia's Shield), *Izvestiya,* August 21, 1998, 1. An anonymous high-ranking officer is quoted as saying, "Instead of round-the-clock control from orbit, we have only six hours." See Aleksei Karelov, "Predmet zasluzhivayuschiy osobogo vnimaniya" (A Subject Which Merits Special Attention), *Vremya MN,* June 16, 1999, 2 (in Russian). According to another media report, the Y2K problem could affect 90 percent of *Kazbek* strategic nuclear command and control system's computers. Due to declining salaries, professional operators have left for better-paying jobs, and they were replaced by recruits, who were told by the commanders, "Never push any buttons" and immediately approach a specialist if an emergency occurred. See Kirill Belyaninov, "Nash chemodanchik nakhoditsya na sklade" (Our Case Is Being Kept in the Reserve), *Novyye Izvestiya,* July 2, 1999, 1, 7 (in Russian).

20. According to another version, the Russian military probably provoked this highly publicized incident in an attempt to halt Norwegian launches, which, they believe, were undertaken for electronic reconnaissance missions as well. Norway did not launch any missiles from January 1995 to the fall of 1998 (talk with Russian missile expert, Moscow, December 1998).

21. The value of this deal was called into question after NATO's decision to bomb Serbia in 1999 over Russian objections.

22. "Russian Premier, His Deputy and Military Discuss Ratification of START-2 treaty." See also interview with Colonel General Vladimir Yakovlev.

23. Although in Helsinki no formal linkage was established between the ABM demarcation agreements and START II's entering into force, it implicitly existed in Russian debates. Later, in 1998, the linkage was fixed in a draft ratification bill.

24. Remarks of Prime Minister Primakov.

25. According to the 1993 constitution, the prime minister must be confirmed by the Duma. If the Duma fails to approve the candidate in three votes, the president can dissolve the Duma, call for new elections, and nominate the prime minister.

26. For example, see remarks of Gennady Seleznyov, the Duma speaker, in *Russky Telegraf,* December 19, 1997, 3 (in Russian).

27. "START II Ratification Is Expected in December," PIR Arms Control Letters, PIR Center, November 13, 1998 (http://www.pircenter.org/acl/index.htm). See also *Parlamentskaya gazeta,* November 11, 1998, 1, 2 (in Russian).

28. Alexander Pikayev, "START II: Better Late than Never," *Carnegie Endowment for International Peace Proliferation Briefs,* 1, no. 16, (December 3, 1998).

29. See full text of the START II draft ratification bill in "Federalny zakon o ratifikatsii Dogovora mezhdu Rossiyskoi Federatsiyei I Soyedinennymi Shtatami Ameriki o dalneyshem sokraschenii I ogranichenii strategicheskikh nastupatelnykh vooruzheniy (proekt)" (Federal Law on Ratification of the Treaty between the Russian Federation and the United States of America on Further Reduction and Limitation of Strategic Offensive Weapons [Draft]), *Yadernoye Rrasprostraneniye,* (Periodic Compilation of Materials and Documents), Carnegie Moscow Center, Issue 27 (December 1998): 76–80 (in Russian).

30. *Izvestiya,* December 16, 1998 (in Russian); *Interfax,* December 8, 1998.

31. *ITAR-TASS* (World Service), December 17, 1998, 16:41 msk (in English). However, Maslyukov visited the Duma the morning of December 17, perhaps in an attempt to save the ratification. *ITAR-TASS* (World Service), December 17, 1998, 17:04 msk (in English).

32. However, later he hinted that under certain circumstances, the Duma might return to treaty consideration. START II supporters were also less explicit. Vladimir Lukin, chairman of the Duma

Committee on International Affairs, stressed that chances for ratification were "very poor in the near future." *ITAR-TASS* (World Service), December 17, 1998, 19:30 msk (in English).

33. Ibid. It should be mentioned that other ranking members were of the opinion that although Iraqi air strikes did make it impossible to discuss START II that day, the delay was not connected directly with them. According to Roman Popkovich, chairman of the Defense Committee, the deputies were not able to become familiar with the strategic nuclear forces modernization program and its financing, which they saw for the first time a day before. Those two documents represented important domestic conditions for treaty ratification, which the Duma had consistently requested from the president since May 1995. The Popkovich statement could also be seen as an attempt to appease hard-liners from his committee after the ratification battle had been lost anyway. If the Communists gave a green light for the decision of the Duma Council—Maslyukov's attendance at the fraction meeting on December 17 was clearly planned in order to neutralize resistance from the radicals— Popkovich, who was loyal to the Kremlin, would certainly follow suit.

34. "Russian Premier, His Deputy and Military Discuss Ratification of START II treaty."

35. Alexander Pikayev, "START II as a Victim of Sexual Scandal in Moscow," March 22, 1999 (http://www.armscontrol.ru/start/publications/ap0319.htm).

36. Gennady Zyuganov, leader of the largest Duma Communist fraction, stated: "There is no point now in looking at the START II Treaty ratification in the State Duma. . . . All the treaties signed earlier have been cancelled out. They simply have no substance." New conditions emerged "that dictate a qualitatively different security doctrine for Russia." *ITAR-TASS* (World Service), March 25, 1999, 13:54 msk (in English).

37. For more details, see Committee on Nuclear Policy, *Jump-START: Retaking the Initiative to Reduce Post–Cold War Nuclear Dangers,* February 1999. The report can be found at (http://www.stimson.org).

—**7**—

A Detailed Analysis of the Urgently Needed New Steps to Control Warheads and Fissile Material[1]

Matthew Bunn

Nothing could be more central to U.S. and world security than ensuring that nuclear warheads and their essential ingredients–plutonium and highly enriched uranium (HEU)—do not fall into the hands of terrorists or proliferating states. If plutonium and HEU find their way onto a nuclear black market, nothing else we do to prevent the proliferation of nuclear weapons will succeed. Similarly, unless stockpiles of nuclear warheads and fissile materials can be secured, monitored, and verifiably reduced, it will be impossible to achieve deep, transparent, and irreversible reductions in nuclear arms. Measures to control warheads and fissile materials, therefore, are central to the entire global effort to reduce nuclear arms and stem their spread.

Today, however, the risk that insecure nuclear materials could be stolen and smuggled to potential proliferators remains unacceptably high—particularly in the former Soviet Union, where controls have been catastrophically weakened by ongoing economic and political upheavals. Moreover, virtually none of the measures that would be required to verifiably reduce stockpiles of nuclear warheads and materials to low, agreed levels are in place.

Since the demise of the Soviet Union, the United States has undertaken dozens of programs costing hundreds of millions of dollars a year to cooperate with the former Soviet states to address these threats. Other nations have also contributed, on a far more limited scale. If judged against the almost total lack of nuclear security cooperation as recently as early 1994, the progress of these efforts is nothing short of dramatic. But if judged against the scale and urgency of the threat, or the opportunities available to address it, current efforts fall woefully short. A "next wave" of targeted cooperative efforts to improve the management of nuclear weapons and weapons-usable nuclear materials is urgently needed, to rapidly reduce the risks of proliferation and provide a firm basis for deep reductions in nuclear arms.

Without doubt, there are enormous obstacles to a major expansion of U.S.-Russian nuclear security cooperation (see "Obstacles to Nuclear Security Cooperation" below). But even within the context of U.S.-Russian relations as they now stand, there is much that could be done. What is needed now is a substantial and sustained increase in high-level leadership coming from the White House. As Senator Joseph Biden (D–Delaware) has recently written, "The war against these 'loose nukes' and 'brain drain' threats is as important as any war in our history . . . it is a war that the United States dares not lose."[2]

This chapter will describe the threats the international community now faces in these areas, assess the steps that are now being taken to address them, and present an outline of a comprehensive strategy to further reduce the risks.[3] The chapter represents an American viewpoint, but the experience of nuclear security cooperation with Russia to date makes clear that these programs will succeed only if they are carried out as true partnerships, serving both Russian and American interests, with Russia playing a major part in their design and implementation.

Obstacles to Nuclear Security Cooperation

There are enormous obstacles to genuine cooperation in sensitive nuclear security areas between former adversaries like the United States and Russia. The souring of U.S.-Russian political relations during 1998 and 1999, accelerated by NATO's bombing of Yugoslavia, has made cooperation even more difficult and the hurdles to be overcome if major new steps are to succeed even higher. The experience of the last several years makes clear that nuclear security cooperation can succeed only if it is approached as a genuine partnership, with experts from both sides contributing their work and ideas to solve common problems together—rather than as an effort by one side to impose solutions on the other.

The most fundamental obstacle to cooperation is that the United States and Russia continue to have many conflicting interests—though they have profound common interests in preventing the proliferation of nuclear weapons and achieving permanent nuclear arms reductions. Russia would like to maintain a cutting-edge nuclear arsenal comparable to that of the United States, and the United States has no interest in helping Russia do that. Both countries' intelligence services would like to find out as much as possible about the other country's nuclear secrets, and both countries are deeply suspicious of the other's intentions in that regard. The United States has an interest in achieving specific non-proliferation and arms reduction goals as quickly and cost-effectively as possible; Russia, while not opposed to that objective, also has an interest in providing as much employment for excess nuclear workers as possible for as long as possible. Substantial segments of the political establishments in both countries—including a large fraction of both countries' legislatures—remain deeply suspicious of the other and skeptical of the whole idea of nuclear security cooperation (which creates a constant danger that problems which arise may be blown out of proportion and spin out of control). Given these differences of interest, disagreements about specific approaches to cooperation are inevitable and need to be resolved patiently with good-faith negotiation and discussion.

Secrecy and limited access to facilities are other serious obstacles faced by essentially all cooperative nuclear security programs with Russia. Enormous progress has been made in breaking down barriers, particularly compared with the early 1990s, when Russia would not allow cooperation on security upgrades at any site with separated plutonium or HEU, even civilian ones—whereas today, cooperation is under way at almost every such site. But enormous barriers still remain, and as political relations have deteriorated, the Russian security services have become more active in restricting access. At the same time, the United States has frequently been reluctant to offer comparable access to its own facilities, and this, too, has slowed progress. The recent furor over Chinese spying and laboratory security in the United States will only make this problem worse.

Competing priorities, bureaucratic disorganization, frequent changes of government personnel, and lack of sustained attention to these issues by the highest levels of government have been serious problems on both sides. It is difficult to do business with a Russian government facing a thousand priorities it considers more urgent, whose prime minister changes every few months, whose ministries often do not communicate, whose nuclear facilities increasingly may not abide by deals cut in Moscow, whose officials often put their industry's commercial interests ahead of non-proliferation interests, and whose senior leadership takes only occasional interest in resolving issues related to these nuclear security cooperation programs. Russian experts have much the same complaints about dealing with the U.S. government.

Another major issue is the difficulty of ensuring that U.S. taxpayers' dollars are being spent as they should be—an issue with several parts. First, there is the widespread corruption in Russia, which makes it essential to structure assistance programs so that the funds cannot simply be raked off into foreign bank accounts. Second, Russia has a dysfunctional payments system, in which, for example, money deposited at a particular bank for use by a joint project at a nearby institute may be seized by the bank to cover the institute's bad debts, or may be seized by tax police to cover the institute's back taxes, or may be used by a desperate institute director to pay salaries of other employees (in the hopes that it can be paid back if the institute's promised government funding ever comes). Third, there is the continuing problem of Russian efforts to impose a variety of taxes, tariffs, and duties on U.S. assistance, in effect, directing a portion of the assistance away from the agreed projects and into the general coffers of the Russian government instead. While the specific situation of each nuclear security program is different, all of them have faced these problems, and even when they have found successful solutions, the fact is that an enormous amount of time, energy, creativity, and political capital is spent following the money trail rather than getting the cooperative work done.

Cultural differences and poor negotiating tactics on both sides have, on occasion, also led to obstacles and disputes, which in some cases have delayed progress by months or years. What may appear from a U.S. perspective to be the minimum necessary audit and examination approach to ensure U.S.-financed equipment is used appropriately may appear from a Russian perspective as unwarranted intrusion and possibly an intelligence mission. A policy change seen on the U.S. side as tightening up lax spending practices of the past may be seen on the Russian side as abrogating the spirit of partnership by ignoring Russian suggestions on how funds should be spent.

Given this list of obstacles to cooperation—which is by no means comprehensive—success in nuclear security cooperation is never guaranteed and the obstacles to initiating major new efforts are substantial. The fundamental ingredients of success are: sustained and energetic leadership; a genuine commitment to working in partnership; a step-by-step approach designed to build trust as progress is made; patience, persistence, and creativity in overcoming obstacles; and consistent follow-through on commitments. With those ingredients and with a willingness to apply additional financial resources, there are opportunities for dramatic new progress to deal with the non-proliferation and arms reduction challenges both countries face, and perhaps even contribute to improving the overall political atmosphere between Russia and the United States.

PART I: THE THREAT

INSECURITY

The possibility that nuclear weapons or their essential ingredients will be stolen and made available on a nuclear black market poses an urgent threat to U.S. and international security. By far the hardest part of making a nuclear bomb is producing the separated plutonium or HEU: most states, and even some particularly well organized terrorist groups, could potentially make at least a crude nuclear bomb if they could get enough of the necessary plutonium or HEU. Unfortunately, the amount of material needed for a bomb is small—4 kilograms of plutonium, an amount smaller than a soda can—and about three times that amount of HEU is potentially enough for a nuclear weapon. Yet these materials exist in both the civilian and military sectors around the world in amounts measured in the hundreds of tons—enough for tens of thousands of nuclear weapons. While the risk of nuclear theft is a global problem requiring a global solution, the risk is most acute today in the states of the former Soviet Union, which are the focus of this chapter.

In the former Soviet Union, a security system designed for a single state with a closed society, closed borders, and well-paid, well-cared-for nuclear workers has been splintered among multiple states with open societies, open borders, and desperate, unpaid nuclear workers—a situation the system was never designed to address. Even Russian Minister of Atomic Energy Evgeniy Adamov has acknowledged that "the weakening of our ability to manage nuclear material has been immeasurable."[4] The economic crisis that followed the August 1998 financial meltdown briefly made a bad situation substantially worse.

The former Soviet states are thought to possess roughly 1,350 tons of weapons-usable nuclear material—plutonium and HEU—of which some 700 tons is in nuclear weapons, and 650 tons is in a variety of other forms, ranging from metal weapons components to impure scrap.[5] These materials are stored in over fifty sites, at which there are estimated to be nearly four hundred buildings containing at least kilogram quantities of plutonium or HEU. All of the nuclear weapons in the former Soviet Union are in Russia, as is some 99 percent of the weapons-usable material, but civilian facilities in Belarus, Kazakhstan, Latvia, Ukraine, and Uzbekistan also have quantities large enough to pose proliferation risks. Serious security problems and risks of theft exist throughout this huge complex of facilities. Indeed, in 1996, the U.S. director of central intelligence testified that weapons-usable nuclear materials "are more accessible now than at any other time in history—due primarily to the dissolution of the former Soviet Union and the region's worsening economic conditions," and concluded that none of the facilities handling plutonium or HEU in the former Soviet states had "adequate safeguards or security measures" in place.[6] In the author's judgment, this remains an accurate assessment today, despite the considerable progress that has been made in improving security and accounting systems.

The security system that existed within the Soviet Union was based heavily on "guards, guns, and gates" at military facilities—a system in which the manager of each area handling nuclear material took "personal responsibility" for the material in that area. The principal threat the system was designed to address was Western spies, rather than homegrown material thieves; close KGB surveillance of everyone was the principal method relied on for dealing with the potential "insider" threat. Hence, a wide range of technologies used routinely in the West to address the insider threat were not used. Few Soviet facilities were equipped with detectors at the doors that would set off an alarm if someone attempted to smuggle out plutonium or HEU (known as "portal monitors"). Simple wax seals were used to indicate whether containers had been opened or material tampered with, making it a simple task for those with the stamps needed to make an identical new seal to open containers and remove material without detection. What little there was in the way of alarms, security cameras, and the like within the buildings relied on open wiring that could easily be cut. While some measurements of material on hand were conducted, few facilities had accurate and up-to-date measurements of all their nuclear material (an essential item if covert thefts are to be detected).

Moreover, purely civilian facilities (where foreign spies were not a concern) often had little security even if they were working with hundreds of kilograms of weapons-usable material. The author has visited facilities, for example, where the only security was provided by a single seated guard behind a desk at the entrance who did not bother to check known workers entering and leaving, and the material was secured in a simple locker with a padlock that could have been snapped in seconds with a bolt cutter available at any hardware store. As one senior Russian nuclear official put it to the author in 1994, "at some of these facilities, we have no one guarding but Aunt Masha with a cucumber."

Despite years of hard work and considerable progress in cooperative programs to address these problems, most still exist today. By the end of the year 2000, if all goes well, modern safeguards and security systems will have been completed at facilities housing one-sixth of the weapons-usable material outside of weapons in Russia, leaving work still under way for the remaining five-sixths of the material. While portal monitors have been installed at many facilities, hundreds of tons of fissile material are in buildings not equipped with portal monitors. Accurate measured inventories of all nuclear material on hand have still not been carried out, and there is still no functioning national inventory system[7]—meaning that if there were material missing, it is quite possible that no one would know. Wax seals are still in wide use as tamper-indicating devices.

The economic crisis in Russia following the August 1998 financial meltdown exacerbated the security problems that were already evident.[8] Unpaid and unfed guards at some facilities left their posts to forage for food, while at other facilities the electricity that is the lifeblood of the alarm and sensor systems was shut off for non-payment of bills. Many facilities simply could not afford to operate and maintain the new security equipment that had been installed with U.S. assistance. However, at least for facilities within the Ministry of Atomic Energy (MINATOM), this emergency situation had stabilized somewhat by early 1999, as the banks had resumed functioning, the decline of the ruble had made the ministry's hard-currency export income go further domestically, and collections of payments for electricity produced at nuclear plants had modestly improved.[9]

As a result of these security conditions, there have been a number of documented cases of theft of substantial quantities of weapons-usable nuclear materials, including 1.5 kilograms of weapon-grade HEU from the "Luch" production association in Podolsk, Russia, in 1992; 1.8 kilograms of 36 percent enriched HEU from the Andreeva Guba naval base near Russia's Norwegian border in July 1993; 4.5 kilograms of material enriched to over 19 percent U-235 from the Sevmorput naval shipyard near Murmansk in November 1993; over 360 grams of plutonium seized in Munich on a plane from Moscow as a result of a German "sting" operation in August 1994; and 2.72 kilograms of essentially weapon-grade (87.7 percent U-235) HEU seized in Prague in December 1994.[10]

Since then, there has been a lull in confirmed cases involving directly weapons-usable material,[11] though there has been a continuing stream of reports of varying levels of credibility. Perhaps the most alarming are the report that 2 kilograms of 90 percent enriched HEU was found to be missing in late 1997 from the Sukhumi research center in the Abkhazia region of Georgia (where a civil war had been under way),[12] and the announcement by the Russian Federal Security Service (FSB, successor to the KGB) in late 1998 that it had foiled an attempted theft of 18.5 kilograms of radioactive material suitable for the production of nuclear weapons components from a facility in the Chelyabinsk region.[13] If this latter incident in fact involved plutonium or HEU, it would be by far the largest confirmed case so far, for the first time involving enough material at one stroke to make a nuclear bomb.

While there is no evidence that enough material for a bomb has yet fallen into the hands of states such as Iran, Iraq, Libya, or North Korea, it is impossible to know what has not been detected. The fact that a large fraction of reports of nuclear smuggling are scams, or turn out to relate to materials with no relevance to nuclear weapons, should not obscure the seriousness of the cases that have occurred.

Security for nuclear materials in weapons in Russia is substantially better than for the "loose" materials just discussed, for reasons relating both to the fundamental nature of nuclear weapons and to the organizational arrangements for their protection.[14] All of the estimated seventeen thousand to twenty-two thousand former Soviet nuclear weapons that still exist have been consolidated within Russia.[15] (Successfully working with the former Soviet states to make this come about was one of the largely unsung non-proliferation success stories of the Clinton administration.) In Russia, the weapons' management and security are the responsibility of the Twelfth Main Directorate of the Ministry of Defense, a trained, professional force of roughly thirty thousand, of whom 45 percent are officers.[16] People working with nuclear weapons are carefully screened, and a "three-man rule" is in place forbidding anyone from working with nuclear weapons either alone or even in twos. Nuclear weapons are large, heavy objects; unlike weapons-usable nuclear material, they cannot simply be carried out in a briefcase or under one's overcoat. Similarly, nuclear weapons are easily countable: the commander of a storage unit is very much aware of whether there are ninety-nine or one hundred weapons in his charge. Inventories are taken regularly, and security forces are regularly tested against a mock terrorist team that attempts to break in.

As the Soviet Union moved toward collapse, the Soviet military rapidly reduced the number of nuclear weapon storage sites, from 500 in the 1980s to less than 100 today, eliminating the risks and costs of having such weapons stored at large numbers of small sites.[17] In 1997, General Eugene Habiger, then commander of the U.S. Strategic Command, led the first American delegation allowed to tour an active Russian nuclear weapons storage facility and view the security procedures there, and he was "impressed," saying that the Russians "go to great lengths" to provide security for nuclear weapons, and that "if what I saw was representative, yes, I have confidence in the safety and security of their nuclear weapon stockpile."[18] Similarly, the CIA concluded in 1996 that security for nuclear weapons in Russia remained effective, in contrast to its conclusions with respect to Russian nuclear material.[19] Despite myriad claims and exaggerated press accounts, there are no confirmed cases of theft or attempted theft of actual nuclear weapons.[20]

Nevertheless, even in the case of nuclear weapons, there are grounds for concern. The top leadership of the Twelfth Main Directorate have testified to the Russian Duma that funding for nuclear weapons security is grossly inadequate[21] (with the Twelfth Main Directorate's budget apparently only half as large as U.S. assistance for Russian warhead security).[22] As the CIA has pointed out, "the threat [of theft] from within the Russian military and the deteriorating economy" mean that the judgment that nuclear weapons remain secure "could change rapidly."[23] Crime is rising rapidly in the Strategic Rocket Forces, and the violent incident in September 1998 when several Twelfth Main Directorate soldiers murdered one of their comrades, took hostages, and attempted to hijack an aircraft suggests that the severe stresses permeating the Russian military in the wake of the August 1998 financial meltdown have been felt within the force that guards nuclear weapons as well.[24] In October 1998, the commander of the Twelfth Main Directorate, while emphasizing that there was no need for concern over the security of Russian nuclear warheads, acknowledged that the directorate's troops had not been given any higher priority in receiving pay than other troops, that they had received the paychecks due them only through July, and that the directorate was helping officers to get vegetables and potatoes for the winter in lieu of cash.[25]

UNDERFUNDING AN OVERSIZED COMPLEX

These security issues are seriously exacerbated by Russia's maintenance of a nuclear complex—both civilian and military—vastly larger than the available funding can support and vastly larger than needed for the complex's post–Cold War missions. On the military side, there remain ten entire cities, home to three-quarters of a million people, built only for the purpose of designing and producing nuclear weapons or nuclear material for them, closed off from the outside world by barbed wire and armed troops. While these cities once got the best of everything the Soviet Union had to offer, their funding has collapsed with the end of the Cold War, and pay there is both meager and intermittent. The nuclear facilities in these cities employ 125,000 people—whose pay, on average, is now less than $100 per month.[26] In late 1996, Vladimir Nechai, director of one of Russia's two premier nuclear weapons laboratories, committed suicide, in part in desperation over his inability to pay his employees' salaries.[27] In November 1998, three thousand workers at Nechai's institute went on strike, protesting "constant undernourishment, insufficient medical service, [and] inability to buy clothing and footwear for children or to pay for their education."[28]

The situation for many civilian nuclear facilities is even worse—particularly for small, isolated research labs that no longer have the funding to do their nuclear research or to provide adequate protection for the material they still have on hand. In visits to a wide variety of nuclear facilities following the August financial meltdown in 1998, the increasing desperation that erodes the performance of security systems while simultaneously increasing temptations for theft was starkly evident.[29] In September 1998, the Russian minister of atomic energy, responding to thousands of nuclear workers protesting unpaid wages, said that the government owed the ministry over $170 million and had not provided a single ruble in two months.[30]

Thus, the threat includes not only weaknesses in technical security and accounting systems but the profound destabilization of the lives of the guards and workers who have access to or provide security for nuclear weapons and materials. To date, the patriotism and dedication to duty of the vast majority of Russia's nuclear workers, even in the face of unpaid wages and shortages of everything from food to medicine, has been the major factor protecting the world from a proliferation catastrophe.

SECRECY

All of these urgent security hazards are taking place within a nuclear complex that remains shrouded in secrecy. After a period immediately following the collapse of the Soviet Union when a substantial amount of new information was released, and Russia seemed positively inclined to pursue nuclear transparency, the opponents of nuclear openness in Russia appear to have regained the upper hand. This pervasive secrecy—symbolized by Alexander Nikitin's arrest and trial for espionage for helping to compile publicly available information relating to the environmental problems of the Russian nuclear navy—poses substantial barriers to cooperation to improve security and even more fundamental obstacles to the kinds of monitoring and openness that would be required to verify deep reductions in nuclear warhead stockpiles.

It is not widely understood, for example, that arms control agreements to date have focused only on delivery vehicles and launchers; once warheads were removed from delivery vehicles, there has been no requirement that they be dismantled, or even accounted for. The United States has never verified the dismantlement of a single Russian nuclear warhead or provided a penny of assistance directly for warhead dismantlement. Nor has Russia ever been permitted to verify the dismantlement of a single U.S. warhead. Nor have the two countries ever told each other how many warheads they now have, how many they plan to retain under future arms control agreements, or how large their stockpiles of fissile material are (though Presidents Clinton and Yeltsin agreed to such a stockpile data exchange in September 1994). Indeed, excessive secrecy is a barrier that both countries, not just Russia, must address—though the prospect for additional openness in the United States seems slim in the wake of the recent scandals over Chinese espionage.

As a result of this survey, U.S. estimates of the size of the Russian warhead stockpile are officially judged to be uncertain to plus or minus five thousand warheads, estimates of the size of the Russian fissile material stockpile are uncertain to more than a hundred tons, and assessments of the security situation at individual facilities are based on information that ranges from nearly complete to virtually nonexistent.

EXCESSIVE STOCKPILES AND CONTINUED PRODUCTION

With the end of the Cold War, Russia and the United States both have far more nuclear warheads than they could possibly need, and far more plutonium and HEU than needed even to support those bloated warhead stockpiles. According to unclassified estimates, the United States still possesses over twelve thousand nuclear weapons and is planning to retain some ten thousand of these (counting both strategic and tactical weapons, both those deployed and those in reserve) even when START I and START II are fully implemented.[31] The United States has an estimated stockpile of nearly 100 tons of plutonium and some 645 tons of HEU.[32] As noted earlier, Russia is believed to have seventeen thousand to twenty-two thousand nuclear weapons remaining, and unclassified U.S. estimates suggest that it has 160 tons of separated plutonium (counting both military and civilian stockpiles) and 1,050 tons of HEU.[33] These remaining plutonium and HEU stockpiles would be sufficient to support a rapid return to Cold War levels of armament.

Yet in Russia, production of new weapons plutonium continues, at a rate of approximately 1.5 tons per year—not because Russia needs or is using the plutonium for new weapons but because the reactors that produce it also produce essential heat and power for nearby communities. Similarly, Russia's civilian spent fuel reprocessing enterprise continues to operate at the RT-1 plant at Mayak, separating in the range of a ton of reactor-grade (but weapons-usable) plutonium each year to add to the nearly 30-ton stockpile already in storage there—again, not because there is any need for this plutonium but because the contracts for this work from foreign countries with Soviet-designed reactors keep nuclear workers gainfully employed.

Finally, there is the problem of what to do with the enormous excess stockpiles of plutonium and HEU in the long run. With HEU, the answer in general terms is straightforward (though implementation has been anything but): it can be blended with other forms of uranium to produce non-weapons-usable, low-enriched uranium, which is a valuable commercial product as fuel for nuclear power reactors. Plutonium can also be blended with uranium to produce fuel, but because of the special handling procedures required by plutonium's radiotoxicity and proliferation hazard, doing so is more expensive than simply buying equivalent low-enriched uranium fuel on the open market, even if the plutonium itself is considered "free." Moreover, in contrast to the situation with uranium, simply blending the plutonium does not solve the proliferation problem, as virtually all mixes of plutonium isotopes are weapons-usable, and plutonium mixed with uranium can be chemically separated from the uranium without great difficulty, at least until it has been irradiated in a reactor.[34]

In short, the problems with management of nuclear material in the former Soviet Union that pose threats to U.S. security boil down to five categories: The materials are insecure; their custodians are on the edge of desperation; their management remains shrouded in secrecy; more weapons-usable material continues to be produced; and no sustainable plan is yet in place for getting rid of the enormous stockpiles of weapons-usable material that are no longer needed. In each of these areas, U.S. cooperative programs to address the problem are making progress, but far more urgently needs to be done.

PART II: THE CURRENT RESPONSE

The United States has two fundamental goals in cooperative programs related to the control of nuclear warheads and fissile material: to reduce the risk of nuclear proliferation and to achieve deep, transparent, and irreversible nuclear arms reductions. The myriad U.S. programs designed to take steps toward these goals can be divided into five categories corresponding to the five problems just described:

- Preventing theft and smuggling of nuclear weapons and material
- Stabilizing the custodians of these stockpiles, providing alternative employment for those no longer needed, and shrinking the nuclear complexes
- Monitoring stockpiles and reductions
- Ending further production of fissile material
- Reducing stockpiles of fissile material

The programs in each of these areas are making significant progress and deserve strong support; they are among the most cost-effective investments in U.S. security found anywhere in the U.S. budget. But what has been accomplished so far pales by comparison with what is needed to address the threat.

PREVENTING THEFT AND SMUGGLING

A variety of programs are in place that are intended to directly improve security and accounting for nuclear weapons and materials in the former Soviet Union and to interdict nuclear smuggling. The United States has (a) a cooperative material protection, control, and accounting (MPC&A) program designed to improve security and accounting for nuclear material in the former Soviet Union, funded by the Department of Energy (DOE); (b) a program to build a secure storage facility for fissile material from dismantled weapons at Mayak, funded by the Department of Defense (DOD); (c) an effort to provide equipment for improving security of nuclear weapon storage and transport, also funded by DOD; (d) programs that have removed weapons-usable nuclear material from selected particularly vulnerable sites; and (e) several programs in Defense, Energy, Customs, and the Federal Bureau of Investigation to cooperate with relevant countries in improving capabilities to stop nuclear smuggling. Other countries have modest cooperative programs contributing to MPC&A (particularly in the non-Russian states of the former Soviet Union), nuclear smuggling interdiction, and (in the case of Japan) containers for the Mayak storage facility.

MPC&A

The MPC&A program has made substantial progress in recent years but has an enormously long road yet to travel.[35] There are now agreements in place to cooperate at virtually every facility in the former Soviet Union where HEU or plutonium outside of weapons is located. The United States had allocated $573 million to this cooperation through March 1999, with the program budget at $140 million in fiscal year 1999 and planned to remain in the $140 million to $145 million range for each of the following five years.[36] Hundreds of U.S. and Russian experts are at work designing and installing improved MPC&A systems, training operators and regulators, drafting and implementing improved regulations, and the like. As of May 1999, security and accounting system upgrades had been declared completed at all of the nine sites in the non-Russian states of the former Soviet Union where separated plutonium or HEU is still located, along with eleven sites in Russia.[37] Security for 30 metric tons of weapons-usable material had been upgraded, with an additional 20 tons expected by the end of 1999 and an additional 50 by the end of 2000.[38] Particularly remarkable progress was being made in working with the Russian navy to secure HEU naval fuel.

Despite this record, the vast majority of the work required remains to be done. Most fissile material in the former Soviet Union is housed in buildings whose security and accounting systems have not been upgraded at all. There are still some sensitive facilities with very large quantities of fissile material that Russia has been unwilling to grant any access to (such as the nuclear weapons assembly/disassembly facilities and the HEU fuel fabrication line at Elektrostal). As a result, upgrades at these facilities have not yet begun (though measures to provide confidence that U.S. assistance is being used appropriately at facilities too sensitive for direct access by U.S. personnel have been developed). While equipment for material accounting is being provided, efforts to conduct real inventories are languishing. Only modest progress has been made in putting in place effective MPC&A regulation with the teeth to fine or shut down facilities that fail to meet standards—without which facility managers have little incentive to devote resources from tight budgets to ensuring adequate safeguards and security. Most significantly, the former Soviet economies remain in deep crisis, and the challenge of ensuring sustainable security after the period of initial upgrading is completed remains a fundamental one. Today, there are facilities in the former Soviet Union where some U.S.-provided equipment is simply not being used, as the facilities do not have the money to operate and maintain it or the incentive to use what little money they have for that purpose.

It is now clear that the MPC&A job will be larger and more challenging than originally anticipated. Early planning envisioned that initial upgrades would be completed by 2002, for a total U.S. program cost of less than a billion dollars. Since those plans were made, expanding U.S.-Russian cooperation has expanded the U.S. understanding of the scope of the work to be done: It has become clear that there are significantly more buildings containing fissile material than had been envisioned, that the scale of required upgrades is even larger than had been thought, and that the need for continued funding for sustainability is much greater than had been envisioned.[39]

Moreover, political and management issues in both Russia and the United States continue to pose significant obstacles to MPC&A progress. As noted above, Russian restrictions on access to facilities have slowed progress at a number of facilities. Worse, virtually all levels of the Russian system, from the president and prime minister to managers of individual areas handling nuclear material, have generally placed only modest priority on improving safeguards and security when allocating their financial and personnel resources. At the same time, Russia has attempted to impose taxes on the U.S. assistance, which reduces both the amount of the assistance available for its intended purpose and the political support for the assistance in the United States. In the United States, the president, the vice president, the national security adviser, and cabinet secretaries have given only sporadic attention to this issue, have allowed problems at the working level to fester, and have only rarely put security for nuclear material at the top of the security agenda with Russia, where it belongs. A prolonged period of interagency disputes over how to implement the program was followed—after full budget and program responsibility was shouldered by DOE in FY1996—by an equally prolonged period of pulling and hauling between different factions with different approaches at DOE headquarters and the DOE laboratories. Only the most modest efforts have been made to coordinate the MPC&A program with the many other fissile-material-related efforts described in this chapter. The personnel resources devoted to the effort have been so slim that many of those involved are suffering from exhaustion and burnout and have no time to work seriously on envisioning and implementing new approaches.

In short, to meet the goal of achieving effective and sustainable security for all the weapons-usable nuclear material in the former Soviet Union within a few years would require a dramatic increase in both financial and personnel resources and political leadership devoted to the problem.

MAYAK STORAGE FACILITY

For years, the U.S. Department of Defense has been helping Russia design and build a storage facility for plutonium and HEU from dismantled weapons at Ozersk (formerly Chelyabinsk-65).[40] After years of delays, the first module of the facility, capable of holding twenty-five thousand fissile material containers (the result of the dismantlement of about eight thousand warheads, as each warhead results in three to four containers of fissile material), is expected to open in 2002. Originally, the facility was planned to have two modules, for a total of fifty thousand containers, and indeed a second facility of equal size was to be built at another site, to accommodate all the excess fissile material from dismantled Russian weapons. However, costs have been rising as delays continue, and while the construction cost was once to have been split fifty-fifty between Russia and the United States, Russia has indicated that it will not be able to pay its half; as a result, the Defense Department has deferred anything beyond the first module of the first facility for now.[41] No agreement has yet been reached on the transparency measures the United States has sought, in return for its assistance, to confirm that (a) the material in the facility comes from dismantled weapons, (b) the material is safe and secure, and (c) the material is not being returned to weapons (see discussion under monitoring, below).

NUCLEAR WARHEAD SECURITY

The U.S. DOD and the Russian Ministry of Defense have been cooperating for several years to improve security for nuclear warheads themselves.[42] The cooperation first focused on transportation, with the provision of security upgrade kits for railcars, secure blankets, "super-containers" for warhead transport and storage, and the like. While that effort continues, efforts are now under way to improve security and accounting for warheads in storage as well, with the provision of computers for creating a real-time accounting system (replacing the paper accounting systems of the past), equipment and training for screening personnel, and improved security equipment for actual warhead sites. A "model" facility is being established at Sergeyev Posad to demonstrate modern equipment, which the United States can then supply at Russian request for installation at actual warhead storage sites. (Here, too, procedures to confirm that equipment paid for with U.S. assistance is being used appropriately at facilities that U.S. auditors will not be allowed to visit are being discussed.) While the transportation security program is nearly complete, the storage security program is still in its early stages, with little if any new security equipment yet installed and operational at Russian warhead storage facilities.

REMOVING MATERIAL FROM VULNERABLE SITES

In some cases, the United States and its cooperative partners in the former Soviet Union have concluded that it makes more sense to relocate the material to a safer location than to try to protect it in place. In November 1994, after more than a year of secret discussions and preparation, nearly 600 kilograms of weapons-usable HEU was airlifted from the Ulba facility at Ust-Kamenogorsk in Kazakhstan to the United States, in what was known as Project Sapphire. The United States paid for the operation, and in effect purchased the material from Kazakhstan with both cash and promises of assistance for other projects.[43] After shipment to the United States, the material was blended to non-weapons-usable LEU under IAEA safeguards. Similarly, in 1997, again after more than a year of secret discussions and preparations, several kilograms of HEU—some fresh and some irradiated—were removed from a research facility near Tbilisi, Georgia, and shipped to the British reprocessing plant at Dounreay for processing (with U.S. funding and assistance), in an effort known as Project Auburn Endeavor.[44] Finally, the U.S. and the Kazakh governments are again working together in a project to ship irradiated fuel elements from a Kazakh breeder reactor located on the shores of the Caspian Sea across from Iran to a more secure site deep within Kazakhstan.[45] These fuel elements are no longer radioactive enough to provide much of a barrier to theft, and contain "ivory-grade" plutonium (that is, plutonium with an even lower percentage of undesirable isotopes than typical weapons-grade plutonium). Although each of these efforts involved relatively modest quantities of material, the intricacies of intergovernment negotiation, long-distance shipment, safety assessments and preparations, and the like required months of effort and cost tens of millions of dollars.

NUCLEAR SMUGGLING INTERDICTION

Once fissile material has been removed from authorized control, much of the battle is already lost. Finding stolen fissile material and detecting and interdicting its passage across borders is a herculean task, in most cases only practicable if good intelligence and police work tell officials where to look. Nevertheless, a "second line of defense" designed to help catch nuclear thieves and interdict nuclear smuggling is an important part of the overall effort, especially as it provides a deterrent effect by increasing thieves' perception of the likelihood of being caught. The United States and other interested states are pursuing limited efforts to exchange intelligence, coordinate responses, and train and equip police, intelligence forces, customs agencies, and border guards in the states in or near the former Soviet Union. A "Programme for Preventing and Combatting Illicit Trafficking in Nuclear Material," agreed to at the P-8 Nuclear Safety and Security Summit in Moscow in April 1996, has focused primarily on developing information exchange mechanisms (still a difficult issue where sensitive police, intelligence, or military nuclear information is involved), expanding the number of countries involved, and conducting a series of conferences and development activities related to "nuclear forensics"—a means to determine the origin of a seized sample of nuclear material.

A variety of U.S. agencies have been providing specific training and equipment to relevant states to deal with nuclear smuggling. The U.S. Customs Service has provided training and equipment to customs officials in key states. Similarly, the FBI has been working to provide training to police and other officials in relevant countries, generally at the International Law Enforcement Academy in Budapest. Between them, these programs are planned to receive $17 million from the Department of Defense over fiscal 2000–2004.[46] The Department of Energy has launched the Second Line of Defense program, which has installed nuclear material detectors at three key border transit points (including Moscow's Sheremetyevo airport and two points on the Caspian Sea), and Russia has requested assistance to equip twenty-two more critical transit points. Several departments—State, Commerce, and Energy, among others—also have programs designed to strengthen export controls more generally, providing an important foundation for nuclear smuggling interdiction efforts. To date, however, U.S. programs that focus on interdicting nuclear smuggling have been piecemeal and have not yet gelled into a comprehensive plan.

STABILIZING NUCLEAR CUSTODIANS

As essential as these efforts to improve security systems for warheads and materials are, they will not solve the proliferation problem if the people who must guard and manage nuclear weapons and materials are desperate, ill-paid, underfed, unable to provide for their families, and embedded in a larger culture of crime and corruption. To address the desperation that could lead to theft of nuclear material or sale of nuclear knowledge, it is critical to (a) help Russia reduce the size of its nuclear complex (both military and civilian) to a level it can afford to maintain safely and securely, including helping to provide alternative employment for the excess nuclear scientists and workers, and (b) work with Russia to ensure that the scientists, workers, and guards who remain as custodians of nuclear weapons, materials, and information are adequately paid, fed, and housed. The second of these objectives is largely something Russia will have to do for itself; taxpayers from other countries cannot be expected to pay for the maintenance of a nuclear stockpile aimed at them. But that makes it all the more essential to help Russia shrink its complex to a size it can sustain on its own, appropriate to the complex's post–Cold War missions—which is every bit as much in Russia's interest as it is in the U.S. interest. From the U.S. point of view, shrinking the Russian complex will not only reduce proliferation hazards but reduce Russia's huge capability to fabricate new nuclear weapons, should circumstances change. Several U.S. and international programs are under way that focus on different aspects of these issues.

THE HEU PURCHASE AGREEMENT AND COMMERCIAL DEALS

Large-scale commercial and quasi-commercial deals are currently the largest sources of hard currency available to stabilize the giant Russian nuclear complex. The U.S.-Russian HEU Purchase Agreement (described below), under which the United States is buying LEU blended from HEU from dismantled Russian nuclear weapons, provides hundreds of millions of dollars a year—the income for most of the remaining workers at several of Russia's largest nuclear weapons complex sites—(though how much of this money goes to MINATOM and how much to the central government is unclear). Similarly, several Russian nuclear sites with commercial contracts to supply enrichment, reprocessing, or fuel fabrication services to foreign customers produce larger income streams than foreign assistance programs generally do.

SCIENCE AND TECHNOLOGY COOPERATION PROGRAMS

The International Science and Technology Center (ISTC) in Moscow, the similar center in Kiev, and a variety of lab-to-lab programs are already employing thousands of former Soviet weapons scientists in useful civilian work.[47] Similarly, DOE's Initiatives for Proliferation Prevention program (IPP, formerly the Industrial Partnering Program), which seeks to furnish initial funds to link Russian and U.S. laboratory technical experts with businesses willing to invest in commercializing their technologies, is also providing temporary employment for thousands of former weapons scientists and attempting to partner Russian institutes with U.S. labs and industry to bring promising technologies to market. But only a tiny number of IPP projects have graduated to being commercially self-supporting; most of the money has historically gone to fund the U.S. laboratory participation, and some of the remainder has historically gone to Russian taxes and overhead (from which the ISTC funds are exempted). Nevertheless, a significant number of IPP projects are now nearing the commercialization stage, and DOE has been undertaking substantial reforms.[48]

NUCLEAR CITIES INITIATIVE

Most recently, the United States and Russia have established a joint "Nuclear Cities Initiative," designed to help downsize Russia's nuclear weapons complex and diversify the economic base of the closed cities of that complex, providing alternative employment for scientists and workers no longer needed for nuclear weapons-related activities.[49] This is an enormous undertaking, and so far U.S. funding for this effort is extremely modest: $15 million in FY1999, with $30 million requested for FY2000. (By contrast, DOE has officially estimated that $550 million over five years—nearly four times currently planned budgets—would be needed to foster sustainable employment for the roughly fifty thousand people that MINATOM has indicated will need new jobs. The fifty thousand figure is itself in all likelihood a substantial underestimate.[50]) By agreement between the United States and Russia, the initial efforts focus on three priority cities—the two weapons laboratories (Sarov, formerly Arzamas-16, and Snezhinsk, formerly Chelyabinsk-70) and one of the plutonium production cities (Zheleznogorsk, formerly Krasnoyarsk-26). As Russia has recently announced that it plans to close two of its four nuclear weapons assembly/disassembly facilities (the Avangard plant, located at Sarov, and the plant at Zarechnyy, formerly Penza-19), DOE hopes to expand the program to facilitate shutdown of these facilities as well.

OTHER U.S. AND INTERNATIONAL PROGRAMS

A variety of other programs designed to achieve other objectives also provide some funding and employment in the nuclear cities. The MPC&A program is particularly prominent, employing several hundred Russian experts in the nuclear cities and providing tens of millions of dollars in either contracts or equipment each year. Construction of the Mayak storage facility is employing hundreds of workers at that site. Programs such as the conversion of Russia's plutonium production reactors and disposition of Russia's excess weapons plutonium may employ hundreds or even thousands of nuclear city workers in the future. Transparency programs, environmental cleanup projects, and a variety of other efforts employ smaller numbers of people at selected sites. Unfortunately, these myriad programs are not coordinated to maximize their overall contribution to providing alternative employment and downsizing Russia's nuclear weapons complex.

MONITORING STOCKPILES AND REDUCTIONS

Progress is even slimmer in bringing transparency to the management of nuclear weapons and nuclear materials, needed to lay the basis for effective long-term cooperation on security and accounting and to achieve deep reductions in nuclear warhead and material stockpiles. While a variety of informal approaches have made some headway—the level of U.S. and Russian access to the other side's nuclear facilities as part of the MPC&A program, lab-to-lab cooperation, and other programs that exist today would have been unthinkable as recently as early 1994—formal transparency discussions between the two governments have produced virtually nothing but a trail of unfulfilled agreements (see "Transparency that Never Happened," page 90).

There have been three fundamental reasons for this lack of progress: (a) the legacy of seventy years of Communist secrecy has made Russia extraordinarily reluctant to open nuclear secrets; (b) there has also been substantial resistance in many parts of the U.S. government to opening key U.S. facilities and operations to Russian examination, which has sometimes manifested itself in demands that Russia accept inspections in return for U.S. assistance, with no reciprocity on the U.S. side—a "pay-per-view" approach that has aggravated Russian suspicions of U.S. motives; and (c) the U.S. government has never offered the Russian government any significant strategic or financial incentives to do the difficult and politically risky work of overcoming the many obstacles to a broad nuclear transparency regime. In short, there is plenty of blame to go around on both sides—and these problems will inevitably be even more difficult to address with souring U.S.-Russian political relations, redoubled Russian reliance on nuclear weapons, and the intense U.S. focus on protecting nuclear secrets in the wake of the China spying scandals. But there remain opportunities, described below, to move transparency forward by ensuring that the measures agreed upon genuinely serve the interests of both sides equally.

Despite the lack of progress on the government-to-government level, there is extraordinarily useful lab-to-lab cooperation under way to analyze and develop technologies and procedures for confirming the dismantlement of warheads while protecting sensitive information. The goal is to have jointly developed approaches already available when formal negotiations begin. This lab-to-lab effort, which also encompasses a number of other transparency issues, is perhaps the most promising U.S.-Russian transparency initiative now under way. But here, too, souring political relations are contributing to difficulties concerning access to information and facilities.[51]

Transparency arrangements for the Mayak storage facility—virtually the only formal U.S.-Russian transparency negotiation still under way as of mid-1999—represent a classic example of the problems with the "pay-per-view" approach. The Russian side, while agreeing in principle early on that in return for its assistance the United States could have access to this facility once it was built, delayed actually beginning negotiations for years on end and has repeatedly raised the issue of the lack of reciprocity at similar U.S. facilities. Formal negotiations are now under way and have largely reached agreement on the straightforward measures that would be implemented at the Mayak facility itself. But since Russia now plans to convert weapons components to unclassified shapes before the material is placed in this facility, the United States is demanding transparency "upstream" at the facility where this conversion would be done to confirm that the material comes from weapons. While the United States argues that the measures it is seeking should not

---

Transparency That Never Happened

High-level U.S.-Russian transparency commitments that have never been fulfilled and initiatives that have never been implemented include:

January 1994:	Presidents Clinton and Yeltsin agree on the objective of ensuring "transparency and irreversibility" of nuclear reductions and establish a working group to negotiate specific measures. None of these measures has ever been implemented.
March 1994:	U.S. Secretary of Energy Hazel O'Leary and Russian Minister of Atomic Energy Victor Mikhailov agree to mutual inspection of fissile materials from dismantled weapons beginning by the end of 1994. The inspections are never implemented.
September 1994:	Presidents Clinton and Yeltsin agree to exchange data on warhead and fissile material stockpiles by the end of the year. The exchanges have never occurred.
May 1995:	Presidents Clinton and Yeltsin reaffirm commitment to transparency and irreversibility, to mutual inspections of material from dismantled warheads, and to warhead and material data exchanges, and agree to have experts explore several other transparency possibilities. None of these measures is ever implemented, and the Russian side cuts off talks in late 1995. By mid-1999, they had not yet resumed.
September 1996:	Secretary O'Leary and Minister Mikhailov announce a "Trilateral Initiative" with the International Atomic Energy Agency (IAEA) to put excess fissile material under IAEA monitoring. (President Clinton had committed to place U.S. excess material under IAEA monitoring as early as 1993, and President Yeltsin had said in April 1996 that he would place the Mayak storage facility being built for Russian excess nuclear material under IAEA monitoring.) While discussions continue, three years later no monitoring under the Trilateral Initiative has been implemented.
March 1997:	At their Helsinki summit, Presidents Clinton and Yeltsin agree that START III should include "measures relating to the transparency of strategic warhead inventories and the destruction of strategic nuclear warheads," and that transparency measures related to sea-launched cruise missiles, tactical nuclear weapons, and nuclear materials will also be explored. Two years later, as a result of the Russian Duma's failure to ratify START II and the U.S. refusal to begin START III negotiations until START II is ratified, no negotiations have begun, and it is expected that these issues will likely be dropped from START III in the interests of simplifying an already complex package of issues such an agreement will have to address.

be considered sensitive, it has refused to offer to implement them at the comparable planned U.S. facility, and the Russian side is balking.[52] Whether transparency measures will be developed and in place in time for the planned opening of the facility in 2002 remains to be seen.

Today, the only fissile material transparency measures actually being implemented on a substantial scale are, not surprisingly, the only ones where there was a large financial incentive to reach agreement—namely, the transparency measures for the $12 billion U.S.-Russian HEU Purchase agreement, designed to provide confidence to the United States that the LEU it is purchasing comes from HEU that in turn comes from weapons, and confidence to Russia that the LEU it is selling is used only for peaceful purposes.[53] Indeed, Russia agreed to the more intrusive aspects of these transparency measures because of its need for large cash prepayments to fund provision of the LEU under the deal. For whatever reason, the United States government has never attempted to apply the basic lesson that transparency success requires some incentive for the Russian side to reach agreement to its broader transparency objectives.

In short, most of the formal government-to-government discussions so far are focusing only on creating one or two "transparency islands" relating to specific projects, such as the HEU Purchase Agreement and the Mayak storage facility. These have been successful where there was a serious Russian incentive to agree. Serious discussions of a broad regime that would be needed to help ensure security and provide a basis for deep reductions in nuclear warhead and material stockpiles have not even begun.

ENDING FURTHER PRODUCTION

Ending continued growth in the stockpiles of weapons-usable fissile material is another critical element of a comprehensive approach to managing these materials. The United States and Russia agreed in May 1995 that no fissile material produced in the future would be used in nuclear weapons, but Russia still has three reactors producing weapons-grade plutonium—because those reactors provide essential heat and power for nearby communities. The 1.5 tons per year of plutonium that continue to be produced are stored in oxide form at the two reactor sites, Seversk (formerly Tomsk-7) and Zheleznogorsk (formerly Krasnoyarsk-26).

In 1994, the United States and Russia agreed to shut down these reactors by the year 2000 and to cooperate in providing alternative sources of heat and power to these communities. Alternative energy sources proved much more expensive than expected, however, and in 1997 the two sides agreed to convert the reactors to a different fuel cycle. In this cycle the spent fuel contains very little plutonium and is suitable for long-term storage without reprocessing. Appropriate monitoring ensures both that the reactors are in fact converted and that plutonium produced before then is not used in weapons. The reactors are expected to finally be converted in 2002, at which point they are expected to have approximately a decade of remaining operational life (after which the issue of providing alternative heat and power sources will arise again). In the spring of 1999, the U.S. government decided to fund development of both LEU and HEU fuels for this conversion program, and to proceed at least initially to convert the cores to use the HEU fuel if, as expected, the HEU fuel becomes available first. The processing, fabrication, transport, and storage of hundreds of thousands of small, easily stealable HEU fuel elements each year could create serious proliferation risks if the most stringent practicable MPC&A measures are not applied throughout the process.[54] Russia's nuclear regulatory agency has raised serious questions concerning the safety of continuing to operate these reactors in general, and the safety of the fuel and core designs being developed for the conversion project in particular. Whether the conversion project will be successfully completed remains quite uncertain.

Meanwhile as noted earlier, Russia's civilian reprocessing at the RT-1 plant at Mayak also continues to separate something in the range of a ton of weapons-usable plutonium every year. No cooperative programs are yet in place to slow or terminate this production. MINATOM is seeking to modify Russian environmental laws to make it possible to accept foreign spent fuel for storage. It would then use the profits to build and operate a large new reprocessing plant known as RT-2, producing still more weapons-usable separated plutonium, at the closed city of Zheleznogorsk (formerly Krasnoyarsk-26). While at this writing it appears likely that the modification to the law will eventually be approved in some form, it still appears highly unlikely that MINATOM will succeed in getting the funds to launch this new reprocessing facility.[55] A number of analysts—including the author—have proposed a different approach in which Russia would accept foreign spent fuel for storage but would use the revenue for non-proliferation and cleanup activities (see "Generating New Revenue for Nuclear Security," page 112).

At the same time, there are no transparency or verification measures in place to confirm that no HEU is being produced—or, for that matter, at reprocessing plants, to confirm that none of the separated plutonium is being used for nuclear weapons. While a global fissile material cutoff agreement that would impose such verification—at least in the U.S. conception—is being discussed at the Conference on Disarmament in Geneva, little progress has been made, and the Russian position on this treaty would exempt most Russian facilities from verification. (See chapter 16, "A Fissile Material Cut-Off Treaty and the Future of Nuclear Arms Control.")

REDUCING FISSILE MATERIAL STOCKPILES

With the end of the Cold War and the consequent dismantlement of thousands of nuclear weapons, both the United States and Russia have enormous stockpiles of plutonium and HEU they no longer need. These huge stockpiles will pose serious proliferation and arms-reduction-reversal risks as long as they remain in readily weapons-usable form. As former Russian minister of atomic energy Victor Mikhailov once said, "Real disarmament is possible only if the accumulated huge stocks of weapons-grade uranium and plutonium are destroyed."[56]

The United States and Russia have both designated hundreds of tons of their fissile material stockpiles as being "excess" to their military needs. The United States has designated 52.5 tons of plutonium as excess, along with 174.3 tons of HEU, for a total of just over 225 tons of excess fissile material.[57] The United States has publicly committed to place this excess material under IAEA verification to confirm that it will never be returned to weapons, but to date, only 12 tons is actually under IAEA safeguards, with an additional 26 tons to be available for verification by the end of 1999.[58] The excess HEU is being blended to LEU at U.S. facilities, for sale on the commercial reactor fuel market (or disposal, in the case of material that is too contaminated to have commercial value).

For the excess U.S. plutonium, a substantial program is in place to demonstrate and implement two complementary disposition paths: Some of it is to be burned as uranium-plutonium mixed oxide (MOX) fuel in existing U.S. reactors, and some of it is to be immobilized with high-level wastes. Recovering plutonium for use in weapons from the massive, highly radioactive waste forms from either of these processes would be roughly as difficult and unattractive as recovering it from the vastly larger quantities of ordinary commercial spent nuclear fuel that already exist—the so-called spent fuel standard.

For either of these approaches, plutonium will have to be converted from weapons components or other forms to oxide; a prototype facility for that purpose was dedicated at the Los Alamos National Laboratory in September 1998, and a full-scale facility at Savannah River is expected to begin operations in 2005. A commercial contract for the initial design stages of the MOX portion of the program—with options for later stages—was signed in March 1999, with a MOX fuel fabrication facility at Savannah River expected to begin in 2006. Full-scale "hot" (radioactive) tests of the immobilization approach are expected in a few years, with operation of a full-scale plant to follow in 2006. While the disposition of the HEU will return funds to the U.S. Treasury from the material's commercial value, plutonium has no value in the current market, as noted above, and hence the U.S. plutonium disposition program is expected to cost in the range of $2 billion.[59]

The MOX track has been criticized by a broad range of nongovernmental organizations on grounds of undermining the U.S. opposition to civilian plutonium recycling; defenders have countered that what the United States has long opposed is making more separated, weapons-usable plutonium, and that using all the available means to reduce stockpiles of separated plutonium is completely consistent with this policy.[60] The politics of the use of plutonium in U.S. reactors remains deeply problematic, however, and whether DOE will succeed in carrying out this part of the program is unclear. Meanwhile, the immobilization track is encountering technical delays related to difficulties with the immobilization of U.S. high-level waste at the Savannah River sites.

Russia has declared 50 tons of plutonium and 500 tons of HEU excess to its military needs. Under the U.S.-Russian HEU Purchase Agreement, the 500 tons of HEU from weapons is being blended to LEU and sold to the United States for resale on the commercial reactor fuel market. This is perhaps the most critical and creative U.S.-Russian fissile material control program: At one stroke, it provides financial incentives to dismantle thousands of warheads, destroys hundreds of tons of weapons-usable material that could otherwise pose risks of proliferation or arms-reduction reversal, gives employment to thousands of Russian nuclear workers, and provides hundreds of millions of dollars a year to the desperate Russian nuclear complex—all at little net cost to the U.S. taxpayer. By the end of 1998, over 50 tons of HEU—enough for thousands of nuclear weapons—had been blended to LEU and delivered to the United States.[61]

This HEU deal has been plagued with a series of problems, however—serious enough to interrupt blending and deliveries for months at a time. These problems were largely caused by placing the deal in the hands of the United States Enrichment Corporation (USEC)—which has no profit incentive to carry out the agreement, since its marginal cost for producing enrichment services is less than what it is paying Russia—and then privatizing USEC in the summer of 1998. USEC privatization caused another rupture in the deal, stopping deliveries for months. This problem was solved only after Congress, in the fall of 1998, under the leadership of Senator Pete Domenici (R–New Mexico), provided a subsidy of $325 million to save the agreement; even then, a final agreement that allowed deliveries to restart was not reached until March 1999. That fix is expected to be temporary, however, and continued U.S. government intervention is likely to be needed as long as the deal remains solely in USEC's hands, with no competition to ensure a fair market price.[62]

There are strong arguments for blending and buying more HEU, and for doing it faster. The 50 tons blended over the six years since the deal began represents less than 5 percent of the Russian HEU stockpile. Although the pace has now increased to 30 tons per year (if all goes well), a decade hence it will still be true that less than a third of the Russian HEU stockpile has been addressed. Indeed, the entire 500-ton deal represents less than half of Russia's total HEU stockpile. Moreover, the deal involves the bulk processing and transport—steps that create new vulnerabilities to possible theft—of tens of tons of weapons-usable material a year with as yet no substantial upgrades to security and accounting at the facilities where the HEU is being processed and blended.

Less progress has been made in dealing with Russia's excess weapons plutonium.[63] The basic options available—use as reactor fuel or immobilization—are the same as in the United States. But Russia lacks both the money to pay for either of these options and the number of modern, safe reactors needed to burn the material rapidly as fuel. Moreover, Russia refuses to consider the immobilization option, considering the plutonium as a valuable national asset produced with thousands of man-years of labor—not something to be thrown away as waste. At their September 1998 summit, President Clinton and President Yeltsin signed an agreement in principle to carry out disposition of 50 tonnes (metric tons) of plutonium on each side and calling for negotiation of a more specific and binding government-to-government agreement laying out how this would be done by the end of 1998. These negotiations did not even formally begin until 1999, but as of mid-1999 there appeared to be at least some hope they would be concluded by the end of the year.

Two fundamental obstacles need to be overcome for this first-step effort to eliminate the fifty tons of plutonium Russia has so far declared excess to be successful. The first problem is financing: Russia has made it clear that it cannot afford to pay the cost of disposition of its excess plutonium (unknown at this time, but likely to be in the range of $1 billion–$3 billion) and will sign no plutonium disposition agreements without a credible financing plan in place; other countries have pledged only a small part of the required funds. Under Senator Domenici's leadership,

Congress put a $200 million down payment on this cost into the fiscal 1999 budget, and the administration has requested an additional $200 million over five years in its Expanded Threat Reduction Initiative. In the spring of 1999, Japan made a pledge of $200 million for submarine decommissioning, reemploying weapons scientists, and plutonium disposition in Russia—but it is expected that only $30 million–$40 million of that amount will be for plutonium disposition, leaving the financing arranged to date still far less than what is needed.

The second major obstacle is the lack of sufficient reactors to burn the Russian plutonium. If all seven of Russia's most modern reactors, the VVER-1000s, and its only operational fast-neutron reactor, the BN-600, were converted to burn partial cores of MOX fuel—which may or may not be possible in the case of some of the older plants—they could burn roughly two tons of plutonium per year. At that rate, even after the years required to get going, it would take twenty-five years longer than the remaining operational years of most of these reactors to burn the fifty tonnes of plutonium Russia has already declared excess, to say nothing of the huge additional quantities that may become excess as disarmament proceeds. Concepts for an international consortium that would buy MOX made from Russian weapons plutonium and market it to reactors in Ukraine, Western Europe, Japan, and Canada are being considered, but no genuinely credible scheme has yet been established.

Yet rapid progress toward a U.S.-Russian agreement is essential, since Congress indicated in the FY1999 appropriations bills that it was unwilling to fund actual construction of disposition facilities in the United States in the absence of any firm agreement with Russia to eliminate its excess plutonium stockpile in parallel. (The $200 million down payment was in part an effort to kick-start these talks by making it clear that at least a substantial portion of the financing could come from the United States.) In short, plutonium disposition is now in the odd situation of being a long-term problem requiring immediate action: if there is not major progress soon on nailing down a Russian plutonium disposition approach—with the necessary financing—the entire U.S. plutonium disposition program may also come to a screeching halt.

Alternative concepts that have been proposed but are not currently being actively pursued include (a) shipping the excess plutonium to storage facilities outside of Russia, regardless of whether it can be used in the near term, as the quickest means to address the security threats it poses; (b) fabricating the Russian plutonium into fuel in existing European MOX fabrication plants, instead of the civilian plutonium they are currently planning to fabricate during that period; and (c) purchasing the Russian excess plutonium and shipping it to the United States for incorporation into the U.S. disposition program.

Finally, if disposition of excess material is ever to meet either its non-proliferation objective or its arms reduction irreversibility objective, far more material will have to be declared excess and moved into the disposition pipeline, which will make the problem of figuring out ways to eliminate these materials that much more problematic. As things now stand, the huge quantities of plutonium and HEU that both the United States and Russia are holding in reserve are easily enough to support a rapid return to Cold War levels of armament, and to pose enormous risks of theft. The United States is keeping in reserve nearly half of its plutonium stockpile (and well over half of its weapon-grade plutonium stockpile), along with nearly three-quarters of its HEU stockpile. Russia is keeping in reserve nearly two-thirds of its weapon-grade plutonium stockpile, along with the majority of its HEU stockpile; in both cases, the amounts remaining in reserve could easily support stockpiles of well over ten thousand nuclear weapons.

The Expanded Threat Reduction Initiative

On January 19, 1999, in his State of the Union address, President Clinton said, "We must expand our work with Russia, Ukraine, and the other former Soviet nations to safeguard nuclear materials and technology so they never fall into the wrong hands. Our balanced budget will increase funding for these critical efforts by almost two-thirds over the next five years."

Unfortunately, it soon became clear that the claimed two-thirds increase in spending for programs to "safeguard nuclear materials and technology" was illusory. The two-thirds increase was not judged by comparison with previous funding levels but rather by comparison with previously planned budget declines—and most of that "increase" went to worthy efforts unrelated to safeguarding nuclear material, from providing civilian jobs for biological weapons experts to dealing with leftover conventional ammunition in the Trans-Dniestr area of Moldova.

The budget for the MPC&A program—the main program most directly dealing with safeguarding nuclear materials—tells the story. In FY1999, when the scope of the nuclear material emergency following the August 1998 financial meltdown became clear, rather than reprogramming additional funds for MPC&A, DOE took funds away, redirecting for work on other projects $12 million of the $152 million Congress had appropriated. The much-vaunted "increase" for MPC&A in the Expanded Threat Reduction Initiative is a request for FY2000 of $145 million—$7 million less than Congress had appropriated the year before (though more, to be sure, than DOE had once planned to request). A substantial amount of bureaucratic infighting was required even to bring the budget to that "not quite flat" level. There is a yawning gap between the administration's rhetoric and its budgeting.

Overall, the Expanded Threat Reduction Initiative package calls for $4.2 billion in spending on a wide range of programs over five years, compared with $2.5 billion that had been previously planned for that period, or somewhat over the $3 billion that would have been spent had FY1999 expenditures (except for one-time initiatives such as the Domenici HEU and plutonium funding) been kept constant for five years. Alternatively, the $4.2 billion can be compared with over $3 billion, which would have been the result of keeping previous spending levels constant for the five-year period, making the result closer to a one-third increase than a two-thirds increase. Roughly two-thirds of the planned spending is for programs related in one way or another, warhead and fissile material control, but in most cases, these programs are not substantially increased compared with the FY1999 funding that existed before the initiative was launched. The "increase," in most cases, represents simply flat funding for programs that had been expected to be phased out as their missions were completed. Table 7.1 compares funding for these programs for FY1999, before the initiative, and the administration's request for FY2000, the first and largest year of the new initiative. As can be seen, most of the programs are held roughly constant; the most substantial increases are for science cooperation programs that provide grants to former weapons scientists (including ISTC, IPP, and CRDF), many of which go to biological, chemical, or aerospace experts rather than nuclear experts.

TABLE 7.1

BUDGETS FOR WARHEAD AND FISSILE MATERIAL CONTROL BEFORE AND AFTER THE EXPANDED THREAT REDUCTION INITIATIVE

	FY1999*	FY2000**
Preventing Theft and Smuggling (in millions)		
MPC&A	$152	$145
DOE "Second Line of Defense"	2 (?)	2
DOD/FBI/Customs nuclear smuggling	3 (?)	4
Mayak storage facility	61	65
Nuclear warhead security	52	55
Stabilizing Nuclear Custodians		
Nuclear Cities Initiative	15	30
IPP	15	30
ISTC	23	95
CRDF	3 (?)	23
Monitoring Stockpiles and Reductions		
HEU purchase transparency	14	15
DOE-DOD warhead transparency[a]	24	26
Ending Further Production		
Plutonium reactor core conversion	30	20
Reducing Excess Stockpiles[b]		
Plutonium disposition	25	25
Converting plutonium components	9	9
Total	**$428**	**$544**

% change (if request fully approved)		+27 %
% change excluding science cooperation programs		+2 %

a. The budget for DOE's Warhead and Fissile Material Transparency Program was $9.5 million in FY1999. In addition, a joint DOE-DOD Integrated Technology Plan to evaluate transparency technologies for START III, Mayak Transparency, and the Trilateral Initiative was initiated in FY1999, funded at just under $20 million (but $4.85 million of that total came from DOE's $9.5 million program). DOE has requested $16 million for its program in FY2000, but it is not yet clear how much funding will be assigned to the total joint program; $26 million is an estimate based on interviews.

b. This does not include the one-time FY1999 congressional add-ons of $325 million for the HEU deal and $200 million for plutonium disposition work with Russia.

* Figures based on data provided by the Departments of State, Defense, and Energy.
**Figures based on Expanded Threat Reduction Initiative.

In short, the Expanded Threat Reduction Initiative will, if approved, provide a modest amount of additional funding for warhead and fissile material control efforts, as well as for other worthy endeavors, and it deserves support. But it falls far short of what is needed to address the urgent proliferation threats posed by nuclear materials in the former Soviet Union and far short of what the president announced to the nation.

PART III: URGENTLY NEEDED
NEXT STEPS

Major action is urgently needed to rapidly reduce the proliferation and arms reduction risks posed by the insecure, oversized, and unmonitored nuclear stockpiles and nuclear complex in the former Soviet Union. New steps are needed in each of the five areas outlined above, but the discussion below focuses in particular detail on the first, and most urgent, of these agendas.

PREVENTING THEFT AND SMUGGLING

A revised and expanded MPC&A program is urgently needed, focused on three strategic goals:

- Consolidating nuclear material at fewer buildings and fewer sites as rapidly as practicable
- Upgrading security and accounting systems at both the facility level and the national level as quickly as practicable, while providing the needed training and services to allow these systems to be effectively used
- Sustaining effective security over time

What is needed is a program designed to reduce the proliferation risk as quickly as practicable unconstrained by funding. This will require substantially larger budgets than are currently planned. Roughly $250 million per year—an increase of roughly $100 million per year over currently planned budgets—for half a decade or more, while the initial consolidations and upgrades are implemented, is a conservative estimate of what is needed.[64] While the pace at which security can be improved is constrained by factors other than money—including the degree of cooperation Russia is willing to permit, the number of experienced U.S. and Russian experts available to carry out the needed programs, and the U.S. and Russian ability to manage the efforts effectively—constrained budgets should not be allowed to slow progress, as is now the case. To protect the U.S. investment, the program should be continued at a modest level—perhaps $50 million per year—for a considerable period after the initial upgrades are accomplished, to ensure that security and accounting systems are sustained and improved and to maintain cooperation and communication concerning the state of MPC&A.

To be successful, a revised and expanded program will have to reinvigorate the sense of partnership between U.S. and Russian participants, and between DOE headquarters and the U.S. laboratories. In recent years, valuable efforts have been made to establish guidelines for which types of security and accounting approaches should be pursued at the various sites where the MPC&A program is working, and to review progress at these sites against the guidelines. But these efforts have included only American experts, and some of the abrupt changes in course imposed by the U.S. side as a result have substantially undermined Russian participants' enthusiasm for cooperation, eroding their willingness to take risks in lobbying their own system for further progress. Ultimately, while the program is being carried out primarily with U.S. funds, the materials are Russia's to protect, and thus integrating a Russian perspective into the design and implementation of all the needed programs is essential. At the same time, however, to maintain budgetary support in the United States, it is critical to focus on implementing the steps that offer the most "bang for the buck" in improving security and accounting as rapidly as practicable. This will inevitably require some patient negotiation to bridge differences between the U.S. and Russian perspectives.

Descriptions of the key steps toward each of the three strategic goals follow.

CONSOLIDATION

Consolidation of nuclear materials is an urgent priority. Protecting fewer buildings and fewer sites means that higher levels of security can be provided at lower cost. When material is removed from facilities completely, the risk of theft at those facilities is eliminated entirely. While the Russian Ministry of Defense has reduced the number of nuclear warhead storage sites from over five hundred to less than one hundred, as discussed above, there has been very little consolidation of weapons-usable material sites. Since late 1998, however, DOE has begun placing increased emphasis on consolidation, and in the aftermath of the August 1998 financial crisis, MINATOM has recognized the need to consolidate its complex to reduce costs. A significant cooperative consolidation effort is now planned. This will focus on both consolidating material at large sites in a smaller number of buildings and areas within the site and removing material entirely from some smaller sites. While such an effort will greatly reduce long-run costs, it will involve significant short-run costs for preparing and transporting material, preparing facilities to receive it, blending it to LEU in some cases, and the like. Many sites—or even individual research areas within sites—are likely to be reluctant to give up the HEU or plutonium they have in stock, given this material's present and historical association with high-level nuclear research; in many cases, financial incentives are probably needed. A consolidation program should include:

- Financing for preparing and transporting nuclear material, and rapidly providing secure storage facilities to which it could be shipped
  An intensive program to purchase small, vulnerable HEU stockpiles that exist at small research reactors throughout the former Soviet Union (see below, "Purchasing Vulnerable HEU Stockpiles")
- Financing to help HEU-fueled research reactors and critical assemblies shift to using LEU fuels (joint development of such fuels for Soviet-designed research reactors is already under way)
- Financing to help some facilities shift away from research requiring either HEU or LEU, or to close facilities completely and provide alternative employment for their workers
- Working toward stringent regulatory requirements for MPC&A of HEU, giving facilities an incentive to avoid the costs of meeting such requirements by giving up their HEU

- Extensive briefings for senior MINATOM officials and site managers on the dramatic savings in safeguards and security costs that are being achieved through consolidation in the United States

Several approaches to rapidly providing appropriate secure storage space for consolidated material can be envisioned. Modest stockpiles of HEU could be shipped to facilities with the capacity to take it out of fuel elements and blend it to proliferation-resistant LEU (such as the Luch Production Association in Podolsk—also the site at which some of the most impressive progress in intrasite consolidation has been accomplished). Where storage buildings with effective security and accounting systems and available space already exist, these could be used. Moreover, technology exists for rapidly deployable secure storage facilities (developed to support deployment of military forces equipped with nuclear weapons), and these types of facilities could be put in place within weeks or months, should a major effort be made to do so; some have already been used. Alternatively, some facilities in the Russian complex have large empty spaces in secure areas, where additional storage facilities could be built quickly and cheaply.[65] Finally, the current legislative restriction limiting the fissile material storage facility at Mayak to hold only materials from weapons could be modified—at least for a portion of the facility—allowing that facility, when completed, to store vulnerable weapons-usable material regardless of whether it comes from dismantled weapons or not. (This would also be an excellent place to store the 30 tonnes of weapons-usable civilian plutonium also in storage at Mayak, if adequate space and cooling capacity could be provided in the new building.)

Purchasing Vulnerable HEU Stockpiles

Currently, the United States is purchasing 500 tons of HEU from dismantled Russian nuclear weapons—which may be among the most secure HEU in the former Soviet Union. It is time to begin purchasing the most vulnerable HEU stocks as well.

Scattered through the former Soviet Union are nearly two dozen small, underfunded civilian nuclear research facilities with HEU—ranging from a few kilograms to hundreds of kilograms or more. Most of these facilities are listed under the categories "Reactor-Type Facilities" and "NIS and the Baltics," in the MPC&A Strategic Plan. Some of these are within Russia, but there are research facilities that still have weapons-usable HEU in Ukraine, Kazakhstan, Belarus, Latvia, and Uzbekistan as well. Many of these facilities no longer have the money to protect the HEU appropriately or to do the research that once required HEU. Indeed, it was at sites like these that some of the worst desperation was observed after the August 1998 financial crisis: guards leaving their posts to forage for food, electricity being cut off because bills had not been paid, and the like.

Simply purchasing the HEU from these facilities offers an opportunity to rapidly reduce the serious proliferation risks they pose. Many of the managers of these facilities would probably be very happy to part with their HEU in return for a million dollars for their facility and a modest amount of assistance for the facility to conduct other research not requiring HEU.

Past efforts to purchase vulnerable HEU stockpiles, such as Project Sapphire, have taken many months of preparation and cost tens of millions of dollars each—partly because of the considerable political and technical headaches of moving material to the

United States or some other country outside the former Soviet Union. A faster, simpler, and cheaper approach for a broader purchase program might be to purchase the HEU and have it blended to proliferation-resistant LEU within Russia—either at the facilities now blending HEU on a large scale for the HEU purchase agreement or at other facilities that have capabilities for small-scale blending of specialty materials like these HEU reactor fuels, such as the Luch Production Association at Podolsk, near Moscow. Secure fissile material transport equipment now being provided to Russia as part of the MPC&A program could be used for the shipment. The value of the LEU after blending could pay, at least in large part, for the costs of shipment and blending, leaving the initial purchase as the principal cost.

The total amount of HEU at the smallest and most desperate facilities where a purchase would be most urgent is probably less than 2 tons. If the price negotiated was similar to the $24 million-a-ton price originally negotiated for the HEU purchase agreement, buying all of these stocks would cost in the range of $50 million. Conceivably, other costs relating to transport, blending, and the like, and additional assistance for these facilities to pursue other research, could double this cost—but ensuring effective security at these many facilities over the long term would inevitably cost still more, and could never provide absolute assurance that thefts would be prevented. One hundred million dollars would be a very small price to pay for permanently eliminating the theft risk at many of the most vulnerable facilities in the former Soviet Union.

This concept has been recommended before in an influential 1997 National Research Council study "Proliferation Concerns: Assessing U.S. Efforts to Help Contain Nuclear and Other Dangerous Materials and Technologies in the Former Soviet Union." The study recommended seeking to purchase and eliminate every former Soviet stockpile of HEU outside of Russia—and a variant of this approach is being implemented on a small scale within the MPC&A program's consolidation effort, with plans to remove all the HEU from one facility in 2000, and two more facilities the following year. So far, however, the managers of the relevant DOE programs have not felt that they had sufficient funds to pursue such an effort on a more substantial scale. Congress should step in and direct DOE to launch a large-scale purchase initiative and provide the funds to do so.

UPGRADES

Installing effective security and accounting systems has been the central focus of the MPC&A program to date. A vast amount of work remains to be done—even if the consolidation effort is extremely successful. In many cases, a greater emphasis is needed on quickly implementing simple, low-cost steps—bricking over windows, piling rocks in front of doors—allowing time later for follow-up with more sophisticated (and expensive) approaches. At the same time, however, the initial emphasis on such physical protection upgrades has to be complemented with improving material accounting and control. As a first step, the United States should work with Russia to put in place a program in which Russia would immediately identify, count, tag, and seal all containers and items with weapons-usable nuclear material throughout the Russian nuclear complex, creating at least a comprehensive record of all the materials that exist; the slower process of performing actual measurements of the nuclear material in those myriad containers and items can proceed in parallel. Redoubled support is also needed for getting an effective national accounting system in place as rapidly as possible. Finally, it is critical to remember that the job is not over when the initial upgrades are declared "complete": not only must the security afforded by the initial upgrades be maintained, but further improvements are inevitably going to be needed to offer effective security at most of these sites. Essentially none of the sites declared completed so far would meet the MPC&A standards to be granted a license to operate in the United States; virtually all are still potentially vulnerable to a well-placed and knowledgeable insider working with a small group of outsiders.[66] Hence the past policy of installing initial upgrades and essentially walking away—already changing slowly—requires a radical overhaul.[67]

SUSTAINABLE SECURITY

Installing modern equipment will not provide a long-term security benefit if that equipment is not operated, maintained, and improved over time; if the people guarding the material and using the equipment are unpaid, untrained, and have no real incentives for good performance; and if there is no "safeguards culture" in which everyone understands that no corners can be cut when it comes to security and accounting for nuclear material. Foreign financial assistance cannot continue indefinitely, and Russian officials and facility managers will ultimately have to be convinced to allocate their own scarce resources to these tasks. The problem of how to move from installing equipment to actually achieving sustainable long-term security is absolutely central to the MPC&A program's long-term success but is by far the most difficult intellectual and policy challenge facing the program.[68]

What is needed is to increase the former Soviet states' *sustainable capacity* to manage nuclear materials securely, and convince them to use that capacity for this purpose.[69] Today, facilities in the former Soviet states have neither the resources (money, appropriate equipment, appropriately trained personnel, and appropriately functioning organizational structures) needed for effective security and accounting for nuclear material over the long haul nor the incentives to use what resources they have for this purpose. Spending on safeguards and security creates no additional products or revenues, so in the absence of effective regulation imposing stringent security and accounting requirements, facility managers in the former Soviet Union facing desperate budget crises have every incentive to cut spending on MPC&A. Beyond the individual facilities is an overall context of dysfunctional governments, a collapsing economy, rampant crime and corruption, and modest high-level attention devoted to MPC&A, all of which makes sustainable security far more difficult to achieve. An expanded MPC&A sustainability effort should focus on three key areas: resources, incentives, and organizations.

SUSTAINABILITY RESOURCES—The United States should:

- Expand and plan for funding of "emergency measures" where needed—funding to keep guards on the job, keep security systems running temporarily, provide backup electricity supplies, and the like—as DOE did on a small scale in the winter and spring of 1998–99.
- Finance the first two to three years of operations and maintenance of sys-

tems installed with U.S. assistance, as an initial settling-in period, with work during that period to reach firm commitments that Russia will pay to keep the systems operational after that.[70]

- Put increased reliance on indigenous personnel and firms to design, build, operate, and upgrade MPC&A systems, building up the indigenous capacities to carry out these missions in the former Soviet states. In particular, the work of designing and building MPC&A systems at individual sites could increasingly be shifted to Russian firms (perhaps initially capitalized with U.S. funds if appropriate firms do not yet exist), with continued oversight by experts from the United States and in-depth cooperation between the firms and the individual sites—increasing consistency in the approaches taken at different sites, increasing indigenous capacity, and reducing costs for and burdens on U.S. personnel.[71]
- Fund the establishment and use of Russian teams to carry out realistic tests of both outsider and insider threats at Russian facilities—with wide dissemination of test results and lessons learned, and funding for fixing problems identified.[72]
- Help finance transition costs (recruitment, training, equipment, and the like) for a shift to more-professional guard forces for nuclear material—either highly trained officer-dominated forces comparable to those that guard nuclear weapons or (at least at civilian facilities) commercial firms such as those that guard Russian banks and nuclear facilities in the United States.
- Finance expanded training programs, including regular training at individual sites as well as the existing national training effort, with a focus on the critical importance to Russia and the world of preventing the spread of nuclear weapons and the key role of effective MPC&A in that effort.
- Explore possible new revenue streams that could finance a robust security and accounting programs for nuclear material in the former Soviet Union after international assistance phases down (see "Generating New Revenue for Nuclear Security," page 112).

SUSTAINABILITY INCENTIVES— The United States should:

- Put nuclear security and accounting at the top of the U.S.-FSU non-proliferation agenda as a fundamental requirement for preventing the spread of nuclear weapons that all states handling weapons-usable nuclear material must meet. The United States should make clear that this is an essential prerequisite for improved nuclear relations, something to be emphasized at every level on every occasion until the problem is adequately addressed (as is now done with issues such as cooperation with Iran, to take one example), and work with other leading nuclear powers to convince them to take a similar approach.
- Increase the priority devoted to strengthening regulation of MPC&A; a realistic prospect of being fined or shut down if MPC&A did not meet stringent standards would create a major incentive for facility managers to invest scarce resources in ensuring adequate security and accounting. The

weaknesses of the regulatory organizations in the former Soviet states require a redoubled effort in regulatory support. MPC&A regulatory support programs need to be beefed up with additional funding and personnel, a new sense of strategic mission, and new ideas, focusing not only on GAN (the Russian independent nuclear regulatory agency) but also on the Ministry of Defense regulatory body that regulates military-related facilities, and on internal self-regulation within MINATOM. In particular, DOE should provide the U.S. Nuclear Regulatory Commission with the funding it needs to continue and expand its regulatory support work in the former Soviet Union.

- Write requirements for MPC&A operations and maintenance, and realistic testing, into MPC&A contracts with facilities, with incentives written into the contracts to fulfill these commitments.
- Give preference in U.S. contracts to facilities with good MPC&A, and use the leverage provided by such contracts to pursue MPC&A objectives. Over time, facility managers in the former Soviet Union should come to understand that excellent MPC&A is part of the "price of admission" for doing business with the United States, just as refraining from transfers of sensitive technology to potential proliferators is—and the United States should work with other leading nations to convince them to take the same approach. At the same time, the United States should seek to use the considerable leverage that funds flowing to Russian facilities from U.S. programs provide to seek additional MPC&A progress—for example, using the fact that some large Russian facilities receive most of their cash income from the HEU deal to convince them to cooperate in ensuring stringent standards of security and accounting.[73]
- Make achievement of high standards of MPC&A a prerequisite for U.S. support for new efforts involving bulk processing or transport of fissile material, which would otherwise increase, rather than decrease, the risks of theft and proliferation. At the same time, the United States should place high priority on working with Russia to upgrade MPC&A for those bulk processing and transport programs that are already under way with U.S. support, such as the HEU deal.

SUSTAINABILITY ORGANIZATION—The United States should work with Russia and the other former Soviet states on a systemic program of reform of the organizations involved in MPC&A designed to ensure that:

- Each facility with weapons-usable nuclear material has a designated office for MPC&A, with appropriate personnel and authority.
- Each national institution with facilities with weapons-usable nuclear material under its control also has a designated office for MPC&A, with appropriate personnel and authority.
- The facility offices communicate appropriately with one another and with the national authorities.
- There are clear and authoritative laws and regulations in place requiring

MPC&A measures that, if complied with in their entirety, would ensure an effective system.

- The regulatory authorities have the authority, independence, personnel, equipment, and procedures required to carry out effective MPC&A regulation, including the authority to impose fines or close facilities for failure to comply with MPC&A regulations.
- There are recruitment, compensation, promotion, and training procedures in place to ensure that highly qualified people are available for all aspects of MPC&A and have incentives for good performance.
- There are effective mechanisms in place for interagency coordination, joint action, and dispute resolution on MPC&A issues.

These are obviously long-term goals that must be approached incrementally, and working with a foreign government on such organization issues is far more challenging than simply providing equipment and training. But these issues are critically important to sustainability: the experience of international development assistance suggests that providing technical assistance alone, without focusing on the broader organizational context, often leads to little lasting benefit. As a first step, DOE should fund a study by nongovernment or laboratory experts to consider what measures toward these ends are most needed and what such programs might cost.

At the same time, governments rarely carry out their functions as well as they might without close oversight. In the U.S. case, embarrassing investigations by journalists, nongovernment advocates, and Congress provided a major part of the impetus for substantial security improvements during the 1970s and 1980s. U.S. nongovernmental organizations—perhaps with some funding from DOE—can play a critically important role in fostering the growth of nongovernmental organizations involved in these issues in the former Soviet states and encouraging journalists and legislators in these states to play an active role in monitoring what is being done and lobbying for change when that is necessary.[74]

STOPPING NUCLEAR SMUGGLING

While the consolidation, security, and accounting measures described above are the highest-priority parts of a program to reduce the risk of potential nuclear theft, new measures are also needed to interdict nuclear smuggling—the "second line of defense" if nuclear materials are stolen. What is most needed now is a well-funded strategic plan integrating the U.S. and international antismuggling efforts, specifying what organizations in what countries should have what capabilities by when, and what resources will be needed to accomplish that objective. It will not be possible to accomplish at once everything that might be done. Hence, the intelligence community should examine where the greatest weaknesses and the highest leverage points for improving the response to nuclear smuggling lie. In particular, goals should include:

- *Establishing trained police units to deal with nuclear smuggling.* Each key country should have at least a small unit of law enforcement officers capable of investigating nuclear smuggling cases. These officers would have the training and equipment to distinguish between, for example, intensely radioactive cesium and weapons-usable plutonium, or between relatively innocuous low-enriched uranium and weapons-usable highly enriched uranium. Other forces that might encounter a nuclear smuggling incident—police, intelligence, border patrols, customs—should be made aware of the existence of this specialized unit and how and when to contact them. Key states could be helped to establish, train, and equip such units relatively rapidly, for a cost in the range of a few millions to a few tens of millions of dollars.

- *Increased intelligence and police cooperation.* All of the principal successes in finding and recovering stolen weapons-usable nuclear materials have been the result of informers and sting operations—which is to say, they have resulted from the efforts of police, intelligence, and "special services." Some nuclear materials have been seized in random searches carried out by border guards and customs agents, but these have been relatively inconsequential in comparison. The lesson is the importance of intelligence, of knowing where to look. Therefore, despite the enormous hurdles faced by any effort to increase cooperation and exchange of information related to sensitive investigations and sources, increased police and intelligence cooperation across borders must be a top priority. For example, the FBI's office in Moscow should include a cadre of experts on nuclear smuggling who could cooperate with Russian counterparts.

- *Training and equipping border patrols and customs.* The immense volume of traffic that crosses international borders every day and the vast and sparsely populated length of the borders between some of the key countries make the task of interdicting nuclear materials as they cross international borders extremely difficult—as evidenced by the massive flows of drugs and other contraband that governments have so far been unable to stop. Nevertheless, border guards and customs agencies in each of the key potential source states and transit states should be provided with sufficient equipment and trained personnel to monitor at the least the main border crossings and international exit/entry points. The steps taken in this direction so far have covered only a few border points in a few states, with little long-term strategic planning of what capabilities should be in what places by what time.

- *Providing regularized mechanisms for forensic analysis of seized nuclear material.* For several years, an international team of experts has been reviewing methods for forensic analysis of seized packages containing nuclear material, analysis that can help identify where the material came from and where it has been since. Only a few labs in the world have the right capabilities for all the various analyses that may be critical. It would be useful to set up more regularized procedures for transferring seized material across international boundaries when necessary for effective forensic analysis.

STABILIZING NUCLEAR CUSTODIANS

To reduce the proliferation risk posed by neglected and demoralized nuclear weapons scientists and workers, and the risk to arms reductions posed by the enormous capacity of the Russian nuclear weapons complex, new steps are needed to cooperatively reduce Russia's nuclear weapons complex to a size Russia can afford to maintain, appropriate to its post–Cold War missions. Part of this mission is helping to provide alternative employment for those displaced nuclear weapons scientists and technicians. A substantial investment (running at perhaps $100 million per year for five years)[75] in the new Nuclear Cities Initiative (NCI) is needed, focused on four critical areas:

- Fostering private-sector job growth in the nuclear cities.
- Employing former nuclear weapons scientists on non-proliferation and arms control policy analysis and technology development.
- Funding Russian, rather than only U.S., scientists to develop technologies for nuclear cleanup, along with other energy and environmental technologies
- Shrinking the Russian nuclear weapons complex. [Note: The details of such a program are described in chapter 5.]

MONITORING STOCKPILES AND REDUCTIONS

The ultimate goal of U.S.-Russian transparency efforts should be an integrated, comprehensive regime that would provide confidence that each side was reducing its total nuclear warhead and fissile material stockpiles to low levels and that these stockpiles were safe and secure.[76] With U.S.-Russian relations as they are in the wake of the bombing of Yugoslavia, however, that goal is a long way off; U.S.-Russian political tensions and renewed concerns over protecting nuclear secrets on both sides are likely to make near-term progress on nuclear transparency extraordinarily difficult. Paradoxically, it appears that the best hopes would be for initiatives that were either very large (so that they might have some chance of addressing Russian security concerns and shifting the political environment in favor of cooperation) or very small (so that they could be pursued informally without drawing undue political attention in either country). A few of the steps that should be pursued are listed below.[77]

NUCLEAR MATERIAL STOCKPILE DATA EXCHANGES

 Achieving a better understanding of the actual quantities, forms, and locations of fissile material in each country is fundamental to cooperative efforts to secure, monitor, and reduce these dangerous stockpiles. The United States has openly published data on its plutonium stockpile and plutonium production and is preparing to publish similar data concerning its HEU stockpile. Preliminary discussions suggest that with creative and informal pushes from the United States, Russia may be willing to take similar steps, as took place when the United States released historical data on nuclear tests. Russian experts, however, do not have funding available to do the work of pulling together this data. The United States should provide the financing necessary for Russia to collect its plutonium stockpile data (probably in the form of a lab-to-lab contract), in return for Russian agreement to share the data with the United States. This informal approach, if successful, could then be applied to HEU, once the United States releases that data. This would provide a rapid means to accomplish a substantial part of the stockpile data exchange agreed to by Presidents Clinton and Yeltsin in 1994 on a contracting basis, without requiring high-level formal negotiations that would draw widespread political attention. The cost would likely be only a few million dollars.

INTERNATIONAL MONITORING OF EXCESS FISSILE MATERIAL

A key issue in the U.S.-Russian-IAEA "Trilateral Initiative" described above is who will pay the costs of monitoring materials in Russia. (To date, the United States has been paying both its own costs and the IAEA's costs of monitoring the small amount of excess material that is under IAEA verification so far in the United States.) Russia is very unlikely to be able or willing to provide the funding to pay these costs, a problem that could stop the initiative in its tracks. The IAEA has proposed the creation of a special disarmament fund to pay for such costs, to which countries might make voluntary contributions, or which might ultimately receive funds from mandatory assessments. The United States could kick-start the effort with an initial contribution to the fund and could agree to pay for Russia's costs to host the IAEA inspections (a cost category very unlikely to be covered by an international fund). U.S. agreement to pay these costs could enable a significant nonproliferation and disarmament initiative to go forward, at a very modest cost (probably a few million dollars per year initially, and less after the arrangement is established).

A MAJOR TRANSPARENT WARHEAD REDUCTIONS OFFER, WITH ASSISTANCE FOR TRANSPARENT WARHEAD DISMANTLEMENT

With the current state of U.S.-Russian relations, there is very little chance that START II will be ratified and formal negotiations completed on START III, incorporating unprecedented transparency for the dismantlement of warheads, before Presidents Clinton and Yeltsin leave office. Informal reciprocal-unilateral initiatives—such as those launched by Presidents Bush and Gorbachev in 1991, which resulted in the pullback and dismantlement of many thousands of nuclear weapons without requiring formal negotiations—represent virtually the only near-term hope for a breakthrough in nuclear arms reductions. (See chapter 17, "Next Steps in Strategic Reductions.") To gain acceptance on both sides in the current political environment, such an initiative would have to address concerns each side has about the other's nuclear stockpile. For example, President Clinton could offer to place a large fraction of the U.S. strategic reserve and tactical nuclear warheads (stockpiles unregulated by arms control to date, and which will represent the vast majority of the total U.S. warhead stockpile under START II) in secure storage open to Russian monitoring and commit them to verifiable dismantlement (with specific procedures to be worked out later) if Russia would do the same with its comparable warhead stockpiles.

This could address Russian concerns about the U.S. maintenance of a large stockpile of warheads that could be rapidly returned to missiles and U.S. concerns about the huge Russian tactical warhead stockpile. Within a few months, the majority of all the warheads in each side's nuclear arsenals could be under reciprocal monitoring and committed to dismantlement.[78] Indeed, technology exists that would make it possible to permanently and verifiably disable these warheads, pending their eventual dismantlement, rather than only subjecting them to monitoring.[79]

As part of this package, the United States should offer to provide financial assistance for warhead dismantlement (e.g., $90 million per year for a dismantlement rate of 3,000 per year, or roughly $30,000 per warhead) in return for Russian agreement to a transparency package that would also be implemented reciprocally at the Pantex dismantlement facility in the United States. The transparency measures would have to be designed jointly by U.S. and Russian experts, to give both sides confidence that while the measures could help confirm that dismantlement was taking place, they would do so without revealing sensitive information or unduly interfering with maintenance of each side's nuclear stockpile. As noted earlier, preliminary U.S.-Russian lab-to-lab work in designing such measures is already under way; U.S. experts have produced reports on the impact of a variety of dismantlement transparency approaches at U.S. facilities, and it would make sense for the United States to help finance a Russian effort to do the same with respect to Russian facilities.[80]

ENDING FURTHER PRODUCTION

The current program to convert Russia's remaining plutonium production reactors, if successful, will end the last production of weapons-grade material in either the United States or Russia. A wide range of obstacles could still delay or derail this program, however. To ensure that the effort genuinely reduces, rather than increases, the proliferation threat, it would make sense to wait the extra year or so that may be required to develop a proliferation-resistant LEU fuel for use in the converted reactors, rather than using HEU—particularly as the HEU fuel is likely to be delayed in any case by the regulatory and safety issues mentioned earlier and therefore there may be no genuine delay from relying on LEU.

Three other key issues relating to fissile material production remain to be addressed:

- The United States should work with Russia to develop and implement reciprocal transparency measures at U.S. and Russian enrichment facilities to confirm that neither country is producing HEU. These measures could provide a test bed for approaches to verifying a fissile cutoff treaty, at a cost likely to be $10 million per year or less.

- The United States should offer to finance the costs of verification of an international fissile material production cutoff at Russian reprocessing plants. Older reprocessing plants never designed for safeguards—as exist in both the United States and Russia—are likely to be the biggest verification challenge for a cutoff, and verification at such plants is likely to cost more than Russia will be willing to pay in the near term, but putting such verification in place would be a sensible security investment, contributing to a global cutoff while improving material control and accounting at Russian reprocessing plants. It would also make sense to begin immediately to carry out small-scale cooperative experiments at U.S. and Russian reprocessing plants to demonstrate technologies and procedures for such verification.[81]
- The United States should offer Russia a cooperative program that would provide alternative employment for reprocessing workers and dry cask storage for spent fuel in return for Russian agreement to a moratorium on civilian plutonium processing, at least until existing excess stockpiles of plutonium (civil and military) have been consumed. Civilian reprocessing in Russia continues to produce roughly a ton of separated, reactor-grade but weapons-usable plutonium per year and is not being addressed by the military reactor conversion program. This effort would have to be handled with extreme care, as civilian plutonium recycling is so central to MINATOM's vision of the future and the disagreements on this subject between the United States and Russia are so sharp that pursuing this issue too aggressively could undermine the atmosphere for other cooperation.

REDUCING EXCESS STOCKPILES

Finally, the vast stockpiles of HEU and plutonium built up over decades of Cold War must be rapidly, safely, and securely reduced to levels sufficient to support whatever agreed warhead stockpiles remain but which can no longer support a rapid return to Cold War levels of armament. The immediate priorities are to provide safe and secure storage for these materials and place them under bilateral or international monitoring to confirm that they will never be returned to weapons—both discussed above. But even after those goals are achieved, far more needs to be done to physically transform these materials into unclassified forms (allowing more intensive monitoring) and ultimately into forms that can no longer be readily used in nuclear weapons, as quickly as practicable.[82] In the case of HEU, in addition to the considerable efforts likely to be necessary to keep the current purchase agreement working—which should be assigned very high priority—new purchases and faster blending of the excess stockpile should be pursued. In the case of plutonium, it is essential to work out a plan to finance the costs of Russian plutonium disposition and negotiate an agreement on how disposition will be done. A variety of modified approaches, achieving these goals from immobilization to plutonium purchases, are worthy of serious consideration. Finally, reductions in these stockpiles need to go far deeper than either the United States or Russia now plan if the goals of substantially reducing theft risks and ensuring the irreversibility of deep reductions in nuclear arms are to be achieved. These steps are elaborated below.

FINANCE RAPID EXCESS HEU BLEND-DOWN

Greatly accelerating the rate at which HEU from Russian weapons is blended to non-weapons-usable LEU would produce a major international security benefit. The current 30-ton-per-year pace of blending for the HEU purchase agreement was determined by what the commercial market could bear, not by what would best serve U.S. or Russian security interests. From a security perspective, it would be desirable to blend all Russian and U.S. excess HEU to non-weapons-usable form—perhaps to an intermediate enrichment level of 19 percent—within a few years, resolving the key non-proliferation and disarmament issues this material poses, even while it continues to be released onto the commercial market at a much lower pace. Significant up-front capital investments in additional or modified blending capacity would likely be required, along with operations costs for implementing the rapid blend-down, and some financial incentives would likely be needed to gain Russian agreement to carry out such a quick blend-down. It would be essential to take care that the blending approach did not interfere with achieving the isotopic mix in the LEU ultimately desired for a commercial product. The additional cost of achieving the blend-down of all excess Russian HEU within for example, five years might be in the range of half a billion dollars (or $100 million per year)—a small price for the large security benefit of accomplishing this objective. DOE should immediately undertake a study, in cooperation with Russia, of what would be required, how much it would cost, and how long it would take to achieve such rapid blend-down. Once the HEU has been converted to forms that could potentially be sold on the market (and thus have commercial value without requiring further work), there may also be opportunities for using the blended-down material as collateral for loans or prepayments, which should also be considered in such a study. The U.S. government should then move rapidly to negotiate and implement an agreement with Russia to blend all the excess HEU in both the United States and Russia to non-weapons-usable form as quickly as practicable.

BUY ADDITIONAL QUANTITIES OF EXCESS HEU

Russia clearly has far more HEU that it does not need for its military stockpile than the 500 tons it has declared excess to date. The United States should offer to buy additional stockpiles of excess HEU, up front rather than at the end of the current deal, with government funds rather than money from commercial firms. The material could be held off the market as a strategic uranium stockpile (rather than flooding the market immediately with still more material from excess HEU). As a first step, the United States could offer to buy an additional 50 tons of HEU (at a cost of roughly $1 billion at the prices currently pertaining in the deal), while stipulating in the contract that a substantial portion of the proceeds be placed in a fund to pay for nuclear security measures (see "Generating New Revenue for Nuclear Security" below). If this first step succeeded, it would make sense to continue with additional steps, ultimately buying all the excess HEU Russia was willing to make available (with transparency to confirm that additional HEU was not being produced, as discussed above).

FINANCE RUSSIAN PLUTONIUM DISPOSITION

Following on the lead Senator Domenici provided with the $200 million down payment for Russian plutonium disposition in the FY 1999 budget, the United States should offer to cover the costs of disposition of Russian plutonium, allowing this effort to finally move forward without being dependent on the complexities of an international finance scheme. The $1 billion–$3 billion cost is small by comparison with the magnitude of the security stakes in eliminating Russia's huge excess plutonium stockpile. This funding would cover the construction or modification of facilities as needed and operations of those facilities to convert Russian plutonium weapons components to oxide, fabricate that oxide into fuel, and irradiate that fuel in reactors.

Generating New Revenue for Nuclear Security

To date, essentially all of the funding for nuclear security in the former Soviet Union has come from government budgets—either the governments of the former Soviet states or foreign governments providing assistance. This is likely to continue to be the dominant source of funding for these activities in the future as well. But there may be opportunities to provide additional sources of revenue that would help improve security in the near term and help the former Soviet states maintain security as foreign assistance phases down over the longer term.

Spent Fuel Storage. A variety of approaches have been proposed in which Russia would establish an international storage facility for spent nuclear fuel from various countries and some portion of the profit would be set aside for non-proliferation and disarmament purposes, ranging from secure storage and monitoring of nuclear material to disposition of excess plutonium. (This differs substantially from MINATOM's proposed approach, in which the profit would be set aside to build and operate a large reprocessing plant.) One of these schemes, put forward by a U.S. entity known as the Non-Proliferation Trust, has reached the point of detailed discussions of actual contracts and could potentially provide hundreds of millions of dollars per year for non-proliferation activities. The income from spent fuel storage should be sufficient to ensure that the storage would be safe and effectively safeguarded. As an alternative, part of the revenues from an international storage site or repository somewhere else might be directed to nuclear security in Russia, as has been suggested by the Pangea group, which is hoping to develop such a facility in Australia.

Additional HEU Sales. As suggested in the text, the United States should seek to buy additional quantities of excess Russian HEU, above and beyond the 500 tons it is currently purchasing. As part of such an additional purchase, the United States should seek to require in the contract that a substantial fraction of the proceeds be spent on specified nuclear security purposes: ensuring nuclear guards and workers are paid, operating and maintaining security and accounting systems, and the like. (If the idea is presented carefully, MINATOM may be favorably disposed to agree to such a requirement, as it would help MINATOM ensure that the funds stay within MINATOM, rather than going to the rest of the Russian government.) While confirming that the funds were spent as agreed would be an issue, there are past precedents of U.S.-Russian agreements with similar requirements. If Russia agreed to spend half the proceeds from the purchase of an additional 50 tons of HEU on nuclear security, this would make available some $500 million for these purposes.

A "Debt-for-Security" Swap. Russia is heavily burdened with foreign debt. Some restructuring of that debt is likely to be essential to economic recovery. In many less developed countries, foreign governments or organizations have negotiated "debt-for-nature" or "debt-for-environment" swaps, in which either a specified area of land is set aside as protected area or a certain quantity of money is set aside in a fund for environmental purposes, in return for forgiveness of a certain quantity of debt. Some of these swaps have already been successful in the former Communist states. For example, in 1991 the seventeen creditor nations of the Club of Paris agreed to a substantial debt-for-environment swap with Poland, in which a portion of Poland's debt was canceled and, in return, Poland made contributions to a newly established independent foundation, the Ecofund, so that the expenditure of the money on the agreed environmental purposes could be easily verified. Under current agreements, the Ecofund is expected to receive over $500 million within a few years. A similar approach could be taken for nuclear security, with a certain portion of Russian debt being forgiven in return for Russia's agreeing to set aside funds for nuclear security into a similar independent fund. As with past debt-for-environment swaps, the amount of money to be placed into the fund would be less than the debt forgiven and would be paid in local currency rather than hard currency, increasing Russia's ability to pay. If Western governments were willing to forgive a substantial quantity of Russian debt, this could potentially provide a large enough revenue stream to support the hundreds of millions per year that it will ultimately cost Russia to ensure high levels of security and accounting for all of its nuclear weapons and fissile material.

   Nuclear Exports within Proliferation Constraints. Much of the revenue the Russian Ministry of Atomic Energy now receives comes from exports of nuclear material, services, and technology, with MINATOM officials estimating that their total exports now amount to over $2 billion per year. (The division of this revenue between MINATOM and the Russian central government is not well understood outside Russia.) At the moment, however, because the United States and other Western countries have imposed stringent trade restraints on Russian exports to their markets, and Western firms dominate many of the markets in states with sound non-proliferation credentials, the growth of MINATOM's export income is sharply constrained, and much of the current income derives from exports to nations of proliferation concern that have been shunned by Western suppliers, such as Iran and India. It would be highly desirable for Western countries to take a number of steps to reduce the barriers to expanded Russian exports to markets with good non-proliferation credentials, in return for specific commitments from MINATOM to apply particular fractions of the resulting revenue to identified nuclear security endeavors. These steps would include: (a) easing trade restrictions on Russian uranium and enrichment exports, (b) encouraging an expansion of Russian fuel fabrication service exports, and (c) ultimately joint design of a new generation of safer, more proliferation-resistant reactors (such as the current Russian-Japanese-French-U.S. cooperation to develop a new high-temperature gas-cooled reactor). All of these would be sensitive, as every piece of market share Russia gains would presumably be lost by a Western supplier. MINATOM's vision of exporting a new generation of simple, cheap reactors to countries all over the world is not likely to be realized. But there remain promising opportunities for action to unlock additional export revenues that could be applied to strengthening nuclear security.

NEGOTIATE AN AGREED DISPOSITION PLAN

As described earlier, the United States and Russia are negotiating a plutonium disposition agreement. Yet key elements of how plutonium disposition would actually be done—including where the financing will come from and what reactors would be used to burn Russian excess plutonium fast enough to match U.S. plans—remain completely undecided. The United States should place redoubled priority on putting together a specific plan and negotiating agreements with all the relevant parties that would allow it to be implemented, within the next year. This would include agreements on whether Russian, Ukrainian, Canadian, European, and/or Japanese reactors would be used, and in what combination. If that is not accomplished, congressional unwillingness to fund construction of U.S. plutonium disposition facilities without a Russian plutonium disposition program proceeding in parallel could cause the entire plutonium disposition effort to come unraveled—and it would then be quite difficult, after years of delay, to convince a future Congress that it was suddenly urgent to provide the funds needed to begin again.

There are several additional approaches to the plutonium problem that deserve serious consideration:

- *Pursuing alternative financing arrangements.* Convincing Congress to provide full funding for disposition of Russian plutonium—or convincing other states to make much larger contributions than they have to date, as the U.S. government currently hopes to do—would require a substantial investment of presidential leadership. If the White House fails to provide such leadership, alternative approaches to providing this funding that might involve less on-budget government expenditure will have to be pursued. One possibility would be to finance plutonium disposition with additional HEU sales. In one concept, for example, a joint venture between MINATOM and various Western fuel cycle and construction firms would be established for the purpose of building and operating the needed plutonium disposition facilities in Russia. MINATOM would provide this joint venture 100 tons of HEU (above and beyond the 500 tons covered by the HEU purchase agreement), and Western countries would agree to modify their uranium and enrichment trade restraints enough to allow this additional increment of material to enter their restricted markets. The joint venture would then have an asset worth roughly $2 billion—enough to pay for blending and delivery of the uranium, as well as construction and operation of the plutonium disposition facilities. The MOX produced would be marketed at prices well below the prices paid by utilities for LEU fuel, to give the utilities an incentive to take it—prices that would be sufficient to cover operations costs for fuel fabrication but not to pay back the initial cost of the plant. By this means, it would be possible to get rid of both Russia's excess plutonium and an additional 100 tons of HEU without the need for additional government appropriations.[83] Another approach would be to use revenue generated from commercial storage of spent fuel in Russia for disposition of excess plutonium.[84]
- *Buying Russian plutonium.* Although plutonium has no value on today's commercial nuclear fuel market, it would make sense for national security reasons to explore with Russia the possibility of buying Russia's excess plutonium. Since plutonium has the same energy value as HEU but is more costly to actually use as fuel, there would be no reasonable argument for a per-ton price any higher than the United States is paying for HEU, resulting in a price of no more than $1 billion for the 50 tons declared excess to date. The most plausible approach would probably be to leave the material in Russia after it was purchased, in a facility owned and operated by the

United States—shipping it to the United States would raise extraordinarily difficult political issues in both Russia and the United States. Wherever the material was located, the United States would then have to pay the cost of storage and disposition as well, which could add $1 billion–$3 billion, as discussed above. In some public statements, Russian officials have indicated that Russia would never sell its plutonium; in some private discussions, however, some senior Russian officials at MINATOM and elsewhere have been willing to at least consider the possibility. Because the United States has never made a serious effort to explore the issue with Russia, no one really knows what Russia's reaction to a real offer would be. The answer might depend substantially on how the offer was made, details of how the transfer of classified information would be avoided, and where the plutonium would eventually end up. A somewhat similar proposal is to offer a substantial financial incentive, perhaps $10,000 per kilogram ($500 million for 50 tons) for Russia to deposit its plutonium in a facility in Russia with international (rather than purely national) guards and monitors and, for reciprocity, to have the United States deposit its excess plutonium in a facility in the United States under similar arrangements.[85] A more radical idea is to set up a single facility in some third country, where all the U.S. and Russian excess material—and perhaps excess warheads as well—would be stored.[86] Obvious obstacles to that concept include obtaining the agreement of Russia, the United States, and the third country.

- *Using MOX plants that already exist.* In Europe, large MOX plants already exist that are fabricating civilian plutonium into fuel, and reactors are already licensed and operating with MOX fuel. If the complex political obstacles could be overcome, therefore, the fastest approach to the disposing of excess weapons plutonium would be to ship both U.S. and Russian excess plutonium to Europe as rapidly as it could be converted to unclassified forms and have these existing facilities (which are now fabricating roughly 10 tons of plutonium into MOX every year) fabricate MOX from weapons plutonium instead of fabricating it from the civilian plutonium they are scheduled to use. This could be done as a "plutonium swap," in which Russia and the United States would effectively give the Europeans title to the excess weapons plutonium in return for receiving title to the civilian plutonium that would be displaced by fabricating the excess weapons plutonium. That civilian plutonium would require disposition eventually but would be reactor-grade material stored in highly secure, well-paid-for facilities in Europe under international safeguards, thereby greatly reducing the proliferation and arms-reduction-reversal hazards the weapons plutonium currently poses more rapidly than other schemes could match. When this concept was publicly broached by Senator Domenici, however, the Europeans strongly opposed it (largely on grounds that it might disrupt their ongoing plans), and it has never been pursued further.[87] But if a significant level of U.S. leadership and some money were put behind such a scheme, the outcome might be very different.

• *Immobilization of Russian plutonium.* Russia has refused to consider throwing its plutonium away as waste, and, therefore, except for some modest joint experimentation on related technologies, there has been little serious pursuit of the immobilization option for Russian plutonium. But even more than in the U.S. case, there are significant risks that the MOX track for Russian excess plutonium could fail, making it critical to have a backup plan in place. If the difficulties in finding enough reactors to burn the Russian plutonium continue to mount, and the costs that would have to be borne by the United States or the international community continue to increase, immobilization may provide a cheaper and simpler alternative. Given official Russian opposition to any plan that does not provide them some benefit for the "value" of their plutonium, perhaps the only possibility for immobilization to move forward on a substantial scale would be for the United States to simply buy the plutonium from Russia (thereby gaining the right to decide what should be done with it) and then pay to have it immobilized in Russia (which would probably be simpler in a variety of respects than shipping it to the United States to become part of the U.S. plutonium disposition program). Given that Russia has an operational high-level waste immobilization facility and large excess plutonium facilities that might conceivably be modified for plutonium immobilization, it is at least possible that the combined costs of purchasing Russia's plutonium and paying for it to be immobilized would be the same as or less than the cost of pursuing the MOX approach as currently planned, and that possibility should be actively examined.[88]

Finally, if disposition of excess material is to make a genuine difference in reducing the risks of proliferation and reversal of arms reductions, it is essential to move toward declaring far larger quantities of material excess, leaving much lower amounts in military stockpiles. The quantities of fissile material the United States and Russia have declared excess to date leave enough material in reserve to support a rapid return to Cold War levels of nuclear armament. If genuine irreversibility is to be achieved, new agreements will have to address these "extra," reserve stockpiles and reduce the total stockpiles of nuclear warheads and nuclear materials to the levels necessary to support the number of deployed warheads permitted by U.S.-Russian agreements. As noted above, verifying the total stockpiles of warheads and fissile materials will be a difficult task, requiring major breakthroughs in transparency and openness. This already tall order will be further complicated by the fact that Russia has larger stockpiles of warheads, plutonium, and HEU than the United States, requiring an application of the START concept of "reduction to equal levels, not equal reductions."

SYNERGIES AND PRIORITIES — THE NEED FOR A STRATEGIC PLAN

The wide range of programs recommended above have many common purposes; the potential for synergy among them is enormous. Some programs require nuclear experts to design and build systems to secure, monitor, and reduce nuclear stockpiles; other programs are seeking to provide jobs for nuclear experts. Some programs require facilities to process plutonium or uranium; other programs are seeking to convert plutonium and uranium processing facilities once used for the weapons program to new missions. Many are dealing with the same Russian nuclear institutions and facilities, often with the same individuals. Mistakes made by one program will color Russian attitudes and affect other programs, just as goodwill generated by one program may make it easier for another to get in the door. While each of these programs has its own unique circumstances, all of them face the common problems and obstacles endemic to nuclear security cooperation with Russia.

Unfortunately, today these programs are being pursued individually, with very little coordination among them and virtually no systematic effort to pursue possible synergies. Officials at the U.S. embassy in Moscow report that it is not at all unusual to have several teams from U.S. laboratories arriving at the same Russian nuclear facility in the same week for completely different purposes, each unaware of the other's trip until they arrive.

Moreover, it is clear that not everything on this broad agenda can be done with equal energy at the same time, yet there has been very little effort to identify which efforts are the highest priorities. Both Russian and U.S. officials working on these programs are suffering from "initiative overload" and are unable to keep track of all the important efforts under way. While there is some virtue in letting a thousand flowers bloom (with the understanding that only a fraction will bear fruit), the need for a clear set of priorities is becoming increasingly obvious. A strategic plan setting such priorities and identifying possible synergies among these programs should be developed urgently and should be coordinated closely with Russian officials.

PART IV: CONCLUSION— THE NEED FOR LEADERSHIP

Unfortunately, there is no single "silver bullet" that will address the myriad risks to international security posed by the gigantic nuclear stockpiles and complex of the former Soviet Union. A broad "next wave" of new measures to reduce these risks is urgently needed. While important progress is being made in nuclear security cooperation with the states of the former Soviet Union, there can be no confidence that the current pace of progress is enough to prevent proliferation catastrophes or to achieve irreversible nuclear arms reductions.

To reinvigorate these efforts with new initiatives, to make them work as a package, to coordinate, prioritize, and integrate them into a strategic plan, and to negotiate them with Russia would require a dramatic increase in sustained leadership from the highest levels of the U.S. government. The current organizational structure of the government, with programs scattered through many departments and no senior leadership engaged on a daily basis at the White House, is simply not suited to the task. Effective and coordinated action to reduce these risks is likely to require designating a senior, full-time point person for the effort, with appropriate staff and resources and with authority deriving directly from the president—on the model of former secretary of defense William Perry's return to government to reshape the

U.S. approach to the North Korean nuclear and missile threat, or even on the model of General Barry McCaffrey's White House office leading U.S. antidrug efforts. Preventing nuclear material from falling into the hands of states like North Korea or Iraq is certainly no less critical to U.S. security; indeed, the entire global effort to prevent the spread of nuclear weapons depends on it. The cost of taking action now to address this threat is tiny by comparison to the cost and risk of failing to act and finding that the essential ingredients of nuclear weapons have found their way into the hands of terrorists or proliferant states.

NOTES

1. An expanded version of this chapter was published as a Carnegie/Harvard joint working paper in February 2000 and can be accessed at: www.ceip.org/npp.

2. "Maintaining the Proliferation Fight in the Former Soviet Union," *Arms Control Today*, March 1999.

3. For previous discussions of the technical and policy backgrounds of these issues, and recommendations to address them, see the list of references in the full Carnegie/Managing the Atom report. While the programs and recommendations outlined in this chapter cover a broad range of activities, they are focused specifically on improving management of nuclear warheads and nuclear material, not on the broader agenda of non-proliferation, arms control, and cooperative threat reduction in which the United States is engaged with the states of the former Soviet Union. Thus, issues ranging from export controls to START II, from de-alerting to biological disarmament, are not addressed here.

4. Nick Wadhams, "Center to Track Russian Nuclear Material," Associated Press, November 4, 1998.

5. See *MPC&A Program Strategic Plan*, U.S. Department of Energy, January 1998, 2 (available at http://www.dp.doe.gov/nn/mpca/frame03.htm).

6. John Deutch, "The Threat of Nuclear Diversion," testimony before the U.S. Senate, Committee on Governmental Affairs, Permanent Subcommittee on Investigations, *Global Proliferation of Weapons of Mass Destruction*, 104th Cong., 2d sess., S. Hrg. 104–422, pt. 2, March 20, 1996.

7. William C. Potter, remarks at the Seventh Carnegie International Non-proliferation Conference, Washington, D.C., January 11–12, 1999 (available at http://www.ceip.org/nnp/potter.htm).

8. See, for example, Bill Richardson, "Russia's Recession: The Nuclear Fallout," *Washington Post*, December 23, 1998; Kenneth N. Luongo and Matthew Bunn, "A Nuclear Crisis in Russia," *Boston Globe*, December 29, 1998; and Todd Perry, "Securing Russian Nuclear Materials: The Need for an Expanded U.S. Response," *Non-proliferation Review* 6, no. 2 (Winter 1999). For a referenced listing of specific incidents suggesting a serious problem in security during this period, see Matthew Bunn, "Loose Nukes Fears: Anecdotes of the Current Crisis," December 5, 1998 (available at http://ksgnotes1.harvard.edu/BCSIA/Library.nsf/atom).

9. Interview with senior MINATOM official, February 1999.

10. For a useful discussion of some of these cases, see William Potter, "Before the Deluge? Assessing the Threat of Nuclear Leakage from the Post-Soviet States," *Arms Control Today*, October 1995, 9–16.

11. Emily Ewell, "NIS Nuclear Smuggling since 1995: A Lull in Significant Cases?" *Non-proliferation Review*, spring–summer 1998.

12. Reportedly, Russian officials gained access to the facility in late 1997 and found it deserted and the reported HEU gone, after failing to visit the facility earlier in the year because of an apparent

bureaucratic misunderstanding. This incident is described on the subscription-only web page of the Center for Non-proliferation Studies at the Monterey Institute for International Studies, at http://cns.miis.edu/db/nisprofs/georgia/facils/vekua.htm.

13. "FSB Agents Prevent Theft of Nuclear Material in Chelyabinsk," *Itar-Tass*, December 18, 1999. The announcement did not indicate what type of material was involved, what facility was involved, or at what stage in the theft attempt the FSB's intervention took place.

14. For a detailed discussion of Russian nuclear weapon storage facilities and storage practices, see Joshua Handler, *Russian Nuclear Warhead Dismantlement Rates and Storage Site Capacity: Implications for the Implementation of START II and De-Alerting Initiatives* (Princeton, N.J.: Princeton University Center for Energy and Environmental Studies. Report No. AC-99-01, February 1999).

15. In 1997, General Eugene Habiger, then commander of the U.S. Strategic Command, estimated that there were 20,000–25,000 warheads remaining in Russia. (Testimony to the Senate Armed Services Committee, March 13, 1997.) A year later, Habiger referred to seventeen thousand to twenty-two thousand as being the number of tactical nuclear warheads alone in Russia, but from other sources it appears that this was a misdescription of the U.S. estimate of the total Russian nuclear warhead stockpile after some additional dismantlement had taken place. See testimony before the Senate Armed Services Committee, March 31, 1998, in *FY1999: Strategic Forces*, S. Hrg. 105–605, pt. 7. See also William Arkin, Robert Norris, and Joshua Handler, *Taking Stock: Worldwide Nuclear Deployments, 1998* (Washington, D.C.: Natural Resources Defense Council Nuclear Program, 1998).

16. "Interview: Igor Valynkin: We'll Do Our Best to Prevent Incidents like That One at the Novaya Zemlya Test Site," *Yaderny Kontrol* (Nuclear Control), 42, no. 6, November–December 1998, Center for Policy Studies in Russia, Moscow.

17. Department of Defense, *Proliferation: Threat and Response*, November 1997, 43.

18. Habiger noted, however, that he had seen only one facility; he observed others on a later visit. He pointed out that the Russians used a somewhat different approach relying more on people and less on high technology. See General Eugene Habiger, "Special Defense Department Briefing," Federal News Service, November 4, 1997; for the later trip, see General Eugene Habiger, "News Briefing," Federal Document Clearing House News Transcripts, June 16, 1998.

19. Deutch, testimony in *Global Proliferation of Weapons of Mass Destruction*.

20. Perhaps the most disturbing allegations of missing nuclear weapons originated with former Russian national security adviser Alexander Lebed, who indicated in several discussions and interviews that while national security adviser to President Yeltsin, he had ordered an accounting of the "suitcase bombs" in the Russian arsenal, and that scores of these weapons were unaccounted for. Lebed's charges were backed by the antinuclear environmental expert Alexander Yakovlev, who had been Yeltsin's environmental adviser early in Yeltsin's term, but they were strongly denied by the Ministries of Defense and Atomic Energy, and Lebed later appeared to back off many of his original charges himself. For an extended discussion of this episode, see Scott Parish and John Lepingwell, *Are Suitcase Nukes on the Loose?* (Monterey, Calif.: Center for Non-proliferation Studies, Monterey Institute of International Studies, 1998) (available at http://cns.miis.edu/pubs/reports/lebedlg.htm). For Lebed's seeming retraction, see Pavel Felgengauer, "Lebed Backpedals on Allegedly Missing 'Suitcase' Nuclear Devices," *St. Petersburg Times*, October 13–19, 1997. The full text of the interview quoted by Felgengauer was posted in October 1997 at the www.msnbc.com website, and is available from the author on request.

21. For an edited English translation of the transcript, see *Yaderny Kontrol Digest*, no. 5 (fall 1997).

22. See statement by General Igor Valynkin, commander of the Twelfth Main Directorate, quoted in "Valynkin Thanks Nunn-Lugar for Russian Nuclear Safety," *Yaderny Kontrol Digest*, no. 10 (spring 1999) (available at http://www.pircenter.org/yke/index.htm).

23. Deutch, testimony in *Global Proliferation of Weapons of Mass Destruction*.

24. For press accounts of this incident, see Bill Gertz, "Yeltsin Orders Nuclear Security Probe,"

Washington Times, October 21, 1998; and Vladimir Georgiev, "Underlying Reason: Crime in the Russian Army Has Rolled Up to Nuclear Munitions Units, but the Ministry of Defense Believes Russia Is Capable of Controlling Weapons of Mass Destruction without Foreign Intervention," *Moscow Nezavisimoye Voyennoye Obozreniye*, September 11–17, 1998, no. 34, 1, translated in Foreign Broadcast Information Service, Central Eurasia, September 23, 1998. For an official reaction from the commander of the Twelfth Main Directorate, see "Interview: Igor Valynkin: We'll Do Our Best to Prevent Incidents Like That One at the Novaya Zemlya Test Site."

25. Mikhail Shevtsov, "Russia Is Capable to Ensure Its Security, General," ITAR-TASS, October 9, 1998. According to Russian officials, a statement in October that troops have only received pay for July means that they are receiving paychecks with some regularity but that the paychecks they received recently only bring them up to what they were supposed to have been paid by July; it does not necessarily mean that they have received no pay at all since July.

26. Igor Khripunov, "MINATOM at the Edge," *Bulletin of the Atomic Scientists*, May–June 1999, estimated $60/month; Minister of Atomic Energy Yevgeniy Adamov reported in the spring of 1999 that average salaries for nuclear industrial workers were 1,800 rubles per month and for scientists approximately 1,400 rubles per month, corresponding to $80 and $60, respectively, at then current rates of exchange. See "MINATOM Reviews 1998, Making Plans for 1999," *Yaderny Kontrol Digest*, no. 10 (spring 1999).

27. For a discussion of the status of the Russian nuclear weapons complex, see Matthew Bunn, Oleg Bukharin, Jill Cetina, Kenneth Luongo, and Frank von Hippel, "Retooling Russia's Nuclear Cities," *Bulletin of the Atomic Scientists*, September–October 1998. See also Igor Khripunov, "MINATOM at the Edge," *Bulletin of the Atomic Scientists*, May–June 1999; The Nuclear Cities Initiative: Status and Issues (Washington, D.C.: Russian-American Nuclear Security Advisory Council [RANSAC], January 1999); and Jill Cetina, Oleg Bukharin, and Frank von Hippel, *Defense Conversion and Small Business Development: A Proposal for Two IFC Projects in Three of Russia's Closed Nuclear Cities* (Princeton, N.J.: Center for Energy and Environmental Studies, Princeton University, Report 306, March 1998).

28. Yevgeni Tkachenko, "Ural Nuclear Workers on Strike, Demanding Wage Arrears," *ITAR-TASS*, November 19, 1998. For a listing of this and many other incidents from the same period, see Bunn, "Loose Nukes Fears."

29. For one published account, see Potter, "Prospects for U.S.-Russian Collaboration for Non-proliferation." Presentation to the Defense and Security Committee of the North Atlantic Assembly, 44th Annual Session, Edinburgh, November 10–13, 1998.

30. David Hoffman, "Russia's Nuclear Force Sinks with the Ruble: Economic Crisis Erodes Strategic Arsenal," *Washington Post*, September 18, 1998.

31. See William Arkin, Robert Norris, and Joshua Handler, *Taking Stock: Worldwide Nuclear Deployments, 1998* (Washington, D.C.: Natural Resources Defense Council Nuclear Program, 1998).

32. See David Albright, Frans Berkhout, and William Walker, *Plutonium and Highly Enriched Uranium 1996: World Inventories, Capabilities, and Policies* (Oxford, U.K.: Oxford University Press for the Stockholm International Peace Research Institute, 1997).

33. Ibid. These estimates of Russia's plutonium and HEU stockpiles have substantial uncertainties; note that their sum is over 100 tons less than the official estimate of the total in MPC&A Strategic Plan.

34. Reactor-grade plutonium can be used to make nuclear weapons at all levels of sophistication. The most detailed unclassified official discussion of the usability of reactor-grade plutonium in weapons is in *Non-proliferation and Arms Control Assessment of Weapons-Usable Fissile Material Storage and Excess Plutonium Disposition Alternatives* (Washington, D.C.: Department of Energy, DOE-NN-007, January 1997), 37–39. This document also provides descriptions of the proliferation hazards posed by the various steps involved in different approaches to long-term plutonium disposition.

35. For an official summary of the MPC&A program, see *MPC&A Program Strategic Plan*. For other recent summaries, see National Research Council, Committee on Upgrading Russian Capabilities

to Secure Plutonium and High Enriched Uranium, *Protecting Nuclear Material in Russia* (Washington, D.C.: National Academy Press, 1999); National Research Council, Committee on Dual Use Technologies Export Control and Materials Protection Control and Accountability, *Proliferation Concerns: Assessing U.S. Efforts to Help Contain Nuclear and Other Dangerous Materials and Technologies in the Former Soviet Union* (Washington, D.C.: National Academy Press, 1997); James Doyle, "Improving Nuclear Materials Security in the Former Soviet Union: Next Steps for the MPC&A Program," *Arms Control Today*, March 1998; Matthew Bunn and John P. Holdren, "Managing Military Uranium and Plutonium," *Annual Review of Energy and Environment*, 1997, vol. 22, 403–86; and Perry, "Securing Russian Materials."

36. For the total, see *Fact Sheet: U.S. Commitment to the Treaty on the Non-Proliferation of Nuclear Weapons* (Washington, D.C.: U.S. Department of State, Bureau of Non-proliferation, May 3, 1999); for projected budgets, see *Expanded Threat Reduction Initiative* (Washington, D.C.: U.S. Department of State, March 1999).

37. *Significant Milestones in Securing and Controlling Nuclear Materials*, Washington D.C.: Department of Energy, May 1999.

38. Briefing by Rose Gottemoeller, assistant secretary for non-proliferation and national security, U.S. Department of Energy, Harvard University, May 11, 1999.

39. See discussion in National Research Council, *Protecting Nuclear Material in Russia*.

40. Some of the background of this facility is summarized in U.S. General Accounting Office, *Weapons of Mass Destruction: Effort to Reduce Russian Arsenals May Cost More, Achieve Less than Planned* (Washington, D.C.: U.S. General Accounting Office, GAO/NSIAD-99-76, April 1999).

41. Ibid.

42. For a useful but somewhat dated description of this cooperation, see Gen. Evgeniy Maslin (former commander, Twelfth Main Directorate), "Russian-U.S. Cooperation on Nuclear Weapons Safety," in John M. Shields and William C. Potter, eds., *Dismantling the Cold War: U.S. and NIS Perspectives on the Nunn-Lugar Cooperative Threat Reduction Program*, Cambridge: MIT Press, CSIA Studies in International Security, 1997. More recent brief descriptions of this cooperation can be found in Gen. Igor Valynkin, press conference, February 3, 1999, Official Kremlin International News Broadcast, *Federal Information Systems Corporation;* and U.S. Department of Defense, "Secretary Tours Russian Defense Facility, Nuclear Weapons Security Projects Viewed at Sergiev Posad," press release, February 1998.

43. For a detailed account, see William C. Potter, "Project Sapphire: U.S.-Kazakhstani Cooperation for Non-proliferation," in Shields and Potter, *Dismantling the Cold War*.

44. See, for example, Michael R. Gordon, "U.S. and Britain Relocate a Cache of Nuclear Fuel," *New York Times*, April 20, 1998; and Toby Dalton, "Tbilisi: The Tip of the Nuclear Iceberg," Issue Brief No. 1, April 23, 1998, available at www.ceip.org/npp.

45. See, for example, Steve Goldstein, "U.S. Plots Move of Plutonium from Risky Site near Iran," *Philadelphia Inquirer*, September 6, 1998.

46. *Expanded Threat Reduction Initiative*.

47. For an account of the ISTC, see Victor Alessi and Ronald F. Lehman II, "Science in the Pursuit of Peace: The Success and Future of the ISTC," *Arms Control Today*, June–July 1998. See also ISTC's website at www.ISTC.RU.

48. For a General Accounting Office review of IPP that was critical on these and other grounds, see General Accounting Office, *Nuclear Non-proliferation: Concerns with DOE's Efforts to Reduce the Risks Posed by Russia's Unemployed Weapons Scientists*, GAO/RCED-99-54 (Washington, D.C.: February 1999). While this report has been portrayed in the press as concluding that the IPP program is useless, in fact it concludes that "DOE's effort to supplement the salaries of former weapons scientists so that they do not sell their services to terrorists, criminal organizations, or countries of proliferation concern is laudable and, we believe, in our national security interests," and

acknowledges that the program is successfully involving thousands of former Soviet weapons scientists in civilian projects. GAO expressed a number of valid concerns over "implementation and oversight" of the program, and made a range of recommendations, nearly all of which DOE has accepted. For a useful response to the GAO report and defense of IPP and the Nuclear Cities Initiative, see Joseph R. Biden, Jr. "Maintaining the Proliferation Fight in the Former Soviet Union," *Arms Control Today*, March 1999.

49. For discussions of the Russian nuclear cities and the Nuclear Cities Initiative, see Bunn et al., "Retooling Russia's Nuclear Cities"; *Nuclear Cities Initiative: Status and Issues; and Nuclear Cities Initiative Program Plan* (Washington, D.C.: U.S. Department of Energy, May 19, 1999).

50. Report to the Congress on the Nuclear Cities Initiative, reprinted in *Nuclear Cities Initiative: Status and Issues*.

51. For a discussion, see *Warhead and Fissile Material Transparency Program: Strategic Plan.* Washington, D.C.: U.S. Department of Energy, May 1999.

52. For a discussion that is critical of the Mayak storage facility because of Russia's refusal to grant this upstream transparency, see General Accounting Office, *Weapons of Mass Destruction: Effort to Reduce Russian Arsenals May Cost More, Achieve Less than Planned*, GAO/NSIAD-99-76 (Washington, D.C.: General Accounting Office, April 1999). For a general description of the types of measurements the United States is seeking, see *Warhead and Fissile Material Transparency Program Strategic Plan.*

53. The specific transparency measures being implemented include: occasional U.S. observation of measurements of containers said to hold HEU components of dismantled weapons, to confirm the presence of HEU with a U-235 content of 90 percent; occasional U.S. observation of the oxidation of metal shavings produced from these weapons components; checking of tags and seals of containers holding purified HEU after shipment to the blending facility; and continuous monitoring of the flow of HEU, blend stock, and blended material at the blending facility, with permanent U.S. presence there. Russia is able to observe the fabrication of the LEU into reactor fuel at U.S. fabrication sites. Because additional blending facilities have been added more rapidly than transparency measures for each facility could be negotiated and implemented, the most complete measures are so far only being implemented at the original blending facility but are planned to be implemented at the others in the future. Because there is not a complete "chain of custody" with tags, seals, and monitoring ensuring continuity of knowledge throughout the entire process, there remain some skeptics who argue that there are possible ways to defeat the transparency regime and provide HEU that did not come immediately from weapons components, or even LEU that was not blended from HEU. (As of mid-1999, a General Accounting Office report expected to be critical of the arrangements for HEU transparency was being drafted.) Given the wide range of information available to the United States at different points in this chain, however—including the ability to measure the isotopic content of the final LEU product, which differs subtly from the isotopic content of newly produced LEU—and given the minor to nonexistent incentives for Russia to provide material other than what has been agreed to and the enormous financial risks to Russia of being caught violating the deal, there appears to be good reason for confidence that the LEU being purchased is in fact blended from HEU, most of which came from dismantled weapons. A brief discussion of these measures can be found in *Warhead and Fissile Material Transparency Program Strategic Plan.*

54. See discussion in Frank von Hippel, presentation to the Sixth International Policy Forum: *Management and Disposition of Nuclear Weapons Materials*, Exchange Monitor Publications, June 7–10, 1999.

55. For a critical summary, see Igor Kudrik, "MINATOM Lobby for Spent Fuel Intensifies," Bellona, April 23, 1999.

56. Statement to the IAEA, quoted in *TASS*, September 22, 1992. As arms reductions proceed, these stockpiles should be reduced in parallel to roughly equivalent levels in the United States and Russia, suitable to support whatever agreed warhead levels remain but not large enough to permit a rapid return to Cold War levels of armament.

57. Feed Materials Planning Basis for Surplus Weapons-Usable Plutonium Disposition (Washington, D.C.: Department of Energy, Office of Fissile Material Disposition, April 1997).

58. *Fact Sheet: U.S. Commitment to the Treaty on the Non-Proliferation of Nuclear Weapons*. Much of the remaining material is in classified forms, or forms that are so contaminated as to be difficult to measure and safeguard, or in facilities that continue to engage in classified activities.

59. These planned dates and cost estimates are from *Cost Analysis in Support of Site Selection for Surplus Weapons-Usable Plutonium Disposition*, Rev. 0 (Washington, D.C.: Department of Energy, Office of Fissile Materials Disposition, July 22, 1998), available at http://twilight.saic.com/md/.

60. For a summary of the critics' view, see Edwin S. Lyman and Paul Leventhal, "Bury the Stuff," *Bulletin of the Atomic Scientists*, March–April 1997; for a summary of the supporters' view, see John P. Holdren, John F. Ahearne, Richard L. Garwin, Wolfgang K. H. Panofsky, and Matthew Bunn, "Excess Weapons Plutonium: How to Reduce a Clear and Present Danger," *Arms Control Today*, November–December 1996. For a direct response to the main criticisms, see Matthew Bunn, "The Case for a Dual-Track Approach—And How to Move Forward from Here," *Nuclear Materials Monitor* 1, no. 5 (July 14, 1997) (available at http://ksgnotes1.harvard.edu/BCSIA/Library.nsf/atom).

61. For an overview of the HEU deal, and a discussion of the problems that have beset it, see Richard Falkenrath, "The HEU Deal," Appendix C in Graham T. Allison, Owen R. Corté, Jr., Richard A. Falkenrath, and Steven E. Miller, *Avoiding Nuclear Anarchy: Containing the Threat of Loose Russian Nuclear Weapons and Fissile Material*, Cambridge: MIT Press, CSIA Studies in International Security, 1996. For a more optimistic official view, see U.S. Enrichment Corporation, "Chronology of the Megatons to Megawatts Contract (as of March 31, 1999)" (available at http://www.usec.com/Structure/Navigation/ThirdTier/newsreleases/08-31-98.htm).

62. For an overview of these events, see Thomas L. Neff, "Privatizing U.S. National Security: The U.S.-Russian HEU Deal at Risk," *Arms Control Today*, August–September 1998 (available at http://www.armscontrol.org/ACT/augsep98/tnas98.htm); the earlier background can be found in depressing detail in Falkenrath, "The HEU Deal."

63. For a detailed discussion of the options for plutonium disposition and the status as of 1997, see Bunn and Holdren, "Managing Military Uranium and Plutonium," and sources cited therein; see also *Final Report of the U.S.-Russian Independent Scientific Commission on Disposition of Excess Weapons Plutonium* (Washington, D.C., Office of Science and Technology Policy, June 1997) (available at http://ksgnotes1.harvard.edu/BCSIA/Library.nsf/atom). A variety of current official program documents and briefings are available at the program website, at http://twilight.saic.com/md/.

64. No detailed analysis has yet been done of what such a funding-unconstrained program would cost; the Department of Energy should undertake such an analysis immediately. The $250 million-per-year estimate arises from adding three figures: Planning for the originally planned $150 million budget for FY1999 made it clear that at least that amount could be effectively spent installing upgrades and providing associated training, while unpublished analyses by participants in the MPC&A program suggest that substantial consolidation and sustainability programs might each cost $50 million per year. Some period would be needed to scale up the effort from the current $140 million-a-year level. Interviews.

65. See, for example, the discussion of the football field-size, concrete-lined underground facility at Krasnoyarsk-26, once intended as an additional reprocessing area, in Bunn and Holdren, "Managing Military Uranium and Plutonium."

66. Interviews with U.S. and Russian MPC&A program participants.

67. All of the non-Russian facilities "completed" in the MPC&A program have been handed over to DOE's international safeguards division for any continued monitoring and work that may be needed—and that division simply does not have the resources to seriously support any further upgrades, or even operations and maintenance of the systems installed. As one DOE MPC&A official put it, "our program has walked away." What approach to take with Russian facilities that are declared "completed" remains under consideration. Interviews.

68. For useful discussions of the difficult challenges posed by MPC&A sustainability, see, for example, James E. Doyle and Stephen V. Mladineo, "Assessing the Development of a Modern Safeguards Culture in the NIS," *Non-proliferation Review*, winter 1998; Oleg Bukharin, *Achieving Safeguards Sustainability in Russia*, Princeton, N.J.: Center for Energy and Environmental Studies, Princeton University, Report No. 305, March 1998; and Todd Perry, "Securing Russian Nuclear Materials."

69. The concept of building a recipient state's capacity to carry out a particular function is one with which there is substantial experience in the international development assistance field, from which the MPC&A program can and should draw important lessons: in general, experience suggests that programs focused only on providing technical assistance for a particular task, without addressing the larger institutional, economic, and political contexts within which that task is performed, usually have only modest lasting benefit. The necessary systemic program of reform requires a systemic understanding of how the system whose capacity is to be built actually functions. See Merilee S. Grindle, ed., *Getting Good Government: Capacity Building in the Public Sectors of Developing Countries* (Cambridge, Mass.: Harvard Studies in International Development, Harvard University Press, 1997). The author is grateful to Stacy VanDeveer for provocative discussions of these points and the opportunity to review a draft paper addressing them.

70. DOE is currently working to ensure that installed systems have "extended warranties" and that adequate servicing capabilities and supplies of spare parts are available, but the proposal to simply pay for the full cost of operations and maintenance during the initial settling-in period would expand this approach substantially.

71. The author is grateful to Christopher Paine for this suggestion.

72. Realistic testing is critically important, as the performance of a system in the real world is almost always different from its performance on paper. Moreover, in the U.S. system, spectacular failures in realistic tests have proved to be an excellent mechanism for convincing high-level officials that more funding for security really was required.

73. Remarkably, although some of the Russian facilities that receive most of their total income from the HEU deal have been among the least cooperative with the MPC&A program, the United States has never sought to link the two.

74. Under the direction of William Potter, the Center for Non-proliferation Studies at the Monterey Institute of International Affairs has already done exemplary work in this area, as have several U.S. foundations, supporting efforts such as the Russian journal *Yaderny Kontrol* (Nuclear Control), but there is certainly more that can and should be done.

75. As noted earlier, DOE has estimated that the cost of providing sustainable employment for 50,000 excess workers in the Russian nuclear weapons complex—possibly an underestimate of the number of excess workers—would be in the range of $550 million. See *Report to Congress on the Nuclear Cities Initiative.*

76. See, for example, the discussion in *Management and Disposition of Excess Weapons Plutonium.*

77. For an excellent recent discussion of transparency measures, with some similar suggestions, see Oleg Bukharin and Kenneth Luongo, U.S.-Russian Warhead Dismantlement Transparency: The Status, Problems, and Proposals (Princeton, N.J.: Center for Energy and Environmental Studies, Princeton University, Report 314, April 1999) (available at http://www.princeton.edu/~ransac).

78. For a description of this concept, see Matthew Bunn, "Act Now, Mr. President," *Bulletin of the Atomic Scientists*, March–April 1998. For a similar proposal applying to active-duty strategic forces, see Admiral Stansfield Turner, *Caging the Nuclear Genie: An American Challenge for Global Security* (Boulder, Colo.: Westview Press, 1997). See also Committee on Nuclear Policy, *Jump-START: Retaking the Initiative to Reduce Post–Cold War Nuclear Dangers* (Washington, D.C.: Henry L. Stimson Center, February 1999) (available at http://www.stimson.org/policy/jumpstart.htm).

79. See Matthew Bunn, " 'Pit-Stuffing': How to Disable Thousands of Warheads and Easily Verify Their Dismantlement," *F.A.S. Public Interest Report*, March–April 1998.

80. See discussion in Luongo and Bukharin, "U.S.-Russian Warhead Dismantlement Transparency."

81. For a recent status report on the fissile cutoff, see chapter 16 of this volume. See also George Bunn, "Making Progress on a Fissile Material Cutoff Treaty after the South Asian Tests," *Non-proliferation Review*, spring–summer 1998. Making progress with Russia on reprocessing verification may require a change in the current Russian cutoff negotiating position, which would exempt most facilities by applying verification only to facilities handling plutonium with a Pu-239 content of 95 percent or more—a proposal that would vitiate the cutoff's effectiveness and verifiability (most U.S. weapons plutonium has a lower Pu-239 content than this). An offer to cover the costs of verification could contribute to Russian willingness to change this position and thereby bring these older plants under verification.

82. For a comprehensive set of next steps for excess plutonium, agreed upon by a panel of U.S. and Russian experts, see *Final Report of the U.S.-Russian Independent Scientific Commission on Disposition of Excess Weapons Plutonium*.

83. See Matthew Bunn, "Getting the Plutonium Disposition Job Done: The Concept of a Joint-Venture Disposition Enterprise Financed by Additional Sales of Highly Enriched Uranium," in *Science for Peace Series Vol. 1: International Conference on Military Conversion and Science: Utilization-Disposal of the Excess Fissile Weapons Materials: Scientific, Technological, and Socio-Economic Aspects*, ed. V. Kousminov and M. Martellini (Como, Italy: UNESCO Venice Office, 1996).

84. For a proposal along these lines, see Matthew Bunn, Neil J. Numark, and Tatsujiro Suzuki, "A Japanese-Russian Agreement to Establish a Nuclear Facility for MOX Fabrication and Spent Fuel Storage in the Russian Far East," BCSIA Discussion Paper 98-25 (Cambridge, Mass.: Kennedy School of Government, Harvard University, November 1998).

85. For a description of this "plutonium bank" idea, see Ashton B. Carter and Owen Coté, "Disposition of Fissile Materials," in *Cooperative Denuclearization: From Pledges to Deeds*, ed. Graham Allison, Ashton B. Carter, Steven E. Miller, and Philip Zelikow, CSIA Studies in International Security No. 2 (Cambridge: MIT Press, 1993).

86. See Brian Chow, Richard H. Speier, and G.S. Jones, A Concept for Strategic Material Accelerated Removal Talks, DRU-1338-DOE (Washington, D.C.: RAND Corporation, 1996).

87. For a description of the basic approach, see Thomas L. Neff, presentation to the Fifth International Policy Forum: Management and Disposition of Nuclear Weapons Materials, March 24, 1998; for a press report of the results of Domenici's discussions with the Europeans on this subject, see Dave Airoso, "Finding Europeans Disinterested, Domenici Gives Up on 'Global Burn,' " *Nuclear Fuel*, July 27, 1998.

88. For a provocative discussion, see Adam Bernstein and Allison MacFarlane, "Canning Plutonium: Faster and Cheaper," *Bulletin of the Atomic Scientists*, May–June 1999.

—ASIA—

8

China's Perspective on Non-Proliferation

Sha Zukang

The good momentum of the international non-proliferation efforts maintained since the end of the Cold War was severely interrupted by the May 1998 Indian and Pakistani nuclear tests. How to repair and consolidate the damaged international non-proliferation regime is a pressing task facing us today. Whether we can cope with it effectively will have far-reaching impact on the future development of the international situation.

The nuclear non-proliferation regime was the hardest hit by the Indian and Pakistani nuclear tests. It is of vital importance that further proliferation of nuclear weapons be prevented. To this end, first and foremost, we must exert all of our efforts to stop and reverse the nuclear development programs of India and Pakistan. The Indian and Pakistani nuclear tests have presented the international community with both a challenge and an opportunity. In a sense, these events have become a litmus test for the effectiveness of the international non-proliferation regime. If the international community could take effective measures to stop or even reverse the two countries' nuclear development programs, the authority and vitality of the international nuclear non-proliferation regime will be immeasurably enhanced.

To achieve this, two things are important. First, the international community should have sufficient patience and perseverance and should not lose hope because of the lack of progress in the short run. Second, the international community, especially the major powers, must achieve consensus and take concerted action on this matter. A robust international non-proliferation regime is in the interest of all countries. If any country seeks to exploit the South Asian situation to obtain unilateral short-term political, economic, or strategic benefits at the expense of other countries and international solidarity and in total disregard for the serious consequences the South Asian nuclear testing has had on the international non-proliferation regime, it can only further undermine the already badly damaged international non-proliferation regime, and, in the end, the long-term interests of that country will also be jeopardized. It is a direct violation of UN Security Council Resolution 1172 to negotiate, or even to discuss, with India India's so-called minimum nuclear deterrence capability. It is also unhelpful to publicly support India's permanent membership in the UN Security Council soon after its nuclear tests. It is obvious that these actions will not help in repairing the damage caused by the South Asian nuclear tests to the international nuclear non-proliferation regime.

Second, the international nuclear non-proliferation regime should be replenished. At present, this includes three main aspects. First is the Comprehensive Nuclear Test Ban Treaty (CTBT). All states concerned should sign and ratify the treaty as soon as possible, so that the treaty can enter into force at an early date. China is accelerating its preparatory work and will submit the treaty to the People's Congress for ratification in the first part of this year, with the hope that the ratification procedures can be completed before September. Second is the Fissile Material Cut-Off Treaty (FMCT). Negotiation should start as soon as possible. All states should make the necessary efforts and demonstrate the necessary political will to conclude a good treaty at an early date that guarantees the adherence of all states capable of producing nuclear materials.

The third aspect is to strengthen the nuclear export control regime. China joined the Zangger Committee in October 1997 and has promulgated the regulations on Nuclear Export Control and on the Export Control of Nuclear Dual-Use Items and Related Technologies. For historical reasons, China has not joined the Nuclear Suppliers Group (NSG) so far, but we support its non-proliferation objectives and have actually incorporated both its control lists, in their entirety, into China's own national regulations. In this connection, we have noted with concern that after the Indian nuclear tests, some NSG members have taken a more proactive stand on issues of nuclear cooperation with India. We hope that these countries could be more cautious in this area.

The fourth issue is that the nuclear disarmament process should be accelerated. The fundamental solution to nuclear proliferation lies with complete nuclear disarmament. We do not believe that there exists a cause-and-effect relationship between the present lack of progress in nuclear disarmament and the Indian nuclear testing, as claimed by the Indian government. But, at the same time, we fully recognize that an accelerated pace of nuclear disarmament will certainly be conducive to consolidating the international non-proliferation regime. The United States and the Russian Federation are duty-bound to take the lead in nuclear disarmament. We hope that START II can be effective and implemented, and the negotiation on START III initiated, as soon as possible. On such basis, the two countries should further reduce their nuclear arsenals so as to prepare the ground for other nuclear weapon states to join in the process.

Last but not least, the role of nuclear weapons should be further diminished. The nuclear deterrence policy based on the first use of nuclear weapons highlights the discriminatory nature of the existing nuclear non-proliferation regime. It does not help to strengthen the international nuclear non-proliferation regime or to dissipate the misconception of countries like India that the possession of nuclear weapons is the shortcut to the status of a world power. We are pleased to note that Germany and

Canada have advocated that NATO should abandon its policy of first use of nuclear weapons. We hope that positive results could come out of the ongoing debates within NATO on this matter.

THE CHEMICAL WEAPONS REGIME

Compared with the nuclear non-proliferation regime, the international regime against the proliferation of chemical and biological weapons, which is based on the Chemical Weapons Convention (CWC) and the Biological Weapons Convention (BWC), is more justified and less discriminatory, but it's by no means problem-free.

With respect to chemical weapons, the relationship between CWC and the Australia Group is a thorny issue. CWC, a treaty which was concluded after extended multilateral negotiations and has as many as 126 state parties, contains in it clear provisions on the export of sensitive chemicals, accompanied with long schedules. We do not deny the right of any country to stipulate stricter export controls than those required by CWC and to establish small groups for that purpose. However, the existence of the Australia Group has resulted in discrepancies in the legal provisions of different countries, which has created a de facto split legal system within the CWC states parties. This inevitably causes confusion and affects the normal international trade of chemicals. This problem is compounded by the seemingly irresistible inclination of certain countries to impose their own standards or even their own domestic legislation on other countries, thus giving rise to unnecessary international disputes. All this has seriously undermined the authority of the CWC. There are only two ways to rectify this situation, namely, to dissolve the Australia Group or to amend the CWC to bring it in line with the requirements of the Australia Group. There must be a single standard rather than two.

The faithful implementation of the existing international treaties is the prerequisite for the strengthening of the non-proliferation regime. CWC has been in force for almost two years, but a certain country has still not submitted its complete declarations, as required by the convention, and has even passed national legislation that openly contravenes the provisions of the convention. Such a practice of putting one's national legislation above international law and refusing to fulfill one's obligations under an international treaty cannot but cause concern.

THE BIOLOGICAL WEAPONS REGIME

With respect to biological weapons, the negotiation on a protocol aimed at strengthening the BWC has entered its final stage. The establishment of any verification system should be guided by the principles of fairness, appropriateness, and effectiveness. Otherwise, verification weakens rather than strengthens the non-proliferation regime. In this connection, there are many lessons to be drawn from the weapons inspections in Iraq. We must have a realistic estimate of the role of verification. The purpose of verification is to deter potential violators from violating its obligations. At the same time, we should be realistic enough to see that no verification regime, however perfect or complete, could provide a 100 percent guarantee that no violations could happen. Therefore, verification measures should be appropriate and feasible. If they are too intrusive and affect the legitimate security or economic interest of the state parties, or are too costly and impossible to sustain in the long run, they will not be able to get widespread support, and in the end the universality of the treaties will be undermined. Such a result would be detrimental to the strengthening of the non-proliferation regime.

THE BALLISTIC MISSILE REGIME

Devoid of any legal basis in international law, missile non-proliferation is the most underdeveloped part of the entire international non-proliferation regime. As the founders of the Missile Technology Control Regime (MTCR) admitted, MTCR is just a time-winning device. Its purpose is to delay missile proliferation rather than provide a comprehensive solution to this problem. Even this limited role was somehow diminished by the regime's lack of objective criteria and by the double standard applied by certain MTCR members in implementing requirements of the regime. Recent developments have shown that the risk of missile proliferation is increasing. It is time for the international community to take a collective look at the missile proliferation issue, including MTCR, and explore better ways to combat this danger.

One cannot discuss missile proliferation without mentioning theater missile defense (TMD). We are deeply concerned about certain countries' efforts to develop advanced TMD or even a national missile defense (NMD), for the following reasons:

First, the development of advanced TMD or even NMD will have negative impacts on the regional or even global strategic stability. Like nuclear weapons, missiles can proliferate both horizontally and vertically. If a country, in addition to its offensive power, seeks to develop advanced TMD or even NMD in an attempt to attain absolute security and unilateral strategic advantage for itself, other countries will be forced to develop more advanced offensive missiles. This will give rise to a new round of the arms race that will be in no one's interest. To avoid such a situation, it is extremely important to maintain and strengthen the Anti-Ballistic Missile Treaty (ABM). During the Cold War, ABM was one of the cornerstones of the strategic stability between the United States and the former Soviet Union, which made it possible for the two countries to make deep cuts in their respective nuclear arsenals. After the Cold War, with the world moving rapidly toward multipolarity, the significance of the ABM Treaty has increased rather than decreased. Some scholars have put forward the idea of making the ABM Treaty a multilateral treaty. This is an idea worthy of our serious consideration. Second, transferring TMD systems to other countries or regions or jointly developing them with other countries will inevitably result in the proliferation of missile technology. Missile and antimissile technologies are related. Many of the technologies used in antimissile systems are easily applicable to offensive missiles. This is one of the main reasons China stands against the cooperation between the United States and Japan to develop TMD and opposes any transfer of TMD systems to Taiwan. We hope that the U.S. government could take a more cautious and responsible attitude on this matter.

China's opposition to U.S. transfers of TMD to Taiwan is also based on another major concern, namely, its adverse impact on China's reunification. TMD in Taiwan will give the proindependence forces in Taiwan a false sense of security, which may incite them to reckless moves. This can only lead to instability across the Taiwan Strait or even in the entire Northeast Asian region.

The proliferation problem cannot be solved without taking the large international environment into consideration. It is important that a fair and just new world order be established whereby all states treat one another with equality. The big and powerful should not bully the small and weak. All disputes should be solved peacefully, without the resort to the use or threat of force. This is the most effective way to remove the fundamental motivations of countries for the acquisition of weapons of mass destruction, thus the best approach to non-proliferation.

—9—

Nuclear Relations in South Asia[1]

Neil Joeck

The strategic landscape of South Asia, and indeed of Asia at large, changed dramatically in 1998 and 1999. With the reciprocal testing of nuclear weapons in 1998 and medium-range ballistic missiles in 1999, India and Pakistan emerged from the world of threshold nuclear status to an overt posture as nuclear weapon states. Although both states enjoyed near-nuclear status since 1990, the overt posture raised a host of new issues. Furthermore, the Kashmir crisis of mid-1999 made clear that the new status each claimed did not remove the danger of war but certainly increased the stakes if war occurred.

A number of important strategic issues are raised by these dramatic events. This chapter will attempt to examine the implications of this new posture for each country and for the region. First and foremost, the decisions to test nuclear weapons and ballistic missiles were a product of each individual state's making a sovereign decision about its national security needs. Both have made clear for a number of years that their attitudes toward nuclear weapons—and, by default, toward nuclear non-proliferation—will not be directed by outsiders. The test decisions cannot be undone, and it now falls on both countries to decide what strategies will best serve them and what obligations they must now assume. They must now reevaluate, if not discard, any assumptions they may have harbored about the stability of deterrence and the unlikelihood of conflict once nuclear weapons were brought out into the open. Issues such as strategic planning, weaponization, deployment, and command and control, which heretofore were relegated to the back burner, may no longer be deferred.

What comes next, therefore, is just as important as the nuclear and missile tests. Neither India nor Pakistan has a ready model to examine for guidance about how best to function in a nuclear deterrent relationship. Some analysts look to the U.S.-USSR Cold War confrontation for parallels or examples, but India and Pakistan's geographical proximity, history of direct conflict, and lack of alliance buffers make their situation quite different—whether for better or worse remains to be seen.

Others argue that India and Pakistan will restrain their competition and do little more than maintain minimum capabilities in order to assure "recessed" or "latent" deterrence. China, watchful and critical of India's actions, is unlikely to make significant changes over the near term but may have to reevaluate its own strategic posture, which could make it more difficult for India to define what a "minimum capability" entails.

Sir Michael Howard said that deterrence rests on a combination of accommodation and reassurance, not on nuclear threats alone.[2] The May 1998 tests certainly made the nuclear threats manifest, but they did not prevent the outbreak of conflict in May 1999. The reciprocal missile testing of early 1999 underscored the threat each posed, but again it did little to prevent conflict from erupting. The elements of reassurance and accommodation must now also be brought to center stage, as they will be at least as important as threats in ensuring national security.

Reassurance and accommodation will involve diplomatic steps that heretofore might have been unnecessary. It will mean each side must engage in a dialogue with the other in the absence of trust, in the knowledge that each must continually monitor what the other does, and in fear that no defense is available to prevent the other from launching a devastating nuclear attack. In this environment, New Delhi and Islamabad will need to find ways to convince one another that each is secure, not just that each is threatened; the relationship must be one of coordination and mutual dependence, not just conflict.

NATIONAL SECURITY AND STABILITY

Acquiring an overt nuclear capability may force both India and Pakistan to reexamine a number of issues that might have been delayed or deferred under conditions of nuclear ambiguity. One important issue is the question of how a nuclear capability, regardless of its configuration, meets the country's broad security needs; a more narrow issue is whether or not to weaponize and/or deploy nuclear forces; a third important question involves the need for command and control.

STRATEGIC PLANNING AND NUCLEAR CAPABILITY

On the basis of their own pronouncements, India and Pakistan took the step to test nuclear weapons in order to enhance security in what they consider to be an insecure region. In April 1998, India's defense minister, George Fernandes, spoke darkly about the menace from China; Pakistan's foreign minister, Gohar Ayub Khan, was equally apprehensive in his assessment of India, even before the Bharatiya Janata Party (BJP) began the nuclear test series on May 11. The BJP evidently long ago concluded that an overt nuclear posture was necessary to confront the Chinese threat, and virtually the whole of Pakistan's defense structure, from conventional to nuclear capabilities, has been a response to the perceived threat from India. Both have presumably concluded that this overt nuclear posture will enhance security, and reduce the likelihood that war will break out and that they will be targeted with nuclear weapons if it does.

TABLE 9.1

NUCLEAR TESTS BY INDIA AND PAKISTAN[a]

INDIA'S NUCLEAR TESTS

Location	Date	Yield
Pokhran, Rajasthan	May 18, 1974	15 kT
Pokhran, Rajasthan	May 11, 1998	• 43 kT thermonuclear • 12 kT fission • Subkiloton
Pokhran, Rajasthan	May 13,1998	• 0.2 kT • 0.6 kT yield

PAKISTAN'S NUCLEAR TESTS

Chagai Hills	May 28, 1998	Pakistan claims that the tests were of a combined explosive force of 40–45 kT of which one was in the 30–35 kT range
Chagai Hills	May 30, 1998	Claimed yield of 15–18 kT

a. Independent analysis of seismic data gathered from the tests, however, has not corroborated the claims of the Indian and Pakistani governments. Estimated total yields for the tests fall well short of official announcements (May 11: 9–16 kt; May 13: 0.15 kt; May 28: 6–13 kt; May 30: 4–8 kt). The smaller estimated yield of the May 11 test would appear to rule out a thermonuclear explosion, contrary to Indian claims. See Terry C. Wallace, "The May 1998 India and Pakistan Nuclear Tests," September 1998, http://www.geo.arizona.edu/geophysics/faculty/wallace/ind.pak/; Brian Barker and Terry Wallace, "Monitoring Nuclear Tests," *Science*, 25 September 1998.

Table prepared by the Carnegie Non-Proliferation Project and does not necessarily represent the views of the author.

Indian and Pakistani strategists alike have argued that nuclear weapons have only been used in the past in situations of nuclear asymmetry—where one state has nuclear weapons but the other does not. Some Indian analysts argue that in situations of nuclear asymmetry, a nuclear-armed state may "blackmail" another, that is, threaten a non-nuclear state without fear of retaliation. By this reasoning, India remained subject to Chinese blackmail, an unstable relationship that needed to be corrected with an overt nuclear posture. Similarly, once India had tested, Pakistan became subject to Indian blackmail, an unstable relationship that also had to be corrected with some in-kind response. The nuclear tests in May presumably corrected the asymmetries and instabilities.

These assumptions about the utility of nuclear weapons in redressing security imbalances should not go unchallenged, especially in light of the BJP's initial indication that it would conduct a thorough strategic evaluation of India's defense needs. Rather than evaluating the utility of nuclear weapons as part of India's defense structure, however, the BJP quickly conducted tests, which stacked the strategic deck before the Strategic Defense Review (SDR) could be conducted. The BJP had also announced that a National Security Council (NSC) would be formed. It was presumably to be the function of this organization to conduct the SDR, and to evaluate India's strategic needs. By testing nuclear devices somewhat precipitately, India made moot the question of whether or not nuclear weapons were even necessary. It was left to the NSC to determine how the nuclear devices already tested fit into a strategic review whose conclusion might otherwise have been that nuclear weapons would ill serve India's needs. The result is that those elements within India that benefit from the nuclear tests—what Itty Abraham calls the strategic enclave[3]—have already dictated the terms of the debate. This was made evident in the hawkish draft nuclear doctrine released in August 1999. It does little to challenge preconceived notions of deterrence, and has been rejected by a number of prominent analysts and policymakers in New Delhi.

Short-circuiting such important issues should be avoided in the future by ensuring that a variety of points of view are represented. It is not at all clear that an overt policy serves India's strategic needs better than the ambiguous option policy, but it is now too late for argument. Even if India wanted to reverse course, Pakistan has been energized to such an extent that neither side will find it easy to back away from its new status. Whether Western countries recognize India as a nuclear weapon state or not, Pakistan does, and will continue to treat India accordingly regardless of what government holds power in New Delhi.

Pakistanis believe that their strategic calculations are somewhat simpler, at least on the surface. Pakistani historians and political analysts argue that Pakistan's vulnerability was made evident in the 1965 and 1971 wars with India, and made it necessary to balance its dependence on outside sources for military assistance and to take steps on its own to counter India's conventional superiority. In 1965, many Pakistanis felt that the United States, when it cut off military assistance to both India and Pakistan during their August–September war, failed to honor its commitments under the terms of the U.S.-Pakistan defense agreements of the 1950s. Then in 1971, both China and the United States "stood by and watched" as India carved Pakistan into two parts, playing midwife to Bangladesh. This line of argument conveniently overlooks Pakistan's internal dislocations and failed policies, but nonetheless undergirds Pakistan's fairly consistent strategic argument that only an independent nuclear capability will (a) remain under Islamabad's exclusive control and (b) deter India from "finishing the job" it began in 1971. Described in these terms, Pakistan feels that it cannot afford to be seen as inferior to India or cowed by Indian behavior. Thus, at every technical turn, Pakistan will attempt to match any Indian development.

Islamabad's external focus, with its preoccupation on the need for nuclear deterrence, overlooks important internal issues that may prove more threatening to Pakistani security than any threat posed by India. The events leading up to the 1971 war provide a cautionary tale for Pakistan. It was not grievances with India that—depending on one's point of view—either forced or allowed India to exploit Pakistan's weakness. Rather, it was Pakistan's inability to resolve its internal ethnic problems that created conditions of insecurity.

Pakistan again faces extremely difficult internal challenges: in Karachi with the disenfranchisement of the Muttahida Quami Movement (MQM); in the Punjab with sectarian violence between Sunni and Shi'a; in Azad Kashmir with terrorist forces who may not respond to Islamabad's agenda; and throughout the country with the influence of the Taliban's success next door in Afghanistan, a success many credit Pakistan with enabling. Nuclear weapons will not solve any of those problems. For some, nuclear weapons provide a unifying symbol of Pakistani statehood, but just as the unifying symbol of Islam was by itself insufficient to hold the state together in the 1970–1971 crisis, so too the symbol of nuclear weapons may be insufficient to hold the country together. Vast economic reforms and social programs will provide a much sounder basis for national security than nuclear weapons, whose utility in serving the security needs of Pakistan is connected entirely to events in the past that were essentially domestic in nature. It may well be that Pakistan's nuclear capability will keep India at bay, but that capability will have no effect on the internal dislocations and failed social policies that again threaten to tear Pakistan asunder.

WEAPONIZATION, DEPLOYMENT, AND STABILITY

After the Pakistani tests, some scientists were quick to claim that the nuclear devices were already "weaponized" and ready to go on missiles. Less was said in India on this score, but in any case, certain questions now ought to be addressed by both sides. What does weaponization mean? Would the steps involved in weaponization increase or decrease stability? Is deployment desirable? What measures will enhance stability? Since the goal in developing nuclear capabilities presumably is to deter rather than to compel, what steps should be taken or avoided to increase stability and to ensure that war never breaks out? Did the overt nuclear posture calm the Kargil crisis once it erupted, or did the confrontation occur because nuclear weapons had been brought into the open? Not all of these questions can be answered here, but the need to address them cannot be avoided by strategic planners in New Delhi and Islamabad.

Although the starting point of weaponization is conceptually and physically different from the end point of deployment, a gray area exists where the two merge. It is also clear that a range of command and control mechanisms would have to come into play as a state moved from the basic step of testing a nuclear device toward more technically complicated measures. By way of definition, weaponization can be thought of as the process of developing, testing, and integrating warhead components into a militarily usable weapon system. Deployment can be defined as the process of transferring bombs and/or warheads to military units for storage and rapid mating with delivery systems at military bases.

The first necessary step in weaponization therefore is to design and test a weapon, which both India and Pakistan have done. The next steps grow increasingly complicated and call for extensive government integration and direction: ensuring that the nuclear devices are accident-proof; designating a delivery vehicle for the tested device; developing the arming, firing, and fusing mechanisms for the weapon; conducting environmental and delivery tests to ensure that the weapon system could survive harsh and diverse conditions; developing handling procedures for the weapon components; assigning responsibility for the weapon systems with respect to storage, physical protection, and delivery; and training the responsible personnel. Perhaps in peacetime, but more likely in time of crisis, it might be deemed necessary to deploy the weapons. This might involve mechanically preparing the delivery vehicles, transporting the weapons (or weapon components) to a staging site, final assembling of weapons, mating weapons with delivery vehicles, and delegating the authority to fire.

On the basis of the foregoing description of this process, it would appear that neither India nor Pakistan has taken steps to weaponize or deploy their nuclear capabilities. Indeed some analysts argue that these steps need not take place and will not take place, because both sides desire only recessed or latent deterrence—for India against China and Pakistan, and for Pakistan against India. Restraint with respect to weaponization and deployment would help to stabilize crises and ensure that nuclear weapons were not used without authorization. Given the lack of any established pattern of high-level communication or crisis management in a nuclear environment between and among these states, it might be highly destabilizing to take some of the weaponization steps. The boundary between a "just-in-case" capability and a "ready-for-use" capability becomes difficult to distinguish as weaponization proceeds. When a country slides into a commitment to prepare weapons for use, it creates enormous uncertainties about intentions and may accelerate the pace of competition while undermining the basis for reassurance and accommodation. All sides would benefit from having a very long fuse on their respective nuclear capabilities should a crisis arise or conflict worsen. Avoiding the heightened readiness associated with weaponization would ensure that when tension rises between the two sides, neither is in a position to take sudden action.

This is all the more true with respect to deployment issues. During a crisis, stability is increased if final assembly has not been completed, if last-minute wiring remains undone, and if weapons are not already mated to delivery vehicles. Avoiding deployment would improve safe handling during periods of high tensions, extend the time available for negotiation, minimize the negative effects of inadequate real-time intelligence, and maintain executive control at all times. Public brandishing of the nuclear capabilities places heavy psychological burdens on executives; the best assurance against early or unauthorized use of these capabilities and the best way to reduce stress are therefore to avoid weaponization and deployment.

COMMAND AND CONTROL

Beyond showing restraint regarding weaponization and deployment, it is not clear what steps, if any, either state has taken to create command-and-control mechanisms to reinforce the kind of stability that nonweaponization and nondeployment would create. China's nuclear program has a lengthy history, and includes established command-and-control mechanisms. Both India and Pakistan have organizations whose responsibility, though somewhat unclear, appears to include at least rudimentary command and control. India's Defense Research and Development

Organization (DRDO) claimed responsibility for the nuclear tests and may now be responsible for the stewardship of India's nuclear capability. The Pakistan Atomic Energy Commission (PAEC) and A. Q. Khan Research Laboratories (KRL) jointly claimed credit for Pakistan's tests, but overall supervision of Pakistan's strategic planning (and therefore its nuclear capability) may fall under the Combat Development Directorate (CDD).

An extensive discussion of command and control can be found elsewhere, but it is worth reiterating that an important value in constructing such control modalities is that they send the message both in peacetime and during crises that the central authorities—with whom negotiations to end a crisis or to provide reassurance will be conducted—remain in full control of the nuclear capability.[4] A balance must be struck between preparing for the possibility that deterrence will fail (in which

TABLE 9.2

INDIAN BALLISTIC MISSILE CAPABILITIES

LAND-BASED MISSILES

Type	First Tested	Range (km)	Payload (kg)	Technological Characteristics	Comments
Prithvi (Army)	Feb. 1988	150	1,000	Single stage, liquid fuel, road mobile	1994 army ordered 75 of which 20–50 have been delivered to the 333d regiment.
Prithvi II (Airforce)	Feb. 1996	250	500	Single stage, liquid fuel, road mobile	1994 airforce ordered 25.
Prithvi III (Dhanush)	Development	350	500	Single stage, solid fuel??	Untested, sea-launched naval version.
Agni	May 1989 (failed) Feb. 1994	2,500	1,000	Two stage, first uses SLV-3, second Prithvi I	Tested to a range of 1,400 km. Successfully validated India's reentry vehicle technology and basic guidance systems.
Agni II	Apr. 1999	2,500–3,000	1,000	Two stage, solid fuel, rail mobile	Tested to a range of 2,000 km on April 11, 1999; 20 missiles under order to be deployed by the end of 2001.
Agni III	N/A	3,500	1,000	?	To be developed using PSLV technology.

SUBMARINE-LAUNCHED BALLISTIC MISSILES

Type	First Tested	Range (km)	Payload (kg)	Technological Characteristics	Comments
Sagarika	N/A	300?	500?	?	Russian aid in development?

Table prepared by the Carnegie Non-Proliferation Project and does not necessarily represent the views of the author.

PAKISTANI BALLISTIC MISSILE CAPABILITIES

LAND-BASED MISSILES

Type	First Tested	Range (km)	Payload (kg)	Technological Characteristics	Comments
M-11	mid-1990 (Chinese test)	290	800	Single stage, solid fuel	30+ stored in canisters at Sargodha Air Force Base near Lahore
Hatf-I	Apr. 1988	80	500	Single stage, solid fuel	Developed with Chinese assistance
Hatf-II	Apr. 1988	300	500	Single stage, solid fuel	Discontinued
Hatf-III	July 1997 (failed)	600	500	Single stage, solid fuel	Based on a Chinese M-9 missile? Failed test flight.
Shaheen (Hatf V)	Apr. 14, 1999	750	1,000	Single stage, solid fuel	Possibly a successful test flight of the Haft-III. Developed by Pakistan Atomic Energy Commission
Ghauri (Hatf V)	Apr. 6, 1998	1,500	700	Single stage, liquid fuel	Tested to 1,100 km. Developed by A. Q. Khan Laboratories.
Ghauri II (Hatf VI)	Apr. 14, 1999	2,000	1,000	Single stage, liquid fuel	Tested to 1,165 km on April 14.

Table prepared by the Carnegie Non-Proliferation Project and does not necessarily represent the views of the author.

case each state will want to be sure it is able to respond) and maintaining civilian political control over the weapons and their delivery vehicles. If deterrence fails, it is in no state's interest to have the result be indiscriminate nuclear attacks on the enemy. At the same time, no side wants nuclear decision making to fall under the purview of groups—such as the military or the scientific community—who lack legitimate authority as well as the broader perspective that political leadership requires. The issue of command and control therefore brings into question the role of the military in both India and Pakistan, as well as the role of their respective scientific communities.

India's uniformed services apparently continue to be excluded from strategic decision making and from nuclear issues. The services have proposed that a National Command Authority be established as a high-level command institution, with a National Strategic Nuclear Command reporting to it and comprising military and technical personnel. Whether this proposal ever is accepted remains to be seen. Pakistan's military already appears to play a central role in developing overall strategy through the CDD. With the move from a covert to an overt nuclear status, it may be all the more important that the management of nuclear capabilities not be excessively compartmented, in order to ensure against accidental or unauthorized use. Keeping the military ignorant does not ensure against unauthorized use. It only guarantees that if and when nuclear capabilities are handed over to military units—in a crisis, most likely—they will be no better prepared to use the weapons than they would be to avoid using them. Even though the probability of untoward or unexpected action is low, the consequence of failing to prevent it is immeasurably high in a nuclear environment.

Although India appears to have chosen to exclude the military, which may increase risks in a crisis, it does have a centralized and coherent scientific community with important responsibilities. Indian analysts have questioned that scientific enclave's accountability and direction, but not its focus. In contrast, Pakistan has evidently involved its military in strategic planning, but has a scientific community that appears at odds with itself, which may create similar risks. As noted above, both the PAEC and the KRL claimed responsibility for the nuclear tests and both are competing in the missile development area as well. Competition between the two institutions, as well as personal animosity, has flared into the open in the past. Islamabad must impose some coherence on these competing bureaucracies to ensure central control in time of crisis.

SOURCES OF INSECURITY

The decisions by India and Pakistan to test nuclear weapons gave prominence to the role of deterrence in addressing their security needs. The sources of insecurity that drove the nuclear programs may also be susceptible to reassurance and accommodation, however, and should be examined with that in mind.

The lack of internal cohesion of the Pakistani state, coupled with the continuing dispute over Kashmir, has created important insecurities in the modern history of the subcontinent. Pakistan's historical concerns about India date from the reluctance on the part of many Indian nationalists in 1947 to support the partition of the subcontinent. Although by now it is rare to hear Indians question that historical fact, the rise to power of the BJP alarms many in Pakistan. The BJP's support for Hindu nationalism awakens memories of the turbulent origins of the two states and reinforces Pakistanis' sense that India is insensitive to the rights of minorities, Muslims included. On India's side, most analysts argue that the existence of Pakistan and the fact of partition are unquestioned realities, while they point to India's constitutional and statutory defense of ethnic and religious minority rights (especially Muslims and in Kashmir) as ample evidence of India's fundamentally democratic approach.

Memories of the creation of Bangladesh in 1971 also continue to create insecurities for many Pakistanis who fear that India will exploit its internal weakness to further destabilize it. Although most Pakistanis acknowledge that the insurrection and disruption within East Pakistan in the late 1960s and early 1970s was created by Pakistan's own policies, many analysts continue to argue that India took advantage of this internal dislocation and may do so again. Indians respond that Pakistan's internal policies in 1970–71, which sent ten million refugees into India, created threats to India's own delicate internal fabric and were tolerated for many months before action was taken.

In any case, so it is argued in New Delhi, the shoe is by now on the other foot as Pakistan continues not only to support insurrection within Jammu and Kashmir but to foment war along the Line of Control (LOC), as was made evident by the Kargil battles in mid-1999. Pakistan insists that the Kashmir dispute can only be resolved when the international community honors the United Nations (UN) resolutions of the 1950s that call for a plebiscite within the state after armed forces have been withdrawn from both the Indian and Pakistani sectors. It is rare that Indians and Pakistanis agree on how to interpret the UN resolutions, and still rarer to find agreement about how to resolve this issue peacefully.

India's concerns with China tend to receive less attention internationally, and indeed within India as well. But it cannot be forgotten that a war was fought in 1962 over border disputes that remain unresolved. Furthermore, conservative Indian strategic analysts are alarmed by a variety of Chinese actions, which, as they see it, portend a more aggressive and militant Chinese foreign policy in the future. China's rapidly expanding economy, nuclear weapon modernization effort, naval expansion, attitude toward the Spratly Islands, coziness with Myanmar, arms acquisitions from Russia, willingness to fire lethal missiles over Taiwan, and lack of democratic process all conspire, in the view of some Indians, to make China a serious threat to India's long-term interests. Against this background, nuclear weapons presumably offer to redress India's insecurities.

For its part, China professes not to understand Indian concerns, and argues that Sino-Indian border discussions had been proceeding favorably before the BJP assumed power. In any case, China's initial reaction of regret at India's tests appeared to be more connected with the challenge India's tests presented to the NPT and the Comprehensive Test Ban Treaty (CTBT) than with the challenge they presented to Chinese security. The Sino-Indian dispute over the McMahon Line, which describes their de facto border, is an issue that, in Beijing's view, is "left over from history" and should not result in armed conflict.

The point in recounting this history is not to assign blame or to seek vindication but to recognize that the problems between India and Pakistan and India and China have not been eliminated. The sources of past conflict continue to be part of the South Asian landscape. As noted above, however, that landscape was transformed by the overt display of nuclear and missile capabilities. The power of the weaponry each side now brandishes has changed by orders of magnitude, yet the potential sources of conflict remain the same.

Some strategic analysts—K. Subrahmanyam in particular—argue that the creation of this capability now makes conflict less likely, as all sides are deterred from hostile acts that could lead to war. As evidence, Subrahmanyam points to the decision by Pakistan to fire on demonstrators on its own side of the LOC to prevent their storming into Indian Kashmir, and to the reluctance of Indian leaders to authorize military pursuit into Pakistan Occupied (Azad) Kashmir.[5] Alternately, analysts like Sumit Ganguly note the problem of the stability-instability paradox, where robust deterrence at the strategic level raises not only the threshold for low-intensity conflict but also the risk of unintended war.[6] Local terrorists, assuming that national governments are prepared to tolerate low-level conflict in a nuclear environment, may therefore escalate their actions with the result that state-to-state relations are worsened and tensions increased.

Until the origins of the 1999 "warlike situation" in Kargil become clearer, it will be difficult to prove either argument. Did Pakistan refrain from going further because it feared escalation? Did local troublemakers create the crisis to insert their own voice into the decision-making process? Regardless of which argument one subscribes to, however, in an environment of overt nuclear competition the stakes of either side being wrong are so great that enormous new burdens are placed on the leadership in India and Pakistan. In an environment where nuclear weapons may be available on both sides, neither New Delhi nor Islamabad can afford to make policy on the assumption that deterrence will always work or that the lid on low-intensity conflict will never blow.

The critical feature that must supplement the new nuclear status is a sustained, institutionalized dialogue. A nuclear confrontation is different because neither side can afford to suffer the consequences if the dialogue fails. The other side to deterrence is defense, and in a world where defense is unavailable against nuclear-armed missiles, it is all the more incumbent on national leaders to keep dialogue open. The point is not that India and Pakistan or India and China must agree, but rather that if they choose to forgo dialogue, contentious though it may be, not only will the issues persist but the consequences of their flaring out of control will pose enormous dangers for which no one is prepared.

REASSURANCE AND ACCOMMODATION

The next steps that must be taken to establish a basis for dialogue involve providing some form of reassurance and accommodation. A number of confidence-building measures have been proposed over the years, and a few have been adopted, but an air of impatience and frustration tends to greet this issue as India and Pakistan in particular talk past each other. The option of falling back on nuclear threats runs serious risks, however, so all sides may want to consider areas where they could perhaps reassure the others about their insecurities, while considering how to accommodate some of the other's concerns. The most prominent concerns, as noted above, involve Kashmir specifically, border disputes in general and internal national cohesion.

Following the near-disastrous Kargil gambit, it would be reassuring to India if Pakistan were to announce that it opposed terrorism in all its forms and supported a peaceful resolution to the Kashmir dispute. In this vein, Pakistan could announce that it was ceasing all logistical and training support to all Kashmiri forces operating within Azad Kashmir, and take meaningful enforcement steps to back that commitment. Pakistan's leaders are extremely sensitive to Kashmir issues, and politicians would risk losing votes by appearing to "abandon" Kashmir. At the same time, however, those within Pakistan who feel that they can interminably bleed India by supporting cross-border terrorism should not be allowed to dictate the terms of Pakistan's policy on Kashmir. The longer Pakistan's elected leaders allow (or support) such activities, the more Pakistan's other domestic problems will fester. Allowing the practice of cross-border terrorism to dictate policy effectively legitimizes the behavior, and Pakistan simply cannot afford to support a policy in Kashmir that if applied within Pakistan's borders would threaten the integrity of the state. The current government's failure to make good on what may have been unwise promises to rename the Northwest Frontier Area Pakhtunkhawa, coupled with the breakdown of its alliance with the MQM in Karachi, makes it and Pakistan as a whole all the more vulnerable if the government fails to condemn external interference elsewhere.

For its part, India could accommodate Pakistani concerns, which are directed at the welfare of Kashmiri Muslims. A clear commitment to draw down forces within the state in response to reduced terrorist violence would benefit the weary people who have suffered for a decade. A reduction in chauvinist and confrontational rhetoric would also help, though Pakistan should be reassured by the BJP's decision not to attempt to force through a conservative Hindu social agenda since it assumed power in 1998. In the changed nuclear environment, however, it is not unfair to ask for more, and a clear statement from New Delhi that it respected and supported Pakistan's internal integrity would provide reassurance to Islamabad on this sensitive point.

Regarding border issues, India could reassure China that its nuclear demonstration was not intended as New Delhi's own way of "blackmailing" China by reiterating that it is committed to the peaceful settlement of the border dispute. Although some conservative Indians argue that the border discussions were less productive than advertised, the principle of negotiation ought to be reinforced, especially following Defense Minister George Fernandes's belligerent statements directed at China, Prime Minister A. B. Vajpayee's indiscreet letter to President Clinton citing China as the reason for India's insecurity, and the nuclear tests themselves.

INSTITUTIONAL MEASURES

The types of reassurance suggested above may be offered, but they are likely to be lost in the noise if not made in an institutionalized form. It could therefore reinforce all parties' commitments to the principle of settling their differences by peaceful means if multilateral institutions were established that codified and raised the status of reassuring statements. It might be useful therefore if standing committees were established to discuss Kashmir and border disputes and if the well-established principle of noninterference in the internal affairs of other states were reinforced. Eliminating indiscriminate firing across the LOC, reducing inflammatory propaganda, providing media access, and safeguarding human rights could all be referred to standing committees in order to provide an ongoing forum for the airing of grievances. In a more general sense, it is important to segregate the causes of conflict in Kashmir from the new nuclear capabilities. Thus it is incumbent on India's and Pakistan's political leaders to address the dangers associated with their recent arms developments forthrightly. The logic of minimum deterrence is insufficient to ensure that war is avoided. When the nuclear programs were kept under a cloak of ambiguity, tacit measures may have been sufficient to provide reassurance. With these programs out in the open, tacit measures must be supplemented with more focused and unambiguous dialogue.

Beyond the role of reassurance on standing disputes, however, lies the question of how to cope with the overt nuclear confrontation created by the tests. Regardless of what else happens, it is extremely important that India and Pakistan in particular engage in some kind of discussion to maintain political control over the scientific and military accomplishments demonstrated in May. (Sino-Indian dialogue should not be ignored, but the nuclear dangers in this relationship still lie somewhere in the future.) After the tests, scientists in both countries may be proud, and military leaders may feel renewed confidence, but political leaders have an increased burden to keep the peace. Peace will not be kept if scientists are encouraged or allowed to develop more and better technical capabilities, while the military's understandable tendency to engage in worst-case thinking has historically produced incomplete analyses of a country's threat environment. Political leaders simply must assert their authority over single-issue bureaucratic actors.

Although joining international regimes is no substitute for direct dialogue, it is salutary that India and Pakistan have declared unilateral moratoria on further testing. In addition, both must engage in good-faith negotiations at the Conference on Disarmament on fissile material controls. This too is not a substitute for direct dialogue, but it is demonstrative of their mutual seriousness of purpose. It would be even more helpful if they now agreed to a moratorium on the production of fissile material while the negotiations proceed. Here they may both pose objections to the extent that they feel that their supplies are inadequate to serve their strategic needs. Again, however, it is important that the scientific and military enclaves not dictate the terms of the debate even before it is engaged. Both India and Pakistan have said they seek only a minimum deterrent. Toward that end, they should be prepared to accept controls on their own fissile material production in order to avoid each side's chasing some impossible answer to the question "How much is enough?" The South African model should be emulated: tight controls were placed on the scientific community, and parts for only seven weapons were actually constructed. India's and Pakistan's political leaders can assert their authority over civilian scientists to ensure that debate over the merits of the Fissile Material Cut-Off Treaty is not hijacked like the nuclear testing debate.

CONCLUSION

With their nuclear and missile tests, India and Pakistan have concentrated the world's and their own attention on a key aspect of security. That aspect alone does not guarantee the security of either nation, a point made clear in the USSR and South Africa, where economic and social security were far more important than military security. It is also clear that nuclear deterrence does not prevent all forms of conflict, as was made evident by the Kargil confrontation. Having decided to emphasize military security, however, India's and Pakistan's nuclear threats must now be complemented by enhanced diplomatic engagement between India and China on one side and India and Pakistan on another. India can certainly take a leading role in this arena, just as it did with the nuclear test series it began in 1998.

In addition to the broad conclusion that nuclear threats must be accompanied by reassurance and accommodation, a number of specific points also emerge:

- Weaponization of nuclear capabilities would increase crisis instability and should be avoided.

- Deployment of nuclear capabilities would be highly destabilizing under any circumstances.
- Military and scientific research and development must be guided and controlled by political decision makers to avoid isolated bureaucratic enclaves from hijacking decision making.
- In the new nuclear environment, which has not eliminated conflict in Kashmir, both sides should commit to resolve that issue without recourse to arms.
- Nuclear "blackmail" cannot substitute for diplomatic dialogue on contentious territorial and other disputes.
- Nuclear capabilities will not solve domestic ethnic and sectarian conflicts, which must be addressed with respect for minority rights.
- Nuclear threats must be accompanied by bilateral discussions across a range of issues, such as:
    a) missile research and development;
    b) military-to-military relations;
    c) crisis communication centers;
    d) scientific exchange and cooperation.

The world is made less safe with the addition of new nuclear-capable nations. India and Pakistan would argue that to the extent this is true, their incremental addition pales in significance when compared with the arsenals of the five declared nuclear weapon states. But the burden of responsibility is a consequence of technical capability, not of stockpile size or nuclear tests. Countries like Japan, Sweden, Germany, Italy, Argentina, Brazil, Kazakhstan, and Ukraine have similar technical capability, yet they have concluded that their national security, and international security, is best served by forgoing developing or maintaining that capability. India and Pakistan have drawn different conclusions, however. They now bear the added burden of ensuring that these new capabilities are never used.

SUPPLEMENT ON FISSILE MATERIAL AND NUCLEAR WEAPONS IN INDIA AND PAKISTAN
By David Albright

Estimating the size of India's and Pakistan's inventory of separated weapon-grade plutonium and highly enriched uranium (HEU) has become more difficult following their nuclear tests in May 1998. Both countries treat the size of their nuclear material stockpiles as highly classified information, partly because such estimates provide a direct indication of the number of nuclear weapons they possess.

In the case of Pakistan, it can be surmised that it has resumed full-scale production of HEU, following a declared moratorium on such production since 1991. Abdul Q. Khan, the father of Pakistan's uranium enrichment program, announced soon after Pakistan's nuclear tests that his country had never stopped making HEU. Although his comment has been greeted skeptically, it indicates that Pakistan may have resumed production of weapon-grade uranium well before its tests in May 1998.

Exactly how long before the tests Pakistan resumed making weapon-grade uranium is not too important in these calculations. During its moratorium, Pakistan produced low-enriched uranium (LEU), which can be upgraded to weapon-grade uranium relatively rapidly. Given the length of the moratorium, this stock of LEU is relatively large and can lead to a rapid increase in Pakistan's stock of weapon-grade uranium.

In addition, in April 1998 Pakistan announced that the Khushab reactor had begun operating. There are few reports, however, indicating whether the reactor is operating consistently, or if its irradiated fuel has been processed into separated plutonium. This reactor, in theory, could make enough plutonium for a few nuclear weapons per year.

With regard to India, information suggests that it is trying to increase the size of its stock of weapon-grade plutonium, and perhaps HEU. There has been some discussion in India of building a new plutonium production reactor. India also may be considering using its civil power reactors to increase its stock of weapon-grade plutonium. In addition, the debate about whether one of the Indian tests used reactor-grade plutonium is unresolved, leaving unanswered whether India considers its civil unsafeguarded power reactors and plutonium stock, at least potentially, a part of its nuclear weapons program.

Faced with a swirling mixture of solid and ambiguous information, the author used a new analytical approach to estimate India's stock of weapon-grade plutonium and Pakistan's stock of weapon-grade uranium. This new approach specifically aims to capture the varying and conflicting information about key parameters affecting estimates of the size of the inventories. Rather than using a best estimate of a specific parameter, such as lifetime reactor operating capacity, a distribution of possible values is derived. In this way, various choices can be assigned a probability of being true. U.S. officials, for example, have recommended strongly that India's Cirus and Dhruva plutonium production reactors have a lifetime capacity factor of about 40 percent. Indian officials have stated that the average capacity factor is significantly greater, as large as 60 to 70 percent. In this estimate, the most likely choice is selected as 40 percent, while values up to 60 to 70 percent are given a diminishing probability of occurring. On the other end, a lifetime capacity factor less than 30 percent is viewed as highly unlikely. In the case of Pakistan's total enrichment capacity at the Kahuta and the newer Gadwal facilities, a wide range of possible values is given equal probability of occurring.

Using Crystal Ball software, these distributions are sampled using a "Monte Carlo" approach to derive a distribution of results. This method varies from previous approaches used by the author, where central or best estimates are derived and an uncertainty is attached by making a judgment about the overall data and information. Although judgments are still necessary in any uncertainty analysis, they can be applied more credibly in this more advanced method.

India's inventory of weapon-grade plutonium is derived by estimating total production in its reactors and by subtracting drawdowns from nuclear testing, processing losses, and civil uses of the weapon-grade plutonium. The median value, which is the value midway between the smallest and largest value, is about 295 kilograms of weapon-grade plutonium at the end of 1998. The range in the values can be understood by considering the set of all values, which in this case vary between 160 kilograms and 460 kilograms. Because values in the tails of the range carry a very low probability of being true, often only the values that fall between the 10th and 90th percentile are considered, which in this case are 240 kilograms and 355 kilograms, respectively. To be more certain that the actual value lies in this range, the 5th and 95th percentiles can be selected, which are 225 kilograms and 370 kilograms, respectively. One way to interpret the results is that, in the latter case, there is 90 percent certainty that the true value lies between 225 and 370 kilograms of weapon-grade plutonium, where the median value is about 295 kilograms. Table 9.4 shows these values and the estimated number of nuclear weapons at the end of 1998.

Pakistan's inventory of weapon-grade uranium is derived by estimating several factors, including total enrichment capacity and the feedstock into the enrichment plant, and by subtracting drawdowns. An important factor in this calculation is that in 1998 LEU, widely reported to have been produced during the HEU moratorium from 1991 to 1998, was upgraded in the enrichment plants to weapon-grade uranium. This significantly increases Pakistan's inventory of weapon-grade uranium. However, this rate of growth in the inventory cannot be sustained because Pakistan will run out of LEU. Table 9.4 shows the results for the end of 1998.

Each country has additional stocks of plutonium and HEU. As mentioned above, Pakistan has started a reactor that can make weapon-grade plutonium. The amount that is separated cannot be estimated, although it is relatively small as of the end of 1998. Similarly, India operates a small enrichment plant that can, in theory, make HEU, although the amount produced so far is unknown. In any case, this amount is believed to be relatively small.

Estimates can also be made of the amount of reactor-grade plutonium in India and Pakistan. These estimates, which are taken from the Institute for Science and International Security's *Plutonium Watch*, are in table 9.4. Their uncertainty is judged to be about 20 percent. Almost all of this civil plutonium is in spent fuel, and is thus not suitable for use in nuclear weapons.

TABLE 9.4

ESTIMATED FISSILE MATERIAL AND NUCLEAR WEAPONS IN INDIA AND PAKISTAN, END 1998

	INDIA	PAKISTAN
IAEA Safeguarded Civil Plutonium—Separated (kgs)	25	0
IAEA Safeguarded Civil Plutonium—Unseparated (kgs)	3,800	0
Unsafeguarded Civil Plutonium—Separated (kgs)	700	0
Unsafeguarded Civil Plutonium—Unseparated (kgs)	3,000	600
Weapon-grade Plutonium (kgs)	225–370	?
Weapon-grade Uranium (kgs)	?	425–680
Nuclear Weapons	40–90	22–43

NOTES

1. Part of this study was carried out for the Department of Energy by Lawrence Livermore National Laboratory, University of California under contract W-7405-Eng-48. The views and materials expressed are the author's and do not necessarily reflect or state those of the University of California or the United States government. Tables 9.1–9.3 presented in this chapter were prepared by the staff of the Carnegie Non-Proliferation Project and do not necessarily reflect the views of the author.

2. Michael Howard, "Deterrence and Reassurance," *Foreign Affairs* 61, no. 2 (winter 1982–83): 309–24.

3. Itty Abraham, "India's 'Strategic Enclave'; Civilian Scientists and Military Technologies," *Armed Forces and Society*, vol. 18, no. 2 (winter 1992).

4. Neil Joeck, "Maintaining Nuclear Stability in South Asia," Adelphi Paper no. 312 (Oxford, U.K.: Oxford University Press for the International Institute for Strategic Studies, 1997), 52–64.

5. K. Subrahmanyam, "Nuclear India," *Indian Defence Review*, 13, no. 2 (April–June 1998): 15.

6. Sumit Ganguly, "Indo-Pakistani Nuclear Issues and the Stability/Instability Paradox," *Defence Today* 4, no. 2, April–June 1996: 185–93.

—10—

The Economic Impacts of the Glenn Amendment: Lessons from India and Pakistan

Daniel Morrow and Michael Carriere

On May 11 and 13, 1998, the BJP government of India conducted a series of nuclear tests in the barren deserts of the Pokhran region. In response to these tests, neighboring Pakistan conducted its own round of nuclear explosions on May 28, 1998, in the Chagai Hills of Baluchistan. As required by law (under the Glenn Amendment), the United States immediately placed both nations under economic sanctions. According to Undersecretary of State Strobe Talbott, who has become the chief U.S. interlocutor with the South Asian neighbors since their respective tests:

> [The sanctions imposed on India and Pakistan] were necessary for several reasons. First, it's the law. Second, sanctions create a disincentive for other states to exercise the nuclear option if they are contemplating it. And third, sanctions are part of our effort to keep faith with the much larger number of nations that have renounced nuclear weapons despite their capacity to develop them.[1]

Just six months after the sanctions were announced, however, the United States had lifted virtually all of the economic sanctions that were imposed on India and Pakistan following their nuclear bomb tests in May 1998. The process of weakening the sanctions in place against India and Pakistan had actually begun in July 1998, when the Senate voted to exempt food exports from sanctions.[2] On October 21, 1998, Congress passed the Brownback Amendment, which gave President Clinton the authority to waive certain economic sanctions in place against India and Pakistan and to resume trade financing and other assistance programs for up to twelve months. President Clinton wasted little time in using this waiver authority. On November 6, 1998, the president's declaration, officially titled the "India-Pakistan Relief Act," waived the prohibitions in place against the activities of the United States Export-Import Bank, the Overseas Private Investment Corporation (OPIC), and the Trade Development Agency in both India and Pakistan. Perhaps most important, the presidential waiver also authorized U.S. officials to support loans to Pakistan from the International Monetary Fund (IMF) and the World Bank.[3] On June 9, 1999, the U.S. Senate voted to extend the waiver authority created by the Brownback Amendment for another five years, in the form of an amendment attached to an approved defense appropriations bill.[4]

While the Brownback Amendment has, for the time being, rolled back almost all of the original sanctions placed on India and Pakistan, the Glenn Amendment—the legislation that required the imposition of the sanctions—remains on the books. Hence, the policy question remains: Should the United States keep the Glenn Amendment—or similar automatic, unilateral sanctions against nuclear proliferators—in place?

It is therefore important to evaluate the impacts of the economic sanctions on India and Pakistan and consider, based on this assessment, whether or not such sanctions might constitute a meaningful disincentive to future nuclear proliferators in the decades ahead. The debate about the future utility of the Glenn Amendment needs to be grounded on such a factual assessment. In this chapter, we seek to establish the facts about what official sanctions were imposed by the United States and others and what direct and indirect effects they had on the Indian and Pakistani economies.

We begin by assembling the facts about what official sanctions were applied and about their specific effects on U.S. transactions with India and Pakistan. Then we consider the changes in capital flows—flows that have become increasingly important in this era of globalization—for each country after their decisions to go nuclear and to what extent these changes might be attributed to the sanctions. The concluding section of this chapter discusses the implications of our findings for the future utility of the Glenn Amendment.[5]

We hope that our assessment of the impact of the economic sanctions on India and Pakistan will contribute usefully to the ongoing debate concerning the efficacy of economic sanctions in general. Even before the South Asian nuclear tests, there was a growing consensus among many foreign policy analysts that the United States now relies too heavily on the use of economic sanctions and that such sanctions efforts have little effect on influencing the behavior of targeted nations.[6] Many argue that globalization has rendered sanctions ineffectual because targeted countries can always find another source for sanctioned trade and finance opportunities. "Globalization multiplies choices of where to invest, produce, buy, sell and cheat in order to achieve national goals," writes the *Washington Post*'s Stephen S. Rosenfeld. "A country blocked on one avenue simply tries another."[7] This notion of globalization's weakening the possible impacts of sanctions is echoed in a recent study done by Richard N. Haass, director of Foreign Policy Studies at the Brookings Institution. According to Haass, "At least in theory, this greater degree of globalization (and the somewhat reduced centrality of the nation-state) ought to have an adverse impact overall on the effectiveness of sanctions. A target state now has many more potential suppliers and markets—and a would-be sanctioner has many more entities to enlist before sanctions are likely to be effective."[8] This study of the impacts of sanctions on the economies of India and Pakistan should shed some light on whether or not globalization does indeed render sanctions ineffective.

THE OFFICIAL SANCTIONS BY THE UNITED STATES AND OTHERS

The United States, under the Glenn Amendment (section 102 of the larger Arms Export Control Act of 1994), was lawfully required to impose sanctions on India and Pakistan after their May 1998 nuclear tests.[9] This legislation, authored by former senator John Glenn (D–Ohio), stipulates that when a non-nuclear weapon state detonates a nuclear explosive device, the U.S. administration must impose an extensive set of sanctions on the offending country, as summarized in table 10.1.

TABLE 10.1

SANCTIONS REQUIRED BY THE GLENN AMENDMENT

The Glenn Amendment to the International Security and Development Cooperation Act of 1985 requires the president to impose these seven sanctions:

- Suspend foreign aid (except for humanitarian assistance or food and other agricultural commodities);
- Terminate sales of any military items;
- Terminate other military assistance;
- Stop credits or guarantees to the country by U.S. government agencies;
- Vote against credits or assistance by international financial institutions;
- Prohibit U.S. banks from making loans to the foreign government concerned; and
- Prohibit exports of specific goods and technology [as specified in the Export Administration Act of 1979] with civilian and military nuclear applications.

Passed into law on April 30, 1994, the Glenn Amendment clarified and amplified previous non-proliferation legislation, that is, the Glenn/Symington Amendments to the Foreign Assistance Act of 1977 and the Nuclear Non-Proliferation Act of 1978.[10] Although the Glenn Amendment does allow the president to delay imposition of the sanctions for thirty days, it includes no provisions for removing the sanctions once they are imposed and grants no authority for waivers of any sort.[11]

The nuclear tests by India and Pakistan triggered these provisions for the first time. Immediately in response to each of these tests, President Clinton quickly announced and reported to Congress that the United States would impose the sanctions required by law. However, since they had never been invoked, working out the details took some time, and the actual sanctions were rolled out over a period of weeks. On June 18, 1998, the U.S. Department of State announced the details, along with the goals, of the sanctions, as summarized in table 10.2.[12]

The U.S. bilateral aid programs that were suspended were minuscule relative to India's public sector budget.[13] The termination of foreign assistance under the Foreign Assistance Act has cost India $51.3 million in aid this year from the United States, including $12 million in economic development assistance and $9 million under the Housing Guaranty program. Another $6 million earmarked for a greenhouse gas program was suspended in India, as was funding for a reproductive health program. Plans for an Indian electrical testing laboratory, to be partially funded by the United States Agency for International Development (USAID) and designed to implement standards for energy consumption and efficiency, were postponed. Following the tests, the Trade Development Agency also announced that it would not be considering any new projects in the region.[14]

United States government lending institutions also severed their ties with India after the May explosions. The U.S. Export-Import Bank (EXIM) estimated that the

---

TABLE 10.2

Summary of Fact Sheet
INDIA AND PAKISTAN SANCTIONS
Released by the Bureau of Economic and Agricultural Affairs
United States Department of State, June 18, 1998

The United States imposed sanctions on India and Pakistan as a result of their nuclear tests in May. Imposing these sanctions, the U.S. sought:
- To send a strong message to would-be nuclear testers;
- To have maximum influence on Indian and Pakistani behavior;
- To target the governments, rather than the people; and
- To minimize the damage to other U.S. interests.

The goals of the United States are that India and Pakistan:
- Halt further nuclear testing;
- Sign the Comprehensive Test Ban Treaty (CTBT) immediately and without conditions;
- Not deploy or test missiles or nuclear weapons;
- Cut off fissile material production for nuclear weapons;
- Cooperate in Fissile Material Cut-Off Treaty (FMCT) negotiations in Geneva;
- Maintain and formalize restraints on sharing sensitive goods and technologies with other countries; and
- Reduce bilateral tensions, including Kashmir.

Accordingly, the United States:
- Terminated or suspended foreign assistance under the Foreign Assistance Act, with exceptions provided by law (e.g., humanitarian assistance, food, or other agricultural commodities).
- Terminated foreign military sales under the Arms Control Act, and revoked licenses for commercial sale of any item on the U.S. munitions list.
- Halted any new commitments of USG credits and credit guarantees by USG entities (including EXIM and OPIC).
- Gained G-8 support to postpone consideration of non-basic human needs (BHN) loans for India and Pakistan by the International Financial Institutions (IFIs) to bolster the effect of the Glenn Amendment requirement that the U.S. oppose non-BHN IFI loans.
- Will issue executive order to prohibit U.S. banks from extending loans or credits to the governments of India and Pakistan.
- Will deny export of all dual-use items controlled for nuclear or missile reasons. Will presume denial for all other dual-use exports to entities involved in nuclear or missile programs.

new prohibition on loans, loan guarantees, and credit insurance immediately affected approximately $500 million of U.S. exports to India in pending transactions. Based on indications of interest received by the bank, an additional $3.5 billion of exports might have been affected if the sanctions had remained in place. OPIC also announced that it too would cease approval of new projects in India. It is difficult to quantify the full impact of this decision: OPIC did not have a figure for the number of potential projects. We do know that India was one of OPIC's top five countries receiving support, an average of $300 million annually from the governmental organization.[15]

The Ex-Im Bank and OPIC sanctions affected several major projects in India. Enron Corporation, in a joint venture with GE Capital and Bechtel Enterprises, has started work on a $2.5 billion power plant south of Bombay with partial funding from both the Ex-Im Bank and OPIC. Following the imposition of sanctions, this project was delayed indefinitely. In the southern city of Mangalore, withdrawal of $350 million in funding from the Ex-Im Bank stalled the San Francisco–based Cogentrix Energy Company's plan for a thousand-megawatt power plant.[16] The contract for a joint telecommunications venture between Hughes Network Systems and the Indian company Ipsat was voided. According to Hughes CEO Jack Shaw: "We invoked the 'force majeure [clause]'[17] because the sanctions deprived the project of political risk insurance from the U.S. Ex-Im Bank on $400 million offshore debt, thereby delaying the financial close indefinitely."[18]

In the case of Pakistan, the loss of U.S. bilateral assistance was not a factor following the May 1998 tests because Pakistan was already under U.S. sanctions imposed by the 1985 Pressler Amendment. This law specified that U.S. aid and government-to-government military sales to Pakistan would be cut off unless the president certifies that Pakistan did "not possess a nuclear explosive device and that the proposed U.S. assistance program will not significantly reduce the risk that Pakistan will possess a nuclear explosive device."[19] In October 1990, the Bush administration declined to make the certification required by the Pressler Amendment and sanctions were placed on Pakistan. Since 1990, both the Bush and Clinton administrations have denied this certification. As a result, there were no bilateral aid flows that had to be cut under the Glenn Amendment.[20]

The Glenn Amendment sanctions also had little effect on the relationship between Pakistan and U.S. government lending institutions, as these associations were still in the formative process at the time of the tests. The Ex-Im Bank had opened for short- and medium-term programs for the public and private sectors in Pakistan in February 1998, and OPIC had only reopened in March 1998. Due to the relatively short amount of time that both institutions had been open for business in Pakistan, only a few projects were postponed by the sanctions.[21]

It was widely assumed in the United States that as has been the case with many other economic sanctions, the United States was alone in this effort to punish the nuclear offenders. This was not the case. Fourteen countries, including Japan, Germany, Australia, Canada, Denmark, and Sweden, suspended bilateral aid programs as a sanction against India and Pakistan. Among these, only the Japanese sanctions involved significant amounts. Japan canceled development loans worth

$1.2 billion to India, as well as $30 million in grant aid. They also suspended all loans to Pakistan, which totaled $231 million in 1997–98, and canceled grant aid of approximately $55 million.[22] The other bilateral programs that were suspended were very small. Germany called off bilateral aid talks with India and put a hold on new development aid worth $168 million. Denmark froze $28 million in aid to India, Sweden canceled $119 million in assistance, and Canada suspended approximately $9.8 million of nonhumanitarian aid to the South Asian country. Australia, a relatively small lender to South Asia, canceled all nonhumanitarian aid to India, $2.6 million. While all of its aid to Pakistan was classified as humanitarian and therefore not canceled, Australia refrained from a planned increase in aid of $2.5 million.[23]

More important, all of the G-7 countries, along with a number of non–G-7 nations, joined the United States in opposing new nonhumanitarian lending by the IMF, the World Bank, and the Asian Development Bank to India and Pakistan. The common stance of the G-8 countries (the United States, the United Kingdom, France, Germany, Japan, Italy, Canada, and Russia) was announced at the G-8 summit in London on June 12, 1998. This was significant because the United States holds less than 18 percent of the voting shares in these institutions. Contrary to a commonly held belief in the United States, the United States does not have de jure veto power over lending by the IMF and World Bank. In fact, together the G-7 countries have only about 45 percent of the votes in the IMF and the World Bank. Other states such as the Nordic countries are required to form a coalition commanding a majority of the voting shares in these two institutions.[24] The consequences of this coalition against nonhumanitarian lending by the IMF and World Bank will be considered below.

EFFECTS OF THE SANCTIONS ON INDIA'S CAPITAL FLOWS

What effect, if any, did these official sanctions have on the economy of the world's second-most-populous nation? The sanctions, if they have had any effect at all, would impact most directly on investments from foreign sources (official or private with official support such as Em-Im Bank financing). Therefore, the most practical approach to this question is examining changes in India's capital account, which records the flows of capital to and from the country, [25] and then considering to what extent any changes might be caused by the sanctions. Among the types of capital flows, the sanctions could potentially have impacts through three distinct channels:

- Changes in financial flows from bilateral creditors and agencies.
- Changes in flows from the international financial institutions (IFIs), especially the IMF and the World Bank.
- Changes in private capital flows as a direct or indirect response to the presence of the official sanctions.

Before examining these three categories of flows, consider the aggregate behavior of India's capital account. There was in fact a sharp decline in capital flows to India during the months following the nuclear tests in May. For April–June 1998 the net inflow was about $4.2 billion less than in the same quarter in 1997. This amount is modest but not insignificant relative to the whole Indian economy: It's equivalent to about 1 percent of GDP and 4 percent of gross domestic investment. Initially, this shrinkage in net capital inflows brought about a decline in India's foreign exchange reserves as shown in figure 10.1. This drop, however, did not induce any panic in the financial or foreign exchange markets because India's initial reserve position was very strong. At the end of April 1998 the foreign exchange reserves of $26 billion equaled about six months' worth of imports, which is considered very healthy. Furthermore, India was able to compensate for this initial loss of capital inflows through the sale of the so-called Resurgent India Bonds to nonresident Indians. This bond issue brought in over $4 billion, and by October 1998 total reserves exceeded the April level.

FIGURE 10.1

INDIAN FOREIGN CURRENCY RESERVES
In US$ Millions, 1998

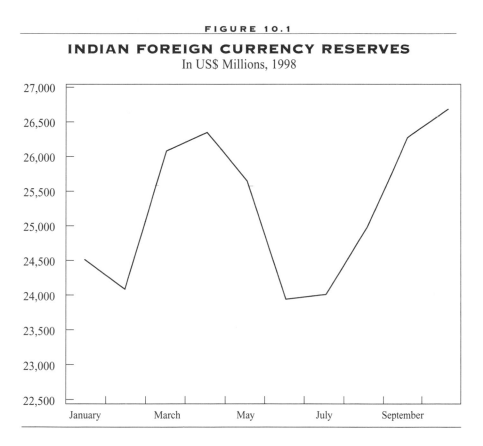

Examining the composition of capital flows, we find that flows of official foreign aid changed very little. According to the balance-of-payments data of the Reserve Bank of India, gross disbursements of external assistance for the period April 1998 through September 1998 were $991 million, compared with $1,066 million for the same period in the previous year. For the Indian fiscal year of April 1998 through March 1999, gross disbursements of $2,726 million were only

5 percent below those of the year before. This may seem surprising since foreign governments imposing sanctions control these external assistance programs most directly. The explanation is that the sanctions affected new commitments, not disbursements of previously contracted loans. At present, official foreign aid to India is "project loans," which normally disburse slowly over several years after commitment. For World Bank project loans, disbursements typically are spread over four to eight years. India, unlike Pakistan, has not been receiving quick-disbursing funds such as IMF financing and adjustment lending by the World Bank, which typically disburse within one to two years. So cutting new commitments of official aid to India would not significantly affect disbursements for several years. For example, World Bank disbursements to India during the six-month period of July–December 1998 were $539 million—about the same pace as previous years.

By contrast, there were notable declines in almost all categories of private flows. As shown in figure 10.2, foreign investment in India fell sharply in May 1998 and remained well below the levels of 1997, and this involved declines in both direct investment and portfolio investments. Receipts from external commercial borrowing were also significantly lower after May 1998.

The key question is how much of the change in private capital inflows was due

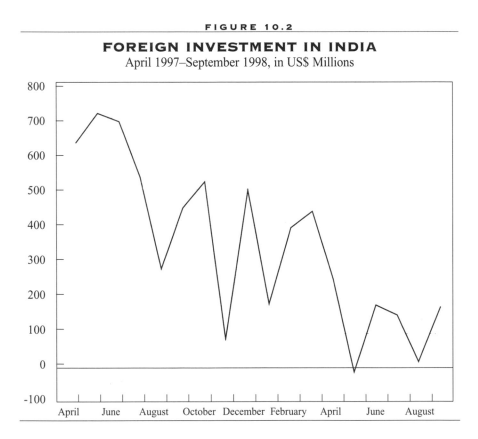

FIGURE 10.2

FOREIGN INVESTMENT IN INDIA
April 1997–September 1998, in US$ Millions

to the sanctions themselves. Of course, in addition to the sanctions, three other, potentially powerful factors could cause such declines in private capital inflows:

- A general decline in international investor appetite for portfolio investments in emerging markets following the Asian financial crisis that began with the Thai baht devaluation in July 1997.
- Fear of possible military conflict in the subcontinent.
- The economic policy announcements by the Indian government that created concerns about a weakening fiscal policy, a possible reversal of liberalization policies, and a generally less favorable climate for foreign investment.

It is impossible to fully untangle these various influences, but some evidence about the relative importance of the sanctions can be gathered from the movements of the markets for publicly traded Indian stocks. Declines in these stock market indices indicate outflow of portfolio investments. We find that the timing of stock market movements and the explanations of those movements by stock market participants indicate that the sanctions themselves were a relevant, although not dominant, factor.

Figure 10.3 shows the movements during 1998 of the Bombay stock market index and also an index of Asian stock markets (excluding India and Pakistan).[26] The Indian market rose sharply from the beginning of the new BJP government in March until the nuclear tests in early May, even though the rest of the Asian markets were almost unchanged. During this period India seemed a relatively safe haven compared with the East Asian countries in crisis and tended to attract foreign portfolio investments.[27] But between the May tests and the end of 1998, the Indian market fell about 27 percent compared with a 4 percent decline in the rest of Asia. We believe that this decline mostly reflects concerns about the economic policy direction of the Indian government. In particular, in June it put forward proposals to raise import tariffs and submitted a budget that indicated an unwillingness to tighten fiscal policy despite accelerating inflation.[28] The fact that the stock market has failed to recover since the lifting of the sanctions confirms that this deterioration in economic policy, combined with the increasing fragility of BJP's governing coalition and hence the poor prospects for better economic policy, was the most powerful factor.

Nevertheless, during June and July, there were some significant market moves that were apparently driven by the sanctions. Surveying both the Indian and the global financial press throughout this period, it is striking that traders paid a lot of attention to the latest news about the scope and potential duration of the sanctions. Immediately following India's tests, as the Bombay Stock Exchange fell 6 percent relative to other Asian markets in three days, there were widespread reports that the movements were due primarily to the impending U.S. sanctions. *Agence France Presse*, in a piece titled "Indian Shares Down amid Fears of Sanctions after Nuclear Tests," quoted Indian stockbroker Gaurav Sanghvi: "The fear of sanctions and its impact on the domestic economy is affecting share prices."[29] This sentiment was backed up the Xinhua News Agency, which reported that the market was falling "in the wake of reports that the U.S. was likely to impose sweeping sanctions on India

FIGURE 10.3

INDIA STOCK MARKET INDEX VERSUS ASIA
(EX-IND AND PAK) INDEX

—— MSCIF India Local

········ MSCIF Asia, Ex-Ind and Pak Index

<u>1998</u>

5/14: First day of market activity after India's second round of nuclear tests.

6/18: Details of U.S. sanctions officially announced.

7/09: U.S. Senate votes to allow agricultural export credits.

7/15: U.S. Senate votes to adopt Brownback Amendment.

9/24: India indicates readiness to sign CTBT.

10/21: President is granted waiver authority.

11/6: President lifts majority of sanctions on India and Pakistan.

for carrying out nuclear tests."[30] Just after the United States announced the details of its sanctions on June 18, the Indian market fell almost 10 percent relative to the rest of Asia. On July 10, 1998, following the U.S. Senate vote of 98–0 to weaken the sanctions by permitting agricultural export credits, the Indian market rose about 12 percent relative to the international market.[31] On July 16, 1998, the day after the Senate approved the Brownback Amendment—legislation that would give the president authority to waive sanctions—the Indian stock market rose 3.7 percent and the *Times of India* headline read, "Shares Sparkle on Sanction Waiver Hopes." The corresponding article reported: "Share prices shrugged off a cautious start to rally sharply at close on Thursday as investors absorbed news of the U.S. Senate's vote to allow President Bill Clinton to stall implementation of economic sanctions against India and Pakistan." According to one dealer at an Indian foreign brokerage house: "It [the vote] was the major trigger to boost the market."[32]

There is another interesting barometer that measures specifically *foreign* investor sentiment toward Indian stocks. This is the market for Global Depository Receipts—called GDRs—which are traded in London. Figure 10.4 shows the movements of the GDR premium. This is the average difference between the GDR price and the price of that stock in the Indian market. According to active participants in this market, the equilibrium difference is about plus 10 percent—reflecting tax and transition cost advantages of the GDRs. On May 8, 1998, just three days before India's first test, the GDR premium stood at 10.49 percent. In the two weeks following the tests, the GDR premium fell to about zero—reflecting a loss of foreign investor interest in Indian stocks. In mid-June, when the United States clarified the sanctions, the premium fell sharply again to about minus 10 percent—but recovered quickly to zero after the Senate voted to allow agricultural export credits. After the sanctions were relaxed, the GDR premium returned to above 5 percent.

There were, of course, other factors that affected market sentiment. In particular, changes in India's credit rating by external agencies caused stock market movements, but these rating changes were to some extent due to the sanctions. On June 19, 1998, Moody's announced its downgrade of the Indian credit rating. While Moody's made clear that its decision was based primarily on India's long-term lack of economic reform, it did state that the presence of sanctions played a role in its judgment. According to Moody's:

> Finally, following India's test explosions of nuclear weapons devices last month, the trade and credit sanctions imposed by the U.S. and other countries are likely to hamper efforts to overcome severe infrastructure constraints. Overall, these circumstances exacerbate concerns about whether growth of the economy and of exports can be sufficiently stimulated to reverse the recent weak performances of the external sector and government finances.[33]

Moody's was not the only credit rating company to downgrade India. On May 22, 1998, Standard and Poor's changed the outlook on India's long-term and local currency issuer credit rating from "stable" to "negative." What led it to this decision? "The change in the outlook reflects the erosion of India's external financial position following the imposition of sanctions by the U.S. and other countries in response to nuclear tests carried out by India last week."[34] Duff and Phelps made a similar down-grade on August 10, 1998. According to Duff and Phelps, the "decision by the United States to impose economic sanctions on India following India's underground nuclear weapons tests could . . . negatively affect India's balance of payments . . . [and] result in lower capital inflows in the coming years."[35] Furthermore, Duff and Phelps cited the fact that the sanctions will force the Indian government to rely on "more costly avenues of borrowing" that may increase the debt burden over time.[36]

The press of India, along with traders and others familiar with the financial

FIGURE 10.4

INDIA GDR PREMIUM,
JANUARY 1998–DECEMBER 1998

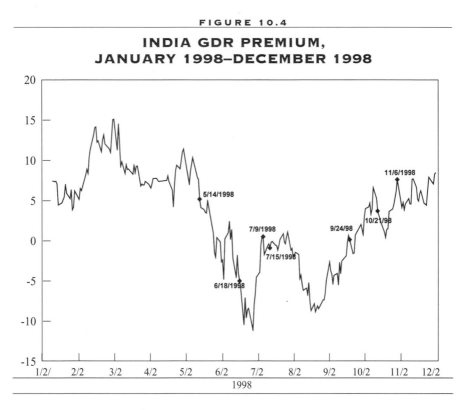

—— GDR Premium (%)

<u>1998</u>
5/14: First day of market activity after India's second round of nuclear tests.
6/18: Details of U.S. sanctions officially announced.
7/09: U.S. Senate votes to allow agricultural export credits.
7/15: U.S. Senate votes to adopt Brownback Amendment.
9/24: India indicates readiness to sign CTBT.
10/21: President is granted waiver authority.
11/96: President lifts majority of sanctions on India and Pakistan.

markets of India, also connected the Moody's downgrade with the imposition of the U.S. sanctions. *The Economic Times,* the *Times of India,* the Economist Intelligence Unit, and *Asiaweek* all reported that the sanctions had played a significant role in the Moody's decision.[37] *Business Today* wrote that "the international credit rating agency, Moody's Investor Services, responded to the sanctions, and downgraded India."[38]

This evidence from the stock market and from the statements by the credit rating agencies suggests that the sanctions themselves—although not the most important driver of market sentiment—were a significant factor. The sanctions themselves contributed indirectly to the observed decline in portfolio investments and in external commercial borrowing in large part through their impacts on the attitudes of agents in the global capital markets. If sustained over time, these reduced capital flows would result in lower economic growth.

Therefore, the bottom line for the case of India is this: sanctions had a marginal—but not negligible effect on the nation's economy. The indirect effects via private capital flows have been far more important than the direct effects of changes in official aid flows. The sanctions would have had greater effect only if they had remained in place for several years and thereby affected significantly not just the commitments but also the disbursements of official creditors such as the World Bank.

THE IMPACT ON PAKISTAN

The story for Pakistan was very different—in terms of the channels by which the sanctions had impact and the magnitude of the impact. In short, a decade of economic mismanagement had left Pakistan heavily dependent on the IMF. When the U.S.-led coalition withheld that support, the resulting collapse of confidence created a balance-of-payments crisis and a significant decline in economic activity.

When the Glenn Amendment sanctions were imposed, the Pakistani economy was extremely vulnerable to the loss of support from the IMF and other IFIs. As stated by an Economists Intelligence Unit report, "Economic mismanagement, fiscal profligacy, rising bank defaults and high levels of corruption in the last ten years [before the bomb tests] have played havoc with Pakistan's economy. . . . On the eve of Pakistan's nuclear test, the economy was already only limping along."[39]

In October 1997, the government of Nawaz Sharif reached agreement with the IMF on an economic reform program supported by an IMF credit of $1.56 billion, to be disbursed in three tranches, and by a World Bank adjustment loan. As of April 1998, $1.2 billion of the IMF funds remained undisbursed. These funds were very much needed to shore up Pakistan's weak external position: in April 1998 its foreign exchange reserves of $1.4 billion equaled only about 90 days of imports, and it needed about $2 billion in net inflows in 1998 to avoid loss of reserves and/or reduced imports.

Following the nuclear bomb tests, the United States and other shareholders in the IMF formed a coalition to block disbursement of the IMF credit and a parallel adjustment loan from the World Bank. In this circumstance, the expectation that the sanctions would block this ongoing IMF support caused a collapse of market confidence, which affected the capital flows, the exchange rate, and aggregate GDP growth in Pakistan. New private inflows virtually stopped. Foreign exchange reserves fell to extremely low levels (see figure 10.5). In early November, just before President Clinton waived a number of sanctions on Pakistan and India, Pakistan's foreign exchange reserves stood at $458 million, a dangerously small amount.[40] The open market (kerb) rate for the Pakistani rupee (Rs.) depreciated from Rs. 45 in early May to Rs. 63 in mid-July—a 28 percent depreciation. By the end of 1998, when most of the sanctions had been lifted, it remained 16 percent below its pretest value.[41] Furthermore, the Pakistani government, which before the sanctions had predicted a GDP growth rate of 6 percent for the 1998–99 financial year (July–June), has recently revised this forecast to 3.1 percent. "We never expected to have that serious impact of the sanctions against Pakistan," explained Pakistani finance minister Ishaq Dar, "and that is why the GDP growth rate ended up at 3.1 percent in 1998–99."[42] Some believe that the Pakistani government's GDP estimate is too optimistic. The Economist Intelligence Unit has forecasted that the GDP growth rate in Pakistan will be just 1.6 percent for this period.[43]

This collapse in confidence was also apparent in the Karachi Stock Exchange (KSE). Figure 10.6 shows that it fell sharply from May; by mid-July it had fallen 34 percent more than the rest of Asian stock markets. This mid-July point is important to note, as it was at this time that it became clear that the sanctions would

FIGURE 10.5

PAKISTAN FOREIGN CURRENCY RESERVES (IN U.S. MILLIONS), 1998

cause the indefinite postponement of IMF funds. On July 10, the Pakistani daily newspaper *The Nation* ran a story that quoted IMF Middle East director Paul Chabrier as saying that the G-8 countries had the last word on IMF funding to Pakistan. On that same day, the KSE reached a then all-time low of 777.26. Three days later, the Pakistani press was reporting that this postponement of IMF funding had led to "the blackest week" in the history of the KSE.[44]

As in the case of India, bad economic policy decisions also contributed significantly to the crisis of confidence and the loss of foreign exchange by Pakistan. In particular, on May 28, 1998, in an attempt to avoid a post-test run of its banks, the government froze all foreign currency accounts in Pakistan. This immediately halted remittances from Pakistanis overseas, which had been a major source of net inflows.[45] However, the timing of stock market movements and the explanations by market participants indicate that—as in the case of India—the sanctions were a very relevant factor.

On June 1, the first day the KSE was open after the nuclear test, the market crashed approximately 15 percent, its worst-ever performance, while all other Asian markets experienced a 4.6 percent drop. According to Associated Press reports, foreign investors were leaving the market due to the threat of forthcoming U.S. sanctions.[46] After the official June 18 announcement of the U.S. sanctions, the KSE proceeded to fall another 13 percent over the next five days, while all other Asian markets fell 4.7 percent.[47] The Pakistani markets also reacted positively to any news regarding the lifting of sanctions. On July 16, the day after the U.S. Senate voted to adopt the Brownback Amendment, the Karachi Stock Exchange jumped up almost 7 percent. This upward trend continued until the end of the week, when the market closed 14.8 percent higher than its opening at the beginning of the week, compared with a 6.8 percent jump in all other Asian markets. The KSE also rallied during the two weeks leading up to the September 1998 UN General Assembly meetings. Among traders in the KSE there was the belief that the UN meetings would result in the easing of the economic sanctions. On the basis of this sense of optimism, the KSE "clawed back 9.5 percent" during the weeks before the UN meetings.[48] Finally, in the wake of the November 7, 1998, waiver announcement that allowed IMF officials to begin to renegotiate with the Pakistani government, the KSE "rocketed 10.5 percent . . . the market's sharpest single-day rise since India and Pakistan conducted nuclear tests in May, prompting the U.S. and other western countries to impose economic sanctions." Concluded Sikandar Khawaja, a representative of the London-based banking and financial services organization HSBC Group: "A positive climate has been created with the belief that the sanctions will be lifted. The sentiment has also been helped by the expectations of a deal with the IMF."[49]

The delay on an IMF support package also thwarted Pakistan's hope of receiving financial support from the Arab world. A $1.5 billion rescue package, consisting of funds from Arab private banks and financial institutions and arranged by the Islamic Development Bank (IDB), was continuously delayed throughout the summer and fall of 1998, as the IDB tied these funds to Pakistan's need to straighten out its relationship with the United States and the IMF. By September 10, 1998, all the IDB was able to offer was $200 million of its own funds.[50]

In summary, because of its prior vulnerability, the Pakistani economy was very

FIGURE 10.6

PAKISTAN STOCK MARKET INDEX VERSUS ASIA (EX-IND AND PAK) INDEX, JANUARY 1998–DECEMBER 1998

——— MSCIF Pakistan Local
········ MSCIF Asia, Ex-Ind and Pak Index USD

<u>1998</u>

6/01: First day of market activity after Pakistan's nuclear tests.
6/18: Details of U.S. sanctions officially announced.
7/10: Sanctions indefinitely delay IMF funding to Pakistan.
7/15: U.S. Senate votes to adopt Brownback Amendment.
9/24: Pakistan indicates readiness to sign CTBT.
10/21: President is granted waiver authority.
11/06: President lifts majority of sanctions on India and Pakistan.

severely affected by the withdrawal of IMF financing by the U.S.-led coalition among IMF shareholder governments, and by the indirect effects of this withdrawal on other capital flows to Pakistan.

IMPLICATIONS FOR THE FUTURE UTILITY OF THE GLENN AMENDMENT

What does this experience with the economic impact of sanctions on India and Pakistan suggest about the future utility of the Glenn Amendment? Should this legal requirement for broad and automatic sanctions remain in place?

The fact that the threat of the U.S. sanctions failed to prevent the nuclear tests by India and Pakistan is certainly not sufficient reason to abandon the Glenn Amendment. The U.S. threat ultimately failed in the case of India and Pakistan, although it might be the case that the threat of sanctions delayed by many years testing of which both nations were capable.[51] A sufficient rationale for executing the threat was, as Undersecretary of State Talbott said, to create a disincentive for other states to exercise the nuclear option if they are contemplating it.[52]

As the millennium draws to a close, it is not obvious which nations might be tempted to go nuclear in the early decades of the next century. At present the states that seem interested in developing a nuclear capacity—in particular, North Korea, Iraq, and, to a lesser extent, Iran—are already isolated from the global economy by their own policies and by existing sanctions. The presence of the Glenn Amendment is irrelevant to their incentives. However, further down the road there may be circumstances in which nations that are more fully engaged in the global economy and that have now pledged to remain nonnuclear are driven by domestic politics or regional pressures to reconsider.

The experience of the sanctions against India and Pakistan suggests that under some but certainly not all circumstances, sanctions such as those required by the Glenn Amendment can impose economic costs on the target nations. These costs might range from mild—as in the case of India—to very severe—as happened to Pakistan. In many cases, these costs are likely to be serious enough to enter into the complex calculus of a state that contemplates going nuclear.

The experience of India is particularly relevant because it indicates that for a country that participates in global capital markets, the indirect effects of sanctions, that is, their impact on the attitudes and expectations of both domestic and foreign economic agents, can magnify the direct effects. For this reason, globalization cuts both ways. As Richard Haass and others have argued, it makes it easier for sanctioned countries to find substitutes for finance or trade that is denied by U.S. unilateral sanctions. On the other hand, globalization also means that U.S. unilateral sanctions can have echo effects throughout global financial markets. Writing in the aftermath of the South Asian explosions, *New York Times* foreign affairs analyst Thomas L. Friedman stated that the economic repercussions of the tests would illustrate

> a fundamental truth about globalization: Globalization does not end geopolitics. Nations, like India, will still defy international norms in pur-

suit of respect, or in response to real or imagined threats, no matter how integrated [into the global economy] they are. But what globalization will do is exact a whole new price for that sort of defiance.[53]

Countries that are very dependent on international capital flow are, ceteris paribus, more vulnerable to these indirect effects. India in 1998 was not particularly dependent on international capital markets, and the indirect effects were correspondingly mild. But nations that might be contemplating the nuclear option a decade hence may be among those that are well integrated into the global economy. The recent experience of India should serve to warn them that in addition to the economic damage caused by increased fear of war, higher military expenditures, and direct U.S. and other bilateral sanctions, there will be adverse repercussions in financial markets. The overall economic cost of these indirect effects of loss of confidence by global financial agents may indeed far outweigh any direct costs of sanctions. But the sanctions are an important catalyst for such effects and therefore a relevant U.S. policy threat.

The case of Pakistan also holds an important lesson. Plausibly a potential proliferator will be a country in a fragile economic position—with high debt, low foreign exchange reserves, and considerable dependence on official assistance. In that event, sanctions by the United States would constitute a powerful disincentive—but only if the United States can successfully create a strong coalition among the shareholders of the international financial institutions (IFIs). When the targeted country has an acute need for quick-disbursing, policy-based lending from the IFIs, sanctions imposed by such a coalition will have very strong and immediate effects that the potential proliferator would undoubtedly have to take into serious account. It may be easier to build a coalition for IFI sanctions than for bilateral sanctions because a priori no one knows whose direct commercial interests are sacrificed by withholding IFI funds. On the other hand, the potential leverage of IFI sanctions could in some situations be undermined by a counterthreat from the targeted nation to withhold repayment of previous obligations to the IFIs.

For U.S. sanctions to create any disincentives, there must be a very strong expectation that they will be enforced. Potential proliferators understand that enforcing unilateral economic sanctions also imposes economic costs on the United States and that once the threat has failed to deter, the U.S. government faces strong domestic pressures not to carry through with the sanctions. Hence, the credibility of the threat—and its potential to deter—depends on maximizing the likelihood that it will be implemented. As Thomas C. Schelling, one of the earliest economists to apply game theory to international politics, has written:

> As a rule, one must threaten that he *will* act, not that he *may* act, if the threat fails. . . . To say only that one *may* carry out the threat, not that one certainly will, is to invite the opponent to guess whether one will prefer to punish himself and his opponent or to pass up the occasion. . . . The key to these threats is that . . . *the final decision is not altogether under the threatener's control.*[54]

On the basis of this reasoning, we believe that maintaining the automacity of the Glenn Amendment—and allowing waivers, if at all, only via an additional act of

Congress rather than at the ex ante discretion of the administration—is critically important. From this perspective, the recent proposal to extend the waiver for India and Pakistan for five years—thereby giving the president broad authority to forgo sanctions against the South Asian neighbors—severely undermines the credibility of the U.S. threat to future would-be proliferators. This argues strongly for keeping the Glenn Amendment in place.

Such automaticity and difficulty in obtaining waivers would also affect the expectations of private economic agents and thereby increase the speed and magnitude of the indirect effects of sanctions. As we have seen in the case of India and Pakistan, markets reacted to the *expectations* about the sanctions: stock markets fell before the details of the sanctions were known, and they rose whenever expectations of a waiver were created.

The economic sanctions of the Glenn Amendment—unless matched by equivalent sanctions by most major countries—will not likely be an overwhelming threat that will certainly prevent future nuclear proliferation. But the experience of the sanctions in the cases of India and Pakistan indicates that the Glenn Amendment does constitute a credible threat in some circumstances and thus does have some disincentive effect against would-be proliferators in certain economic circumstances. Such a threat is likely to be a useful complement to other means by which the United States can seek to limit the number of nations with nuclear weapons. It is better than no economic threat, better than deciding on economic sanctions only after the fact of proliferation, and better than being forced to rely solely on military action against a proliferator.

NOTES

1. "U.S. Diplomacy in South Asia: A Progress Report," remarks given at the Brookings Institution, November 12, 1998.

2. "Senate Votes to Exempt Food Exports from Sanctions on India, Pakistan," *Washington Post*, July 10, 1998.

3. "Senate Passes Budget Bill, Clinton Makes It Law," *Los Angeles Times*, October 22, 1998; "U.S. Lifts Sanctions on India, Pakistan," *Washington Post*, November 7, 1998. The Clinton administration dropped its objection to World Bank loans to India in February 1999. See "Americans Won't Block Indian World Bank Loans," *Washington Post*, February 18, 1999.

4. "US Senate Votes for 5 Yr Suspension of India/Pak Sanctions," *Asia Pulse*, June 10, 1999. This defense appropriations bill still needs to be approved by the House of Representatives and President Clinton before it becomes law. Under the original Brownback Amendment the president was given the authority only to waive the sanctions against India and Pakistan for up to one year—the sanctions legislation itself remains law.

5. Our findings relate solely to the efficacy of the Glenn Amendment. We do not wish to make any blanket statements regarding the efficacy of economic sanctions—sanctions policy should be studied by a case-by-case approach. Too many recent studies on sanctions wish to reach sweeping conclusions in terms of their effectiveness (or, as the current trend seems to be, ineffectiveness). See, for example, Douglas Johnston, Jr., and Sidney Weintraub, *Altering U.S. Sanctions Policy: Final Report of the CSIS Project on Unilateral Economic Sanctions* (Washington, D.C.: Center for Strategic and International Studies Press, 1999). Such an approach, while often citing some type of need for sanctions policy, fails to highlight crucial differences between country cases in its quest to

portray sanctions as highly flawed policy, and frequently ends up undermining the effectiveness of all sanctions efforts.

6. See, for example, Gary Hufbauer, "The Snake Oil of Democracy: When Tensions Rise, the U.S. Peddles Sanctions," *Washington Post*, July 12, 1998. The U.S. business community has played a predominant role in helping this perspective gain credence in the recent debate surrounding the efficacy of sanctions. Organizations such as USA Engage, a coalition of over 600 U.S.-based companies, have launched a powerful public relations campaign to convince lawmakers that there are "more effective ways of reacting to objectionable actions and policies of foreign governments other than by imposing unilateral sanctions." Quote taken from USA Engage's home page, www.usaengage.org. American commercial interests, in fact, were the driving force behind the July 9, 1998, legislation to exempt food exports from the sanctions on India and Pakistan. For coverage of anti-sanctions organizations and their impact on the sanctions debate, see "U.S. Backs Off Sanctions, Seeing Poor Effect Abroad," *New York Times*, July 31, 1998; "Second-Guessing Sanctions: The Price of Pressure," *CQ Weekly*, August 15, 1998; and Jesse Helms's "What Sanctions Epidemic?," *Foreign Affairs*, January–February 1999. The collection of materials housed at the USA Engage home page is particularly useful in helping one understand the antisanctions position that is prevalent in the U.S. business community. For a more academic (as well as more thoughtful) presentation of this skeptical outlook on sanctions, see Richard Haass, ed., *Economic Sanctions and American Diplomacy* (New York: Council on Foreign Relations, 1998).

7. "Sanctions Frenzy," *Washington Post*, June 12, 1998.

8. Haass, 1998, 5–6. For more on the relationship between globalization and sanctions, see Robert A. Pape, "Why Economic Sanctions Do Not Work," *International Security*, fall 1997.

9. For an excellent history of the Glenn Amendment, see Randy J. Rydell's "Giving Nonproliferation Norms Teeth: Sanctions and the NPPA," *Nonproliferation Review*, winter 1999, 1–19.

10. Rydell, 1999, 2.

11. This automaticity was not based on some general notion about assuring the credibility of the sanctions and thereby strengthening their deterrence effect. Leonard Weiss, who was the senior staff person for Senator Glenn, has explained that when the initial version of the Glenn Amendment was approved in 1981, ". . . because the Reagan Administration appeared so hell-bent to fight a proxy war with the Soviets using the Mujahein, there was concern whether a nuclear test by Pakistan would result in a U.S. sanction while the Afghanistan war was being pursued. So Ronald Reagan was given no waiver to exercise in the event of a nuclear test by Pakistan." Remarks by Leonard Weiss, "The Current Debate over Sanctions and Non-Proliferation," Seventh Carnegie International Non-Proliferation Conference, Washington, D.C., January 12, 1999.

12. However, on June 18, it was not at all clear how to implement the provision that U.S. private banks could not make loans to the Indian and Pakistani governments. The interpretation of this provision was debated throughout the summer, and the U.S. Treasury eventually found a way to interpret the law that exempted U.S. banks from this requirement. Harvard University's Devesh Kapur notes that such a development actually undermined the bite of the sanctions. See Kapur's "The Domestic Consequences of India's Nuclear Tests," paper presented to a conference on "South Asia's Nuclear Dilemmas," Weatherhead Center for International Affairs, Harvard University, February 1999.

13. In the text we present details of the economic sanctions. The Glenn Amendment also required termination of various military aid programs. *Jane's Defense Weekly* reported that the first test flight of the Indian Air Force's Light Combat Aircraft (LCA) has been postponed indefinitely, due primarily to sanctions imposed on the craft's American-made engines and flight-control system. India's newly established Badmal Ordnance Factory, created to produce ammunition for a 155-mm towed howitzer using U.S. equipment, has been forced to shut down. There have also been reports that the sanctions postponed the Indian development of the Advanced Light Helicopter (ALH), as the ALH was designed with a U.S.-made turboshift engine in mind. However, as the French and Russian defense industries are reportedly eager to step in, it is likely that these disruptions to the Indian military will be only short-term.

14. "Fact Sheet: India and Pakistan Sanctions," released by the Bureau of Economic and Agricul-

tural Affairs, U.S. State Department, June 18, 1998; "Implementation of Glenn Sanctions for India and Pakistan," U.S. Agency for International Development (USAID) Fact Sheet, July 15, 1998; and "CERC's Project Hit by US Sanctions," *Economic Times*, July 14, 1998.

15. "India Economy: Tallying the Cost of Sanctions," *Economist Intelligence Unit Country Briefing*, July 6, 1998.

16. "India Braces for a Backlash," *Time* (International Edition), June 1, 1998; "India's Nuclear Test Left Cloud over Economy," *Los Angeles Times*, July 12, 1998.

17. Such a clause is meant to cover unexpected circumstances like adverse weather or labor strikes that prevent the parties from fulfilling the terms of a contract and may allow parties to suspend their contractual obligations until the conditions improve.

18. "Hughes Pact in Crossfire of India Sanctions," *Los Angeles Times*, July 29, 1998; and "Briefing—Asia Telecommunications," *Asia Pulse*, August 19, 1998.

19. Quoted in Rodney W. Jones, Mark G. McDonough, Toby F. Dalton, and Gregory D. Koblentz, *Tracking Nuclear Proliferation 1998: A Guide in Maps and Charts* (Washington, D.C.: Carnegie Endowment for International Peace, 1998), 132.

20. Ibid.

21. "Ex-Im Closes for New Business in Pakistan," Export-Import Bank of the United States, press release, June 1, 1998.

22. "Ground Zero," *Newsweek*, May 25, 1998; "And Now for the Fallout," *Business Week*, May 25, 1998.

23. Gary Clyde Hufbauer, *Economic Sanctions Reconsidered*, 3d ed. (Washington, D.C.: Institute for International Economics, forthcoming); "Inquiry into Nuclear Testing by India and Pakistan," joint submission by the Department of Foreign Affairs and Trade, the Australian Defence Organisation, and the Australian Safeguards Office to the Senate Foreign Affairs, Defence and Trade References Committee, June 1998.

24. The very strong tradition in these institutions is to avoid voting within their boards of executive directors. Instead, if the management determines through consultations that shareholders with a majority of voting shares oppose a loan, that loan is not presented to the executive directors for approval.

25. It is not feasible to approach this question by considering changes in GDP or other measures of aggregate economic activity. The sanctions, if they had any effects at all, primarily impacted investment activities, and there are substantial lags between changes in investment and changes in GDP.

26. The index used here is the Morgan Stanley Asian Index. The published index is based on a set of stocks including those from India and Pakistan. We have constructed an adjusted index that eliminates the Indian and Pakistani components of the overall index so that we can compare movements of these two markets against the rest of the Asian markets.

27. According to a 1998 United States Trade Information Center report on India, "the Southeast-Asian crisis will only have an indirect and relatively limited effect on the Indian economy. India is seen as a related but separate market, and Southeast Asia's problems are not likely to be replicated in India." Taken from the Trade Information Center's Internet website (http://infoserv2.ita.doc.gov/tic.nsf).

28. It should be noted that the failure of the Indian government to adequately address the potential costs of the sanctions in their June 1998 budget played a predominant role in criticisms of the plan.

29. "Indian Shares Down amid Fears of Sanctions after Nuclear Tests," *Agence France Press*, May 12, 1998.

30. "Sensitive Index on BSE Loses 77.37 Points," *Xinhua News Agency*, May 12, 1998.

31. "Senate Votes to Exempt Food Exports from Sanctions on India, Pakistan," *Washington Post*, July 10, 1998.

32. "Shares Sparkle on Sanctions Waiver Hopes," *Times of India*, July 17, 1998.

33. "Global Credit Research Report," *Moody's Investors Service*, June 19, 1998. Similar downgrades, along with similar market movements, occurred in postnuclear Pakistan. Once again, the sanctions played a significant role in the decision to downgrade. See, for example, "Pakistan Downgraded as Concern over Ability to Service Debt," *Standard and Poor's CreditWeek*, October 21, 1998.

34. "India's Fiscal Problems Prompt Rating Downgrade," *Standard and Poor's CreditWeek*, October 28, 1998.

35. "DCR Downgrades Sovereign Ratings on Republic of India," *Duff and Phelps Press Release*, August 10, 1998.

36. Ibid.

37. See "Moody's Cuts India's Sovereign Rating by Two Notches to 'Speculative,' " *Economic Times*, June 20, 1998; "Moody's Ratings May Choke Firms' Borrowings Ahead," *Times of India*, June 23, 1998; "India Economy: Tallying the Cost of Sanctions," *Economist Intelligence Unit Viewswire*, July 6, 1998; and "Surviving the Aftershock," *Asiaweek*, July 3, 1998.

38. "Fretting and Fuming in the Fiftieth," *Business Today*, August 22, 1998.

39. Economist Intelligence Unit, *Country Report on Pakistan*, Third Quarter, 1998, 8.

40. "Forex Reserves Fall to $458m," *Dawn*, November 6, 1998.

41. All rupee data have been culled from the Pakistani-based publication *Business Recorder*. The aftermath of the nuclear tests also led the government of Pakistan to devalue the official currency rate by 4.2 percent on June 28, 1999. See "Pakistan Devalues as Asian Turmoil Spreads," *Financial Times*, June 29, 1998. For the connection between the sanctions and the depreciation of the rupee, see "Pakistan Economy: Traders Face Somber Future in Wake of Sanctions," *Economist Intelligence Unit*, June 4, 1998.

42. "Pak Economic Performance Remains Dismal," *Xinhua News Agency*, June 11, 1999. The GDP growth rate for 1997–98 was 5.3 percent.

43. Economist Intelligence Unit, *Country Report on Pakistan*, June 1, 1999.

44. "G8 Has Last Word on ESAF Revival, Warns IMF Director," *The Nation*, July 10, 1998; "The Blackest Week in History of KSE," *The Nation*, July 13, 1998.

45. It is important to note that this economically unsound act of freezing foreign currency took place mere hours after Pakistan's nuclear tests. The Pakistani press has reported that the Sharif government undertook this process in response to the belief that the blasts, along with the sanctions that would follow, would cause massive investor flight. Other reports indicate that Sharif froze all currency accounts in an attempt to counter the negative financial effects of the sanctions, by keeping as much currency in Pakistan as possible. See "Continuous Depreciation of Pak Rupee," *Dawn*, August 24, 1998.

46. "Panic Selling as Pakistan Stock Market Reopens," *AP Online*, June 1, 1998.

47. "Karachi Stock Exchange Index Goes Down," *Xinhua News Agency*, June 19, 1998.

48. "Power Deal May Boost Karachi," *Financial Times*, September 22, 1998.

49. "Pakistan: Karachi Default Worries Recede," *Financial Times*, November 11, 1998.

50. "Pakistan: IMF Team Due to Arrive for Talks," *Financial Times*, September 11, 1998.

51. Rydell, 1999, writes that calculations among Indian officials about international reactions played a crucial role in discouraging India from testing nuclear weapons on more than one occasion. According to former Indian president Venkataraman, "All preparations for an underground nuclear test at Pokran had been completed in 1983 when I was the defence minister. It was shelved because of international pressure and the same thing happened in 1995."

52. Talbott, 1998.

53. Thomas L. Friedman, "What Goes Around . . . ," *New York Times*, June 23, 1998.

54. Thomas C. Schelling, *The Strategy of Conflict* (New York: Oxford University Press, 1960), 187–88. Italics in original.

—THE MIDDLE EAST—

—11—

Inspecting Iraq

Richard Butler

Following Iraq's expulsion from Kuwait, it became clear that the Saddam Hussein government had created a truly alarming range and quality of weapons of mass destruction (WMD), and a very considerable long-range missile force to deliver those weapons. There was also concern about Iraq's nuclear weapons program, which the International Atomic Energy Agency subsequently demonstrated was advanced. For these reasons, the Security Council imposed very heavy, very strict requirements upon Iraq for the destruction, removal, or rendering harmless of those weapons under international supervision. Those obligations were supported by heavy sanctions.

The actions that were taken to try to ensure the fulfillment of Iraq's obligations included the establishment of a unique organization and set of mechanisms, namely, the United Nations Special Commission on Iraq (UNSCOM). It was envisaged that UNSCOM's job in the disarmament of Iraq's weapons of mass destruction would take a relatively short time, possibly as little as a year. It has taken eight years, and the job is still not completely finished.

The reason for this distressing lag is that Iraq did not fulfill its obligations:

- Iraq did not make accurate disclosure statements of its prohibited weapons and weapons capability.
- Although the law required that all destruction be conducted under international supervision, Iraq unilaterally destroyed weapons in order to ensure that the commission would never know the full nature and scope of its WMD capabilities.
- Iraq pursued an active policy and practice of concealing weapons and proscribed components from the commission.

In addition to the envisaged disarmament of Iraq, the Security Council decided to establish a system of ongoing monitoring and verification to ensure that Iraq did not reconstitute its prohibited weapons in the future. The first version of that system has been in operation since 1994. However, the monitoring system will need further, and perhaps substantial, development when it is decided by the Security Council that the disarmament phase has concluded, and thus when certain, if not all, of the sanctions are lifted, Iraq's economic and financial capacity, including the capacity to acquire dual-use materials that may be diverted for WMD, will be reconstituted.

TABLE 11.1

IRAQI DENIAL AND DECEPTION EFFORTS: DECLARATIONS ON BIOLOGICAL WEAPONS

April 1991	Iraq declares it has no BW program.
May 1992	Iraq provides its first Full, Final and Complete Disclosure (FFCD) for its biological weapons program.
July 1995	Iraq admits to an offensive program but denies weaponization.
August 1995	Following the defection of General Hussein Kamel, Iraq withdraws its third "final" FFCD and admits to a far more extensive BW program which included weaponization.
September 1997	Iraq provides its fifth FFCD. An international panel of experts unanimously finds it incomplete, inadequate, and technically flawed.
Spring 1998	Team of technical experts concludes that Iraq's latest FFCD is deficient in all areas, including history of the BW program, organization, acquisition of raw material, research and development, agent production, and weaponization.

Table prepared by the Carnegie Non-Proliferation Project.

Dismantling Iraq's WMD program has intrinsic and extrinsic implications. Intrinsically, there is a need for the international community to manage the array of weapons created and obtained by Iraq. Physical disarmament is especially important given Iraq's past behavior with respect to its use of weapons and also given the particular characteristics of the Middle East.

Extrinsically, Iraq is a wider test case of the ability of the international community to maintain non-proliferation regimes. If the intrinsic case of Iraq were lost, something of deeper and wider importance would also be lost: the faith of states in many parts of the world in the non-proliferation regimes.

The concept and treaties of the non-proliferation regimes have three aspects: a moral commitment, a political decision, and a system of verification and common assurance. The moral commitment is the view or value judgment that the weapons involved are inadmissible. This commitment can be seen in the Nuclear Non-Proliferation Treaty (NPT), the Chemical Weapons Convention, and the Biological Weapons Convention (BWC). Each of these asserts, elementally, that no state should have, or seek to acquire, the weapons involved.

When governments embrace the moral commitment, this is followed by a political commitment to give effect to what has been agreed upon at the moral level. Typically, political commitment is expressed in the development of a treaty or convention and the decision to join it.

That decision is deeply influenced by the third feature: the perception of states of whether or not treaty adherence by partners can be relied upon. The key way in which that assurance is given is through a verification system of compliance with the terms of the treaty and its obligations.

Although verification can never be 100 percent effective, there is a discernible point of intersection between a relatively high degree of credible verification, expressed largely in technical terms, and a similarly high degree of political confidence derived from credible political commitment. This point of intersection of objective fact and subjective political judgment, if both are done properly, shows results in a climate of confidence that would then underpin the non-proliferation objective.

Every day that passes in which states see their neighbors keeping their promises, they then recommit to keeping their own. As every year passes, the original moral commitment and the behavioral implications flowing from it solidify to the point where, as the NPT has largely demonstrated, it becomes unthinkable for most states to take the extraordinary decision to back away from the moral and political commitment and begin to acquire prohibited weapons.

This conceptual structure and reality that have grown in strength during the last thirty years are most deeply threatened by what may be called the "worst nightmare" of treaty partners or potential treaty partners: that a state will cheat from within. The problem of states remaining outside the non-proliferation system is well known and not small. Yet there is an obvious sense in which cheating from within—the behavior by states to join a given treaty while clandestinely seeking to make the weapons prohibited by that treaty—is the larger problem. This is a "nightmare" problem because it threatens the whole non-proliferation concept and structure at the most fundamental level.

Iraq is a party to the NPT and the BWC but has cheated on and/or sought to cheat on both. Iraq has made the nightmare problem more than theoretical. Iraq's behavior in respect of its obligations, principally under Security Council Resolution 687, has also raised very grave challenges both to the authority of the Security Council and to the credibility of efforts to verify compliance with the non-proliferation regimes.

The Security Council alone can address the first of these challenges. Regarding efforts to verify compliance, two points may be raised. First, UNSCOM developed groundbreaking means of inspection and verification. These demonstrated that much can be achieved if the organization involved is endowed with the required technical skills and flexibility of operation. These facts and lessons should be valued in the context of work under the non-proliferation regimes. It is important to note that UNSCOM's verification and monitoring rights are far more extensive than those of any current disarmament and verification agency.

TABLE 11.2

IRAQI BIOLOGICAL AND CHEMICAL WARFARE PROGRAMS

BW AGENT PRODUCTION AMOUNTS[a]

BW Agent (Organism)	Declared Concentrated Amounts	Declared Total Amounts	Comments
Anthrax (Bacillus anthracis)	8,500 liters (2,245 gallons)	85,000 liters (22,457 gallons)	UNSCOM estimates production amounts were actually three to four times more than the declared amounts but is unable to confirm.
Botulinum toxin (Clostridium botulinum)	19,400 liters (10x and 20x concentrated) (5,125 gallons)	380,000 liters (100,396 gallons)	UNSCOM estimates production amounts were actually two times more than the declared amounts but is unable to confirm.
Gas Gangrene (Clostridium perfringens)	340 liters (90 gallons)	3,400 liters (900 gallons)	Production amounts could be higher, but UNSCOM is unable to confirm.
Aflatoxin (Aspergillus flavus and aspergillus parasiticus)	N/A	2,200 liters (581 gallons)	Production amounts and time frame of production claimed by Iraq do not correlate.
Ricin (Castor bean plant)	N/A	10 liters (2.7 gallons)	Production amounts could be higher, but UNSCOM is unable to confirm.

BW-FILLED AND DEPLOYED DELIVERY SYSTEMS (NUMBER)

Delivery Systems	Anthrax	Botulinum Toxin	Aflatoxin	Comments
Missile warheads Al-Husayn (modified Scud B)	5	16	4	UNSCOM cannot confirm the unilateral destruction of these 25 warheads due to conflicting accounts provided by Iraq.
R-400 aerial bombs	50	100	7	Iraq claimed unilateral destruction of 157 bombs, but UNSCOM is unable to confirm this number. UNSCOM has found the remains of at least 23.
Aircraft aerosol spray tanks (F-1 Mirage modified fuel drop tank)	4			Iraq claims to have produced 4 but may have manufactured others.

a. **Total** refers to the amount of material obtained from the production process, while **concentrated** refers to the amount of concentrated agent obtained after final filtration/purification. The concentrated number is the amount used to fill munitions.

continued on next page

table 11.2 continued

CW AGENT STOCKPILES

CW Agent	Chemical Agents Declared by Iraq	Potential CW Agents Based on Unaccounted Precursors	Comments
VX	At least 4 metric tons	200 metric tons	Iraq denied producing VX until Hussein Kamel's defection in 1995.
G Agents (Sarin)	100 to 150 metric tons	200 metric tons	Figures include both weaponized and bulk agents.
Mustard	500 to 600 metric tons	200 metric tons	Figures include both weaponized and bulk agents.

CW DELIVERY SYSTEMS (NUMBER)

Delivery Systems	Estimated Numbers before Gulf War	Munitions Unaccounted For[b]	Comments
Missile warheads Al-Husayn (modified Scud B)	75 to 100	45 to 70	UNSCOM supervised the destruction of 30 warheads.
Rockets	100,000	15,000 to 25,000	UNSCOM supervised the destruction of nearly 40,000 chemical munitions (including rockets, artillery, and aerial bombs), 28,000 of which were filled.
Aerial bombs	16,000	2,000	
Artillery shells	30,000	15,000	
Aerial spray tanks	Unknown	Unknown	

Source: U.S. Government White Paper, located at www.state.gov/www/regions/nea/iraq-whitepaper.html. Paper released on February 13, 1998.

b. All of these munitions could be used to deliver CW or BW agents. The numbers for missile warheads include 25 that Iraq claims to have unilaterally destroyed after having filled them with biological agents during the Gulf War. UNSCOM has been unable to verify the destruction of these warheads.

Second, Iraq's behavior has illustrated another point of irreducible significance. All of the non-proliferation treaties accept that the responsible actor is the sovereign independent state. In a world of sovereign states, recalcitrance on the part of any state and refusal to provide the modicum of cooperation required by the treaty regime can be a major and possibly insuperable obstacle to the achievement of common objectives.

At present, Iraq is again challenging the concept of cooperation on the grounds that cooperation will not bring results, such as the lifting of sanctions. But cooperation is essential to the conduct of UNSCOM's work and thus to the fulfillment of the requirements of the Security Council, including, presumably, any sanctions decision.

Various solutions are being suggested for this problem. Work is under way at very high levels, but it is not yet clear what solution will be chosen to end the present crisis. My hope and belief are that the solution decided upon will be consistent with the advancement of what is one of the great achievements of the international system in the second half of the twentieth century: the establishment of a tapestry of treaties that express the determination to ensure that weapons of mass destruction do not proliferate.

SUPPLEMENTAL INFORMATION

BACKGROUND INFORMATION ON IRAQ'S ABILITY TO RECONSTITUTE ITS WMD CAPABILITIES[1]
(Prepared by the Carnegie non-Proliferation Project)

At the conclusion of the Persian Gulf War in 1991, United Nations Security Council Resolution 687 ordered the government of Iraq to halt development and destroy existing stockpiles of all nonconventional weapons and any ballistic missile capable of a range in excess of 150 kilometers. The Security Council established the UN Special Commission on Iraq to direct and monitor the destruction of ballistic missiles and chemical and biological weapons, and tasked the International Atomic Energy Agency (IAEA) to investigate and supervise the destruction of Iraq's nuclear program. The inspection and monitoring regime conducted by UNSCOM and the IAEA has generally been successful, overseeing the destruction of more prohibited weapons than were destroyed by coalition forces during the Gulf War. The painstaking efforts of the IAEA and UNSCOM have been hailed as evidence of the viability of intrusive verification regimes such as those embodied in the Chemical Weapons Convention and foreseen for the Biological and Toxin Weapons Convention.

Despite UN inspection efforts, Iraq's WMD declarations have been inconsistent, and Iraq has repeatedly obstructed inspection and monitoring activities. In late 1997, Iraq ordered the expulsion of all Americans working with the Special Commission, precipitating a crisis that led to the complete withdrawal of UNSCOM inspectors that November. Again, in winter 1997–98, Iraq blocked access to what it called "Presidential and Sovereign Sites," areas that UNSCOM had targeted for inspection. Under threat of U.S air strikes, Iraq signed a deal with UN Secretary-General Kofi Annan that would allow inspections to continue.

The fall of 1998 brought yet another crisis. In October, Iraq unilaterally decided that all UNSCOM activities would cease. UNSCOM inspectors once again were withdrawn and a U.S.-led coalition prepared to use military force. As U.S. B-52 bombers were en route, President Hussein once again pledged to allow UNSCOM inspections to resume. Although UN weapons inspections resumed on November 18, Iraq's cooperation with UNSCOM was again short-lived. By December 15 Chairman Richard Butler was forced to report to the Security Council that Iraq had not met his requests for documents related to chemical and biological weapons and had consistently blocked access to several facilities. "Iraq's conduct ensured that no progress was able to be made in the fields of disarmament," Butler stated.

On December 16, U.S. and British aircraft initiated a three-day bombing campaign. U.S. President Bill Clinton argued that "instead of the [UN weapons] inspectors disarming Saddam, Saddam has disarmed the inspectors. This situation presents a clear and present danger to the stability of the Persian Gulf and the safety of people everywhere." In addition to degrading Iraq's WMD ability and Iraq's ability to threaten neighboring states, the strikes were intended "to demonstrate the consequences of flouting international obligations.".

RECONSTITUTION POTENTIAL

UN inspectors have been barred from Iraq since December 16, 1998, when the United States and the United Kingdom began their bombing campaign. While some reports suggest that Iraq has not actively pursued reconstitution of its WMD programs since, that does not preclude Iraq from seeking these capabilities again in the near future.[2] Shortly after he resigned his post as chief of UNSCOM's concealment and investigation unit in August 1998, Major Scott Ritter testified before the U.S. Senate Armed Services and Foreign Relations Committees that absent continued inspections, "Iraq will be able to reconstitute the entirety of its former . . . capabilities within six months."

Iraq's former WMD capabilities were substantial. Prior to the Gulf War, Iraq maintained one of the most deadly chemical and biological weapons (CBW) capabilities in the developing world. According to UNSCOM findings, Iraq deployed seventy-five 600-kilometer-range Al-Hussein ballistic missiles tipped with biological or chemical warheads. Iraq possesses extensive experience developing and producing such agents. At its peak, the Iraqi CBW arsenal included over thirty thousand liters of deadly biological agents (anthrax, botulinum toxin, and aflatoxin) and a demonstrated capability to produce and deploy a variety of chemical weapons as well (VX, mustard gas, sarin). Iraq probably maintains the necessary precursor chemicals and documentation for the production of chemical agents, especially VX, and commercial production facilities could be readily adapted for such an effort. According to Major Ritter, UNSCOM has information suggesting that CW "precursor and possible agent production are taking place inside Iraq."[3] A similar effort could result in a near-term limited production capability of biological agents, and Major Ritter believes that Iraq has hidden "several Al-Hussein warheads filled with a dry BW agent, probably Anthrax," as well as a mobile BW production facility.[4]

A renewed ballistic missile program could also pose a major threat to regional stability. While 817 of the known 819 prohibited ballistic missiles had been accounted for by the end of 1997, Iraq has presumably continued its efforts to develop a medium-to-long-range ballistic missile capability. Major Ritter maintains that Iraq probably has between five and twelve missile assemblies and missile components for up to twenty-five missiles apparently salvaged from destroyed stockpiles.[5] Under the guise of work on allowed short-range missile systems, Iraq could acquire the expertise and materials for the breakout production of longer-range variants within six months. An extensive network of covert procurement companies has been set up to import both dual-use and prohibited material, including machine tools, liquid and solid propellants, and engine components, all of which would be essential for renewed development and production.

TABLE 11.3

IRAQI BALLISTIC MISSILE PROGRAM

IRAQI BALLISTIC MISSILES (NUMBER)

Item	Initial Inventory	Comments
Soviet-supplied SCUD missiles (includes Iraqi modifications of the SCUD: the Al-Husayn with a range of 650 km and the Al-Abbas with a range of 950 km)	819	UNSCOM accepts Iraqi accounting for all but 2 of the original 819 Scud missiles acquired from the Soviet Union. Iraq has not explained the disposition of major components that it may have stripped from operational missiles before their destruction, and some Iraqi claims—such as the use of 14 Scuds in ATBM tests—are not believable. Gaps in Iraqi declarations and Baghdad's failure to fully account for indigenous missile programs strongly suggest that Iraq retains a small missile force.
Iraqi-produced SCUD missiles	Unknown	Iraq denied producing a completed Scud missile, but it produced/procured and tested all major subcomponents.
Iraqi-produced SCUD warhead	120	Iraq claims all 120 were used or destroyed. UNSCOM supervised the destruction of 15. Recent UNSCOM inspections found additional CW/BW warheads beyond those currently admitted.
Iraqi-produced SCUD airframes	2	Iraq claims testing 2 indigenous airframes in 1990. It is unlikely that Iraq produced only 2 Scud airframes.
Iraqi-produced SCUD engines	80	Iraq's claim that it melted 63 engines following acceptance tests—53 of which failed quality controls—are unverifiable and not believable. UNSCOM is holding this as an open issue.
Soviet-supplied missile launchers	11	UNSCOM doubts Iraq's claim that it unilaterally destroyed 5 launchers. The Soviet Union may have sold more than the declared 11 launchers.
Iraqi-produced missile launchers	8	Iraq has the capability to produce additional launchers.

In terms of its nuclear program, Major Ritter claims that Iraq maintains the components for several "implosion-type" nuclear devices (lacking only the fissile material) and that most of the intellectual infrastructure of the nuclear program remains in place. According to Khidhir Hamza, an Iraqi nuclear scientist who defected to the United States in 1995, Iraq still employs twelve thousand scientists and technicians in its nuclear program.[6] However, it would take much longer for Iraq to deploy nuclear weapons than it would to renew its other nonconventional weapons development programs. Iraq's nuclear weaponization and uranium enrichment infrastructure was heavily damaged during the Gulf War. Iraq does retain the technical knowledge, however, and is suspected of retaining hidden machine tools and nuclear feedstock, which would be necessary should it again attempt uranium enrichment.

Even assuming an immediate return to pre–Gulf War conditions, Iraq is probably five to seven years away from the possession of enough highly enriched uranium for a rudimentary nuclear explosive device. But, as David Albright, a scientist who was the first nongovernmental IAEA inspector in Iraq, noted, "with the right kind of assistance, Iraq could be making annually enough highly enriched uranium for a nuclear explosive within a short time—perhaps a few years." Alternatively, if Iraq were to acquire weapons-usable fissile material from another country, "Saddam Hussein could have nuclear weapons within a matter of months."[7]

AN END TO INSPECTIONS

The clear consequence of the airstrikes that began in December 1998 has been the discontinuation of UNSCOM's work in Iraq. The Security Council has been deadlocked, unable to find consensus on a new approach to Iraq. In January 1999, France broke from the U.S. and British position, proposing that the Security Council end the embargo on Iraqi oil sales and replace the intrusive inspection regime with a new monitoring system aimed at preventing Iraq from reconstituting its WMD program. The French plan called for replacing or modifying UNSCOM with a new commission for preventive, long-term weapons monitoring that relies on sensors and cameras; ending the sanctions on the sale of Iraqi oil, which would otherwise remain in place until Iraq's dismantlement is complete; and prohibiting the sale of materials that Iraq could divert for weapons development.

While Russia and China supported this plan, the United States rejected most major points in the French proposal, insisting that the oil embargo should not be lifted until existing disarmament requirements have been satisfied and that monitoring methods should include intrusive inspections.

In June 1999, the United Kingdom and the Netherlands offered a competing resolution suggesting that UNSCOM be replaced with a new United Nations Commission for Investigation, Inspection, and Monitoring. Iraq would give the new commission "unrestricted access and provision of information" and "immediate, unconditional, and unrestricted access to any and all areas, facilities, equipment, records and means of transportation which they may wish to inspect." Sanctions would be suspended if Iraq answers remaining disarmament questions and cooperates with the new commission. The commission would give Iraq a specific list of outstanding issues.

As of mid-1999, it did not appear that the inspection issue would be resolved in the near future. The continuing Security Council disagreement over how best to address the Iraq problem seems far from resolution, especially when the status quo—a strong sanctions regime and no apparent efforts by Iraq at WMD development—requires no further diplomatic efforts.

NOTES

1. Carnegie Endowment Project associate Toby F. Dalton prepared the background material provided here, with the assistance of Matthew Rice and Janice Sung. Janice Sung prepared the tables in this chapter. The views expressed in this background material do not represent the views of Ambassador Richard Butler or of the United Nations Special Commission on Iraq.

2. See Karen DeYoung, "Baghdad Weapons Programs Dormant," *Washington Post*, July 15, 1999, A19.

3. Scott Ritter, *Endgame* (New York: Simon and Schuster, 1999), 217.

4. Ibid., 219.

5. Ibid., 222.

6. Interview by Charlie Rose, *60 Minutes II*, January 27, 1999.

7. Institute for Science and International Security press release, "Military Strikes in Iraq: Inspections, Sanctions Must Stay in Place to Prevent Nuclear Weapons Program Reconstitution," December 17, 1998.

—12—

Iran-Russia Missile Cooperation

Richard Speier, Robert Gallucci,
Robbie Sabel, Viktor Mizin

BACKGROUND
By Richard Speier

The international policy on missile non-proliferation is called the Missile Technology Control Regime, or MTCR. That policy was secretly negotiated by the seven Western economic summit nations during the 1980s and then publicly announced in 1987. In the years since, the membership in the regime has more than quadrupled, from seven to thirty-two.

The regime has one central tenet, and that is to create a strong presumption to deny the export of ballistic or cruise missiles whose capabilities represent a threat to deliver nuclear, chemical, or biological weapons. The regime also has a strong presumption to deny exports of major components, production equipment, technology in the form of floppy disks or blueprints, or technology in the form of people traveling and giving engineering assistance for such programs. The regime has not only a strong presumption of denial but also a flat prohibition against the export of complete production facilities for these systems or their complete production technology, including engineers helping people build complete production facilities. The regime also has a strong presumption of export denial for missiles of any range or payload or for any of a long list of items if they are intended for chemical, biological, or nuclear delivery.

On the very same day the regime was announced in April 1987, the United States had three special meetings—with Russia, China, and Israel—because these countries were key potential suppliers of missile technology whose support would be very important to the success of the regime. In the intervening years all three of those nations stated their support for the regime. Indeed, in the early 1990s, Israel and Russia actually put into their regulations the export controls of the MTCR.

It was not until 1995, however, that Russia became a full member of the MTCR. (Full membership entitles a nation to participation in the decision making of the regime and to the exchanges of information within the regime.) Within a few months of Russian MTCR membership, troublesome reports started appearing of Russian missile guidance equipment discovered in Jordan, headed eventually for Iraq. Other stories focused on Russian exports to India for a submarine-launched missile. Most troubling, about a year after Russia joined the regime, reports surfaced in Israel that Russian entities were helping Iran to develop ballistic missiles.

In 1998, Iran tested a Shahab-3 ballistic missile with a range of 1,200 km. There are reports that Iran is developing a longer-range Shahab-4. In August, Iran displayed a mock-up of a space launch vehicle, which is usable as an intercontinental ballistic missile (some called it the Shahab-5). It is clear that Iran has a very broad missile program.

The issue has involved intense high-level diplomacy on a triangular basis among the United States, Israel, and Russia. Following, three officials intimately involved in this dialogue explore the positions of each nation in depth.

A UNITED STATES VIEW
By the Honorable Robert Gallucci*

In 1997, the issue of Russian entities' assistance to Iran in the area of ballistic missiles found itself prominently featured on the agenda of the Gore-Chernomyrdin Commission. After collecting information about this assistance to Iran for more than a year, the United States gave it a prominent place in the Gore-Chernomyrdin context.

These entities are in some cases institutes, in some cases universities, in some cases for-profit organizations that have roots in the Soviet Union. Some of these names are well known: the Moscow Aviation Institute, the Baltic State Technical University, the Scientific Research and Design Institute of Power Technology (NIKIET). They have been mentioned many times in the open literature. The assistance in question is sometimes material shipped from a Russian entity to Iran that may be used for parts of a ballistic missile, maybe for the warhead, maybe for the fuselage. Sometimes components are shipped that may have to do with guidance. These entities have also been training Iranians in Russia in the development, design, and manufacture of ballistic missiles. Russian missile experts have also traveled to Iran to help with development of long-range ballistic missiles.

In August of 1997, about eight months after the Gore-Chernomyrdin Commission first discussed this issue, a direct channel was established on it. Ambassador Frank Wisner was named for the U.S. side, and Mr. Yuri Koptev, head of the Russian Space Agency, was appointed on the Russian side. The channel was designed to deal specifically with this issue, put particular emphasis upon it, and then report the results of the meetings to the Gore-Chernomyrdin Commission.

Through this process, the United States made démarches to Russia about activ-

* The views expressed are those of the author and do not necessarily reflect the position of the United States government. These comments have been adapted from a presentation at the Carnegie Non-Proliferation Conference, January 1999.

ities that the U.S. officials observed, and shared information and intelligence about interactions between Russian entities and the Iranian ballistic missile program. For one full year, from the summer of 1997 through the summer of 1998, the process achieved steady progress, whether measured by input indicators—improved Russian export control—or output indicators—less evidence of assistance.

In terms of input indicators, the United States succeeded in persuading the Russian government of the wisdom of putting certain provisions in place, such as the Decree of January 22, 1998 (the so-called Catch-All Decree), which allowed the Russians not only to control those items listed under the Missile Technology Control Regime Annex but also to look at the end user and end use—in other words, to give Russia a tool to control more of the activities that were of concern.

Many consultations took place at the expert level on export controls, with U.S. experts going to Russia and Russian experts coming to the United States to improve their ability to execute the control of this technology. In the summer of 1998, the Russian government announced the investigation of nine Russian entities for possible proliferation activities, particularly with respect to Iran.

In terms of output indicators, when the dialogue with the Russians began in the summer of 1997, there were a dozen or so cases under discussion that the United States wanted Russia to act upon. That number was slowly whittled away, and there were actually cases of goods being stopped. In some cases, U.S. observers no longer saw any activity, at least activity that was of concern. Over time, the number of problem cases that were under discussion diminished.

Later in 1998, however, this progress came to a halt, as measured by both input and output. In terms of input, the export groups and technology groups that were supposed to meet following the Moscow summit in September 1998 really have not met effectively. The investigation of those nine entities that was launched with such optimism in July 1998 has not produced any real results, such as a conclusion that anyone acted inappropriately or illegally; there has been no prosecution.

On the output side, in the summer of 1998, Iran tested its so-called Shahab-3, an MRBM. Many of the problem cases that the United States had identified as much as a year ago continued, while some new cases of assistance were identified. The United States continues to raise this issue at the highest levels of the Russian government. The two presidents have spoken about it, and the dialogue has also continued with the foreign minister and with Director Koptev. This issue is front and center on the diplomatic agenda between the United States and Russia.

Despite the process of gradual improvement through the summer of 1998, the U.S. Congress passed a sanctions resolution aimed at Russian entities cooperating with Iran on missiles. The resolution was vetoed by the president, and the Senate chose not to override it, no doubt because of the actions the U.S. and Russian governments took. Indeed, the day after the nine entities were identified for investigation by the Russians, the United States named seven of them against which trade action would be taken. In January 1999, three more entities were subject to trade action.

What is the significance of Russian-entity assistance in the Iranian case? Iran's ballistic missile program did not receive assistance exclusively from Russia. Iran received very material assistance from North Korea, providing a substantial boost to allow them to develop the Shahab-3.

But Russian assistance was extremely important in shortening the amount of time in which the Iranians would be able to develop, manufacture, and deploy their own MRBMs, and do so presumably with some improvement in quality. Continued Russian assistance will allow not only for the rapid deployment of the Shahab-3 but also for the Iranians to move on to IRBMs and ICBMs.

Of course, MRBMs—whether No Dongs, Shahab-3s, or extended-range SCUDs like the Iraqis were developing—are not of much use in a military sense for the delivery of conventional munitions. They become interesting and very dangerous, provocative, and destabilizing, though, when they are mated with weapons of mass destruction—chemical, biological, or nuclear.

Russia is also assisting Iran with its nuclear development efforts and is currently the only nation providing assistance to Iran in the nuclear area. Notwithstanding Iran's status as a member of the Non-Proliferation Treaty (NPT), no other country besides Russia believes that it is prudent or wise to engage in nuclear cooperation with Iran. Russia is helping Iran complete the Bushehr reactor, and there is concern that the assistance will go beyond that reactor and contribute to Iran's ability to develop a nuclear weapons capability. So it is the combination of Russian assistance to Iran with ballistic missiles and in the nuclear area that creates a most troubling and new development in the region.

The international regime created to control ballistic missile proliferation, the MTCR, has been broadly successful, much as the NPT regime has been broadly successful: There are relatively few states that act contrary to the regimes. This success only highlights those cases where a treaty regime like the NPT, or an informal agreement, like the MTCR, is unsuccessful. India and Pakistan come to mind in the nuclear area. And in the missile area, there are three cases of transfers that particularly stand out: those occurring from China, North Korea, and Russia. Each of these cases involved transfers to both the Middle East and South Asia and has had destabilizing results.

Like the nuclear issue, the ballistic missile issue has thresholds. In the nuclear area, the acquisition of a nuclear weapon is the principal threshold, notwithstanding the observation that students of nuclear proliferation usually make: that proliferation is a process, that there is a real difference between a simple fission device, a boosted device, and a thermonuclear weapon. Several orders of magnitude of destruction do indeed separate these types of weapons. Still, the sharpest firebreak is between no nuclear capability and the acquisition of a first nuclear device.

Similarly, in the missile world, there are firebreaks. There are two in particular. First is the acquisition of an MRBM, particularly if the range of that MRBM is sufficient to allow the state to reach its principal adversary for the first time or to launch from more secure locations. In the case of India and Pakistan, and perhaps in the case of Iran, it seems as though this might be true. The second firebreak is the mating of that MRBM with a weapon of mass destruction, particularly a nuclear weapon. In the South Asian context, it seems that the threshold has been breached: both India and Pakistan have deployable nuclear weapons, and both are working on deployable MRBMs. In the Middle East, that threshold is widely thought to have been breached by Israel. Iran has demonstrated an MRBM capability, but not a nuclear capability. It is not at all clear how long this will remain true.

THE ISRAELI VIEW
By the Honorable Robbie Sabel

Iran is an important regional state and should be treated as such. The policies of the Iranian government may be objectionable to Israel, but the Iranian norms are clearly a world apart from the aberrant behavior of Saddam Hussein, the Iraqi dictator. Nevertheless, and notwithstanding such a caveat, the combination of three nefarious elements in present-day Iranian policy should set alarm bells jangling loud, not only in Israel but also throughout the world.

The three elements of Iranian policy that fuse together to form this nefarious danger are: the development of weapons of mass destruction (WMD), the development of missiles capable of delivering such weapons of mass destruction, and, finally, the hate-inspired policies of the Iranian government toward Israel. Taken as a whole, there is indeed cause for concern.

Israel recognizes the Islamic Republic of Iran and the right of the Iranian people to choose their own form of government. Israel seeks no dispute with the Iranian people or with its government. Needless to say, Israel has no territorial dispute with Iran, and there are no bilateral issues that deeply divide the two nations. In the past, Israel has had close relations with Iran.

Israel encounters from Iran, however, a total negation of Israel that transcends any difference there might well be over their respective foreign policies. Israel is officially branded the "Small Satan." Iran opposes all attempts by Israel at reaching peace with its neighbors. Iran supports terrorism against Israeli and Jewish targets worldwide. The Iranian involvement in the bombing of the Israel Embassy in Buenos Aires and the Jewish Community Center there is now a matter of record. It certainly causes anxiety when the Shahab-3 missile was paraded in Tehran on September 25, 1998, with the inscription on the missile carrier declaring that "Israel should be wiped off the map." The Iranian minister of defense, Ali Shakhmani, declared during the parade that Iran would not use its military capability against anyone with the exception of the "Zionist regime." Extremist slogans by themselves may be dismissed as harmless verbal fireworks, but when they are combined with extensive development of missiles and weapons of mass destruction, it is time to pay attention. In assessing Iran, Israel looks principally at capabilities and not at rhetoric. But inevitably one must attempt to assess intentions as well, and the combination of expressed hostile intent and capability gives Israel cause for grave concern.

The massive Iranian investment in missiles and weapons of mass destruction is particularly striking when it is appreciated that because of the slump in oil prices, Iran is in dire financial straits. A country that diverts its scarce financial resources from economic development to long-range ballistic missiles is worthy of very careful attention from the international community.

Iran is developing weapons of mass destruction. From the recent declaration made to the Organization for Prohibition of Chemical Weapons the international community received confirmation of what has long been suspected, namely, that Iran has developed a chemical weapon capability, presumably including poison gas. Iran has yet to make a full declaration in accordance with the Chemical Weapons

Convention, and of course no inspections have taken place. There is reason to believe that Iran has developed a biological warfare capability and is attempting to obtain more technology and know-how from Russian sources in this area.

In the long term, the developments in the nuclear field are perhaps the most alarming. Iran, desperately short of cash yet awash with oil, is spending some $800 million on the nuclear reactor facility in Bushehr. This is clearly not tied to Iran's energy needs. Furthermore, Iran has attempted to purchase from Russia a heavy-water research reactor and other equipment. It has unsuccessfully attempted to obtain technology for uranium enrichment and conversion from China. Since low-enriched uranium is freely available at low prices, it is difficult to find a non-military justification for such efforts. Iran also failed at clandestine attempts to purchase nuclear technology from Britain and specialized metals from Russia. The recent visit to Tehran by Yevgeny Adamov, the Russian minister of atomic energy, appears to portend more intensive and open Iranian purchases from Russia in the nuclear field. There is no economic justification whatsoever for such purchases. The only purpose is to build a nuclear infrastructure that in the future can be diverted to weapon construction. The international community has seen from the bitter Iraqi experience that adherence to the Nuclear Non-Proliferation Treaty (NPT) by itself is not sufficient to prevent such diversion. Iraq in fact used the NPT as a cover for its clandestine activities.

A useful step to assuage the anxiety over such possible diversion would be for Iran to adhere to the IAEA enhanced inspection protocol—the so-called 93+2 agreement. There has been talk of such adherence, and even reports that Iran has tried to obtain further nuclear technology in exchange for such adherence. But so far Iran has continued to abstain from actually adhering to the protocol, which if applied, would seriously curtail Iran's ability to develop nuclear weapons.

The third element is the development of missiles by Iran. Iran has tested a prototype of the 1,300-kilometer-range Shahab-3. There is no reason to believe that it was not a successful test. Iran may claim that it requires missiles to counter a possible Iraqi missile threat. The Shahab-3, however, could travel far beyond Iraq. It is a strategic weapon, and the inscriptions attached to it in the Tehran parade leave no doubt as to the envisaged target. An even longer-range missile, the Shahab-4, is planned, and would place large parts of Europe within range.

Such missiles make no military sense if armed with conventional high-explosive warheads. Their inherent inaccuracy from 1,300 kilometers makes them of marginal importance if all they can do is deliver a high-explosive warhead. Were they to be armed, however, with chemical or biological warheads, they would become immensely effective terror weapons against civilian targets. Were they to be armed with nuclear warheads, they would irrevocably change the face of the Middle East.

Can the development of missiles be halted? The answer is a qualified yes. The Shahab-3 is still an unreliable prototype. A state can accept less than absolute reliability for a missile carrying conventional warheads. If a conventional warhead explodes off target, the damage is manageable. But a missile carrying a nonconventional warhead must be absolutely reliable. It is safe to assume that Iran would be extremely reluctant to use a missile with a nonconventional warhead unless it was sure of the reliability of such a missile. The danger of a nonconventional missile's exploding over one's own territory, or over that of a friendly state, is not a danger that Iran is likely to ignore.

For the Shahab-3 to enter Iran's arsenal, the missile has to be produced in usable quantities. Iran is not yet in a position to do so. The missile has to be completely reliable. Iran has not yet developed it to this stage. The missile will, presumably, be adapted to carry nonconventional warheads. This has not yet been done and requires sophisticated technology. All these additional refinements require, in the foreseeable future, outside help. That help can only come from Russian companies and entities.

Iran plans to produce the 2,000-kilometer-range Shahab-4; it could be armed with a 1,000-kilogram warhead with a shorter range. Such a large warhead would expand the possibilities of using different types of nuclear warheads. A longer range, possibly using Russian engine technology, would require even more advanced technology. Again, outside help is required and Russia is the likely source. There has been talk from Iranian sources of developing the Shahab-5, an intercontinental ballistic missile. Such missiles, of course, are for ranges far beyond Israel.

At present, Russian companies and entities continue to provide assistance to the Iranian missile development project and to the development of an Iranian nuclear infrastructure. The U.S. government has devoted considerable efforts to trying to persuade the Russian government to prevent such proliferation. Russian colleagues acknowledge their awareness that it is not in Russia's interest to see Iran with long-range missiles equipped with nonconventional warheads. Yet, is Russia doing everything in its power to prevent such leakage of technology, know-how, and material?

The Russian government is not making such an all-out effort. There may in fact be elements in Russia that believe there is economic and even strategic gain in such deadly trade. Despite the acknowledged internal problems of the Russian government, proliferation could be prevented if the will existed. If the Russian government reached the conclusion that such proliferation is a dire threat to Russia, the leakage would be prevented. Instead there is an opposite trend, and the much-publicized trip of Russian minister Adamov to Tehran appears to be flaunting nuclear ties rather than limiting them.

It is still not too late to prevent Iran from developing long-range missiles with nonconventional warheads. The Missile Technology Control Regime (MTCR) is not a complete answer, but it certainly plays a useful role in limiting proliferation. It is clear that there have been violations of the MTCR by Russian entities in regard to Iran.

How does one bring about cessation of violations? Iran and Russia have to believe that Western and other states see such proliferation as a very real threat to world security and are willing to take the necessary steps to prevent such proliferation. Such steps need to involve elements of both impedance and inducements. If Iran and Russia face firm, united opposition to such proliferation, these two states will conclude that such proliferation is not in their interest. It is not yet too late.

THE RUSSIAN VIEW
By Dr. Viktor Mizin*

Iran is probably the most demonized country in American political culture. To Russia, Iran is just a country that is a major regional power and, as described by Mr. Zbigniew Brzezinski, a door to Eurasia. Unlike Iraq, Iran is not under international sanctions, but rather unilateral sanctions by the United States government.

To understand Russian attitudes toward Iran, it is important to distinguish three major groups in the Russian political elite. The first could be termed proliferation zealots or proponents. These are the people who exchange a flurry of memos with the U.S. government and who formulate official Russian positions on non-proliferation, including the Iran case, which basically do not differ much from the official American approach as described by U.S. national security adviser Sandy Berger (see chapter 4 of this volume).

Then there are the people who manufacture armaments, and they could be called neutrals. Finally, the last group opposes any kind of export control or non-proliferation. They view such regimes as some sort of sly ruse devised by the U.S. government under the pressure of U.S. companies to squeeze out Russian armament makers from lucrative world markets.

While the first group, the zealots or proponents, is engaged in endless consultation with Americans and signs all kinds of papers, the third group is constantly undermining the regime Russia signed onto.

It is also important to understand the difference in U.S. and Russian approaches to proliferation concerns. While certain people in Russia pay lip service to the politically correct notion that proliferation is dangerous, if one looks at the countries that are known as "rogue states" (in official Russian parlance, Moscow rejects the notion of rogue states), all of those countries are former clients of the Soviet Union: North Korea, Libya, Iraq, and others. And unlike the situation faced by the United States, the deployment of any ballistic missiles does not threaten Russian troops stationed abroad. There is also no political community in Russia—as there is in the United States—strong enough to influence the voting in the parliament.

That is why one always hears very politically correct words from Russian political scientists about the concerns that Iran is developing missile capabilities. No one in the Russian political elite is seriously considering the threat of this development. For example, it was the same case with Saudi Arabia developing an IRBM potential.

Iran remains a very important market for the remnants of the Russian military industry. The collapse of the economy in Russia literally prods the best of Russian industry (the most technologically saturated companies), which have now lost state government procurement orders, to search for clients abroad. Russia officially considers the Bushehr reactor deal, for example, legitimate because Iran is under IAEA safeguards.

Iran is also a very important market for Russian conventional armaments, and as it is well known, this issue slowed Russian adherence to the Wassenaar Arrange-

---

* The views expressed are those of the author and do not necessarily reflect the position of the Russian government.

ment. Many arms experts in Russia believe that Iran is another untapped market for Russian weapons, and therefore there is no rational basis for ending arms sales to this country, even after fulfillment of current contracts as was agreed in bilateral U.S.-Russian talks. These experts now consider Iran, since the death of Ayatollah Khomeini, just another country that actually has ceased supporting terrorist activity and is no less democratic than some U.S. allies in the Middle East. These feelings are quite widely shared by the Russian political elite.

It is interesting that the U.S. government actually opened the eyes of the Russian government after an article appeared in *The Los Angeles Times* detailing Iranian efforts to procure Russian missile components, and with information provided by Israeli intelligence. It is also interesting that the Russian official reaction moved from official denial from the Ministry of Foreign Affairs and Mr. Chernomyrdin, to reluctant recognition, and then to reports of the successful apprehension of some Iranian spies that contacted Russian missile manufacturers.

This shows that this is not a clandestine program supported and maintained by the Russian government, but rather the adventurous activities of some cash-strapped Russian defense manufacturing facilities. Of course, in Russia, like in many other countries, there is no such thing as a private or independent defense manufacturing facility. They are independent, but still tightly controlled by the Ministry of Defense.

The problem is, how does one stop this process? What could be done in the future? The logical answer is to improve existing export controls. Unfortunately, as the recent revelations show, export controls in Russia are not operational. The problem is enforcement, enforcement, and enforcement.

So the emphasis should be placed on providing more competent personnel on export control services, equipping them with state-of-the-art technology, ensuring the real-time exchange of data and information from Moscow to custom checkpoints. Also, another problem is the bureaucratic wrangling. Russia needs a governing body to oversee export controls.

Finally, a significant part of the proliferation problem is the people. The major threat is that missile specialists will flee abroad because they are unemployed at home. One possible solution is the development of a joint U.S.-Russian project that could employ these Russian specialists. For example, many years ago President Yeltsin proposed that the United States and Russia jointly develop what was termed a "Global System of Protection," that is, an antiballistic missile or another sort of space tracking system. This would be a good idea in the context of future discussions of Russian export controls. Another project that was discussed was the employment of Russian missile scientists in joint commercial efforts, similar to efforts in the nuclear sphere. American companies could employ the best and brightest Russian missile engineers and foremen, thus preventing them from fleeing to proliferant countries.

These are very optimistic solutions. For the time being, however, the good example of cooperation between the Russian Ministry of Atomic Energy and U.S. Cooperative Threat Reduction program should be followed and applied in the missile non-proliferation sphere.

—13—

Middle East Arms Control and Regional Security Dilemmas

Benjamin Frankel, Ariel Levite,
Khidhir Hamza, Bruce Jentleson

The Arab-Israeli conflict in the Middle East has been the principal focus of international attention to the region. Increasingly, however, attention is turning to the development of weapons of mass destruction (WMD) and ballistic missile capabilities by Iraq and Iran. Soon, these nations may challenge Israel's strategic regional monopoly. As the peace process moves forward, arms control in the regional security context will become an increasingly important requirement for a lasting peace.

BACKGROUND
By Benjamin Frankel

The nuclear situation in the Middle East has, until now, been different from nuclear developments in other regions for four reasons.

First, unlike the nuclear competition between the superpowers during the Cold War, or the current situation in South Asia, nuclear weapons and other WMD were sought and acquired in the region against the backdrop of an official state of war between Israel and its neighbors.

Second, one country has a nuclear monopoly, a monopoly it has worked very hard to maintain during the last thirty years. Israel engaged in covert action against Egypt in 1961–63 to prevent Egypt from acquiring nuclear weapons, and attacked the Iraqi reactor at Osiraq in 1981. Challenges to this unique monopoly might make Israel more amenable to seriously rethinking its policy options.

Third, Israel has enjoyed a remarkable immunity from U.S. pressure. The United States exerted tremendous pressure on South Korea and Taiwan in the mid-1970s to abandon their nuclear pursuits, and on Pakistan during the previous twenty years.

During the Carter administration, the United States pressured Germany not to co-operate with Brazil. Israel, with very few exceptions in the early 1960s, has remained untouched by such pressures.

Finally, the Middle East is a region of multiple rivalries. Not everything revolves around the Arab-Israeli conflict. Efforts to resolve one conflict may exacerbate another. The military weakening of Iraq, for example, may lessen Israel's security anxieties and make it more amenable to make concessions to the Palestinians. A weak Iraq, however, may inflame Iran's expansionist designs and encourage Kurdish and Shi'a separatism, which, in turn, may lead to increased Turkish and Saudi anxiety and military assertiveness. There is thus an additional complexity in trying to negotiate through this minefield of multiple rivalries that does not exist in other WMD competitions.

In the last fifty years two developments in the region, each leading in a different direction, have pushed the issue of nuclear and WMD control onto the diplomatic and political surface. One set of developments may be viewed as positive. This is the fact that two Arab countries, Egypt and Jordan, have peace treaties with Israel. The Palestinians now have a measure of peace with Israel, and there is some normalization of relations between Israel and a few other Arab countries. In the context of peace and normalization, many of these countries, led by Egypt, insist on some kind of accounting of Israel's WMD capabilities. It is perfectly normal for countries at peace to expect a relationship that is peacelike rather than warlike.

There are negative developments as well. Countries such as Iran, Iraq, and Syria have been investing large sums of money and many resources to acquire WMD capabilities. Just as Israel is being asked to have its capabilities monitored in some fashion, it needs to be mindful of the similar capabilities emerging in other states.

These developments will erode Israel's monopoly, because there is very little it can do on its own to retard the development of WMD capabilities in other states. As Iran and Iraq continue efforts to develop such capabilities, it is increasingly likely that the United States will be forced to reexamine its hands-off policy toward WMD capabilities in Israel. Change is coming.

AN ISRAELI PERSPECTIVE
By Ariel Levite

Nineteen ninety-eight was a bad year for proliferation in general and in the Middle East region in particular. The closing years of this century are likely to be a lot worse. The Middle East is currently presenting a very acute case of proliferation-induced instability. The region is at a critical juncture where things are not developing incrementally or slowly, but rather quickly. This instability will continue for a while longer.

The Middle East will undergo a dramatic transition that may well be reversible, and will turn the Middle East in a very different direction—needless to say, in a very adverse direction. The gravity of the present situation stems primarily from developments around Iran and Iraq. The potential for spillover from that part of the region is very real, both within the Middle East and beyond the Middle East to Europe, as well as to India.

The current situation has little to do with the Arab-Israeli conflict. Therefore, there isn't that much hope that even if considerable progress was made toward a resolution of the Arab-Israeli conflict, starting with the Palestinians and extending to the Syrians, things would get a lot better. Too much hope should not be pinned on the Arab-Israeli peace process without dealing effectively with the problem of Iran and Iraq.

IRAN

Currently, Iran benefits from an outpouring of WMD and ballistic missile technology from the Russian Federation. The assistance from the Russian Federation continues unabated, despite the three-year sustained effort by the U.S. government to convince the Russian Federation to curb its assistance. With the government of Prime Minister Yevgeny Primakov, combined with deteriorating economic conditions, things have only worsened.

There is nothing to suggest that this is likely to dramatically change anytime soon. Furthermore, Iran is also on the receiving end of considerable North Korean assistance in the missile domain. Once again, there is nothing to suggest that this assistance will slow down. American efforts to try to bring North Korea in line with nuclear and missile issues are progressing slowly, especially in the missile domain, where very little progress at all appears to have been made.

In fact, the successful tests of the North Korean missiles have done nothing but whet Iran's appetite for further missile assistance. Since North Korea funds its indigenous missile development through exports, there is nothing to suggest that it will stop that activity. This assistance is no longer with 300- to 500-kilogram missiles but in the intermediate range.

Iran also professed, in a recent statement by its minister of defense, to be driven by a strong desire to influence events throughout the region and beyond. Iran would extend its deterrence to cover the entire Arab world, implying ambitions of not just intermediate-range missiles (IRBMs) but intercontinental missiles (ICBMs). The Iranians are cooperating not only with parties outside the region but also with parties in the region.

Those who hoped that internal developments in Iran, particularly with the ascendancy of a more moderate president, would somehow affect the course Iran pursues with weapons of mass destruction have been disappointed. Changes in attitude toward the peace process, Israel, and terrorism have thus far proved elusive, with some indication of a worsening situation. Either because of the weakness of the president or because he does not dispute the policy, greater emphasis has been placed since his election on WMD and missile programs.

It is quite remarkable that this has occurred even in a period of deep financial crisis inside Iran. The financial crisis has affected many other sectors of Iranian society, including its ability to repay some of its debts. The crisis has not, however, affected Iran's pursuit of a WMD and ballistic missile capability.

Even less reassuring is the fact that some U.S. allies, particularly in Europe, have rushed in to try to do business with Iran, regardless of the Iranian government's other activities. The only bright spot when it comes to trading with Iran may be the People's Republic of China, which for a variety of reasons has elected, by and large, to stop cooperating with Iran in many of those critical areas.

IRAQ

Some of Iraq's capabilities have been set back by the combination of the seven-year effort by UNSCOM and military actions. Clearly, Iraq retains a residual WMD and ballistic missile capability, which is tightly concealed, as well as a very solid infrastructure base, which could be used to restart its WMD efforts.

Renewal of Iraq's WMD program is expected for several reasons. First, the nature of the Iraqi political regime has not fundamentally changed in any way; it is determined to try to keep whatever capability it had, despite the sanctions. Second, its crippling of the disarmament effort by initially expelling UN inspectors, and then upon their return limiting their activities, has left the situation in limbo. Indicators do not bode well for reviving the verification efforts in Iraq. Third, the Iraqis themselves are unlikely to be positively affected by what they see is happening across the border.

REGIONAL IMPLICATIONS

There is considerable potential for spillover from Iran and Iraq in many ways, not just into other countries but also to nonstate actors. Those who would like to see global arms control really making a difference in the programs of Iraq and Iran have little to celebrate. There is slight evidence to suggest that global arms control arrangements are having an effect on the Iranian and Iraqi thirst for weapons of mass destruction and ballistic missiles.

At the same time, the regional arms control and security process, which showed such promise for changing things in the long term, has been completely frozen now for three years because of Egyptian dissatisfaction with the agenda. There is a profound anxiety in the region about what these trends may imply. This is directly attributable to what is happening in Iran and the fact that the Egyptians cannot afford to stay behind when they see Iran becoming nuclear. Also, part of the recent acrimony between Iraq and Egypt suggests that the Egyptians cannot be indifferent to what is happening with Iraq.

The anxiety is increasingly being transferred to the overall outlook on the region, and within the region. The other countries in the region have to choose between trying reconciliation with Iran and/or with Iraq and trying to consolidate their defense links with the United States. Countries are weighing their options to a degree that it is beginning to cloud the outlook of the peace process above and beyond the problem of adherence to either the Syrian or the Palestinian arrangements. This is increasing defense expenditures and changing priorities in spending. Higher expenditure in all of these areas is likely to occur if conditions do not change for the better soon.

AN IRAQI PERSPECTIVE
By Khidhir Hamza

The impetus in the Middle East for establishing a weapons of mass destruction capability is Israel. Israel's huge arsenal of nuclear weapons provides legitimacy to any Arab power intent on developing a nuclear arsenal. Even so, most Arab countries no longer pose a serious threat in their pursuit of a nuclear weapons capability. In general, there is no viable Arab nuclear weapons program other than Iraq's.

Egypt has yet to start a serious nuclear weapons program. The Egyptian program remains fragmented, underfunded, and understaffed. There were signs of the beginning of an Algerian program, now abandoned. The Syrian nuclear weapons program is nearly nonexistent. Both the nuclear technology knowledge and the support base are weak. Syria's lack of nuclear prowess was highlighted when Israel planted a listening device powered by a nuclear battery onto the Syrian telephone network. The device was subsequently discovered, but Syrian technicians had serious difficulties dealing with it. The Syrian threat lies primarily in the lower technology of chemical and biological programs.

Iran's nuclear program does not have the scientists and human capabilities to compare with those of Iraq's, the largest program in the Middle East. It was estimated that the Iranian program was only one-tenth the size of the Iraqi program. In 1975, Iraqi scientists visited Iran, and at that time the Iranians displayed total inability to create a viable nuclear program. Not only was their reactor often shut down, but also their program had dwindled in size since its peak level of some 120 to 130 people working on designing a nuclear weapon.

Iran took a different approach toward achieving a nuclear capability: It began by purchasing expertise. Iraq's program, on the other hand, was generally indigenous except for a piece of the nuclear program that had been transferred to the military—uranium enrichment using centrifuge technology. Iraq's leaders believed that buying expertise would compromise the reliability and continuity of the program. The Iraqis believed that their nuclear program should be totally indigenous and totally self-reliant.

This approach, though, was not universal among Iraq's programs. The chemical and biological programs relied on foreign expertise.

Iran's revival of interest in a nuclear capability is driven more by Iraq than by Israel. The Israeli arsenal, which has existed for twenty to thirty years, cannot explain the recent acceleration of the Iranian program. The most likely reason for this acceleration is the discovery of the size of the Iraqi program.

Iraq's nuclear ambitions can be understood by examining its unique security situation. Iraq's water, controlled by Turkey, has been cut off in the past. The Euphrates River periodically dries up. It was recently almost dry for five years, during which time most of the river's basin agriculture was destroyed. It is almost guaranteed that Iraq's water supply will dry up over the next century. Again in 1998 and 1999, the Euphrates is almost dry, and the situation in the Tigris River is worsening.

Iraq has no natural resources except for oil, and even this has been greatly restricted. Sanctions aside, almost all of the Gulf outlets are controlled by Iran. Oil pipelines must pass through either Turkey or Syria, and both have stopped the flow in the past.

Iraq perceives enemies on all fronts, and when it is not vying for regional power, it is fighting for regional continuity. In the East, the Iranians present themselves as defenders of the Shiites. The majority of Iraqis are Shiite, but they are dangerously underrepresented. This poses a serious security problem for the Iraqi government, controlled by the Sunnis.

The possibility of a confrontation with Israeli is a fringe issue. Egypt's President Mubarak reinforced this view by repeating a portion of a conversation he had with Iraq's president. "We have no borders with Israel," said Saddam Hussein. "Since we have no borders with Israel, it is not our problem. It is your problem."

Iraq's strategy against these perceived threats can be split into two groups, tactical and strategic. Chemical and biological weapons are regarded as tactical. They can potentially be defended against, especially with advances in biotechnology and other sciences. The main goal is to develop a strategic nuclear weapon. The intent to use a radiation weapon was there during the Iran-Iraq war, but not enough radioactive material was produced to build one.

The Iraqi nuclear program was planned to have the capability to protect against local wars similar to the Iran-Iraq war. It would offer to Iraq some kind of deterrence against Israel and hegemony in the area over other countries. Plans were made and designs drawn for an eventual production of about 100 kilograms of weapons-grade uranium, enough for about six bombs, in five to ten years. The idea was not to build a bomb or two, but for Iraq to become a nuclear power equal to Israel.

The importance placed upon Iraq's different strategies is reflected by the allocation of resources. Before the Gulf War, about seven thousand people worked in the nuclear program. Now the number has been increased to twelve thousand, with an estimated total expenditure for the program of $10 billion for the period preceding the Gulf War. Only about four hundred people work in the chemical program and a couple of hundred in the biological programs.

After the Gulf War, the nuclear weapons program increased in size. To avoid detection by international inspectors, the nuclear program's staff was dispersed around the country. A positive side effect was that this gave the scientists and engineers an opportunity to redeem themselves after having failed to provide a bomb for the Gulf War. They began working on reconstructing Iraq's civilian sectors. They took over the tasks of rebuilding civilian industries and services such as electricity and telephone networks, even water and sewer. They rebuilt refineries, factories, and even Saddam's palaces. As a result, today, the nuclear program is more focused, better organized, and better run.

ARMS CONTROL AND REGIONAL SECURITY
By Bruce Jentleson

There are three types of challenges that are crucial to the Middle East region when it comes to non-proliferation.

First, how should a nation that fundamentally and blatantly challenges the non-proliferation regime and the Arab national community be dealt with? In the case of Iraq it is important to see the larger issues and not just those that are specific to the particulars of the case.

Second, how should the international community respond to a nation whose foreign policy intentions may be in transition, in which there is the potential for moderation, as well as some signs of behavior and policy that continue to threaten U.S. interests, U.S. allies, and indeed international non-proliferation?

Third, how should experts think and talk about the Middle East as a region, and the importance of developing regional processes, agreements, and institutions for dealing with regional security, arms control, and non-proliferation? In this case it is instructive to look at the Madrid peace process that was begun in 1991, and at one of the multilateral working groups in particular. The work of the arms control regional security group (ACRS) reveals some interesting lessons, both in the progress that it made and the problems that it ran into, and leaves some important implications that are crucial for thinking about the region.

The first issue is to continue to emphasize the proliferation threat that Iraq poses. This is very well established. If one examines the course of interaction with Iraq over the last twenty years, it is fundamentally an issue that tests the will, capacity, and credibility of the international community to deal with such challenges and it has broad implications in terms of precedents that were set. In the 1980s, before the invasion of Kuwait, there was a fair amount of intelligence and other information available to the West about the Iraqi effort to develop its WMD capacity. This information was not acted upon sufficiently because of certain flawed assumptions and perhaps some self-delusion about what was possible in the relationship. But it also clearly demonstrated the leakiness of the international regime. This did not just start with the discovery of Iraq's WMD capacity and infrastructure in 1991. One must think about how it got to the point before that.

When UN Security Council resolutions were passed and the Special Commission (UNSCOM) on Iraq was formed in the first part of the 1990s, it was, in addition to creating an effective way to deal with the immediate problem of Iraq, an affirmation by the United Nations and by major countries that sovereignty would not be a strict shield behind which nations could hide. Sovereignty, of course, provides rights, but it also comes with responsibilities. Indeed, this issue has come up in many other contexts as well, for instance, with military interventions and peacekeeping. But in a sense, that is really what UNSCOM has been about—a member state of the United Nations simply cannot invoke sovereignty to shield policies and practices that threaten others in the region and the international community.

The reverse is also true. Now that inspections have ceased, the precedent created by UNSCOM will be lost if the international community does not sustain the political will needed to seriously and effectively deal with such a major WMD threat. If the international community cannot deal with this strong threat now, it poses serious questions about what can be achieved in the future.

In terms of Iran's place in the region, and in the global community, there are two different approaches, but they are not necessarily mutually exclusive. One track is on the specific issue of WMD, and includes the sanctions against Russian companies. The second is on the U.S.-Iran relationship, and how to interpret changes in Iran.

There is no question that there are forces at work within the country that are pushing for changes, but how quickly and in what ways those are manifested in terms of WMD issues and other areas of foreign policy are much more difficult to answer. Moreover, there is the problem that certain actions might be well meaning but could boomerang and produce the opposite of the effect intended.

In principle, there need to be three guidelines for efforts in this area. The first is reciprocity: that as the relationship develops between Iran and others in the international community, there must be some basis of understanding that measures have to be taken on both sides to improve relations.

Second is proportionality. This is something we lost sight of with Iraq in the 1980s in an effort to play the "enemy of my enemy is my friend" game. Many measures were taken that not only allowed Iraq to resist defeat by Iran in the Iran-Iraq war but indeed contributed significantly to the dual-use technologies in other parts of the WMD infrastructure discovered in February 1991. There needs to be proportionality in the measures taken, with an eye still kept on the importance of dual-use technologies, monitoring, and end-use verification.

Third is the importance of mixed strategies. A position of standing deterrence can be maintained through what inevitably, in a best-case scenario, would be a fairly significant transition period. It should be understood that cooperation has its benefits, but also that noncooperation has its consequences.

Turning to the region in general, it is extremely important (and this was the basis for the Madrid process and for the ACRS working group) that even if Israel and the Palestinians achieve an agreement, even if Israel and Syria achieve bilateral agreement, even if the Iraq and Iran issues are solved today, there still is a need for a broader regional security process. This process could begin to create the norms, procedures, institutions, and relationships to deal with the proliferation, arms control, and broader security issues that affect the region. The Middle East should become no different than any other region in which these processes are becoming increasingly important in the post–Cold War world. The proliferation issue, in this connection, cannot really be addressed effectively outside the context of regional security. One cannot surgically extract or totally hone in on the WMD issues on a broad regional basis without dealing with the other dimensions of regional security.

There are a couple of inherent problems in doing this. First is the "one step behind rule" vis-à-vis the bilaterals: that whatever success might result from multilateral negotiations in the region, it always has to stay at least one step behind the bilateral negotiations. When the bilateral negotiations start not to just stall but to go backward as they have over the last few years, it becomes even more difficult to stay in such a process.

Second, there are strategic asymmetries in the region that make mutuality of national security inherently problematic. It relates to the character of weapons inventories, to geostrategic issues, issues of strategic depth.

Third, there is a fundamental difference in basic approaches to regional security cooperation in terms of sequencing and emphasis. The general Arab view that was advocated most strongly by Egypt has tended to give priority to direct arms control measures, and within that category, to the nuclear issue in particular. Israel, on the other hand, has stressed the need to start with confidence-building and security-building measures, in order to first establish greater political trust and make some tangible improvements in regional security, and then take some additional arms control steps. This tension in approaches still exists and needs to be resolved.

Fourth is the problem of the nonparticipants. Syria boycotted all of the multilateral talks. Lebanon did too. Syria's presence at any future efforts to deal with regional security is extremely important.

Fifth, the definition of the region, of what constitutes the Middle East, becomes extremely difficult. For example, Iran and Iraq were excluded from the ACRS. Perhaps the formula of Israel, the Arab League, plus Iran is a fairly reasonable formula for how to define the region.

The ACRS group actually made some progress before it fell apart, and there are lessons to learn from the progress that was made. The very creation of a multilateral process for arms control and regional security in a region where no comparable process ever existed was in itself a significant achievement. The group did not begin to define a working agenda on issues like a WMD-free zone, confidence- and security-building measures, conventional arms control, regional security center, regional communications networks, or a security declaration of principles. It did, however, reach a point of actually working on negotiating initial agreements for first-generation measures in this area.

The ACRS eventually fell apart, and it is important to note that it fell apart prior to the election of the Israeli government led by Benjamin Netanyahu. It broke down over the Egyptian-Israeli conflict on the nuclear issue and over a number of other issues as well. It is crucial that efforts be made, not necessarily to reconstitute ACRS but to try to start a regional security process that would provide a forum and a basis for the countries in the region to begin work on measures for military-to-military exchanges, for efforts in mutual familiarization, for confidence-building measures, for laying the basis for arms control.

Global norms and regimes will be necessary, but not sufficient, to bring about this regional forum, and having these regional processes will be crucial. The United States has an important role to play in that leadership, but other expert regional parties, such as the Europeans and the Canadians, also need to be involved as well. In essence, unless this regional security process sets up the beginnings of institutionalization, there will not be a sufficient basis for dealing with fundamental arms control and non-proliferation problems in the Middle East region.

—INTERNATIONAL—
LAW AND AGREEMENTS

—14—

Can the Missile Technology Control Regime Be Repaired?

Richard Speier

Is missile non-proliferation a lost cause? Since 1998 an increasing number of commentators seem to think so. This chapter describes the reasons for the growing belief that missile non-proliferation has failed. It examines the developments in missile non-proliferation policy that may have contributed to its purported failure. In particular, it examines the dichotomy that has been posed between missile defense and missile non-proliferation. Finally, it proposes policy measures to repair the regime.

HAS MISSILE NON-PROLIFERATION FAILED?

The headlines of 1998 and 1999 announced missile tests of increasing ranges by India, Iran, North Korea, and Pakistan. Some advocates of deploying a national missile defense (NMD) system warned that missile proliferation is now uncontrollable. The thoughtful July 1998 report unanimously issued by the bipartisan Rumsfeld Commission expressed similar sentiments.

> Since the end of the Cold War, a number of developments have made ballistic missile and weapons of mass destruction (WMD) technologies increasingly available. They include:
>
> - A number of nations have chosen not to join non-proliferation agreements.
> - Some participants in those agreements have cheated.
> - As global trade has steadily expanded, access has increased to the information, technology, and technicians needed for missile and WMD development.
> - Access to technologies used in early generations of U.S. and Soviet missiles has eased. However rudimentary compared with present U.S. standards, these technologies serve the needs of emerging ballistic missile powers.
> - In those countries of concern to the United States, commerce in ballistic missile and WMD technology and hardware has been growing,

which may make proliferation self-sustaining among them and facilitate their ability to proliferate technology and hardware to others.[1]
- Ballistic missiles armed with WMD payloads pose a strategic threat to the United States. This is not a distant threat. Characterizing foreign assistance as a wild card is both incorrect and misleading. Foreign assistance is pervasive, enabling, and often the preferred path to a ballistic missile and WMD capability.[2]

Although the Rumsfeld Commission investigated the ballistic missile threat, a similarly grim prognosis could be given with respect to cruise missile proliferation.[3] Not only are cruise missile technologies becoming more widely available, but the United Kingdom, France, and Russia appear ready to export their most advanced versions.[4]

With such developments continuing to occur, it is easy to be pessimistic about the future of missile non-proliferation generally and its key international policy in particular—the Missile Technology Control Regime (MTCR).

THE MTCR FINDS ITS TARGET

The establishment of the MTCR by the G-7 governments was announced over 12 years ago, after secret negotiations lasting $4\frac{1}{2}$ years.[5] As described at its public announcement on April 16, 1987, the MTCR was an international export control policy and associated arrangements to limit the proliferation of nuclear-capable missiles. In January 1993 its guidelines were amended to address the proliferation of missiles capable of delivering nuclear, biological, or chemical weapons.[6]

The MTCR began as a small regime with a limited but well-defined objective—to "hinder" (President Reagan's word) the proliferation of rockets and unmanned air vehicles exceeding the capability to deliver a 500-kilogram payload to a range of 300 kilometers. These parameters corresponded to the weight of a first-generation nuclear warhead and to the strategic distances in the most compact theaters where nuclear-armed missiles were thought likely to be used.

In 1993 this objective was expanded to limit the proliferation of missiles of any range and payload if they were "intended" for the delivery of nuclear, biological, or chemical weapons.

In the first years of its existence the regime realized notable successes in delaying Brazilian and Indian space launch vehicle (SLV) programs and in dismantling the Condor missile program, the South African SLV program, and some programs in former Warsaw Pact states.

Moreover, these visible successes were accompanied by far less obvious progress. The regime blocked the export of hundreds of components, technologies, and production capabilities for missiles. These export denials caused schedule and budget overruns and unreliability problems that deferred and complicated proliferator programs, diminished their effectiveness, and in some cases discouraged them altogether. Coupled with these physical restraints, the MTCR's establishment of an international norm against missile proliferation prevented governments from enjoying a political free ride in developing such systems.

But within a few years of its announcement, the regime began to suffer serious problems.

THE MTCR LOSES ITS AIM

Several decisions over the lifetime of the MTCR have been so important that they can be said to constitute turning points in the regime.

REINVENTING THE REGIME

Within a year of its announcement, the regime was bombarded by proposals for converting it from an export control policy supported by the most significant suppliers to a universal regime. Suggestions have repeatedly arisen to underpin the MTCR's export controls with a global missile non-proliferation treaty that would establish a universal consensus binding suppliers and recipients. The MTCR is the only non-proliferation supplier regime not underpinned by such a treaty. Proposals have ranged from a global intermediate nuclear forces treaty to a zero ballistic missile treaty to a Canadian proposal to MTCR members for a ballistic missile ban.[7]

One of many problems with such ideas is that the negotiation process between "haves" and "have-nots" invariably produces demands for some concessions from the "haves." Most of the proposals have anticipated this by incorporating a plan to share SLV technology. Because of the interchangeability of SLVs and ballistic missiles, such proposals could only undercut the non-proliferation value of the effort.

Other problems involve the variety of definitions of a missile (as in the INF treaty, which uses definitions far more limited than those of the MTCR)—leading to a possibility of venue shopping for the most favorable set of international rules. The consideration most compelling to the negotiators of the original MTCR was the difficulty of setting rigid rules dividing hardware and technologies for desirable missiles (e.g., defensive systems) from proscribed missiles. The MTCR's strong rules restricting transfers of a short list of items and case-by-case rules for other items would be difficult to translate into a more inflexible treaty arrangement. And some commentators feared that the most important "have-nots" would simply stay out of a global treaty arrangement.

The Canadian proposal collapsed in the face of a near consensus of opposition at an ad hoc meeting of MTCR members in 1995. But proposals to reinvent the regime continue to arise, frequently including questionable notions for safeguarding SLVs.[8] The result has been a continuing diversion of potential support for the regime and of the limited staff resources to implement it.[9]

EXPANDING THE MEMBERSHIP

By 1989, the implicit objectives of the regime were starting to change. Stung by accusations that the regime was a failure because no new governments had adhered to it, the G-7 began a massive expansion of membership. The first new members—treaty partners in NATO, the European Space Agency, and the European Union, as well as Australia and New Zealand—could be justified because existing treaties and defense arrangements included the sharing of missiles and their technologies. As the expansion continued, however, a tension emerged between the size of the regime's membership and the MTCR's basic principles.

There are now thirty-two regime members, at least two others (Israel and South

Korea) that unilaterally adhere to its guidelines without being a party to the information exchanges among members, and China with unusual claims of adherence.[10]

The expansion, however, resulted in two troubling consequences. First, efforts
were diverted away from the non-proliferation of real-world systems. The SCUD
and its increasingly sophisticated derivatives were the centerpiece of most of the
missile proliferation of the 1990s; but no concerted effort against SCUD proliferation, analogous to that made against the Condor, was undertaken in the late 1980s
and early 1990s, when SCUD enhancements were still in their infancy.[11]

Second, the expansion of membership appeared to become an end in itself, a
diplomatic certificate of a government's international acceptance. The price of this
practice was a set of increasingly obfuscated and weakened standards.

ADMITTING PROSCRIBED PROJECTS INTO THE REGIME

The first obfuscation of the MTCR's clear and simple objective came with the 1993
change in U.S. policy toward membership—permitting SLV programs formerly
opposed by the regime to be brought into the regime and assisted by other members. Brazil, always a bellwether for missile non-proliferation policy, was the first
nation to join the regime and enjoy the change in the status of its SLV program from
proscribed to tolerated.

The rationale behind admitting Brazil's SLV program into the regime was a
combination of high hopes and low bureaucratic maneuvering. The high hopes
were epitomized when the president of Brazil announced that in joining the regime,
Brazil would abandon all efforts to acquire ballistic missiles. This laudable intention could, of course, change in the future—especially once Brazil had acquired
ballistic missile capabilities through its SLV program. After all, its SLV program
had been initiated in tandem with its nuclear weapons program, casting suspicion
on the true intent of its efforts.

The low bureaucratic maneuvering involved the resolution of a battle between
the U.S. Departments of Defense and State in the late years of the Bush administration and early in the Clinton presidency in the State Department's favor. The
State Department found its diplomacy encumbered by the necessity of resisting
SLV ambitions in friendly nations—with Brazil enjoying especially vigorous support within the U.S. bureaucracy. By caving in to these ambitions, inventing a physically meaningless distinction between offensive missiles and other, interchangeable
projects such as SLVs, and promising a study of the possibility of safeguarding
SLVs, the United States realized short-term diplomatic benefits. But long-lasting
costs quickly followed.

The Brazil case appeared to send the message to Ukraine and South Korea that
membership could legitimize and assist bigger missile programs. Ukraine won a
U.S. concession that as a member it would have the right to develop missiles with
a range of 500 kilometers—versus the 300-kilometer limit that the United States
had insisted on with respect to other new non-nuclear weapons state members.
South Korea was limited to a 180-kilometer range under a long-standing agreement
with the United States. In negotiations on MTCR membership (not concluded at the
time of this writing) Korean officials reportedly secured U.S. agreement to a 300-

kilometer range and then raised the ante by demanding a 500-kilometer range for indigenous missile development and, moreover, the right to develop SLVs.[12]

One might try to defend the South Korean demands on the grounds that South Korea is merely seeking a limited degree of symmetry with a North Korea that is bristling with missiles of far longer range. But this symmetry, whatever its merits on the Korean peninsula, is likely to lead other governments to demand the same rights. The first governments likely to make these demands are those that gave up proscribed programs to join the regime: Argentina with its former Condor program, South Africa with its former SLV, and former Warsaw Pact members with their Scuds and SS-23s.

The United States itself may be applying a dangerous degree of symmetry to its missile negotiations on the Korean peninsula. A statement by the Department of State in 1997 and more recent reports in the South Korean press suggest that the United States may be discussing MTCR membership not only for South Korea but for the North as well.[13]

One can hope that these statements are confused and that the United States is merely urging North Korea to "adhere" to the MTCR, that is, unilaterally to observe its restrictions. Admitting North Korea into the MTCR, given its history of noncompliance with the Nuclear Non-Proliferation Treaty and its missile infrastructure, would distort the functioning of the regime to the point of ineffectiveness.

The result of this policy shift has been to alter the motives of regime members toward using their membership to acquire larger missiles rather than to prevent missile proliferation. And the restraint of members toward intraregime transfers has been correspondingly weakened.

ADMITTING RUSSIA

The next obfuscation came with the 1995 admission of Russia into the MTCR as a formal member. For the first time the MTCR included a major missile power without the ability, and perhaps without the will, to limit its missile-related exports. Even as Russia was admitted to membership, Russian exports for India's missile program were being reported. Some two years after Russian membership, Russian exports for Iran's ballistic missile program were reported—initially by Israel—and became a major issue between the United States and Russia.

Membership shielded Russian firms from most of the impact of U.S. sanctions laws, leading to congressional efforts in 1998 to pass new legislation, a presidential veto of this legislation, and a gradual buildup of U.S. sanctions imposed on Russian firms by executive order and unilateral space launch policy.

By the time these steps were taken, however, much of the damage had already been done. Russia repeatedly blocked consensus within the regime, and discipline—as seen by the British-French offer of stealth cruise missiles—began to erode.

THE EFFECTIVE CESSATION OF U.S. SANCTIONS

United States law first adopted missile proliferation sanctions in 1990. These sanctions complemented the provisions of the MTCR by imposing penalties for certain international transfers between nonmembers of the regime.

The sanctions were imposed, with significant effect, on Russia and China in the early 1990s. But the last such sanction, imposed against China in 1993, was reinterpreted by the executive branch to reduce its economic impact by 90 percent. In spite of repeated reports of Chinese contributions to missile proliferation, the Clinton administration imposed no further sanctions on China.

No other significant missile non-proliferation sanctions were imposed until India's and Pakistan's missile tests of 1998, at which time India and Pakistan were both slapped with sanctions. Egypt, which was reported since the 1980s to be engaged in SCUD cooperation with North Korea, escaped sanctions until 1999.

The five-year hiatus in missile proliferation sanctions had an unfortunate but predictable effect. For example, the U.S. weakening and then cessation of missile sanctions on China over the last six years, and the U.S. drive for Chinese membership in the MTCR, suggested that the MTCR and complementary measures were becoming increasingly hollow. As a result of these and other steps, the regime now serves more of a representational than a non-proliferation function.

In the real world the spread of missiles was occurring at an accelerating rate with export controls hemorrhaging and sanctions weak and unpredictable. Missiles are immensely complicated systems that almost always depend on first-rate foreign assistance if they are to be reliable and, thus, could be one of the easiest targets of non-proliferation policy. They continue, however, to proliferate at an unprecedented pace.

A FALSE DICHOTOMY

As a result of these developments, it was easy to conclude that missile proliferation was uncontrollable. Some advocates of national missile defense said as much and insisted, successfully, that the United States government step up its missile defense efforts.[14] Meanwhile, some advocates of non-proliferation argued that such proliferation as had occurred really was not all that serious or that missile defenses, particularly those currently banned by the Anti-Ballistic Missile Treaty, would force proliferators to develop offensive countermeasures, thus increasing rather than controlling proliferation.

The proponents of these positions, however, were falling into a false dichotomy: that missile non-proliferation and missile defense excluded each other. In fact, from the earliest days of the MTCR, many advocates of each had seen the other as substantially complementary.

In the earliest MTCR briefings to the U.S. missile defense community, the complementarity was expressed in terms of targeting. Missile defenses target the boost, midcourse, and reentry phase of a missile's flight. Missile non-proliferation targets the research, development, and production phase. They both shoot at the same missile.

The details of this interplay are subtler. Missile defenses, if they are even perceived as being effective, raise the cost of a missile offense. They force the development of more or less expensive countermeasures, or they increase the number of offensive missiles that must be launched in order to maintain a given degree of confidence in destroying a target. Missile non-proliferation efforts also seek to raise the cost of a missile offense. Both hope to raise the cost to the point where the proliferator is discouraged from even attempting to develop an offensive force.

Missile non-proliferation is valuable to missile defense in other ways. To understand the details, however, it is essential not to view non-proliferation as having failed if there is a single test or if there is the development of a small force of missiles of uncertain reliability. By raising not only the cost but also the development time and the unreliability of the offensive force, missile non-proliferation allows missile defense to become more effective. By limiting the sophistication of the threat, missile non-proliferation raises the feasibility of successful missile defense.

Arguably, by these more subtle measures, missile non-proliferation has so far succeeded in many important cases. The major missile technology to have proliferated to date is SCUD technology—a 1950s technology derived from the 1940s German V-2 ballistic missile. SCUD technology is relatively unsophisticated, and attempts to make it more sophisticated in order to increase its range have drawbacks that can be exploited by missile defenses. Ground systems are relatively elaborate, launch time is relatively long, acceleration is relatively slow, radar cross sections are relatively large, payload is relatively limited, and accuracy is relatively poor. Missile defenses can exploit many of these vulnerabilities.

The missile proliferation that has not yet occurred—such as the sophisticated Pershing II technology embodied in the Condor ballistic missile sought by Argentina and Iraq (and also by Egypt, which is reportedly still trying)—would be far more stressing to missile defenses. For missile defense advocates, that is why the many elements of missile proliferation that are still controllable should be viewed as worth controlling.

What needs to be done to repair the missile non-proliferation regime?

FUTURE DIRECTIONS

There are four major and complementary approaches that could be used to restore the effectiveness of missile non-proliferation policy:

1. STOP DOING HARM

Some bad ideas have crept into the policy, and they need to be pushed back out. One is that SLVs and other "nonoffensive" missiles can somehow be distinguished from "offensive" missiles and handled more permissively. The Indian conversion of an SLV to the Agni first stage and the recent North Korean launch of a so-called SLV should serve as a reminder of the unavoidable physical fact that the hardware, technology, and production infrastructure for SLVs are interchangeable with those for ballistic missiles. The same is true even for some "defensive" missiles in the hands of proliferators. The Russian SA-2, a huge air defense missile, has served as the basis for offensive missiles in China, India, Iran, Iraq, and even Serbia. The only way to control missile proliferation effectively is to apply the MTCR's restrictions, in the words of its guidelines, "regardless of purpose."

Another bad idea is that membership in the regime should be offered to an increasing number of missile-capable states, regardless of their willingness or capability to control exports. Membership numbers should not be used as a measure of the success of the MTCR. Tenacity in opposing proliferation is the appropriate criterion.[15]

Other bad ideas, more systematic in their proposed effects on missile non-proliferation, arise every few years. One is safeguards on SLVs or other systems that have the physical capability to exceed MTCR parameters. Safeguards, a seductive term that has never quite been defined, would supposedly impose physical and institutional barriers to prevent the misuse of missile hardware. But safeguards would allow a potential proliferator to gain training, experience, access to hardware, and even a production infrastructure. All these could be turned to any use after good intentions had evaporated.

The most frequent bad idea is a universal treaty on missile non-proliferation. This might seem to offer the prospect of symmetry with the other non-proliferation regimes and a global agreement between the "haves" and "have-nots." But the fine print usually includes the offer of SLV technology as an incentive to the "have-nots"—aggravating rather than reducing the proliferation problem.

Even if SLV technology were not offered as a sweetener for joining such a treaty, the dangers would be considerable. The history of negotiations for such treaties implies that the restrictions of the MTCR would serve as a ceiling rather than a floor on the restrictions in a treaty. The process of negotiations would inevitably lead to compromises with the objective of international security. And the difficulty in securing restraint on transfers among parties to the treaty, given the disparity of practices within the MTCR, could easily turn the treaty regime into a "missile supermarket." Indeed, if such a treaty realized its objective of securing universal membership, it is difficult to envisage how effective missile technology export controls could survive.

The first step to arresting the decline of the MTCR is to stop promoting these bad ideas. Then, some positive steps can be taken.

2. BE CLEAR ON THE OBJECTIVE

The stated objective of the MTCR is to limit the proliferation of missiles capable of delivering mass destruction weapons. The objective is not to replicate the United Nations General Assembly or to reward governments for close diplomatic relationships. The objective is not to facilitate access to missile technology by MTCR members.

In piling diplomatic and economic objectives on top of the MTCR's security objectives, the work of non-proliferation becomes hopelessly encumbered. The focus of the MTCR should be returned to stopping real-world "projects of concern." If the MTCR has become a missile supermarket, those governments opposed to missile proliferation should make every effort to close down the market and restore the regime to its original purpose.

Technical precision has given the MTCR much of its effectiveness. An engineer knows whether the system triggers the regime's restrictions. But loose rhetoric about missiles has created a vague set of international notions that, in some cases, poses significant dangers.

Focused concern over *ballistic missile* proliferation created a climate in which cruise missiles were ignored in the cease-fire terms for the Gulf War, resulting in a legal Iraqi cruise missile industry, one installation of which was bombed in December 1998. The concern with cruise missiles is not a technical quibble, but should be considered to address the next great missile proliferation threat. The MTCR addresses this threat, but the governments responsible for enforcing the MTCR need to ensure that the cruise missile controls contained in that regime are uniformly and vigorously applied.

In practice, the actions of the United States set an upper limit on the actions by most other governments in opposing proliferation. This means that the United States, before anyone else, must regain its clarity of purpose.

3. ACT WITHIN AND OUTSIDE OF THE MTCR

The dismantling of the Condor missile program has been successful for at least a decade. This success resulted from actions inside and outside the regime. The seven members of the regime applied the MTCR provisions through their export control and internal enforcement mechanisms. But beyond the MTCR's provisions, the quiet threat of sanctions (even before the United States had legislated it), the indefatigable application of diplomatic pressure, and the use of an array of other instruments rolled up most of the network of front companies and covert activities that contributed to the Condor.

Today, Israel—not a member of the MTCR—generates much of the pressure for export restraint and sanctions against Iran's ballistic missile program. The fact that the MTCR is an international standard makes it easier for governments to support Israel's efforts. But the case demonstrates that effective actions need not be confined to MTCR members or the workings of the MTCR.

Sanctions are not a part of the MTCR, but they can be an enormously effective instrument. In the words of U.S. senator John Glenn, sanctions are a means for "taking the profit out of proliferation." The U.S. sanctions laws have, in recent years, been honored more in the breach than in the observance. But the United States is not alone in having available the instrument of sanctions. Japan has gone beyond the letter of the MTCR in imposing sanctions on North Korea for its recent Taepo-Dong 1 launch and threatening additional sanctions if North Korea launches again.

As the MTCR becomes diffused in purpose and bogged down by the diversity of its members, it becomes all the more important for serious governments to act unilaterally or multilaterally without necessarily waiting for the blessing of all the MTCR members. Sanctions, focused diplomacy, and the interdiction of dangerous exports can still take the profits out of missile proliferation. With appropriate action inside or outside the regime any proliferation that does occur will take longer, cost more, and result in far less reliable and less militarily significant missile threats. If the action delays proliferation long enough, proliferator governments will change. As has happened many times in the past decade, a new government may abandon a program that its predecessor labored to preserve. Even existing missile programs may be abandoned.

4. INTEGRATE MISSILE NON-PROLIFERATION AND MISSILE DEFENSE POLICIES

Missile defenses cost tens of billions of dollars. Missile non-proliferation staffs are small and limited to resources thousands of times smaller. Missile defenses and missile non-proliferation both entail political and diplomatic costs, but they impact different political and diplomatic interests.

Does it make sense to spend tens of billions of dollars for missile defenses and not impose more effective sanctions on the entities contributing to missile proliferation? To the best of our knowledge, this question is not even addressed at high political levels. The National Security Council staff has different individuals handling missile defenses and missile non-proliferation; at best, they appear only to be "aware" of each other's activities.

Advocates of missile defenses should call for stronger non-proliferation measures, if for no other reason than to limit the sophistication of the offensive systems that the defenses are meant to counter. Advocates of missile non-proliferation should view missile defenses—if they are cost-effective—as another means of discouraging proliferators. The two advocates should talk to each other when their efforts seem threatened.

Counterproliferation, as envisaged in the early 1990s, treated proliferation prevention as part of a consistent spectrum with deterrence, counterforce, active defense, and passive defense. Policymakers need to pay more than lip service to the integration of those concepts.

PROGNOSIS

This chapter began with the question "Is missile non-proliferation a lost cause?" It is not. The development of missiles is expensive, complex, and difficult for the proliferator. Non-proliferators, if they will maintain the necessary tenacity, can continue to take advantage of these problems. Missile proliferation can be controlled, at least to the extent that it is delayed, reduced in sophistication, made more vulnerable to missile defenses, and—in some cases—discouraged altogether.

But the title of the chapter is "Can the MTCR Be Repaired?" It should be clear that the MTCR is not synonymous with missile non-proliferation. Although the MTCR is currently the international centerpiece for missile non-proliferation, there are other instruments for pursuing the same objective. This is a fortunate fact because the MTCR is badly broken. It is not clear whether the thirty-two disparate governments now in the MTCR can pull together the resolve to repair the regime. U.S. leadership would be essential to such an effort, but the United States itself has led the MTCR into many of its present difficulties.

To repair the MTCR, the United States and the other key members would need to make a high-level political decision to stop using the regime as a diplomatic bauble. Such a decision is always possible. But the trend of the last decade does not offer cause for optimism.

NOTES

1. *Report of the Commission to Assess the Ballistic Missile Threat to the United States, Executive Summary* (Washington, D.C.: Government Printing Office), July 15, 1998, 17.

2. Ibid., 25.

3. For American and Russian perspectives on the cruise missile proliferation threat see M. Dennis Gormley, "Hedging against the Cruise-Missile Threat," *Survival*, spring 1998, 92–111; Gennady Khromov, "The Threat of Cruise Missile Proliferation Requires Urgent Coordinated Actions," *The Monitor* (Center for International Trade and Security, University of Georgia, Athens) fall–winter 1998, 3–5. Also, see Carnegie Endowment for International Peace Non-Proliferation Roundtable, "Cruise Missile Proliferation: Threat, Policy and Defenses," October 9, 1998 (http://www.ceip.org/-programs/npp/cruise.htm).

4. Douglas Barrie, "Missile Puts U.K. on Spot," *Defense News*, September 14–20, 1998, 1, 50; Douglas Barrie and Barbara Opall-Rome, "Britain Will Allow U.A.E. Black Shahine Sale," *Defense News*, October 26–November 1, 1998, 3, 42; Douglas Barrie and Philip Finnegan, "U.A.E. Missile Buy Advances with British OK," *Defense News*, November 30–December 6, 1998, 3, 34. Also, see Nikolai Novichkov, "Russian Anti-Ship Missile Targets Multi-$B Market," *Jane's Defence Weekly*, June 9, 1999, 13.

5. The group of seven industrialized countries known as the G-7 includes Canada, France, the Federal Republic of Germany, Italy, Japan, the United Kingdom, and the United States. They announced the MTCR in April 1987.

6. For a fuller description of the MTCR and a discussion of recent missile proliferation developments see Rodney W. Jones et al., *Tracking Nuclear Proliferation: A Guide in Maps and Charts*, 1998 (Washington, D.C.: Carnegie Endowment for International Peace, 1998). An excellent website for following developments in missile proliferation is maintained by the Centre for Defence and International Security Studies, Lancaster University, U.K., at (http://www.cdiss.org).

7. Speier, Richard H., "A Nuclear Nonproliferation Treaty for Missiles?" in Henry Sokolski, ed., *Fighting Proliferation: New Concerns for the Nineties* (Maxwell Air Force Base, Ala.: Air University Press, September 1996).

8. For a discussion of the concept of SLV "safeguards" see Brian G. Chow, *Emerging National Space Launch Programs: Economics and Safeguards* (Santa Monica, Calif.: RAND Corporation, 1993), RAND/R-4179-USDP.

9. For the most recent versions of this hardy perennial see Jonathan Dean, "Step-by-Step Control over Ballistic and Cruise Missiles," *Disarmament Diplomacy*, no. 31, October 1998 (http://www.-gn.apc.org/acronym); and Barbara Opall-Rome, "Chinese Official Urges Broader, Revised MTCR," *Defense News*, January 19, 1999, 1.

10. China's unusual formulation of adherence—to the "guidelines and parameters" of the regime—has raised questions as to whether China applies MTCR controls only to complete missile systems or also to components and technology, as required by the regime. China's October 1994 agreement to "not export ground-to-ground missiles featuring the primary parameters of the MTCR" left open these questions as well as the question of how China's policy applied to Category 1 systems, such as ship-to-ground missiles and SLVs.

11. It was widely maintained that Scud proliferation was unstoppable even in the late 1980s. But the United States has now discovered that many ingredients for the improvement of Scuds, such as specialty steels, are worth trying to stop even at this late date. See, for instance, Bill Gertz, "Missile Parts Sent to North Korea by Chinese Companies," *Washington Times*, July 20, 1999; and Bill Gertz, "Technology Transfers a Concern, U.S. Says," *Washington Times*, July 21, 1999.

12. Kwon Dae-yul, "Kim Seeks 500km Missile Range," *Chosun Ilbo* (Seoul), July 4, 1999.

13. Nicholas Burns, U.S. Department of State press briefing, April 8, 1997: Q: "Would you like them [North Korea] to join the MTCR? . . ." BURNS: "Obviously, we want to see the broadest possible inclusion of countries in the MTCR, because that's the major international regime that

governs that tries to limit the proliferation of missile technology and missiles themselves. But, if you'd like, I can consult with Deputy Assistant Secretary of State Einhorn and see if we can get you something more specific before these talks are held." Also, "US 'Reluctant' to Allow ROK Development of Missile," Seoul, *Korea Times* (Internet version) in English, 0813 GMT July 28, 1999: "The United States has urged North Korea to stop ballistic missile production, halt missile exports, and join the Missile Technology Control Regime (MTCR)."

14. In January 1999, Secretary of Defense William Cohen announced the addition of $10.5 billion to the Pentagon's five-year planning budget for a national missile defense system. A decision on whether to deploy such a system is to be made in June 2000.

15. See Richard Speier, "Russia, Ukraine, and the Nth Member Problem," in *Missile Proliferation and MTCR: The Nth Member and Other Challenges*, ed. Victor Zaborsky and Scott Jones, (Athens: Center for International Trade and Security, University of Georgia, June 1997).

—15—

Chemical and Biological Weapons

Jonathan B. Tucker, Brad Roberts, Elisa Harris

In the latter half of the 1990s, concern increased over the threats posed by the proliferation of chemical and biological weapons. The Chemical Weapons Convention (CWC), signed in 1993 and ratified by the United States in 1997, has promised to revolutionize arms control verification techniques and reliability. The Biological Weapons Convention (BWC), on the other hand, remains mired in negotiations over the addition of a real enforcement mechanism.

Three expert views are presented here on critical aspects of this problem. The technology for the production of biological weapons is perceived to be so widespread it is often assumed non-proliferation measures can do little to prevent their development. Jonathan Tucker reminds us of the serious risks represented by biological warfare materials and expertise that were once a part of the Soviet Union's offensive biological warfare (BW) program. He outlines measures that can prevent the materials and expertise from spreading outside Russia and the other states of the former Soviet Union. Brad Roberts examines the potential threat and the corresponding implications for the use of biological weapons in warfare, noting that many existing constraints may be gradually disappearing. Finally, Elisa Harris presents an alternative view: that the risk of chemical and biological weapons use may actually be waning.

BIOLOGICAL WEAPONS PROLIFERATION FROM RUSSIA: HOW GREAT A THREAT?
By Jonathan B. Tucker

For nearly two decades, the Soviet Union and then Russia maintained an offensive biological weapons (BW) program in violation of the 1972 BWC. In addition to five military microbiological facilities under the control of the Soviet Ministry of Defense, a parallel network of nearly fifty biotechnology institutes and production facilities worked on biological weapons under the cover of the Ministry of Agriculture, the Ministry of Health, the Soviet Academy of Sciences, and an ostensibly civilian pharmaceutical complex known as Biopreparat.

The Communist Party Central Committee established the Biopreparat organization in 1973, a year after the Soviet Union signed the BWC but before it ratified the treaty.[1] A secret Interdepartmental Scientific-Technical Council on Molecular Biology and Genetics coordinated the flow of information among the various agencies and state scientific organizations involved in the BW program.[2] Biopreparat was placed under the civilian cover of the Main Administration of the Microbiological Industry (*Glavmikrobioprom*).[3] In addition to some peaceful development of drugs and vaccines, the Biopreparat institutes engaged in offensive BW research and development. Because the first director of Biopreparat was General Vsevolod I. Ogarkov, the top-secret complex was known informally as "the Ogarkov system" but officially only by its postal designation, "P.O. Box A-1063." Ogarkov's successors were Colonel General Yefim Ivanovich Smirnov, a former Soviet minister of health,[4] and Major General Yuri Tikhonovich Kalinin, who had previously served in the chemical troops of the Soviet army.[5]

The Biopreparat complex comprised forty-seven facilities, including eleven research institutes.[6] Major research and development centers were located in Moscow, Leningrad, Obolensk (near Moscow), Lyubuchany, and Koltsovo (Siberia); mothballed production facilities were in Omutninsk, Pokrov, Penza, Kurgan, Berdsk, and Stepnogorsk (Kazakhstan); and an open-air test site was situated on Vozrozhdeniye Island in the Aral Sea. (The leading Biopreparat institutes and production complexes are listed in table 15.1.)

TABLE 15.1

SELECTED BIOPREPARAT RESEARCH INSTITUTES AND PRODUCTION COMPLEXES

State Research Center for Virology and Biotechnology "Vector," Koltsovo
State Research Center for Applied Microbiology, Obolensk
Institute of Immunology, Lyubuchany
Institute for Scientific Biological Instrumentation, Moscow
Institute for Highly Pure Biopreparations, St. Petersburg
Institute for Biochemical Engineering, Moscow
Research and Design Institute for the Biotechnology Industry "Biotin," Kirov
Scientific Experimental and Industrial Base, Omutninsk
Biologics Plant, Pokrov
Scientific Design Institute and Factory of Biopreparations Complex, Berdsk
Progress Plant, Stepnogorsk

At the peak of the BW program, Soviet scientists weaponized about a dozen anti-personnel and anticrop and antilivestock agents. Beginning in 1984, the top priority in the five-year plan for the Biopreparat research institutes was to alter the genetic structure of known pathogens, such as those that cause plague and tularemia, to make them resistant to Western antibiotics.[7] To plan for large-scale production of BW agents in wartime, the Biopreparat organization established a "mobilization" program and department.[8] Recent reports suggest that the Soviets were also working to develop entirely new classes of biological weapons, including "bioregulators" that could modify human moods, emotions, heart rhythms, and sleep patterns.[9]

A large number of scientists and technicians worked on several BW programs in the former Soviet Union:

- Biopreparat employed more than thirty thousand people, of whom about nine thousand were scientists and engineers;
- The Fifteenth Directorate of the Ministry of Defense had about fifteen thousand employees at the five military microbiological institutes under MOD control;
- The Ministry of Agriculture had about ten thousand scientists working on development and production of anticrop and antilivestock weapons;
- Several institutes of the Soviet Academy of Sciences employed hundreds of BW scientists;
- Other scientists were engaged in BW-related research for the Anti-Plague Institutes of the Soviet Ministry of Health and other state institutions;
- The Third Directorate of the Ministry of Health developed agents for assassination and special operations under the code name *Flayta* ("flute").[10]

Thus, a total of about sixty thousand people were working on BW activities.[11] Although Ph.D.-level scientists were in the minority, technicians acquired sensitive knowledge about virulent strains or the design of special bomblets employed for the dissemination of biological agents.

THE SPECTER OF "BRAIN DRAIN"

During the Soviet era, weapons scientists received higher living standards and the chance to do research but forfeited the right to travel abroad. This rule was strictly enforced by the KGB, which carefully monitored their movements. After the breakup of the Soviet Union in 1991, however, the economic crisis took a severe toll on scientific organizations that once had been lavishly funded by the state.[12] Although U.S. officials worried about the leakage of dangerous materials, equipment, technical data, and know-how from the vast Soviet military establishment, their focus was almost exclusively on improving security for nuclear weapons and scientists. Only with the defection to the West of top scientists from the Soviet BW program did the U.S. intelligence community learn that the program was far more extensive and deadly than had been suspected. This realization led to concern that former Soviet bioweapons experts, suffering economic hardship, might be recruited by proliferant states or even terrorist groups.

Russia did not officially acknowledge the existence of an offensive BW program until April 1992, when President Boris Yeltsin admitted there had been a "lag in implementing" the BWC by the Soviet Union and then Russia. Yeltsin then issued an edict to dismantle all offensive capabilities. In September 1992, the United States, the United Kingdom, and Russia signed a joint statement creating a Trilateral Process to resolve lingering concerns about the elimination of the offensive BW program and to demonstrate the defensive nature of Russia's remaining capabilities. After initial reciprocal visits to selected facilities in each of the three countries, however, the governments were unable to agree on satisfactory procedures for more extensive mutual inspections, and the Trilateral Process ground to a halt.[13]

As a result of economic hardship and Yeltsin's edict, the operating and research budgets of many biological research centers were slashed. Salaries of thousands of scientists and technicians were delayed for three to six months and stagnated at a time of soaring inflation. This financial hardship led to an internal "brain drain" from the Biopreparat institutes. Between 1990 and 1996, for example, the State Research Institute for Applied Microbiology at Obolensk lost 54 percent of its staff, including 28 percent of its top scientists.[14] The downsizing of the BW complex raised fears in the West that former bioweapons scientists might be recruited by outlaw states and terrorist organizations.[15] According to 1992 congressional testimony by then CIA director Robert Gates, the most serious problem involved BW experts whose skills had no civilian counterpart, such as bioengineers specializing in the weaponization of BW agents.[16]

Detailed open-source information about the whereabouts of former bioweapons scientists is scarce, but the anecdotal data are not encouraging:

- More than three hundred former Biopreparat scientists have emigrated from the Soviet Union to the United States, Europe, and elsewhere.[17] But no one knows how many weapons scientists have moved to countries of proliferation concern in the Middle East, East Asia, or South Asia.
- In 1994 some BW scientists from the Russian Ministry of Defense visited North Korea; the purpose of this visit is still unknown.[18]
- On August 27, 1995, the *London Sunday Times* reported that the recruitment of Russian BW experts had enabled Iran to make a "quantum leap forward" in its development of biological weapons, allowing Tehran to proceed directly from basic research to production and to acquire an effective delivery system.[19]
- Even senior bioweapons scientists have had difficulty finding employment. In a 1995 memoir, former Obolensk deputy director Igor V. Domaradskij reported that in March 1992, desperate for work, he offered to sell his services to the Chinese Embassy in Moscow. In May 1993, he sent a similar offer to Kirsan Ilyumzhin, president of the Kalmyk republic within the Russian Federation. However, he received no response in either case.[20]

Some institute directors have sought to keep their top talent intact by dismissing more junior scientists and technicians. Yet because of the economic crisis, which worsened in August 1998 with the collapse of the ruble, even high-level scientists are not being paid, much less being assured a good standard of living.

IRANIAN RECRUITMENT EFFORTS

Iran has been particularly aggressive about recruiting bioweapons scientists in Russia. Shortly after the 1991 Gulf War, Iran tried to recruit BW experts from leading laboratories such as Obolensk and Koltsovo. When this effort largely failed, Iranian agents turned their attention to smaller research institutes. An investigation by the *New York Times* found that Iran had offered former BW scientists in Russia, Kazakhstan, and Moldova jobs paying as much as $5,000 a month—far more than most ex-Soviet scientists make in a year at home. Many of the initial contacts were made by Mehdi Rezayat, an English-speaking pharmacologist who claimed to be a "scientific adviser" to Iranian president Mohammed Khatami.[21]

Iranian officials who approached the Russian scientists usually expressed interest in scientific exchanges or commercial contacts, but two scientists were asked specifically to help Iran develop biological weapons. Of particular interest to the Iranians were microbes that could be used in war to destroy crops, and genetic engineering techniques. Although most of the Iranian offers were rebuffed, Russian scientists said that at least five of their colleagues had gone to work in Iran in recent years. One scientist described these arrangements as "marriages of convenience, and often of necessity."[22]

Shortly after the *Times* article was published, one of the Russian scientists who had been mentioned by name as working in Iran, Dr. Valery Bakayev of the Institute of Medical Biotechnology in Moscow, strongly denied that he was conducting BW research for Tehran.[23] Nevertheless, it appears that the basic thrust of the allegation is correct and that a significant amount of know-how related to biological weapons has been transmitted from Russia to Iran.

NOVEL FORMS OF BRAIN DRAIN

Some early assumptions about Russian brain drain have proved wrong. Although some scientists have left, the predicted mass exodus of weapons specialists has not materialized. One reason is that unless severely pressed, few Russians want to leave family and friends and move to an alien culture, even if they are paid handsomely for their services. For this reason, foreign governments are not only recruiting Russia's underpaid weapons experts to emigrate to those countries but are enlisting them in weapons projects within Russia's own borders. Weapons scientists living in Russia have been approached by foreign agents seeking information, technology, and designs, often under the cover of legitimate business practices to avoid attracting attention.[24]

A second new form of brain drain is based on modern communication techniques, such as e-mail and faxes, which are available at some of the Russian scientific institutions. As a result, it has become possible for weapons scientists to "moonlight by modem," supplementing their meager salaries by covertly supporting foreign weapons projects on the margins of their legitimate activities.[25] The scale of this problem is difficult to assess from open sources.

A third form of brain drain is to sell access to, or copies of, sensitive documents. For example, a detailed "cookbook" of proven BW production techniques would be of great assistance to a country seeking to acquire its own biological arsenal. According to an article from the Russian press, despite Yeltsin's edict requiring the elimination of the offensive BW program, archives related to the production of BW agents have been removed from the MOD facilities at Kirov and Sverdlovsk, and from a number of Biopreparat facilities, and preserved for long-term storage.[26]

POTENTIAL FOR LEAKAGE OF BW AGENTS

Another disturbing possibility is that ex-bioweapons scientists could smuggle Russian military microbes to outlaw countries or terrorist groups seeking a BW capability. Obtaining such seed cultures is not essential for making biological weapons, since virulent strains can be obtained from natural sources. Russia genetically engineered a number of disease agents to be particularly deadly, however, by rendering them resistant to standard antibiotic therapies and environmental stresses. Because a seed culture of dried anthrax spores could be carried in a sealed plastic vial the size of a thumbnail, detecting such contraband at a border is almost impossible. Unlike fissile materials, biological agents do not give off telltale radiation and they do not show up in X rays. According to one assessment, "Stealing BW is easier than stealing change out of people's pockets. The most widespread method for contraband transport of military strains is very simple—within a plastic cigarette package."[27]

That military strains can be smuggled out of highly secure facilities in Russia has already been demonstrated. In 1984, when security within the Soviet biological warfare complex was intense, a military scientist named Anisimov, working at the military microbiological facility at Sverdlovsk, developed a genetically altered strain of tularemia that was resistant to antibiotics. He was transferred to the Institute for Applied Microbiology at Obolensk but wanted to get a Ph.D. degree for his work, so he stole an ampoule of an antibiotic-resistant strain of tularemia and brought it to his new lab. According to an account of this incident in Igor Domaradskij's memoir, *Troublemaker*:

> Literally within a month after the appointment of Anisimov as head of the Tularemia Section at Obolensk, I happened to learn that he had succeeded in achieving a high resistance to tetracycline, the "stumbling block" of all our work. Naturally this came as a surprise to my colleagues, and rumors circulated that he had in fact brought this strain with him "in his pocket" from his previous place of work at Sverdlovsk-19. But Anisimov claimed that he had done it all "from memory. . . . " Pursuant to the then-current "regulations for working with highly infectious pathogens" (including tularemia), such research was possible only in special facilities, from which it was categorically forbidden to remove any cultures. . . . The Institute set up a commission to compare our strains with those of Anisimov. In the course of its deliberations, it was discovered that . . . Anisimov's strain bore an important marker that was peculiar to the Sverdlovsk strain, namely sensitivity to nalidixic acid [a rare antibiotic]. . . . The fact of theft of a strain from the Sverdlovsk institute could be considered as having been proven.[28]

Because of concerns about the possibility of theft of military seed cultures, the U.S. government is currently providing funds to upgrade physical security at Obolensk and the Vector virology laboratory in Koltsovo, which serves as Russia's germ bank for strains of smallpox and other deadly viruses.[29]

EXPORTS OF DUAL-USE PRODUCTION EQUIPMENT

In the fall of 1997, weapons inspectors with the United Nations Special Commission (UNSCOM) uncovered evidence of a July 1995 agreement by the Russian government to sell Iraq sophisticated dual-use fermentation equipment that could be used to produce biological weapons. A confidential document seized by the inspectors at an Iraqi government ministry described lengthy negotiations between official delegations from the two countries leading to a deal worth millions of dollars. Although the Iraqis claimed that the equipment would be used to make single-cell protein for animal feed, UNSCOM determined that before the 1991 Persian Gulf War, Iraq had used a similar plant at a site outside Baghdad called Al Hakam as a cover for the production of deadly BW agents, including anthrax and botulinum toxin.[30] It appears that the Russian equipment ordered by Iraq was never delivered. This troubling report suggests, however, that the Russian government should be pressured to tighten its export controls on sales of dual-use production equipment to known BW proliferators such as Iraq and Iran.

EFFORTS TO STEM BIOLOGICAL BRAIN DRAIN

One effort to address the brain drain problem is the International Science and Technology Center (ISTC) in Moscow, which became operational in August 1992 and funds civilian research projects by former Soviet weapons scientists. This program, supported by Russia, the United States, the European Union, Japan, South Korea, Norway, and private companies, distributes research grants worth about $400 to $700 a month to Russian weapons scientists so that they can remain at home, engaged in the peaceful application of their expertise.

Although the initial focus of the ISTC was almost exclusively on nuclear and missile scientists, in 1994 the center expanded its efforts to include former BW facilities and specialists. Even so, in 1996, only 4 percent of the projects funded by the ISTC involved former bioweapons scientists.[31] This proportion jumped to 8 percent in 1997, 15 percent in 1998, and 17 percent in 1999.[32] Although support for peaceful research by former BW scientists is likely to grow further, the level of funding is still not proportionate to the severity of the threat.

Another initiative, initiated in 1996 by the U.S. National Academy of Sciences (NAS) with funding from the Department of Defense, supports joint research projects at former Biopreparat institutes directed at the epidemiology, prophylaxis, diagnosis, and therapy of diseases associated with dangerous pathogens such as those causing anthrax, glanders, plague, and viral hemorrhagic fevers. This program is run by a joint committee of DoD and the NAS, and receives funds from both the Department of Energy and the State Department.[33] The rationale for this effort is to stem brain drain, learn more about the Soviet BW program, gain access to previously secret laboratories, benefit from Russian advances in biodefense, and help reconfigure the former Soviet BW complex into a "less diffuse, less uncertain, and more public-health oriented establishment."[34]

To counter the recruiting of Russian scientists by Iran and other states of proliferation concern, the United States has recently expanded its effort to keep former

BW experts and institutes gainfully employed in peaceful research activities. These activities include scientist-to-scientist exchanges, joint research projects involving Russian and American experts, and programs to convert laboratories and institutes formerly associated with Biopreparat.[35] Although the stipends provided by these programs are less than what Iran is offering, U.S. officials believe that they are attractive because they allow Russian scientists to remain in their country and collaborate with respected Western scientists on peaceful projects. In 1998, about one hundred former Soviet BW scientists visited laboratories and institutes in the United States and an equal number of American scientists visited laboratories in Russia. The program appears to have had some initial success in that Obolensk has ended its contacts with Tehran.[36] Joint research programs in the field of biotechnology are also likely to yield innovations and products that eventually should benefit the Russian economy.

Some conservatives, such as Representative Floyd Spence (R–South Carolina), chairman of the House Committee on National Security, worry that collaborative research on dangerous pathogens might be counterproductive by helping to keep Russia's BW development teams intact.[37] Former Biopreparat chief scientist Ken Alibek also warns that Russia will never entirely abandon a program in which it had military superiority, no matter how many cooperative programs it joins. Because the line between offensive and defensive research hinges largely on intent, ambiguities and suspicions about the Russian program will persist. Given the inevitable dual-use concerns about research on dangerous pathogens, it is essential that such scientific collaborations be highly transparent and include regular, unimpeded access to facilities, personnel, and information.[38]

POLICY RECOMMENDATIONS

The following steps would help to address the lingering concerns associated with proliferation from the former Soviet BW program:

- The Russian government should declassify and release detailed information about the history of the Soviet/Russian BW program.
- The Russian government should increase the transparency of its current BW defense programs by agreeing to reciprocal visits by U.S./U.K. teams to microbiological facilities controlled by the Ministry of Defense.[39]
- The Russian government should strengthen its export controls on sales of dual-use fermentation equipment to countries of BW proliferation concern.
- Western countries should invest greater resources in addressing problems of BW-related brain drain, not only in Russia but in other former Soviet republics such as Kazakhstan, Uzbekistan, Ukraine, and Georgia.

THE PROSPECTS FOR BIOLOGICAL WARFARE

By Brad Roberts

When discussing BW, three questions are often raised:

- How likely is the use of biological weapons in a war against the United States?
- What would the effects be?
- What are the implications for arms control?

LIKELIHOOD OF BW USE

There can be no certainty that biological weapons will be used against U.S. forces, interests, or targets; nor can there be certainty that BW will not be used. The history of nonuse, the potential U.S. response, and the low military utility of BW are frequently used to argue that BW use is unlikely. However, each of these points is misleading.

The first argument is that BW will not be used in the future because they have not been used in the past. This is not historically accurate: Imperial Japan used biological weapons in its invasion of China in the 1930s, and the Soviet Union evidently also used them surreptitiously to slow the German invasion in 1940. There may be a renewed debate over allegations that the United States used biological weapons against North Korea and China in the 1950s. The debate will be rekindled by a new book that utilizes documents in Chinese archives to support the allegations. The counter side will be presented by the Cold War History project at the Woodrow Wilson Center, where a case study drawing heavily on Soviet archives argues that the allegations were trumped up by the KGB.

The fact that biological weapons have not been used frequently in modern times does not imply that states have not taken seriously the possibility of biological warfare. Some have actively prepared for the offensive use of such weapons. Over the last few years, a great deal has been learned about the offensive BW capabilities of the Soviet Union, Iraq, and even South Africa. The growing list of revelations strongly suggests that other states have been more interested in biological warfare, and have invested heavily in preparations for it, than experts on proliferation have assumed.

The United States and other governments make the assessment that approximately a dozen states are engaged in preparations for biological warfare. Many of these states are in the Middle East and Northeast Asia, regions where the United States deploys military forces in support of security guarantees to friends and allies.

In sum, the historical record may not be a good indicator of the future, not least because the historical record is misleading. Nonuse does not equate with noninterest. Among a handful of states, interest and preparations have been high. This does not imply that use of such weapons is likely, but it makes it harder to dismiss such use as very unlikely.

A second argument commonly used to support the notion that BW use is unlikely is that no state would attack the United States with BW due to the threat of retribution, that is, a nuclear reply from the United States. However, Sweden's ambassador Rolf Ekeus, who served as the chairman of UNSCOM, contended that Saddam Hussein completely dismissed nuclear threats from Washington (though not from Tel Aviv), assuming that there was no condition under which a U.S. president would kill millions of Iraqi civilians.

A third argument involves the reputed low military utility of BW. This belief is based on Washington's decision to abandon biological weapons in 1969. Having evaluated the tactical and strategic utility of BW, the United States concluded that biological weapons are not efficient battlefield weapons and are strategically redundant to nuclear weapons. However, regional aggressors may not weigh the utility of such weapons in these terms. Aggressors may consider the possible utility of BW in various stages of asymmetric conflict against the United States. Biological weapons have come to be seen as the weapon of choice for a state attempting to fight and escape a military confrontation with the United States; biological weapons may be seen as more effective and reliable for these purposes than chemical or conventional weapons and less risky than nuclear attack on U.S. forces or allied populations.

EFFECTS OF BW USE

The effects of a BW attack cover the spectrum of possibilities. It is conceivable that a BW attack may have no effect. The Japanese sect Aum Shinrikyo reportedly conducted at least nine failed attacks with biological weapons, some of which were intended to cause literally millions of fatalities. Their failures related to the strains of agents produced and the method of delivery. Experience suggests that an effective biological attack may be more difficult than suggested by those who argue that there are essentially no technical barriers to effective use of biological weapons.

Alternatively, the effect of a BW attack may be very limited operationally—but significant strategically. For example, a terrorist-style attack, not attributable to the attacking party, might weaken the commitment of the members of a coalition to undertake war to overturn an act of regional aggression or to prosecute that war to the point of putting the aggressor regime at risk. Few may be killed, but if the coalition action is crippled, the strategic effect would be significant.

A third scenario is a BW attack that is massively disruptive but not massively destructive. Conceivably, biological agents causing high morbidity but low mortality may be used to cripple a military intervention or to collapse a neighboring state. Such non-lethal BW agents have been explored by some countries.

Last, the effects of BW attack could well exceed the effects of nuclear attack. Against unprotected forces, BW agents offer the prospect of wide area coverage that nuclear devices do not—especially the fission-style weapons that might conceivably find their way into the arsenals of regional powers. Against unprotected civilian targets, effectively aerosolized BW agents could kill huge numbers of people.

To illustrate this point, consider the possible consequences of an Iraq that has had five years to re-create its WMD arsenal after the lifting of sanctions. As a reasonable worst-case proposition, Iraq might succeed in assembling a handful of fission-style weapons but substantially more than a handful of long-range delivery systems (perhaps as many as three hundred) for which BW agents could readily be produced in the necessary quantities. Within range of Iraq's delivery systems are more than sixty cities with populations of more than one hundred thousand. Obviously, nuclear devices could be used to attack only a handful of those targets. With fission-level effects, these devices would not be expected to annihilate the populations. But there would be a sufficient number of BW delivery systems to repeatedly attack all of those targets. A thumbnail sketch of possible casualty levels suggests that the casualties resulting from BW attack would be at least on an order of magnitude larger than those of the posited nuclear attack. This scenario illustrates the fact that biological weapons may give regional powers mass destruction capabilities beyond what can be achieved at the nuclear level.

This entire discussion of effects of use assumes the aggressor's use of noncontagious biological warfare agents. The use of contagious agents would change this calculus profoundly. A lethal flu outbreak occurred in 1918; three strains of the flu killed over twenty million people over the following year (total casualties—not fatalities—in World War I were approximately fifteen million).

IMPLICATIONS FOR ARMS CONTROL

The first implication is that the control of biological weapons should not be merely an afterthought for those interested in arms control. To take BW arms control seriously is to move beyond the platitudes that are normally offered up on this subject. Reports like that from the Canberra Commission on the Elimination of Nuclear Weapons do little service to the cause of BW arms control by adding a sentence calling for implementation of an effective regime. The problems of building an effective regime of BW control differ fundamentally from those in the nuclear domain. Arms control is no panacea for the BW problem, but it is also indispensable to reinforcing the anti-BW norm and to limiting the number and sophistication of BW proliferator programs. A viable regime requires conclusion and implementation of the compliance protocol for the Biological Weapons Convention now under negotiation. It also requires dealing with extant problems of noncompliance as well as a viable export restraint system.

The second implication is that the BW threat is not simply something concocted by those who are seeking new ways to legitimize the retention of nuclear weapons. To be sure, there is a large debate about the specific nature of the BW threat—it is inherently difficult to calibrate the capabilities and intentions of BW possessors. But enough is known that the problem is real and cannot be wished away. To do so on the argument that it has been cooked up to keep nuclear weapons around seems likely only to ignore a set of problems that could lead to a much more substantial proliferation of all weapons of mass destruction in the years ahead. The BW problem requires good answers if regional security is to be preserved and if the global treaty regime is to remain efficacious.

For the United States, part of the current "answer" is a nuclear threat: The United States does not *rely* on nuclear weapons to deter biological attack, but nor does it entirely write them out of the equation of deterrence and retaliation. Those interested in reducing the role of nuclear weapons in U.S. defense strategy and international relations more generally should be strong supporters of the other tools of deterrence—active defenses, passive defenses, and counterforce. But for many in the non-proliferation community, counterproliferation remains an objectionable concept. There is no better illustration of the mutually reinforcing nature of non-proliferation and counterproliferation than their application to the BW problem. Working with only one or the other tool of policy, the problem is not soluble. Working with both, there is some hope of making headway.

THE NATURE OF THE THREAT
By Elisa Harris

There is a widespread view that the CBW proliferation problem, defined as the threat of CBW acquisition and use by nation-states, has grown worse since the end of the Cold War and continues to grow. However, arguably, it is not the threat itself that has changed but the perception of the CBW threat.

During the Cold War, Soviet and Warsaw Pact CBW capabilities dominated U.S. attention. Although CBW programs existed in many countries outside of Europe and the Soviet Union, attention centered on the Soviet Union and the Warsaw Pact because these were the key threats to U.S. interests. Most countries of CBW proliferation concern today have programs dating back to the 1970s, the 1980s, or even earlier. Nevertheless, the perception is that the proliferation problem has grown worse since the end of the Cold War.

This perception is founded on several factors. First, a number of events in recent years have brought CW and BW to the public's attention.

- Details of the Soviet BW program, in which dozens of agents, including plague and anthrax, were researched, produced, and, in some cases, weaponized (in some instances for delivery on ballistic missile warheads), have become public.
- Extraordinary revelations about Iraq's BW program and a series of continuing crises over the disposition of its BW capabilities have occurred.
- The Aum Shinrikyo cult, which launched a CW attack in the Tokyo subway, reportedly produced and attempted to use BW.

Each of these events brought attention to the CBW issue, contributing to the perception of an increased threat.

There have also been technological developments of importance. First, the diffusion of dual-use chemical technology has facilitated acquisition of indigenous chemical weapons programs by proliferators. Advances in biotechnology have facilitated BW production and also potentially the nature of the BW agents that may be produced in BW programs.

Notwithstanding this perception and these developments, one could argue that the CBW proliferation problem has, in fact, declined since the end of the Cold War. There are several points supporting this argument.

First, extraordinary political changes have greatly reduced the dominant CBW threats to U.S. and allied interests. Today, it is virtually inconceivable that Soviet chemical weapons or residual BW capabilities would be deliberately used against U.S. military forces or allies. Instead, the main threat is the theft of weapons or the brain drain of scientists to the Third World. This underscores the importance of U.S. programs for assisting in chemical weapons destruction in Russia, for helping dismantle former CBW facilities, and for working with the Russians to redirect people to cooperative peaceful purposes.

Second, U.S. military capabilities for dealing with CBW threats have increased as well. The United States today has an unsurpassed conventional military force structure. The United States is investing in tactical missile defenses against CBW threats and is giving increased and much-needed attention to passive defenses, measures aimed at detecting and protecting troops from these weapons' effects.

Although still vulnerable, the United States is clearly better positioned today to operate in a chemical or biological environment than any other force around the world. These military capabilities, the conventional, and the passive and active defense clearly must affect an adversary's calculation as to whether or not to use CBW against U.S forces.

Third, export control efforts, interdiction efforts, and sanction policies are informed by increasingly better intelligence on proliferation programs. These have helped slow down and, in some cases, limit proliferators' CBW capabilities. Export controls cannot stop a determined proliferator, but export controls and interdiction efforts are having a major effect on some of the proliferation programs of concern.

Successes in this area are often classified because of the sensitivity of intelligence; however, John Gannon, the head of the National Intelligence Council, said at a recent conference that preventing Libya from obtaining needed chemicals and equipment and technical expertise has set back the Libyan CW program by some ten years. This example is one of the successes of export controls and interdiction efforts being targeted by an increasingly more robust body of intelligence information.

A fourth reason why one could argue that the CBW threat is less today is arms control efforts such as the Chemical Weapons Convention (CWC). The CWC has helped cap the bulk of the theoretical CW proliferation problem by legally binding countries not to acquire chemical weapons. Today there are 126 state parties to the CWC.

The CWC has also begun to help roll back CW proliferation programs. South Korea and India are two very good examples. Both countries were not publicly identified or acknowledged as chemical weapons proliferators. Both have acknowledged the development, production, and possession of chemical weapons; these programs are in the process of being dismantled under the CWC.

The CWC is giving the United States and the international community new tools for dealing with CW proliferation threats and for things like challenge inspections. Under this treaty, the United States has an opportunity to pursue CW program concerns in countries like Iran.

The picture is considerably more ambiguous on the BW arms control side. The

Biological Weapons Convention (BWC) has been in force since 1975. However, the BWC has no enforcement provisions and no verification provisions. There have been reports that a dozen or so countries have or are seeking to acquire biological weapons. Some of those countries, the key ones, are parties to the BWC. It is clear that this convention has not prevented proliferation. What is left to consider is whether or not the problem will be worse in the absence of the BWC.

There is clearly a CBW proliferation problem. But because of a combination of forces—some beyond our control, like political change in the Soviet Union and in South Africa, others arising from policies consciously pursued by the U.S. government on the military side, export controls, intelligence, interdiction, arms control—the CBW proliferation threat has been mitigated. Not eliminated, but mitigated since the end of the Cold War.

Clearly the United States must continue pursuing non-proliferation policies that seek to deter not only the use of chemical and biological weapons but also the acquisition of these weapons in the first place. This is a policy goal that the United States only began to add into its calculations with the Iran-Iraq war and the revelations about how the Iraqis acquired their CW and BW capabilities.

Deterring acquisition as well as use is going to require continued reliance on a range of military and nonmilitary instruments. On the military side, there are three key ones: strong conventional forces, robust active defenses, and robust passive defenses. The United States also needs to be prepared on the military side to provide assistance to friends and allies that might be threatened or attacked with a CBW.

On the nonmilitary side, the United States needs to ensure adequate funding for CBW-related redirection and dismantlement efforts in the former Soviet Union—Russia, in particular—in order to reduce the likelihood that expertise or materials contribute to more CBW proliferation and acquisition efforts.

The United States also must continue to invest in intelligence collection and analysis to better characterize the threat and guide export control efforts, interdiction efforts, and sanctions efforts. It is critical that the United States continue to reject efforts by Iran and a handful of other countries to eliminate national and multilateral export control regimes like the Australia Group.

Finally, on the arms control front, the United States needs to work with other state parties to implement the CWC effectively. This tool can bring great benefits, but it will require considerable political will for the United States and other state parties to achieve all potential benefits. And the United States should move forward in efforts to negotiate—as the president has challenged us to do—a compliance protocol to the Biological Weapons Convention.

Ultimately, success against the CW and BW proliferation problem will be determined by how aggressively all these instruments, military as well as nonmilitary, are pursued.

NOTES

1. Even prior to formal ratification, the Vienna Convention on Treaties forbids signatories from undermining the aims of an agreement.

2. Sergei Pluzhnikov and Aleksei Shvedov, "Terrible Secrets of the 'Ogarkov System,' " *Sovershenno Sekretno*, no. 4 (1998): 12–14.

3. Sergey Leskov, "Plague and the Bomb: Russia and U.S. Military Bacteriological Programs Are Being Developed in Deep Secrecy, and Present a Terrible Danger to the World," *Izvestiya*, June 26, 1993, 15, translated in JRPS-TND-93-023, July 19, 1993, 22–23.

4. V. Umnov, "The Danger of a Biological War Remains," *Komsomolskaya Pravda*, September 19, 1992, 3, translated in JPRS-TAC-92-030, October 8, 1992, 32–35.

5. "Interview with Biopreparat Official," *Pravda*, October 15, 1992, 4, translated in JPRS-TAC-92-035, December 5, 1992, 23–25.

6. National Academy of Sciences, Institute of Medicine, National Research Council, *Controlling Dangerous Pathogens: A Blueprint for U.S.-Russian Cooperation* (Washington, D.C.: NAS, October 1987).

7. John Barry, "Planning a Plague?" *Newsweek*, February 1, 1993, 40–41.

8. Milton Leitenberg, "The Biological Weapons Program of the Former Soviet Union," *Biologicals* 21, no. 3 (September 1993): 187–91.

9. Judith Miller and William J. Broad, "Germ Weapons: In the Soviet Past or in the New Russia's Future?" *New York Times*, December 28, 1998, 1.

10. Ibid.

11. Author interview with Dr. Kenneth Alibek, Monterey, Calif., November 6, 1998.

12. David Hoffman, "Idled Arms Experts in Russia Pose Threat," *Washington Post*, December 28, 1998.

13. Amy Smithson, "Concerns Renewed about Russia's Bio Weapons Program," *CBW Chronicle* 2, no. 4 (May 1998).

14. Judith Miller and William J. Broad, "Bio-Weapons in Mind, Iranians Lure Needy Ex-Soviet Scientists," *New York Times*, December 8, 1998, A1, A12.

15. R. Adam Moody, "Armageddon for Hire," *Jane's International Defence Review*, February 1997, 21–23.

16. Robert Gates, testimony [as CIA director] before the Senate Governmental Affairs Committee, Hearing, *Weapons Proliferation in the New World Order*, January 15, 1992. See also R. Jeffrey Smith, "Gates Fears Soviet 'Brain Drain,' " *Washington Post*, January 16, 1992, A22.

17. Author interview with Dr. Kenneth Alibek.

18. Ibid.

19. *Sunday Times* [London], article on August 27, 1995, cited in *Chemical Weapons Convention Bulletin*, no. 30 (December 1995):17.

20. Igor V. Domaradskij, *"Troublemaker" or the Story of an Inconvenient Man* (Moscow, 1995).

21. Miller and Broad, "Bio-Weapons in Mind, Iranians Lure Needy Ex-Soviet Scientists."

22. Ibid.

23. MSNBC, "Russian Denies Iranian Germ Link," January 4, 1999.

24. R. Adam Moody, "The International Science Center Initiative," in *Dismantling the Cold War: U.S. and NIS Perspectives on the Nunn-Lugar Cooperative Threat Reduction Program*, ed. John M. Shields and William C. Potter (Cambridge: MIT Press, 1997), 277.

25. Alan Cooperman and Kyrill Belianinov, "Moonlighting by Modem in Russia," *U.S. News &*

World Report, April 17, 1995, 45.

26. Pluzhnikov and Shvedov, "Terrible Secrets of the 'Ogarkov System.' "

27. Ibid.

28. Domaradskij, *"Troublemaker" or the Story of an Inconvenient Man*.

29. Judith Miller and William J. Broad, "Dollars Are Weapons of Choice in the War on Bacteria Peril," *New York Times*, December 8, 1998, A12.

30. R. Jeffrey Smith, "Did Moscow Try to Skirt Sanctions?" *Washington Post*, February 13, 1998, A2; Judith Miller, "Official Confirms 1995 Russian-Iraq Deal," *New York Times*, February 18, 1998, 8; R. Jeffrey Smith, "Russians Admit Firms Met Iraqis," *Washington Post*, February 18, 1998, 16.

31. Richard J. Seltzer, "Moscow Science Center Lauded," *Chemical and Engineering News*, December 23, 1996, 28–31. See also International Science and Technology Center, *Report on ISTC Projects in the Field of Biotechnology and Life Sciences* (Moscow: ISTC, June 1997, GB-XIII-012 Attachment K2).

32. Miller and Broad, "Dollars Are Weapons of Choice in the War on Bacteria Peril."

33. Laurie Garrett, "US Funds Research at Former Soviet Germ Warfare Labs," *Boston Globe*, August 10, 1997, 2.

34. National Academy of Sciences, *Controlling Dangerous Pathogens*, October 1997, 6–9.

35. Miller and Broad, "Bio-Weapons in Mind, Iranians Lure Needy Ex-Soviet Scientists."

36. Miller and Broad, "Dollars Are Weapons of Choice in the War on Bacteria Peril."

37. Miller and Broad, "Germ Weapons: In the Soviet Past or in the New Russia's Future?"

38. National Academy of Sciences, *Controlling Dangerous Pathogens*, p. 18.

39. On December 17, 1998, U.S. and Russian military experts met for the first time at the Military Academy of Radiological, Chemical and Biological Defense, in Tambov, Russia, and agreed in principle to a series of military scientific exchanges in 1999 that may eventually provide direct Western access to four military microbiological facilities at Sergiev Posad, Kirov, Yekaterinburg, and Strizhi. See Miller and Broad, "Germ Weapons: In the Soviet Past or in the New Russia's Future?"

—16—

A Fissile Material Cut-Off Treaty and the Future of Nuclear Arms Control[1]

Camille Grand

The essential ingredient for all nuclear weapons is a core of highly enriched uranium (HEU) or plutonium, known as fissile material.[2] Since the end of the Cold War, the five nuclear weapon states are all assumed to have stopped (or almost stopped) the production of fissile material on a unilateral basis.[3] Moreover, four of them (the United States, Russia, France, and the United Kingdom) have declared unilateral, unlimited moratoriums on future production.[4] Taking this good news for granted, some have argued that the need and the momentum for a Fissile Material Cut-Off Treaty (FMCT) have vanished in terms of nuclear disarmament.[5]

Moreover, the other benefits expected in the field of nuclear non-proliferation are often portrayed as either negligible or counterproductive, as the proposed FMCT does not address existing stockpiles of material. It would accordingly signal a de facto recognition of the three nuclear-capable states (Israel, India, and Pakistan) and thus undermine the Non-Proliferation Treaty (NPT) and the regime as a whole.

Finally, many non-nuclear weapon states and nongovernmental organizations do not see the need to formalize an agreement and would prefer the international community and the Conference on Disarmament to focus on nuclear disarmament itself.

The establishment of an ad hoc committee by the United Nations Conference on Disarmament (CD) in August 1998, after years of failed attempts, has thus appeared as less good and important news than one would expect, at least beyond arms control expert circles. From a skeptical perspective, it seems to typify the false arms control promise: When you wanted it you could not get it, and now that you can get it, you do not really need it.

After an overview of the fissile material negotiations I will argue, on the contrary, that an FMCT is not only a most needed step in international security, in spite of the many pending issues in the negotiations, but also a useful tool for further nuclear arms control measures and a key negotiation issue in defining the security landscape of the future.

EARLY ATTEMPTS TO ADDRESS
FISSILE MATERIALS

Addressing nuclear arms control via the issue of fissile material is not a new concept. During the entire Cold War, many initiatives focused on fissile material as a tool to put an end to the ongoing nuclear arms race. Most of these attempts failed, as the countries involved refused to accept a control or a ban on production that would leave them in a state of inferiority versus the other nuclear weapon states.

As early as 1946, the centerpiece of the Baruch Plan[6] was the creation of an international "Atomic Development Authority" that would legally be the owner of all fissile materials. In 1954, India proposed a universal, nondiscriminatory convention to end the production of fissile material.[7] Two years later, in 1956, a fissionable material cutoff became a centerpiece of U.S. arms control policy with President Eisenhower's proposal to end the production of nuclear weapons. It remained an important part of U.S. nuclear diplomacy until 1969. In the 1980s, new proposals were issued by nongovernmental groups,[8] the Soviet Union proposed a phased disarmament program in 1982 that included a halt in fissile material production, and the United Nations General Assembly passed several resolutions in favor of a freeze on fissile material production.

In spite of some limited successes in 1964 (statements on fissile material production restraint issued simultaneously by the United States, the USSR, and the United Kingdom), these proposals and negotiations never got very far.

FROM THE CLINTON PROPOSAL TO
THE SHANNON MANDATE

It is only in the 1990s that the cutoff gained a new momentum with the end of the Cold War and the new, growing concern about nuclear proliferation.[9] In 1992, when President George Bush announced a halt in fissile material production, the United States became the first country to declare a unilateral and unlimited cutoff on future production. This moratorium allowed President Bill Clinton to call for a multilateral convention banning the production of fissile materials for nuclear explosives in a September 27, 1993, speech before the United Nations. In his speech, President Clinton emphasized both the non-proliferation and the arms control benefits from a FMCT. It is to this date the most important initiative taken by the Clinton administration in the field of multilateral arms control. The only other issue that would come close is the Clinton administration support for the Comprehensive Test Ban Treaty (CTBT), but the CTBT is not per se a Clinton initiative, while the FMCT will remain a Clinton legacy in the field of nuclear arms control.

The Clinton proposal took place not only in a new strategic environment but also at a time when most nuclear weapon states had stopped or were getting ready to stop fissile material production after having built up large stockpiles (see table 16.1). The unilateral U.S. initiative on halting production has indeed been followed by Russia (1994), the United Kingdom (1995), and France (1996).

The Clinton speech played a decisive role in the later UN resolution (UNGA 48/75L) on the "Prohibition of the Production of Fissile Material for Nuclear Weapons or for Other Explosive Devices," adopted by consensus on December 16, 1993.[10] This resolution called for a "non-discriminatory, multilateral and internationally and effectively verifiable treaty banning the production of fissile material for nuclear weapons or for other explosive devices" as "a significant contribution to nuclear non-proliferation in all its aspects."

Following this breakthrough, Ambassador Gerald E. Shannon of Canada was appointed in September 1994 by the CD to lead consultations on "the most appropriate arrangement" to negotiate an FMCT. On March 24, 1995, after a year of consultations, Ambassador Shannon released his report and suggested a mandate (known as the "Shannon mandate") for the ad hoc committee, primarily focusing on fissile material production but leaving the door open to other options for the negotiators.[11] In spite of a major Western push to establish the ad hoc committee quickly (before the 1995 NPT Review and Extension Conference), negotiations in the CD stalled over the issue of existing stocks, the members failed to appoint Ambassador Shannon as the chair, and, thus, they failed to truly establish the ad hoc committee.

Even though the NPT Conference attempted to give a new impetus to the talks by putting the FMCT in the concluding "Principles and Objectives" document, the FMCT became the orphan of arms control negotiations for three years. As one observer noted, "No one care[d] for it very much any more, although nobody [would] say so openly."[12] Indeed, after a failure in 1996, the CD failed again to establish an FMCT committee in 1997, even though the delegates should have been more ready to focus on the issue, with the CTBT negotiations having come to a successful conclusion.

It was only in August 1998 that the CD was finally able to establish an ad hoc committee,[13] after the last opponents (Pakistan and Israel) reversed their position. Since this important turn, however, the CD has been unable to truly start the negotiations. As an insightful follower of arms control diplomacy has recently written: "The problems are structural and political, with the sad fact that valuable though it would be, the fissban has no sufficiently strong driving force behind it to overcome the persistently placed obstacles of linkage and protection of nuclear privileges."[14] Most arms control analysts would nevertheless subscribe to the views expressed by a leading expert: "It would be tragic if [the treaty] were lost at a moment in history when a window of opportunity appears to have opened up through which it could be finally achieved."[15]

TABLE 16.1

STOCKPILES OF WEAPONS-USABLE FISSILE MATERIAL IN METRIC TONS

Country	Military HEU (declared excess)	Date Production Stopped	Military Plutonium (declared excess)	Date Production Stopped	Declared Unilateral Moratorium on Future Production of Fissile Material
United States	750 (174)	1988	99.5 (53)	1964	1992
Russian Federation	1,050 (500)	1987	131 (50)	1994[a]	1994
United Kingdom	21.9	1963	7.6 (4.4)	1995	1995
France	25	1996	5	1992	1996
China	20	1987 (?)[b]	4	1991(?)[b]	No
Israel[c]	?	—	0.5	Production continues	No
India[c]	Negligible	—	0.33	Production continues	No
Pakistan[c]	0.2	Production continues[d]	Negligible	Production may have started	No
Totals	1,700 (674)		230 (107.4)		No

Sources: The figures for stockpiles are taken from Frank von Hippel, "The FMCT and Cuts in Fissile Material Stockpiles," *Disarmament Forum*, no. 2 (1999), an update from the major source on plutonium and HEU stockpiles: David Albright, Frans Berkhout, and William Walker, *Plutonium and Highly Enriched Uranium, 1996: World Inventories, Capabilities and Policies* (SIPRI/Oxford University Press, 1997). The dates have been compiled by the author from various sources, including the table in Annette Shaper, "A Treaty on the Cut-Off of Fissile Material for Nuclear Weapons: What to Cover? How to Verify?" *PRIF's Reports*, no. 48 (July 1997): 21.

Note: Due to a lack of transparency, Albright, Berkhout, and Walker assign a high level of uncertainty to these figures (from 20 percent up to 50 percent) for all countries, except the United States and the United Kingdom.

a. Three Pu–producing reactors are still in use, but under the Gore-Chernomyrdin amended agreements, weapon-grade plutonium is no longer extracted and the reactors are to be modified by the year 2000 and shut down in 2009–2010.

b. As the Chinese government has refused to declare a moratorium, the dates given are subject to caution and should be handled carefully. Fissile material production could resume, may even have continued.

c. The production of the three nuclear-capable states is likely to have increased since these estimates, as production continues.

d. Pakistan claims to have stopped production of HEU from 1991 to 1997.

A MOST NEEDED STEP IN
INTERNATIONAL SECURITY

The FMCT negotiation is a complicated and technical issue; even the purpose of the treaty remains hotly debated.[16] Is it primarily targeted at strengthening nuclear non-proliferation as the traditional U.S. approach would suggest?[17] Or does it only make sense as the first step of a phased nuclear disarmament, as many among the nonaligned and nongovernmental groups are supporting? Could it even be turned into a plutonium ban as antinuclear activists have suggested and as nuclear reprocessing industries fear?

In fact, the FMCT debate is raising many different issues and needs to remain focused. Some have strongly and rightfully made the case that the FMCT was "neither a non-proliferation nor a disarmament measure factually";[18] it is, however, a critical measure for the future of both nuclear non-proliferation and disarmament.

The FMCT is, in my view, needed for four reasons of almost equal importance to international security:

- Opening a new era for the relations among the P-5 through enhanced transparency.
- Strengthening the non-proliferation regime.
- Building confidence and security in nuclear regional frameworks.
- Preventing the spread of fissile material to nonstate actors.

A NEW ERA AMONG THE NUCLEAR STATES

So far, the nuclear arms control process has primarily been a bilateral U.S.-Russian effort combined with a set of unilateral steps taken by the three medium nuclear-weapon states. The FMCT, together with the CTBT signed in 1996 (and one should take this opportunity to stress the utmost importance of an early entry into force of the CTBT, so far ratified only by Britain and France among the nuclear-weapon states and the nuclear-capable states), is a unique opportunity to engage the medium nuclear weapon states in the negotiating process defining the role of nuclear weapons in the new decade.

These two treaties offer a nondiscriminatory regime imposing equal obligations on nuclear weapon states, nuclear-capable states, and non-nuclear weapon states that will primarily be supported by the nuclear weapon states and the nuclear-capable states. The treaties intend to put an end to both the qualitative and the quantitative arms race by forbidding nuclear tests and further production of nuclear weapons. One can certainly argue that the stockpiles of fissile material accumulated over the years are more than sufficient and that the nuclear weapon states and nuclear-capable states preserve their ability to remain nuclear in the midterm. But this is not the main point, which is in fact the following: with the FMCT, the real and giant step is that nuclear weapons will enter a finite universe and the nuclear arms race of the last fifty years will be, one hopes definitely, closed in a verifiable manner.

The exact content of the FMCT is yet to to be defined. But it will in any circumstances offer an opportunity for enhanced transparency among the nuclear weapon states and the nuclear-capable states at a stage in nuclear arms control when it becomes a need.

As the START process slims the arsenals of the Big Two, the other three nuclear weapon states have to commit themselves to stopping the growth of their existing arsenals in order not to create destabilizing situations. As its arsenal goes down, Russia has to be sure that the other three, which are still perceived as potential adversaries, do not continue an arms buildup that could wreck the fragile START stability. As far as France and the United Kingdom are concerned, the existing relative transparency and commitments are reassuring, but could potentially be reversed.

The case of China is more troubling.[19] The exact size of the Chinese nuclear arsenal is unknown to the international community (with estimates ranging from a few hundred warheads to a couple of thousand[20]), and it is assumed that it is still growing in size and capability. A verified freeze in Chinese fissile material production going beyond the present supposed, but unconfirmed, halt in production would be a very important step in this framework.

Moreover, in the definition of a stable nuclear environment, the enhanced transparency offered by an FMCT verification regime would certainly contribute more broadly to building confidence and trust among the P-5 and, as such, open the way for further reductions, as my conclusion will try to demonstrate.

STRENGTHENING THE GLOBAL NON-PROLIFERATION REGIME

Far from weakening the regime, the FMCT is a tool to repair the non-proliferation regime—not the only tool but certainly an important one. First of all, it could strengthen the current non-proliferation verification regime by providing the means to control facilities now neglected by the International Atomic Energy Agency (IAEA) safeguards systems, including indigenously built reprocessing or enrichment facilities. With an FMCT in force, undertaking covert nuclear activities will become more difficult. This applies to non-NPT parties as well as to parties tempted to undertake a clandestine program.

Second, the FMCT is fulfilling a commitment made at the 1995 NPT Conference. In 1995, the "Principles and Objectives" called for the "immediate commencement and early conclusion of negotiations on a non-discriminatory and universally applicable convention banning the production of fissile material for nuclear weapons or other nuclear devices." During the three preparatory committees to the 2000 NPT Review Conference, many delegations have recalled these objectives in the NPT framework.[21] The regime needs these promises to be kept before the 2000 NPT Conference in order to build trust among the 187 parties to the treaty.

On a more controversial level, it offers a way to address the nuclear-capable states issue, by capping the development of their nuclear capability at a minimum level. As William Walker puts it:

> There is no doubt that India, Pakistan, and Israel represent a problem toward achieving negotiations. If the whole process of negotiating this

treaty really requires prevention and prestige, then [the treaty] could be very valuable in encouraging restraint in South Asia and in influencing the ways in which they shape their deterrent strategies. It also gradually shifts the Israeli policy in a useful direction towards more transparency.[22]

In the current international situation, the three nuclear-capable states will not sign the NPT, and the NPT cannot be amended to welcome them as nuclear weapon states with any special status without jeopardizing the entire regime. The FMCT thus appears as a way to engage Israel, India, and Pakistan in the global regime and, for the first time, to associate the three nuclear-capable states with an arms control agreement both capping their ability to engage in an arms race and taking into account the current nuclear framework.

It is not a best-case scenario for the arms control community, but it is certainly the best solution in the present situation, especially since the FMCT is also likely to help build trust and confidence in regional frameworks.

BUILDING TRUST AND CONFIDENCE IN REGIONAL FRAMEWORKS

Regional security is an often forgotten element of a cutoff agreement. The lack of confidence among the states involved in one or another regional security issue is often the most challenging to begin solving the dispute.

In Southern Asia, the FMCT would provide triple reassurances within the China-India-Pakistan triangle and avoid a costly arms race among the three, India trying to balance Chinese superiority, China trying to ensure the continuation of its overwhelming superiority, and Pakistan doing its best to achieve a pseudoparity with India. With a freeze on future fissile material production, the three would need to stick to the present minimum nuclear equilibrium. If the FMCT looks in sight, we will certainly face a last-minute fissile material stockpile buildup—at least in India and Pakistan, where a buildup is already under way. However, if all states involved have good reasons to believe and secure ways to verify that the others have stopped production of HEU and plutonium, they are more likely to accept a lower equilibrium and to develop trust- and confidence-building measures in other related fields.

In the Middle East, a verified Israeli commitment to freeze its supposed fissile material at a certain level—and hence its nuclear arsenal—would certainly be a critical first step in building trust in the region. In return, the Israelis would get a treaty that would further prevent acquisition of nuclear weapons by other regional actors.

The Korean peninsula could be another example of the regional benefits induced by a FMCT, which would help countries involved feel more confident about the freeze of the North Korean nuclear program and thus prevent further nuclear temptations in the region.

A cutoff agreement in itself is surely not enough to build trust in a regional conflict situation. It is, however, an interesting and important tool for increasing regional confidence.

PREVENTING THE SPREAD OF FISSILE MATERIAL
TO NONSTATE ACTORS

Increased monitoring of nuclear facilities and the end of further production fissile material would, last but not least, certainly help prevent traffic of nuclear material. The theft from vast existing stockpiles, for instance, in the former Soviet Union, will remain a problem, but a FMCT will make it more difficult for terrorist groups to acquire fissile material, as the accounting and safeguarding of the remaining stockpiles are likely to increase with time.

PENDING ISSUES IN THE FMCT NEGOTIATIONS

As needed as it might be, the FMCT faces several major issues in the months to come, even when the negotiations are finally launched in Geneva. Paradoxically, the talks are currently held back primarily for political reasons even though the challenges are more technical than anything else (with serious political side effects). Ambassador Mark Moher of Canada has recently identified before the CD the three types of challenges facing the FMCT: "conceptual parameters" (stocks, characterization of state parties, moratoria on current production), "strategic issues" (scope, definitions, and verification), and "structural matters" (governance, verification machinery, financing).[23] Reading through the debates at the CD and the statements made at the NPT preparatory committees, one can shortlist the pending issues into several topics: scope, stocks, and verification. At first sight, these debates are technical, but the following questions are in fact highly political: Exactly what fissile material should the FMCT prohibit? How should it deal with the issue of stocks? What is the proper verification regime?[24]

WHAT FISSILE MATERIALS SHOULD
THE TREATY PROHIBIT?

On this first point, some approaches might prove too ambitious to be productive and are under any circumstances likely to raise the opposition of the nuclear-weapon states or the countries with large nuclear industries. As pointed out recently by Japan's ambassador Akira Hayashi, a difficult point about the FMCT is that it "is bound to be of very technical nature, understood only by experts."[25] To summarize the debate, one could divide the answers to the question of what material to cover into a maximalist approach and a more incremental (and, in my opinion, more reasonable) view. In the first case, some countries and nongovernmental organizations try to prohibit the production of most fissile materials, arguing that most fissile materials are dangerous. The others try, on the contrary, to establish a distinction between weapons-usable fissile materials and other materials.[26]

In-depth consideration of the technical debate aside, one point is clear: The nuclear weapon states and some countries with large nuclear industries such as Japan or Germany will not accept the broadest definition of fissile materials. The FMCT is not the treaty to address the issue of the reprocessing industry's good faith. Some side issues, like HEU for naval or research reactors, will need to be clarified, but trying to achieve a comprehensive ban on future production of pluto-nium and HEU for civilian purposes is counterproductive.

To avoid unnecessary and time-consuming controversies about what are "fissile materials," South Africa has put forward the term *nuclear weapons material*, which, if properly defined, could become acceptable to everyone.[27] The most appropriate and less ambiguous wording would probably be *nuclear weapons fissile material*.

A last point sometimes raised about the scope is the issue of tritium, which, "in the IAEA classification, does not count as a nuclear material."[28] Because of strate-gic needs due to tritium's shorter life, a ban on tritium production would in any case not be acceptable to the nuclear weapon states. More important in the long term, tritium is also likely to have more and more civilian uses in the future, even though these applications are at present still in the research and development phase.

There might be a need to clarify and organize the list of fissile materials between direct-use materials and others,[29] but the FMCT should focus on the materials that have been used to build bombs over the past fifty years (plutonium-239 and urani-um-235). It cannot, and should not, address the wider debate about the nuclear fuel cycle and the even broader debate about the future of the nuclear industry altogether.

WHAT ABOUT STOCKS?

Because of its highly political nature, the issue of stocks is more controversial. For the many countries pressing for some form of inclusion of stocks, it is a way to en-sure that the fissban will indeed be a disarmament measure (this is the reason they press for their preferred "Fissile Material Treaty" title rather than a Fissile Material *Cut-Off* Treaty). For the nuclear weapon states and the nuclear-capable states, it is going much beyond the acceptable scope of the proposed treaty, which is not a nuclear weapons convention. As Harald Müller has put it, "One has to walk the tightrope between overburdening the fissban with too much of the disarmament agenda, and depriving it of much its value by too timidly ignoring the stockpile issue."[30]

Many more or less realistic proposals have been put forward to address the issue of stocks. Some countries want a stockpile provision to be included in the treaty imme-diately. Some have suggested a phased approach with the inclusion of stockpiles at a later date, possibly with a compulsory provision in the FMCT. However, for those who do not want to jeopardize the entire negotiation, the stockpiles are more likely to be addressed as a side issue.

On a unilateral basis or possibly through joint statements, the nuclear weapon states and nuclear-capable states could accept certain principles meeting some of the demands of the non-nuclear weapon states. This could include a better accounting of past production, a higher transparency on fissile materials holdings, and a commit-ment to place under safeguards excess materials. All these steps would contribute to the irreversibility of the disarmament process parallel to the FMCT and increase confidence among nuclear weapon states and between nuclear weapon states and non-nuclear weapon states.

These provisions do not need to be included as a provision of the FMCT itself but should rather take the form of incremental steps declared and taken by the nuclear weapon states. This would allow each nuclear weapon state to move faster on the measures that suit it best. For instance, because of their larger stockpiles, the two nuclear superpowers can be expected to declare more excess materials than the others. The three medium nuclear weapon states could insist on the irreversibility of the unilateral steps taken. The most opaque nuclear states (China and the three nuclear-capable states) can be expected to put the emphasis on transparency.

Finally, there are other major issues that are left aside by so much insistence on stocks and that are probably more important for irreversibility. The future of production facilities is one of them. France is so far the only country to have started to dismantle its production facilities. If this move were to be followed, it would mean more in terms of irreversibility than the inclusion of small amounts of excess stockpiles. Is not the first goal of the fissban to halt production forever in a verifiable manner? And, accordingly, is not the dismantling of facilities dedicated to such production a priority?

Strong political gestures by the nuclear weapon states on the issue of stocks can be expected by the non-nuclear weapon states as they engage fully in the negotiations. However, insisting on the inclusion of current stockpiles will just lead the FMCT negotiations into a deadlock. Once again, the fissban cannot be expected to resolve all pending issues in the nuclear field: It is only a very important step in a broader and longer process.

WHAT VERIFICATION REGIME?

The last major issue for controversy in the FMCT negotiation—the verification regime—is of the utmost importance if we are to ensure the credibility of the treaty.

Some—including some of the strongest supporters of the FMCT logic, such as the U.S. administration—are tempted to accept a focused verification regime in order to ensure an early entry into force. This would mean focusing on the most visible facilities (enrichment plants and reprocessing facilities). This approach might prove counterproductive in the longer term.

If, for the time being, the risks of cheating are relatively low and are rather well covered by the existing NPT safeguards, the FMCT should aim to reinforce these safeguards and apply them to more states. Accordingly, a tough inspection regime monitored by the IAEA would be preferable. As noted by several Australian experts, it might indeed be "politically and financially nonviable, at this stage in the nuclear disarmament process, to attempt to apply a full-scope safeguards regime."[31] It is, however, important to try to achieve the most comprehensive regime possible in order to meet two objectives: nondiscrimination and verifiability. These are major political and technical objectives.

The verification provision must certainly take into account the specific problems raised by the monitoring of nuclear facilities in nuclear weapon states. It must also carefully structure inspections conducted by non–nuclear weapon state inspectors in the nuclear weapon states in order to reduce proliferation-associated risks. But an intrusive regime is needed for the treaty to make sense. As estimated by Annette

Schaper, the costs of a comprehensive verification system would be annually only $140 million.[32] This would double the current IAEA Department of Safeguards budget (currently about $70 million), but it would be a small price worth paying to have a treaty gifted with a serious inspection regime. Investing in inspections of the nuclear-weapon states might seem pointless at first sight, but it is an important step in shifting nuclear mentalities toward more accountability and, again, a small price for achieving a high non-proliferation payoff from the FMCT. Without a proper verification regime, the FMCT would lose many of its virtues.

There are more pending issues in the negotiations, such as the entry-into-force provision, but these can be left to the last steps of the discussions. The current objective is to go beyond the deadlock in Geneva and get the negotiation started in earnest. Besides the obvious need for a little more political will from the states involved, the current problems can be solved through a more positive approach. If some unnecessary linkages were dropped, the FMCT talks could have a fairly good chance of commencing soon and fulfilling its important role as an integral part of a global nuclear arms control regime.

A TOOL FOR FURTHER ARMS CONTROL

Together with the CTBT, an FMCT will for the first time create a nuclear verification regime on a nondiscriminatory basis. First- and second-tier nuclear weapon states, nuclear-capable states, and non–nuclear weapon states will all be treated equally. As such, an FMCT provides a useful tool for defining the basis of the nuclear-weapons regime in the new decade: increased transparency, universality of obligations, tighter limits on nuclear arsenals.

On transparency, there are still many reservations on the exact scope of the FMCT. The United States, Russia, and more recently the United Kingdom have unilaterally revealed more information on their current stockpiles of fissile material. Even though France is the only country to have so far taken the path of irreversibility by dismantling its fissile material production facilities, it today appears more reluctant to accept increased transparency in the current framework. Moreover, China and the three nuclear-capable states still prefer to preserve a very opaque nuclear ambiguity in this field.

The treaty is unlikely to impose on states parties a complete transparency of past production, as most nuclear-weapon states are unlikely to accept it. It will, however, for the first time, induce nuclear-weapon states and nuclear-capable states to accept inspections in the very heart of their nuclear complexes (as the CTBT also will do, once it enters into force, for testing related activities). This is a very new and challenging task for the FMCT. Nuclear establishments in every country are reluctant to accept inspections. It took years of implementation of the Intermediate Nuclear Forces (INF) Treaty and the START agreements to create a fairly confident environment between the United States and Russia. The FMCT is a unique opportunity to develop such a climate among the P-5 and beyond. Increased nuclear transparency is not an end in itself, but it is a critical tool for increasing international and regional security.

The FMCT would also impose equal obligations on all state parties, which is typical of the new era opened by the Chemical Weapons Convention and the CTBT. The non–nuclear weapon states are unwilling to accept treaties that preserve nuclear inequalities. The FMCT, on the contrary, puts most of the burden on nuclear weapon states and nuclear-capable states, not as such but because they are the ones with the most facilities involved. On the nuclear weapon states side, signing the FMCT is admitting that the international landscape has changed and that to preserve the legitimacy of their nuclear status, they have to demonstrate a new openness. In this case it involves a verifiable commitment not to produce fissile material, thus admitting, at first theoretically, that their arsenals will not go beyond certain limits defined by the current stockpiles.

Because of these characteristics, the FMCT is not so much a Cold War arms control measure finally signed as it is a key event defining the future of nuclear weapons in the next decades: an end to nuclear arms races, tighter limits on existing weaponry, and enhanced transparency of the nuclear complexes.[33] A future upon which those who favor elimination and those who see a role for nuclear weapons in the medium to long term can certainly agree.

CONCLUSION

This chapter, I hope, has presented some convincing reasons for seriously negotiating an FMCT and for ensuring its early entry into force. The FMCT has many virtues, but too much should not be put on its shoulders. This would kill the treaty. Among other things, the FMCT scope should not be expected to address all issues pending at the CD, including nuclear disarmament *stricto sensu*, via the issue of stocks. Transparency of the existing stockpile is also more likely to be a side effect of the treaty than its primary objective.

Instead of focusing on political issues, the key element for a successful FMCT is obviously its verification regime, which should be the responsibility of an experienced body of inspectors. The IAEA accordingly seems the most appropriate structure to fulfill this task. The range of activities covered by the treaty should keep a balance between a focused approach that could leave too many nuclear activities out of the FMCT scope and an overstretched ambition too costly to be truly verifiable.

Altogether, the tasks of the negotiators are not easy and the establishment of the ad hoc committee is only a first step on a difficult road. Innovative solutions, a spirit of compromise, and political will are needed from all the countries involved in Geneva and beyond. It is, however, a commitment that the FMCT deserves.

NOTES

1. An earlier and shorter draft of this chapter was presented at the panel "Negotiating a Cut-Off of Fissile Material Production" of the Seventh Carnegie International Non-Proliferation Conference (Washington, D.C., January 11–12, 1999). The author wishes to thank his copanelists (Ambassador Mark Moher, Rebecca Johnson, Michael Guhin, and Professor William Walker) for their insightful

presentations. This chapter would not have existed without Joseph Cirincione's trust and support at the Carnegie Endowment for International Peace. Of course, the author takes sole responsibility for all the shortcomings in this text. The views expressed in this paper should not be taken to represent the views of any institution, in France or elsewhere.

2. Nuclear fission is the splitting of the nucleus of an atom into two (or more) parts. Fissile material, principally uranium-235 and plutonium-239, is capable of allowing this fission to cascade into a chain reaction. In a chain reaction, when a neutron hits the nucleus of the atom, the nucleus splits and emits two or more neutrons, which in turn induce nearby nuclei to fission, sustaining and accelerating the process and releasing tremendous amounts of energy in a very short time.

3. These five nations are also the five permanent members of the United Nations Security Council and are often referred to as the Permanent Five, or, for short, the P-5.

4. For further details on existing stockpiles and the moratorium, see table 1.

5. As, so far, the agreed purpose of the negotiation is production of fissile material, I will stick to the classical FMCT acronym, even though some state parties to the talks prefer to refer to a Fissile Material Treaty (FMT) in order not to preclude the inclusion of stocks. Another frequently used nickname is "fissban," first coined by Rebecca Johnson and adopted by other leading analysts in this debate such as Annette Shaper.

6. Based upon the Lilienthal-Acheson report of 1945, the plan was presented by the United States representative Bernard Baruch to the UN Atomic Energy Commission on June 14, 1946. On these early efforts see Jean Klein, *L'entreprise du désarmement 1945–1964* (Paris: Cujas, 1964); and John Taylor, *Restricting the Production of Fissionable Material as an Arms Control Measure—An Updated Historical Overview* (Albuquerque: Sandia National Laboratories, 1987). For a comprehensive bibliography on FMCT issues, refer to Daiana Cipollone, "The Fissile Material Cut-Off Debate: A Bibliographical Survey," Research Papers, no. 38 (Unidir, 1996).

7. As recalled in Savita Datt, "Fissile Material Cut-Off Treaty: A Critique," *Strategic Analysis*, February 1998.

8. See for instance the proposals issued by the Thirty-First Pugwash Conference in 1981, quoted in *The Arms Control Reporter* 17 (1998): 612.A.5.

9. To understand the renewed interest in the FMCT, refer to the still very stimulating contributions by Thérèse Delpech, Lewis Dunn, David Fischer, and Rakesh Sood in "Halting the Production of Fissile Material for Nuclear Weapons," *Research Papers*, no. 31 (Unidir, 1994).

10. For the full text of the UN resolution and other key documents and commentaries on the FMCT, see the website of The Acronym Institute (http://www.acronym.org.uk/fmctdesc.htm). The Federation of American Scientists also maintains a comprehensive FMCT website (http://www.fas.org/-nuke/control/fmct/index.html).

11. CD/1299, March 24, 1995.

12. See Rebecca Johnson, "Little Orphan Fissban," *Bulletin of Atomic Scientists*, May–June 1997, 4.

13. For the agreement, see CD/1547, August 11, 1999.

14. Rebecca Johnson, "Geneva Updates No. 45," *Disarmament Diplomacy*, March 1999, 28.

15. Harald Müller, "A Ban on Production of Fissile Materials for Weapons Purposes: Doomed Prospects?" PPNN Issue Review, no. 13 (April 1998): 7.

16. The best study of the technical (and political) problems raised by the cutoff remains the report by Annette Shaper, "A Treaty on the Cut-Off of Fissile Material for Nuclear Weapons—What to Cover? How to Verify?" PRIF Reports, no. 48 (July 1997).

17. For a good example of this approach, see William H. Kincade, "Nuclear Weapons Grade Fissile Materials: The Most Serious Threat to U.S. National Security Today," *INSS Occasional Paper 8*, January 1995.

18. Harald Müller, "A Ban on Production of Fissile Materials for Weapons Purposes," 2.

19. There are even concerns about Chinese willingness to negotiate an FMCT in the first place. See Lisbeth Gronlund, Yong Liu, and David Wright, "The China Card, Will China Agree to Cut Off Fissile Material Production?" *Nucleus* 17, no. 2 (summer 1995).

20. The recent and comprehensive Carnegie Endowment non-proliferation study notes that China has "enough fissile material for approximately 2,700 nuclear weapons." Rodney W. Jones, Mark G. McDonough with Toby F. Dalton and Gregory D. Koblentz, *Tracking Nuclear Proliferation: A Guide in Maps and Charts*, 1998 (Washington, D.C.: Carnegie Endowment for International Peace, 1998), 54.

21. As examples, see the specific statements and proposals made by Australia, Canada, Egypt, Japan, and South Africa at the third NPT prepcom, New York.

22. For insightful remarks on the policies of India, Pakistan, and Israel regarding an FMCT, see the presentation delivered by William Walker at the Seventh Carnegie International Non-Proliferation Conference, January 11–12, 1999, Washington, D.C. (http://www.ceip.org/programs/npp/walk er.htm).

23. Ambassador Mark Moher, statement before the Plenary of the Conference of Disarmament, Geneva, March 18, 1999.

24. The most serious and constructive studies of these issues have been written by Annette Shaper, "A Treaty on the Cut-Off of Fissile Material for Nuclear Weapons—What to Cover? How to Verify?" *PRIF Reports*, no. 48 (July 1997): 18–29. See also her proposals to tackle the issue of stocks in "The Fissban: Stocks, Scope and Goals," *Disarmament Diplomacy*, no. 34 (February 1999): 13–16. One should also refer to the recent special issue of *Unidir's Journal* titled "Fissile Materials: Scope, Stocks and Verification," *Disarmament Forum*, no. 2 (1999).

25. Statement by H. E. Akira Hayashi, representative of Japan at the third NPT prepcom, New York, May 13, 1999.

26. That is, primarily plutonium-239 and highly enriched uranium (HEU with more than 20 percent of U-235). There are also technical debates about the likely inclusion of other special nuclear materials like neptunium.

27. Statement by the Republic of South Africa at the third NPT prepcom, New York, May 13, 1999.

28. Annette Shaper, "A Treaty on the Cut-Off of Fissile Material for Nuclear Weapons," 19.

29. For a proposal, see ibid., 20–25.

30. Harald Müller, "A Ban on Production of Fissile Materials for Weapons Purposes," 4.

31. Victor Bragin, John Carlson, and John Hill, "Verifying a Fissile Material Production Cut-Off Treaty," *Non-Proliferation Review*, fall 1998.

32. Annette Shaper, "A Treaty on the Cut-Off of Fissile Material for Nuclear Weapons," 42.

33. On the characteristics of this new era, see Camille Grand, "The Current Deadlock in Nuclear Arms Control: A Difficult Mutation to a New Era?" *Disarmament Diplomacy*, no. 34 (February 1999): 10–13.

—17—

Next Steps in Strategic Reductions

Michael Krepon, Thomas Graham Jr., Bruce Blair, Robert Bell, Alexei Arbatov

The negotiated nuclear arms reduction process, embodied in SALT and START, has been a central component of the U.S.–Soviet/Russian relationship for the past thirty years. The process held great promise for rapid progress on deep reductions at the end of the Cold War, but it is now essentially stagnant. This lack of progress poses a serious threat to the non-proliferation regime, which is conditioned in large part on the pledge made by the nuclear powers to reduce and eventually eliminate their nuclear arsenals.

Over the past few years many experts have issued detailed reports with proposals for more quickly and effectively realizing strategic arms reduction. In this chapter Ambassador Thomas Graham, Jr., and Dr. Bruce Blair describe, respectively, proposals for deep cuts in nuclear arsenals and the de-alerting of deployed forces. Robert Bell, special assistant to the president for defense policy and arms control at the National Security Council, describes his reaction to this agenda and the obstacles to further negotiated reductions. The Honorable Alexei Arbatov, director of the Center for Political and Military Forecasts and a member of the State Duma of the Russian Federation, provides a Russian perspective on this debate.

JUMP-STARTING THE PROCESS
By Michael Krepon

Nuclear dangers do not remain in equilibrium or in a steady state: if there is not progress in reducing these dangers, backsliding will occur.

There was much progress from the second Reagan administration until the second Clinton administration. Since 1996, however, there has been a considerable loss of momentum, followed by significant backsliding. Much effort will be required to regain lost ground. Part of the problem has been the Clinton administration's regrettable policy of waiting for the Russian Duma to ratify START II before new initiatives on strategic arms reductions could be pursued. The United States has been waiting for the Duma since January 1993. In the interim, many complications have arisen. It should now be clear that a "waiting for the Duma" approach has not led to a reduction of nuclear dangers. Quite the reverse is true.

The Committee on Nuclear Policy, a working body of over forty experts (including Thomas Graham, Bruce Blair, and Alexei Arbatov) from the nongovernmental community, has come to a different conclusion. The committee supports the treaty ratification process and would like the Duma and the United States Senate to act expeditiously. But committee members have come to the conclusion—some with great reluctance—that the formal process of negotiating and ratifying treaties is now more of a hindrance than a help for the nuclear threat reduction agenda.

Given current circumstances, the committee has concluded that the United States and Russia should proceed with parallel, reciprocal, and verifiable steps to reduce deployed nuclear forces, whether or not the Duma ever ratifies START II. Over time, treaties to confirm these reductions might be ratified. But it no longer makes sense to hold this process hostage to legislators in the Duma who have other agendas to pursue.

DEEP CUTS
By Ambassador Thomas Graham Jr.

Deep cuts in the existing nuclear arsenals are crucially important to reducing a number of the most dangerous threats to international security. Further progress toward nuclear disarmament is crucial to the continued viability of the Nuclear Non-Proliferation Treaty (NPT) regime. In addition to eroding confidence in the NPT, the retention of excessively large nuclear arsenals exaggerates the political value of nuclear weapons, making them more attractive to additional states. Furthermore, each nuclear weapon retained, especially on high alert, constitutes some risk of accidental or unauthorized use. Deep cuts in the nuclear arsenals have always been desirable, but more and more they are becoming indispensable to international security. In the long run, we will have to do more than we have in the past to move toward nuclear disarmament if we are to move away from the threat of nuclear proliferation.

Once more, the START II ratification process appears to be on hold after the interventions in Iraq and Kosovo. Even after approval by the Duma, START II must return to the U.S. Senate for approval of the recent amendments, and there it will be tangled up in the debate over the ABM Treaty agreements. So, even with the best of outcomes, entry into force of START II is some time off. This represents a serious challenge both to efforts to reduce global stockpiles of nuclear weapons and to the NPT regime's efforts to prevent the proliferation of nuclear weapons. This challenge must be addressed in a creative way, perhaps with informal arrangements for the short term. We cannot wait forever for START II. We may have to wait for START II to catch up. Time is limited; we must move forward.

TABLE 17.1

JUMP-START: RETAKING THE INITIATIVE TO REDUCE POST–COLD WAR NUCLEAR DANGERS

Recommendations:
The United States should:

Deep Reductions

- Supplement formal arms control treaties with paralled, reciprocal, and verifiable reductions

- Immediately declare U.S. intention to reduce, alongside Russia, to 1,000 deployed strategic nuclear weapons within a decade

- Offer cradle-to-grave transparency on the status of all U.S. and Russian nuclear weapons as the basis for reciprocal reductions

- With reciprocal verification, subsequently reduce to 1,000 total nuclear weapons on each side

- Seek agreement from the other nuclear weapon states on a ceiling on their current deployment levels and begin multilateral talks on reductions once the United States and Russia reach 1,000 total nuclear weapons

Removing the Hair Trigger

- Immediately stand down, alongside Russia, nuclear forces slated for destruction under START II

- Declare its intention, with a parallel, reciprocal commitment from Russia, to eliminate the launch-on-warning option from nuclear war plans

- Begin discussions among the five nuclear weapon states on verifiably removing all nuclear forces from hair-trigger alert

- Declare its intention, with a parallel, reciprocal commitment from Russia, to verifiably eliminate massive attack options from nuclear war plans

Fissile Materials and Warhead Controls

- Help install modern security and accounting systems and provide resources and incentives for sustaining effective security at all Russian nuclear facilities

- Help consolidate Russia's weapons-usable materials into the smallest possible number of locations

- Help shrink the Russian nuclear weapons complex

- Promote alternative employment in Russia's nuclear cities

- Build a cradle-to-grave transparency and monitoring system for all warheads and fissile materials

- Negotiate reductions in fissile material stocks in excess of that needed to support a 1,000-warhead stockpile

- Triple current funding for fissile materials controls

Source: The full text of the Committee on Nuclear Policy report *Jump-START: Retaking the Initiative to Reduce Post–Cold War Nuclear Dangers* is located at *www.stimson.org/policy.*

If this challenge can be overcome, however, in the medium to long term, the START process may be able to continue serving as the foundation for substantial cuts in the numbers of nuclear weapons possessed by the nuclear weapon states. The plan for START III, which it is agreed can begin to be addressed once the Duma approves START II, is a level of 2,000–2,500 deployed warheads and significant agreement with Russia on transparency. Since Defense Minister Igor Sergeyev has stated publicly that Russia will be at 500 strategic systems for economic reasons by 2012, it would appear unlikely that Russia would make a deal on transparency, their major bargaining asset in these negotiations, unless the United States is prepared to consider a level of forces closer to where Russia must be. However, the United States would only consider deep cuts of this sort if the Russians were prepared to negotiate complete transparency.

Beyond this, if the NPT is to survive and remain effective over the long term, a deep-cuts negotiation involving all five nuclear-weapon states, which will bring the level of total weapons for the United States and Russia down into the low 100s (less for the other three), should happen in the next ten to fifteen years.

Accordingly, consideration should be given to proposing for START III a level of 1,000 deployed strategic nuclear warheads, which would come close to the possible Russian level of 500 in 2012, and this should facilitate constructive negotiations on transparency. Already, at 2,000–2,500, U.S. strategic force levels are likely moving below a true Russia-wide hard-target kill capability (as opposed to a city-busting strategy), and thus a move to 1,000 probably would not have a fundamental impact on strategy. In the agreement to this first phase of reductions there would be a commitment to a second-phase level of 1,000 weapons total, bringing in Russian tactical nuclear weapons as well as reserve weapons.

Once the second phase is complete, the U.S.-Russian level would then be low enough to make possible a five-power negotiation to very low residual levels, which could be the end point until the world has changed sufficiently to permit contemplation of a prohibition on nuclear weapons. Discussion of the verification requirements of a deep-cuts treaty regime should be included in these five-power negotiations, and the three threshold states should be involved in some way. This residual level could be 300 each for the United States and Russia, 50 for the United Kingdom, France, and China, and zero for India, Pakistan, and Israel, but with their fissile material kept on their territory under International Atomic Energy Agency safeguards so as to permit reconstitution should the agreement break down. As an essential part of this, the non–nuclear weapon states would all pledge again their non-nuclear-weapon status and agree to joint action against any state that should violate this norm.

A medium- or long-term plan to enact deep cuts, however, may not be possible or prudent without short-term efforts aimed at preventing the further proliferation of nuclear weapons. Statements made by Prime Minister Atal Bihari Vajpayee after the Indian nuclear tests to the effect that "India is a big country" now that it has nuclear weapons are evidence that a troubling psychology still exists. The perceived political value of nuclear weapons remains too high, and the 1945-era

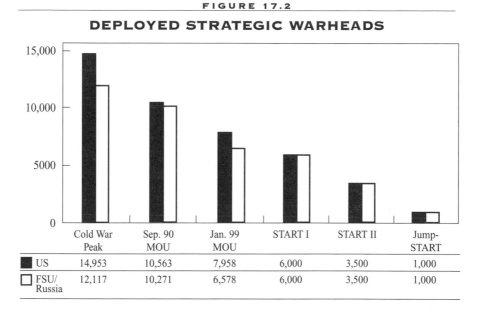

FIGURE 17.2

DEPLOYED STRATEGIC WARHEADS

	Cold War Peak	Sep. 90 MOU	Jan. 99 MOU	START I	START II	Jump-START
■ US	14,953	10,563	7,958	6,000	3,500	1,000
☐ FSU/ Russia	12,117	10,271	6,578	6,000	3,500	1,000

The graph above details the levels of U.S. and Soviet/Russian deployed strategic nuclear warheads. Each nation maintains a total stockpile of nuclear weapons (including nondeployed and tactical warheads) that is much larger than the number of deployed strategic warheads counted by START I (current total stockpiles are estimated to be 12,070 for the United States and 22,500 for Russia). The Cold War peak level refers to the highest number of strategic warheads each side deployed during the Cold War. The United States deployed its highest numbers in 1987, while the Soviet Union reached its peak deployment in 1989. [From the Natural Resources Defense Council: http://www.nrdepro/datainx. html.]

Every six months the United States and Russia declare their START-accountable nuclear arsenals in a START Memorandum of Understanding (MOU). These declarations are based on very specific counting rules laid out in the START agreement, but do not always reflect the actual deployed forces. [For a description of the differences between START counting rules and actual deployed forces, see *Nuclear Successor States of the Soviet Union* (Washington, D.C.: Carnegie Endowment for International Peace and Monterey Institute of International Studies, March 1998), 9. For estimates of the current number of deployed warheads, see "NRDC Nuclear Notebook," in *The Bulletin of Atomic Scientists*, and "Nuclear Numbers" at the Carnegie Non-Proliferation Project website:www.ceip.org/npp].

START I and START II impose limits of 6,000 and 3,500 warheads, respectively. Initial discussions between the United States and Russia on START III have identified a limit as low as 2,000–2,500 warheads. The Jump-START proposal from the Committee on Nuclear Policy recommends a reduction of deployed nuclear forces to a level of 1,000 warheads, and, over time, a reduction to a total force of 1,000 warheads (both deployed and nondeployed).

technology required to produce them is too simple, to be confident that a condition will not develop that could prompt a string of nations to try to enhance their international standing by acquiring nuclear weapons.

In addition to deep cuts, further action should be taken to reduce the political value of nuclear weapons, such as the adoption of a no-first-use policy. The 1997 Report of the National Academy of Sciences, *The Future of U.S. Nuclear Weapons Policy*, linked deep cuts and the adoption of a no-first-use policy. The report argued that nuclear weapons should be limited to the core deterrence role of deterring their use by others. This would do a lot to reduce the political value of nuclear weapons should the five nuclear weapon states adopt such a policy. This would be an important corollary action to the arms reduction effort that would help the world understand that the nuclear weapon states are committed to and actively working toward disarmament. It would also be important for our nuclear non-proliferation policies since retaining the first-use option is inconsistent with the security assurances the nuclear-weapon states gave in 1995 in connection with the indefinite extension of the NPT (except for retaining a first-use option against Russia, China, India, Pakistan, Israel, and Cuba—nuclear weapon states and states not party to the NPT). The nuclear weapon states promised in these assurances, which are an important part of the NPT regime, never to use or threaten to use nuclear weapons against non-nuclear weapon state NPT parties (some 181 countries) unless attacked by them in alliance with a nuclear weapon state.

Through the NPT, all but four of the world's nations are legally bound to work toward the elimination of nuclear weapons; it is essential that this commitment be maintained and strengthened. The arms reduction process must continue and be multilateralized on the road toward ultimate nuclear disarmament. Deep cuts in the nuclear arsenals, coupled with other actions by the nuclear weapon states to reduce the political value of nuclear weapons, will be necessary if the NPT is to survive in the long term, and if widespread nuclear proliferation is to be averted.

REMOVING THE HAIR TRIGGER ON NUCLEAR FORCES
By Bruce Blair[1]

Hair trigger is a characterization of the strategic postures that capture basic operational truths. First, the emergency procedures for authorizing the transmission of a launch order emphasize speed, split-second timing, and decision making by rote. Checklists, not rational deliberation, dominate the process to such an extent that the players, including the presidents, would, under canonical scenarios, be enacting a prepared script designed to elicit a quick assent and effect a rapid missile launch before any incoming missiles arrived at their targets. The time constraints on this fateful decision process would be measured in seconds and minutes. The command systems allow only a few minutes to detect and assess an attack, and allow their presidents only a few minutes to receive advice from their top advisers and decide whether to authorize nuclear retaliation. (Emergency procedures require the duty commander at the North American Aerospace Defense Command, NORAD, to give his assessment of the validity of missile attack indicators within about three minutes after receiving the initial sensor report. The procedures give the duty commander at Strategic Command about thirty seconds to brief the U.S. president on his options and their consequences.)

Hair trigger also means that large numbers of missiles stand at maximum readiness to fire; only a short set of computer commands stands between their peacetime vigil and their immediate launch. For example, the U.S. land-based missile force sitting in silos in the Great Plains is fully fueled, gyroscopes running, and ready to lift off as soon as they receive computer commands. These commands amount to little more than punching in passwords and stroking "enter" three times in succession. Once the full complement of codes passes from the launch center computer (the launch crews are required to perform the launch sequence and issue these codes within a brief period) to the missile computer, the silo lid instantaneously blows off and the missile booster instantly ignites (although many missiles wait for some seconds or a few minutes on an automatic terminal countdown in order to ensure a staggered salvo). Today upward of 5,000 U.S. and Russian warheads remain poised for immediate launch.

The Committee on Nuclear Policy's proposal emphasizes taking nuclear forces off hair-trigger alert, so that they cannot be fired on a massive scale at a moment's notice. The committee recommends:

1. Immediately standing down U.S. and Russian forces slated for elimination under START II.
2. Immediately beginning five-power discussions on removing all nuclear forces from hair-trigger alert.
3. Immediately eliminating the launch-on-warning option from U.S. and Russian nuclear war plans.
4. Committing to the eventual elimination of all massive attack options from their nuclear war plans.

In the current situation, the hair trigger on one side locks the other side into the same nervous stance. Despite the 1994 Clinton-Yeltsin pact not to aim missiles at each other, the missiles on both sides remain loaded with wartime targets that can be activated in seconds (ICBMs) or minutes (SLBMs). If a launch order went out right now, the ICBM launch crews in the field could decode and validate the order, activate wartime targets in the missile's memory, send arming codes to the missiles, and launch them—all within a couple of minutes. Submarine crews on alert boats would take only ten minutes longer (the extra time is needed to spin up the missiles' gyroscopes). The result: 4,000 strategic ICBM warheads fired in a matter of a few minutes (2,000 on each side), and another 1,000 SLBM warheads break water ten minutes later.

The most recent illustration of this skittish force interaction and its associated risk of accidental launch was the Russian nuclear false alarm triggered by a NASA rocket fired from Norway on January 25, 1995. Coincidentally, a virtual duplication of this NASA rocket launch was scheduled to occur sometime during the period between January 11 and January 25, 1999. The 1995 false alarm resulted in part from the failure of Norway's prior diplomatic notification to reach the operators of the Russian early-warning system. In December 1998 Norway notified Russia of the impending second launch, and the U.S. Department of Defense received assurance from Norway that the notification was given to Russia. It is uncertain whether the Russian operators actually received the notification.

As a first step toward uncoupling these forces from mutually reinforcing hair-trigger alert, and reducing the danger of their mistaken or unauthorized launch, the committee recommends taking off alert the hundreds of U.S. and Russian missiles (carrying thousands of warheads) to be eliminated under the START II treaty. In 1997, at Helsinki, the presidents agreed to "deactivate" these missiles by 2004 on a reciprocal basis after START II is ratified. The committee recommends that they be stood down immediately, this year, and that the two presidents order this action whether or not the Russian Duma ratifies START II. A key advantage to this approach to reducing nuclear danger is that de-alerting steps could be taken immediately upon the direction of the presidents in their capacity as commanders in chief, as was demonstrated by Presidents Bush and Gorbachev in 1991 when they stood down many thousands of strategic and tactical nuclear weapons within a matter of days to months. They did not conduct elaborate, time-consuming negotiations or submit their decisions for Congress or Duma ratification. They ordered the de-alerting of the strategic weapons slated for elimination under START I, even though that treaty had not yet been ratified (it had only just been signed on July 31, 1991).

The United States should initiate the process in order to encourage reciprocity by Russia, and, moreover, the United States should match the larger number of weapons that Russia would de-alert under this formula. Both sides' alert arsenals would thus decline from about 2,500 today to 500 weapons tomorrow.[2] The need for verification would be minimal because both sides would still possess a large, secure, and invulnerable deterrent force. Although retaliation by the de-alerted forces would be delayed, any prospective aggressor would draw scant comfort from the knowledge that a day or so might pass before suffering the devastating response of the victim. However, this recommendation could be well monitored by national technical means supplemented by the already existing extensive rights under START I for inspecting each other's missiles on a random, short-notice basis.

The committee's second recommendation seeks a total stand-down of the nuclear arsenals possessed by all the P-5 nuclear states. Britain, France, and China should join the United States and Russia to discuss this. Since the former three countries are basically already operating on a low-alert level, the key change for them would be making their alert status transparent. Such transparency by Britain, France, and China would satisfy a precondition for Russia's standing down its total force.

The committee's third recommendation is that the presidents of Russia and the United States immediately announce that they are eliminating the accident-prone option of launch on warning from their strategic war plans. Initially, these declarations would be implemented by procedural changes of the sort that currently preclude the United States from launching missiles on warning against Chinese targets.

Such changes would be no more verifiable than declarations that strategic missiles are no longer targeted at each other's country. However, deterrence does not require the ability to launch on warning in any case, and therefore transparency is not essential. To the extent that verification is desired, the declaration would gradually become practical, concrete, and transparent as various de-alerting measures such as removing warheads from missiles are instituted.

The committee's fourth and last major recommendation calls for eliminating the massive attack options from the nuclear war plans. In the current U.S. strategic war plan, many scores of small-scale options involving 1 to 100 warheads (in round numbers) exist, but the major options involve strikes against a minimum of about 1,000 and a maximum of 3,000 targets in Russia.[3] The major strike plan would hurl weapons at over 1,000 nuclear targets; at about 500 units of the ragtag, half-starved, unpaid Russian regular (non-nuclear) army; at 500 factories in Russia's dysfunctional economy; and at nearly 200 so-called leadership targets, despite the virtual absence of leadership in Russia. Targeting dogma carried over from the Cold War encourages planners to aim many hundreds of U.S. nuclear weapons at the Moscow metropolis. In the recent past they assigned 69 nuclear warheads to one lonely installation on its outskirts—the Pushkino radar site. Today, the Russian target list covered by the major U.S. options is actually about 20 percent longer than it was during the mid-1990s, even after removing several former Soviet states from the list last year.

What purpose do these massive options serve, other than to rationalize the activities and large arsenals of our nuclear establishments? What real security problem do they solve?

The standard, pat response is that they deter a deliberate, cold-blooded massive attack. But does this threat still exist nine years after the fall of the Berlin Wall? Technically, it does, but politically, it surely does not. Such a premeditated genocidal attack by either the United States or Russia against each other is implausible and unthinkable, almost as absurd as a British or French attack on the United States. This Cold War scenario is simply not a reasonable basis on which to shape the post–Cold War nuclear postures of our countries.

Large-scale attack plans indeed create far bigger problems than they solve. The current postures create or perpetuate a host of problems, beginning with their adverse effect on mutual trust and reassurance. These postures technically project an apocalyptic threat that is entirely incompatible with U.S.-Russian political relations, and that arguably impedes the complete normalization of our relations.

More important, the alert practices are dangerous. The real danger today is not a failure of deterrence but a mistaken or unauthorized launch. The hair-trigger postures are inherently dangerous in these terms, and they are becoming more so as Russia grows to rely more on nuclear weapons and on their quick, early use in a crisis.

Despite the denials and reassurances given by both the Russian and U.S. governments, the stress and strain on the current nuclear control system in Russia already raise strong doubt whether it can preserve adequate standards of operational safety. Further deterioration of Russia's system in physical, organizational, and human terms appears inevitable in the absence of an economic miracle that arrests it and ushers in military reform and revitalization. As a consequence, the negative trend in Russian nuclear control represents one of the most serious current threats to international security, and it is increasingly doubtful that the control system can endure the growing pressure without incident. Deterrence could be amply satisfied, and operational safety could be much better served, by far smaller options and arsenals on far lower alert.

This fourth recommendation of eliminating massive attack options must be reciprocal and verifiable. If the three preceding recommendations are adopted, the fourth will become much more feasible.

Among the many benefits, standing down the arsenals on a parallel, reciprocal basis would:

- Reduce the susceptibility of Russian and U.S. forces to accidental, illicit, or mistaken launch.[4]
- Eliminate the hypothetical specter of a sudden, massive, deliberate attack.
- Smooth over the emerging wrinkle of sharp numerical inequality favoring the United States, a development that could derail arms control and sour relations.[5]
- Strike a better balance between deterrence and operational safety.
- Strike a better balance between deterrence and reassurance.
- Preserve, for the foreseeable future, the presidential flexibility in the matter of nuclear options.
- Yet still project, over the long run, the ultimate elimination of nuclear weapons, which in turn would strengthen U.S.-Russian diplomacy in the area of non-proliferation.
- Help create an international norm of operational safety that would apply universally, to all nuclear states, making it taboo for any nation to keep nuclear forces in a launch-ready configuration.
- Create momentum for establishing an exact accounting and monitoring arrangement for nuclear warheads, which would also enhance their security against theft and diversion to rogue states or terrorists.

In conclusion, removing the hair trigger on nuclear forces is a long-overdue adjustment to the end of the Cold War. By ending the alert practices they carried over from the Cold War, the former adversaries can finally expunge the darkest suspicion from their political relationship and lay the groundwork for a truly productive partnership. They can also better protect their citizens from a catastrophic failure of nuclear control. The virtues of de-alerting should weigh heavily in crafting the next steps in strategic reductions.

THE CLINTON ADMINISTRATION PERSPECTIVE
By Robert Bell

The experts represented on the Committee on Nuclear Policy have concluded that the administration has "lost a considerable amount of momentum," indeed, that we are in a period of "backsliding," in our mutual pursuit of nuclear reductions. In *Arms*

Control Today, however, a year-end assessment by John Isaacs of the Council for a Livable World called 1998 a year of "status quo." He notes no major progress, but also that where things could have gotten much worse, they did not.

John Isaac's assessments are closer to mine than are those of the committee. In many ways we were on defense in 1998 with regard to the ABM Treaty and missile defense. That fact cannot be glossed over. The fact that we were able to rebuff the attack successfully should be no less of a concern than any disappointment over the lack of progress some might attribute to this administration. What these facts suggest is that there is a whole other audience out there that must be reached. Experts need to help keep the administration honest (and that is the real value of this conference), and the other challenge is to expand our horizons so we are not just talking to ourselves.

We were not, of course, just on defense in 1998. We made great strides in implementing START I. That sounds like a throwaway line, but you need to remember that when you sign treaties, even when you get them ratified, they do not just happen. There is the hard work of getting down to the ceilings, and the good news is that as of now, four years after START I entered into force, the United States and Russia are two years ahead of schedule in terms of accountable warhead reductions.

Both are now well under 7,000 accountable warheads. The United States is close to 6,000; Russia is close to 6,500 en route to the final accountable level of 6,000, which is not due until December 2001.[6] These facts should counter the notion that we are in a "strategic pause" or that we are paying a price for the regrettable delay in Duma ratification of START II.

This administration has also been very active in terms of trying to ensure the safety and security of those warheads that are coming off missiles as we make the START I reductions. At the September 1998 Moscow summit, Presidents Clinton and Yeltsin approved an important agreement on fifty tons of excess plutonium and how to safely dispose of such material. There are some new ideas being developed to enhance U.S. policy in these areas.

We worked very hard and very quietly in 1998 to try to facilitate START II ratification. The September summit itself was meant to be a key, if not the key, catalyst to achieving that result. Before, our position had been that the president would not go to Russia if START II had not been ratified. We moved with regard to this linkage position, and it was almost a success. On the eve of our intervention in Iraq, in terms of my assessment and where the vote count appeared to be, for the first time I really believed this was going to happen and that, in fact, it might have been a Christmas Day event. The strategy to ratify START II was on track in 1998. The circumstances involving Saddam Hussein and Iraq were not under our control in the arms control sense.

We have not been sitting on our hands with regard to the issues concerning either "de-alerting" or the START II–START III linkage. In both cases, there have been some intensive reviews within the administration and some new ideas in these areas may soon be revealed.

We did resolve some issues in those reviews. In particular, I would remind you of the agreement reached at the September summit on sharing missile early-warning data. I have spent about eight days since the summit in Moscow negotiating the missile early-warning agreement. The Russians have very different ideas of the scope and scale of that and certain details, such as the cost. So as wonderful as it is to say, "Just do this and just do that," there is a necessary phase that has to follow, to figure out exactly what that means, how we are going to do it, and with what obligations, costs, and responsibilities.

We worked very hard in 1998 to prepare the way for expeditious progress on START III. We are now in the last two years of the Clinton administration, and the president very much wants START III to be part of his legacy.

And to that end we not only reached an agreement in 1997 with the Helsinki framework, but we are tasked by our president to continue the conceptual dialogue with our Russian counterparts to elaborate those principles in the Helsinki Agreement, and we are doing that.

It is difficult to prepare an opening position for a major arms control negotiation, but we have done it. The Presidential Decision Directive that set the strategy and the specific proposals for START III has been worked through interagency consensus, has been reviewed and approved by the president, and is on the shelf ready for us to get on the next plane after START II ratification. This includes the opening statement that will be made in that first negotiating round.

That was a lot of work in 1998. I do not think it is a record of "inaction" or "backsliding." I will, however, grant John Isaacs this point: This was not the breakthrough year that we had hoped for. We do not yet have approval for START II and immediate movement into START III. So, where does that leave us?

In a sense I am tempted to say, "I feel your pain." I have worked a long time on START II. I drafted for Senator Nunn the Senate Armed Services Committee's report on START II in July 1992. There is no one that wants to get this done more than I. The issue is: What is the appropriate balance between a treaty track and a unilateral track with a fair amount of independent initiatives? My sense is that if you conclude that START II just is not in the offing, if the "last, best chance" for the treaty was before the Iraq situation arose in December 1998, obviously the balance is going to have to shift further in the direction of other initiatives.

But in the context of opportunities to shift the balance more in the direction of unilateralism and less formalism, it seemed to me that the Committee on Nuclear Policy's proposed numbers and rates of movement are past the point that our policy or political consensus could support. There are, however, some common themes here that we can agree on.

First is the fundamental point that we need a combination of treaties and less formal initiatives. I think we need both. The question is the balance between the two. Do you let one become the enemy of the other to the exclusion of progress that is otherwise available? I think it's important to avoid that.

Second, it seems to me that there is a strategic relationship between the question of deep cuts and how low you can go in central strategic numbers, on the one hand, and what is possible with respect to the future of tactical nuclear weapons, warhead disposition, and transparency, on the other.

At Helsinki, that triad was fundamental to the framework established there. The question, though, is the sequencing. Tom Graham said that you cannot expect Russia to get serious about transparency until the United States starts talking about deep cuts. There are others within the interagency that would say that you have it backward, that we have to see the color of their money with respect to transparency, particularly with tactical nukes where there are huge uncertainties about how many they have, let alone where they are, before we can assess the deep-cuts question.

My sense is that it is best to take all three in their interrelationships, and that is our plan. We will get on the next plane after START II is approved and begin START III negotiations with these three parts, and then make the decisions in their interrelationship.

Now, there is one assumption that was central to Bruce Blair's presentation—in fact, he was quite explicit on it—that I did think was different between where the committee is coming from and what we believe, and that was his statement that it is as "implausible, unthinkable and almost as absurd" to think about Britain or France attacking us as it is to imagine a Russian nuclear strike.

I do not say that because I think it is plausible, thinkable, and not absurd to imagine that. It is unimaginable to think that Russia would do that today, tomorrow, next week, next month, next year. The issue, though, is how far you can carry that progression. We have a National Security Strategy, most recently issued in October and signed by the president. Our strategy says that while it is unthinkable today, and while we are going to do everything in our power to help Russia down the road to democratization and free market economic reform, we have to hedge against the remote but not impossible prospect of a reversal in which intentions change much faster than capabilities could be restored. That does not mean we harbor any animosity toward Russia at all. It means that we are being prudent.

Now if you were to conclude that it is "implausible, unthinkable and almost absurd" to imagine a strategic exchange with Russia, not only today, next week, next year, but, into the next decades of the twenty-first century, if it really is over forever with very high certainty, then of course much more would be possible in terms of reducing the central strategic numbers. The numbers that were agreed to in Helsinki, in my view, represent the outer edge of the envelope for the old paradigm where we are still hedging against a reversal that would require us to mount a more robust deterrent rather than maintaining a hedge posture. If we can move past that, if we make that progress with Russia and that becomes the political consensus in the United States, then I believe a lot of the committee's recommendations are possible. But I do not think that is politically feasible or practical at this point.

Last, we have to wrestle with this issue of balance. If the conclusion should be to assume that despite our best efforts, START II is just not in the cards, before we conclude that treaties are now more of a hindrance than a help, we should remember what the value of treaties really is.

Treaties make it much harder, although not impossible, to reverse decisions. All treaties have a supreme national interests clause. A rather specific guarantee of withdrawal under certain circumstances has been central to a lot of arms control politics on the Hill and a lot of arms control decision making in the interagency.

So, imagine what would have happened with President Reagan's Strategic Defense Initiative if we had not had the ABM Treaty, but instead just a posture with regard to strategic defenses established only as a matter of unilateral policy. Imagine what courses might now be in the offing if the Conventional Forces in Europe Treaty was not in place in the context of NATO enlargement. Imagine if the MIRVed ICBM ban that is central to START II—indeed championed as the great accomplishment of START II—were not a matter of codified law in that treaty. You could forget that restriction if it were just a policy. It would come under pressure as Russia struggles to mount high numbers of strategic warheads with an economy that is in real trouble.

Imagine that the Comprehensive Test Ban Treaty is not legally in force in the year 2001. It is just subject now to national moratoriums, including in this country where the Hatfield-Exon-Mitchell legislation has been automatically repealed by its own terms because of India's testing. Imagine that—consistent with its last party platform—the Republican Party of this country ran a campaign against CTB and called for continued nuclear testing. Clearly, there is value to getting these provisions down in treaties.

Treaties give you an equality of outcome. That is a fundamental truth about negotiations in which the devil really is in the detail and the legislatures of each country are looking over your shoulders.

Treaties also bring verification. Verification can be difficult because it prolongs negotiations. But it also builds confidence, and confidence is important as a stabilizing measure during times of crises.

There is a reason our Founding Fathers said these things should be done by treaties and that treaties should require a super majority or two-thirds vote. It was to invest the country corporately in these deals in the same way that the country needs to invest corporately in "go to war" decisions. You pay a price if you have policies in place on less than that degree of consensus, less than the closure and consensus we got with the Chemical Weapons Convention. What you get is a Congress that is tempted to have it both ways. For example, Congress passed legislation on START II early deactivation, which says you can still negotiate understandings but you cannot spend any money unless you submit a report that explains how it is reciprocal, verifiable, and irreversible. If you cannot certify all these points, then you can only do the agreement if you invoke a national interest waiver, in which case Congress will be very critical.

Now, it may be that the "Plan B" the committee has proposed is the best we can expect given the current political lineup in the Duma. But I hope that we see a change.

BRIDGING THE GAP IN WESTERN-RUSSIAN SECURITY AGENDAS
By Alexei Arbatov

There is no sense in pretending any longer that a decade after the end of the Cold War, Russian and Western security priorities are the same or of the same order. They are different, because the objective situation of Russia and the West is different, as is the experience of each over the past ten years. Moreover, relatively friendly relations between the leaders of Russia and the United States cannot help in resolving these differences and rather are a handicap by making tough and pragmatic bargaining more difficult.

Besides its domestic political instability and economic decline, Russia feels vulnerable in the south, threatened in the west, potentially endangered in the east, and progressively inferior on the global strategic level. In contrast, the West is domestically robust, invulnerable, and superior vis-à-vis Russia, but terrified by the prospect of weapons of mass destruction (WMD) and missile technology proliferation to the rogue regimes in the Third World, or even to terrorist groups.

Hence, to avoid further controversies and a complete disintegration in all arms control and security regimes, a "grand bargain" should be brokered. This deal should include Western concessions to Russia on the security issues most important to Moscow, and be reciprocated with Russian concessions on the problems most important to the United States and its allies.

DIVERGING PERSPECTIVES

The non-proliferation of WMD and their means of delivery no longer occupies a top place in the list of Russia's security priorities. In contrast to what was practiced by the USSR, Russia does not deploy forces outside the former Soviet territory; the separation of Trans-Caucasus and Central Asia has geographically moved Russian borders to the north, farther from Asian areas of proliferation concern. This makes Moscow less concerned by limited WMD and missile capabilities that relatively remote Third World countries could obtain. Also, Russia's own substantial nuclear deterrent provides some guarantee against possible WMD attack launched by any state proliferator against the national territory (or what was the national territory until the end of 1991).

On the other hand, Russia's growing strategic nuclear inferiority to NATO, conventional forces inferiority to both NATO and China, its continuing economic crisis, disintegration of the federal regime, and proliferating conflicts across post-Soviet space, including Russia's own territory, are all much higher on the Russian list of security threats.

Meanwhile, non-proliferation is occupying a much higher place on the security watch list of Western countries. Traditional concerns about Moscow's nuclear and conventional superiority and potential aggression have faded away. On the other hand, European and Japanese reliance on the U.S. security guarantees makes nonaligned states more sensitive to possible blackmail from potential proliferators, since they are left without the ability to deter such states from using WMD. Also, the acquisition of WMD and missile technology by certain regional actors could effectively block the Western interventionist options in areas of vital importance, like the Mediterranean, the Middle East, and the Persian Gulf. The United States, due to its geographic advantages, is able to effectively use the threat of proliferation as a motivator for the development of missile defenses, further affecting Russian security considerations.

In this sense, for Russia the worst has already happened, as its territory has been within range of nuclear weapons developed by third countries for a long time:

first with Britain, and later with France, China, Israel, and, now, potentially India and Pakistan. To a certain extent, this means that for Moscow, non-proliferation is not a very useful motivating instrument for achieving its main security concerns.

However, non-proliferation does represent an important, if not unique, tool for Russian participation in building the Euro-Atlantic security architecture. Russia's abundant stockpiles of nuclear and chemical arms, weapons materials and technologies, and WMD and missile production capabilities and know-how make it a vitally important participant in any non-proliferation regime. Without Moscow's involvement, such regimes would hardly be sustainable. This situation has opened doors for Russia to various prestigious Western clubs and, simultaneously, provided it with convincing arguments that could be relevant for promoting its interests in other areas.

RUSSIA'S SECURITY AGENDA

For Russia, the growing imbalance in strategic weapons is of serious concern, since this is one of the very few—if not the only—remaining pillars of its status and role in the world. There is a commonly accepted perception in Moscow that without this pillar Russia would be ignored by the West altogether (or in the view of Communists and nationalists, treated like Yugoslavia or even Iraq).

Without a robust nuclear deterrent, Russia would feel even more vulnerable in the face of conventional superiority across its borders in the west and in the east, and proliferating local conflicts in the south. Thus, for Moscow, START III negotiations are aimed at correcting the deficiencies of START II. As a matter of fact, the value of START II is not so much in its terms but in its opening the door to the follow-on treaty.

In order to avoid an expensive buildup of single-warhead ICBMs, Moscow wants an agreement to achieve lower ceilings for weapons, far below the limits of 2,000–2,500 agreed to at the U.S.-Russian summit in Helsinki in March 1997. The preferred ceiling now looks closer to 1,000 weapons. Otherwise, continued deployment of MIRVed ICBMs would be much harder to resist for Russia. Moreover, the possible unilateral withdrawal from the ABM Treaty by the United States creates additional strategic reasons for keeping MIRVs deployed.

Second, in Russia's eyes, the new START agreement must also solve the problem of asymmetric breakout potential. Under START II, the United States does not have to physically destroy the majority of its weapons and is able to fulfill reductions largely by downloading, that is, removing warheads from their missiles and converting part of strategic bombers for so-called non-nuclear missions. There is no requirement to physically destroy removed warheads, which will likely be placed in storage for some time. This fact would permit the United States to quickly upload warheads onto missiles. Through such a redeployment, the United States could easily reconstitute its strategic forces to a size even exceeding the START I ceilings. Russia, on the contrary, has to physically destroy the vast majority of its missiles in the course of reductions, making such a ramp-up impossible. This puts Moscow in a very disadvantageous position.

Finally, with START III, Moscow wants to achieve more tangible assurances than those contained in START II provisions that the United States will not eventually withdraw from the ABM Treaty unilaterally. India's and Pakistan's nuclear debuts in 1998, as well as the probable Chinese reaction of accelerating its own strategic program, contribute to this probability. Such steps by China would radically change Russia's strategic environment, since in the extreme case China might be able to inadvertently achieve something close to nuclear parity with Russia after 2010. The combined effect of an Indian-Pakistani-Chinese offensive missile expansion would make some sort of U.S. national strategic defense unavoidable, thus affecting Russian security calculations.

Although in Helsinki the two presidents agreed to synchronize deadlines for implementing both START II and START III by December 31, 2007, Washington refuses to initiate formal negotiations on the new treaty before START II enters into force. For its part, Moscow is ready to commence the actual START II reductions only after getting some certainty with regard to START III. The situation is further complicated by disputes between the executive branches and legislators in both countries. As a result, the future of strategic arms control remains uncertain.

Unfortunately for START II proponents, U.S.-British air strikes in Iraq took Russian Duma Communists off the hook. Under pressure of the coalition government of Prime Minister Primakov they had been bracing themselves for a vote on START II ratification in December 1998. However, if there is no further deterioration of U.S.-Russian relations or new regional crisis with ensuing unilateral Western use of force, this issue would reappear sooner or later.

In the meantime, a compromise or "grand bargain" could be based on the following points. Russia would declare that even in the absence of a ratified START II, it will go along with reductions according to its schedule, and verification will be ensured by START I procedures. The United States, in its turn, should go along with intensive and full-scale START III negotiations with the principal goal of reducing the warhead levels to 1,000 to 1,500 by the year 2010. As soon as the new treaty is negotiated, Russia would simultaneously ratify START II and START III, and the United States would, at the same time, ratify START III and 1997 New York protocols (on theater missile defense and a START II extension schedule).

Also, there would have to be an agreement that the United States would not unilaterally withdraw from the 1972 ABM Treaty. If the security situation requires it, revision of the treaty and development and deployment of strategic ballistic missile defenses should be undertaken cooperatively between the United States and Russia, which might also be joined by their allies.

Another problem is theater nuclear weapons and U.S. forward-based systems in Europe. The 1997 Helsinki summit opened the door for formalizing the tactical nuclear arms control arrangements made in 1991 unilaterally by President Bush and President Gorbachev and the nonbinding NATO-Russia Founding Act. The United States and Russia agreed that negotiations covering tactical nuclear weapons, as well as long-range sea-launched cruise missiles, could be conducted separately from the START III process. Russia's approach to the issue is shaped by two main considerations. On the one hand, it is interested in binding provisions that would prevent nuclear deployments in new NATO states and that could lead to the dismantlement of U.S. long-range sea-launched cruise missiles. On the other hand, Russia's tactical nuclear weapons not only balance nuclear forces of the other side but also counter superior NATO (and Chinese) conventional capabilities.

Moreover, there are significant technical challenges in negotiating a tactical nuclear arms control agreement. Here, very different principles of control and accounting will be needed, as compared with the strategic arms control process. The counting rules and verification provisions for nuclear arms control were focused on deployed delivery systems, whereas all carriers of tactical nuclear weapons are dual-use, and warheads attributed to them are not constantly kept on delivery vehicles. Thus, a future agreement would require establishing procedures for controlling nuclear storage sites, which are likely to be much more intrusive and complicated than those for monitoring airfields and missile and submarine bases. Such an agreement would also require verification measures on warhead dismantlement, another extremely sensitive issue. Hence, it would be advisable to continue separating strategic and theater nuclear arms control efforts.

Another important step could be aimed at formalizing the Founding Act provision preventing the deployment of nuclear weapons on the territories of the new NATO members and across the whole area of Central and Eastern Europe. For Russia, this would represent legally binding and verifiable guarantees against such deployments. In exchange, NATO would receive a guarantee that nuclear weapons would not be returned to Belarus or the Kaliningrad region. The agreement would also consolidate the international non-proliferation regime: a new nuclear-free zone would be de facto established, and for the first time a part of the territory of a nuclear power could be proclaimed a nonnuclear weapon sanctuary.

On a broader level, the enlargement of NATO should be de facto, if not de jure, channeled into predominantly political parameters, without involving considerable military alterations. This could hardly be translated into any formal commitments, as initially requested by Russia, but could be assured by some less formal agreements. For example, the CFE Treaty adaptation should be accompanied by significant—say, 50 percent—reductions of the existing personnel and Treaty Limited Elements (TLE) numbers. This would be the most impressive argument against Russia's fears and suspicions associated with NATO's push eastward.

There is no possibility, nor any need, for Russia to maintain parity with the whole of NATO in postconfrontational Europe (in contrast to demands of the West with respect to the East in the 1980s). However, the joint goal of NATO enlargement should be a reduction, as opposed to an increase, in the alliance's military advantage over Russia. Otherwise, suspicions and noncooperative moods would be hard to avoid in Russia.

Russia should also be more actively linked to the modernization of the armed forces in East Central Europe. This would alleviate Russia's military-industrial complex opposition to NATO enlargement and could shift domestic political perceptions of this issue. The interests of potential Western suppliers might suffer, although not excessively, as they would keep a monopoly on all sophisticated equipment, whereas Russia's involvement would be focused upon more traditional items, such as heavy weapons.

For example, tactical ballistic missile defenses might become an extremely important joint pan-European project for Russia. Such cooperation would be an essential step toward minimizing Russia's concerns on the erosion of the existing

ABM limitation regime. Even more important, Russia's reemerging threat perceptions with respect to NATO would be thus practically eliminated (since joint air and missile defense is by definition only possible between nonenemies). Also significant is the fact that Russia's involvement in the project would by no means be symbolic, since the superb S-300 and S-400 air defense systems might eventually constitute the core of such a system.

WESTERN SECURITY AGENDA

In response to Western concerns, Russia must establish much more stringent domestic control on the export of nuclear/chemical materials and equipment, and missile and dual-use/sensitive technology. Russia's strict adherence to the Non-Proliferation Treaty as a nuclear-weapon state and its membership in several multilateral discriminatory export control regimes, like the Wassenaar agreement, the Missile Technology Control Regime, and the Nuclear Suppliers Group, are indispensable to securing Western cooperation on Russian security concerns.

Without reneging on Russian-Iranian or Russian-Indian cooperation, Moscow should be more sensitive to Western objections. This nuclear cooperation, as well as analogous deals by the West, must be more transparent and a subject for stringent IAEA control regimes. In particular, Russia and the United States (preferably together with China) should jointly apply pressure on India and Pakistan with the aim of putting all civilian and military nuclear projects under comprehensive IAEA controls and ending the production of fissile materials for weapons purposes. In the same way, India and Pakistan should be induced to join the CTBT to curtail the nuclear arms race on the subcontinent. If necessary, those regimes may be made more comprehensive and restrictive, and in this whole area Russia should go along with the respective demands of the West.

Beyond these steps, Russian-Western cooperation on nuclear materials, as well as their joint projects with third parties, should be enhanced even further. In this regard, commercially motivated complications in implementing the U.S.-Russian highly enriched uranium deal should be avoided. One other area of important cooperation is the dismantling of decommissioned nuclear-powered submarines in the Russian northern region and the Far East. This may bind Russia and the West much closer and with fewer domestic controversies, than, for example, verifying the elimination of nuclear warheads.

NOTES

1. The author of this chapter is indebted to Frank von Hippel for his large creative contribution to this analysis, and to his colleagues at the Committee on Nuclear Policy for their suggestions.

2. In order to match the lower Russian level of alert weapons, the U.S. Trident submarines would no longer assume a quick-launch readiness after leaving port for patrol. Their missiles would be kept on "modified alert," about eighteen hours from launch-ready condition.

3. A noteworthy recent addition to the smaller options (Limited Attack Options): China. China has reappeared in the U.S. strategic war plan after a hiatus lasting nearly two decades. (China had

been removed in the early 1980s following normalization of U.S.-China relations.) A year ago, administration officials quashed media speculation that President Clinton's new nuclear guidance issued in 1997 (NSDD-60) would result in China's reinstatement in the U.S. Single Integrated Operational Plan (SIOP). Nevertheless, the speculation proved correct. Meanwhile, the United States expresses little if any sympathy for India's claim to feel sufficiently threatened by neighboring China to want a nuclear arsenal to protect itself.

4. Feeding U.S. early-warning data into the Russian network, as envisioned by the data sharing agreement signed at the September 1998 Moscow summit, may help mitigate the effects of Russian false alarms but it hardly removes the risks. De-alerting is a superior solution to the dangers posed by hair-trigger alert.

5. Russia's economic plight has sealed the fate of the country's nuclear arsenal on a path toward oblivion. The tailspin will leave Russia with an arsenal no larger than 200 strategic weapons within ten to fifteen years, and perhaps smaller than 100. Russia will be in the same league as Britain, France, and China. Western governments appear oblivious to this imminent change in the strategic situation. While the United States concentrates on its long-standing priority of encouraging Russian ratification of START II, the profound demographics of Russian missile aging and the inability of Russia to finance replacements render asunder the treaty's core relevance. Obsolescence is outpacing mandated arms reductions to such an extent that the START process as we know it cannot begin to keep pace. The ceilings established by START II and by the Helsinki agreement (outlining a lower ceiling for START III) are in fact so unrealistically high for Russia that the START process is becoming counterproductive. In the main, it only works to keep the Russian arsenal at an artificial high, well above its natural lower plateau.

6. A July 1, 1999, START Memorandum of Understanding states that the United States has 7,815 deployed, START accountable warheads, and Russia has 6,546. The aggregate numbers are available on the U.S. Department of State web site at http://www.acda.gov/factshee/wmd/start1/startagg.htm.

—18—

Constructing a New Agenda

Darach MacFhionnbhairr, Patricia Lewis, Marina Laker, Luiz F. Machado

Progress in building the non-proliferation regime has historically depended on the agreement of the nuclear weapon states. But progress does not necessarily begin with these states. For example, Ireland introduced the original resolution, unanimously approved by the United Nations General Assembly in 1961, calling on all states to negotiate the international agreement that ultimately became the Non-Proliferation Treaty (NPT). Mindful of the catalytic role non-nuclear weapon states can play, the ministers for foreign affairs of Brazil, Egypt, Ireland, Mexico, New Zealand, Slovenia, South Africa, and Sweden in June 1998 launched a "New Agenda" initiative to resuscitate the disarmament process. They expressed their deep concern "at the persistent reluctance of the nuclear-weapon states to approach their Treaty obligations as an urgent commitment to the total elimination of their nuclear weapons" and urged them, as first steps, to abandon their hair-trigger nuclear alert postures and to remove nonstrategic nuclear weapons from deployed sites.[1] They outlined several other practical and achievable objectives in a short statement and pledged to "spare no efforts to pursue the objectives." If other nations rally to the initiative, this could become a welcome catalyst.

Below, Darach MacFhionnbhairr from Ireland and Luiz Machado from Brazil discuss the New Agenda Coalition, Marina Laker from Canada discusses her nation's Human Security Agenda, and Patricia Lewis, director of the United Nations Institute for Disarmament Research, provides an overview of these new initiatives and the role of nongovernmental organizations.

THE NEW AGENDA COALITION
By Darach MacFhionnbhairr

The New Agenda Coalition brings together government representatives from the main nuclear disarmament traditions and approaches. The foreign ministers, who jointly addressed the current complacency over the retention of nuclear weapons in their June 9, 1998, declaration and with the United Nations General Assembly Resolution [reprinted at the end of this chapter] adopted on December 4 of the same year, did so from the standpoint that nuclear weapons have no place in the aftermath of the Cold War. Central to the initiative are:

- A refusal to accept the premise that nuclear weapons can be retained indefinitely and not used whether by accident or intentionally.
- A concern that the lack of decisiveness in proceeding to the elimination of these weapons will ultimately result in the erosion of the non-proliferation regime.

The timing of the initiative is the result of a shared perception that a unique opportunity is now being squandered and that we cannot by the inaction of the international community allow the goal of a nuclear weapon–free world slip past us forever.

The recent achievement of universal adherence to the NPT by the non–nuclear weapon states (Cuba excepted) brings one of the goals of the treaty within reach. This positive outcome is in stark contrast to the absence at present of any substantive indications by the nuclear weapon states that they intend to proceed with determination to achieve the other goal in this balanced treaty, namely, the early elimination of nuclear weapons.

The unlimited extension of the NPT agreed in 1995 will only strengthen the non-proliferation goal if the future implementation of the obligations under the treaty results at an early date in a nondiscriminatory environment where all states are non–nuclear weapon states. Article VI of the treaty clearly sets a term to the retention of nuclear weapons, and no treaty that is based on inequality of treatment for its subjects can be permanent.[2]

It is not surprising, therefore, that the non–nuclear weapon states, flush from the universality of their adherence to the NPT, feel empowered in calling for the setting of the agenda and demanding immediate action from both the nuclear weapon and nuclear-capable states. This can be through bilateral, plurilateral, or, where appropriate, multilateral means with a view to ridding the world of these weapons. The New Agenda Coalition is representative of this sense of empowerment. Our governments consider that the international community has reached that juncture when we must embark on the final push toward the full and complete implementation of the purposes and provisions of the NPT by all states.

The drafters of the New Agenda did not anticipate the developments of 1998. However, these events inevitably require a radical reappraisal of the pace of nuclear disarmament. If India, Israel, and Pakistan are not to be factored in as nuclear weapon states—which would pull the NPT asunder—the five permanent members of the United Nations Security Council (China, France, Russia, the United Kingdom, and the United States, or P-5) must now seriously weigh the option of persisting with the retention of nuclear weapons in the medium term. Or alternatively they must adopt the non–nuclear weapon states' interpretation of article VI as an obligation for early and definitive action, and consequently for engaging in negotiations for the rapid elimination of their nuclear weapons.

The Joint Ministerial Declaration and its adaptation as a resolution of the General Assembly set down actions required by all governments to fulfill the implementation of their respective obligations under the NPT or, in the case of India, Israel, and Pakistan, actions in conformity with its goals. It sets out the necessary constituents of the nuclear disarmament process and the proposed modalities for its realization. It does not fall hostage to the presumption that there is one unalterable way to proceed. It gives due weight to each element in the process: bilateral, plurilateral, and multilateral.

The debate on the draft resolution demonstrates the extent of political commitment to a more forceful nuclear disarmament agenda among the non–nuclear weapon states. The reaction of the non–nuclear weapon states in the alliance was particularly significant in this connection and consistent with recent efforts by many of these states for an early and fundamental reappraisal of the role of nuclear weapons.

The broad range of nonaligned countries likewise embraced the proposals, which, while different in approach and emphasis from more traditional strategies for nuclear disarmament, were viewed as a constructive opening that might initiate action on the nuclear disarmament agenda.

On the other hand, the reception of the resolution by the nuclear weapon states demonstrated that:

- The control of the nuclear disarmament agenda continues to be viewed by the nuclear weapon states as exclusively their prerogative, both as regards forums and content.
- The currency of the arguments advanced for the retention of nuclear weapons remains rooted in the Cold War.
- A focus on vertical proliferation is now viewed as detracting from the fight against horizontal proliferation.

The reaction of the nuclear weapon states to the draft resolution therefore focused on defending the adequacy of the measures undertaken by them to date and the seriousness of their commitment to the specific performance of their NPT obligations. They rejected both the proposals urging purposeful early and conclusive bilateral negotiations as well as those for appropriate multilateral negotiations in the context of a universal nondiscriminatory world free of nuclear weapons. They claimed that proposals for the consideration of interim measures relating to existing nuclear weapons deployment, such as de-alerting, no-first-use, and nonstrategic nuclear weapons, undermined strategies fundamental to existing security arrangements. Proposals for specific action by the nuclear-capable states—India, Israel, and Pakistan—in the nuclear disarmament scheme were viewed as opening the avenue to recognition of these countries as nuclear weapon states.

We can conclude from the adoption of the draft resolution that there is a growing unwillingness on the part of the non–nuclear weapon states to accept the continuing assertion by the P-5 that they, rather than their non–nuclear weapon state partners, will continue to set the nuclear disarmament agenda. The importance attached to the proposal of so many governments suggests that the resolution is perceived as containing a realizable approach premised on a serious commitment to the elimination of nuclear weapons that will stand the test of time. We must of course equally conclude that the extent of nuclear weapon state resistance to the resolution demonstrates their concern that such an initiative indeed represents a threat to current nuclear weapon state positions.

While the New Agenda initiative was governmental in its genesis, its proposals are for the most part the currency of the analysis that has emerged over the past number of years. They have emerged through developments such as the Advisory Opinion of the International Court of Justice, the Canberra Commission on the Elimination of Nuclear Weapons and a broader debate among governments and in civil society. There are clear parallels between the approach of the New Agenda Coalition and those nongovernmental organizations that have been at pains to reinvigorate the nuclear disarmament agenda. Of particular importance in this connection are the organizations that have coalesced around the Middle Powers Initiative, which brings together organizations with diverse approaches but an overarching commitment to the resuscitation of the nuclear disarmament agenda. The contribution of civil society is fundamental to the pursuit of the New Agenda, although it must be added that nuclear disarmament is not currently a focus for civil society at large.

The impact of the New Agenda on nuclear disarmament in the future will depend on the success of the advocacy of the past year in shaping concerned governments' approaches to nuclear weapons. Developments at the Conference on Disarmament (CD), at the International Atomic Energy Agency (IAEA), and at the NPT preparatory committee meetings will provide early indicators of the results of our activities to date. There are of course other forums—at which the New Agenda governments are not represented—that have a critical role in actions fundamental to achieving the purposes of the initiative.

The perspective of the 2000 NPT Review Conference is central to our efforts. While it reviews implementation of treaty objectives set in 1995, the conference will be able to report that the Comprehensive Test Ban Theory (CTBT) has been concluded and that Fissile Material Cut-Off negotiations are, we hope, in progress. It is questionable whether there will be any satisfactory development to report on the third and fundamental action element of the 1995 NPT Review, namely, "the determined pursuit by the nuclear weapon states of systematic and progressive efforts to reduce nuclear weapons globally." It also remains to be seen what will emerge on nuclear issues that can be advanced in the alliance.

Hence, when we revisit the objectives in 2000 to set out a new program of action for the following period, we must anticipate that the non–nuclear weapon state parties will insist on securing more detailed undertakings by the nuclear weapon states. It is likely that these will focus especially on the elimination of nuclear weapons and the expeditious pursuit of negotiations premised on the early elimination of these weapons. In the absence of serious movement toward fulfilling such commitments in the near future, the authority of the international community acting as the parties to the NPT will be seriously eroded, resulting ultimately in harm to the treaty itself. The New Agenda Coalition will, for its part, continue to develop and elaborate on the initiative launched in 1998 with a view to maintaining the momentum it promises and broadening the base of governmental support.

THE ROLE OF NONGOVERNMENTAL ORGANIZATIONS
By Patricia Lewis

There are a number of initiatives aimed at establishing a new agenda for the pursuit of non-proliferation goals. These include the New Agenda Coalition (NAC) and their First Committee Resolution, the Canberra Commission on the Elimination of Nuclear Weapons, and Japan's Tokyo Forum. We are undoubtedly going to see others. Initiative-itis is something that could become catching over the next few years, as many share deep concerns about the future of the NPT and about the future of international security regimes.

Nongovernmental organizations will undoubtedly continue to promote such initiatives. One can think immediately of the Middle Powers Initiative and also some of the new work that is being done on de-alerting nuclear weapons and on new approaches toward nuclear disarmament beyond the START process. There are also some very new ideas from experts and diplomats like Ambassador Jonathan Dean and others on the prevention of war, which ties in very closely with the idea of a human security agenda.

Of the new agenda initiatives, what exactly is new? Some of the ideas contained within the June 9 NAC statement, the First Committee Resolution, and the Canberra Commission are new, but there are some very old ideas as well. What's really new is the approach these initiatives are taking. What we see now is a very realistic approach across the board, with the very notable exceptions of the nuclear weapon states. We see very pragmatic approaches such as the recognition of power centers and the recognition of NATO as an important player in nuclear disarmament and non-proliferation. NATO is viewed not necessarily as something to confront, but perhaps as an organization that may be harnessed and brought into some form of partnership to help push these issues forward.

Some savvy politics has been involved in developing this new approach. There is some very clever wording, for example, in the First Committee Resolution. The wording in this document made it very difficult, if not impossible, for a number of states to vote against it, and even made it difficult to merely abstain—as witnessed by the detailed justifications provided by those states that did abstain.

The new agenda shakes off the old agenda, by jettisoning some of the rigidity of the old agenda—for example, the proposal to establish a time-bound framework for nuclear disarmament coming from one side, while the other side maintains that only the P-5 should negotiate these issues.

The new agenda approach forms a middle ground. There is fluidity because of its plurilateral, multilateral, and unilateral approaches, as well as the inclusion of the old approaches. Although there is much technical work involved, this new approach shows considerable strategic thought. It is fleshing out many of the key objections to what everyone rhetorically agrees to: nuclear disarmament.

It is also part of a new approach to security. By looking at what human beings actually need and discussing security in a wider context, it provides a firm basis for the approach in human rights. It integrates a wide variety of aspects of security from the individual to the community, from village to global aspects, as well as bringing into account economics, environment, education, and trade—in other words, all aspects of human security. Academics have been working on this approach to human security for several years, but now it is filtering up to the political level, becoming something real and tangible.

Within that approach is a spectrum of armaments, which means that we have to take a spectrum of approaches to disarmament as well. From small arms at one end to nuclear weapons at the other, they are all part of what UNESCO has called the "culture of violence." We need to turn this fabric of violence into a culture of peace.

We have to look at the problems in the context of the whole. When there is movement in one part of the fabric of violence, it affects the rest of the fabric. These issues are connected. We need to recognize these connections and be aware of the wider security issues in order to be able to make progress on the individual security issues.

We are also beginning to see in these new approaches new creative partnerships and new tools for diplomacy, for example, the recent agreement between Canada and Norway, the Lysoen Declaration, announced in late 1998. These partnerships between countries also need to involve civil society—the key aspect of the new approach to security. We need partnerships with governments, with nongovernmental organizations, and with the media. For example, leading up to the Ottawa convention on land mines, the media played a very important role in the campaign. The media—a critical part of civil society—became, in a sense, a partner in that process.

The United Nations is a forum that can play an important role in these new partnerships. We must be aware, however, that there are many other forums that we can use. Indeed, one part of a pragmatic, multistranded approach is that we can and should use a number of different forums.

Some key problems need to be highlighted. For example, the groups of like-minded states that have been forming over a number of issues can be very constructive and move things along. But what has happened, and is likely to happen again, is that other states that are not like-minded can present very large obstacles and actually prevent consensus.

Another difficulty, if we just take nuclear disarmament and consider the possibilities of partnerships between governments and NGOs, is that there is a wide range of views within the NGO community. The NGOs are by no means all in agreement. For example, they do not agree on the pace and scope of discussions and negotiations. On the issues of no-first-use of nuclear weapons or ballistic missile defense, for example, there is a wide range of opinions and big differences on the eventual end point. Not all NGOs believe that complete nuclear disarmament is desirable or feasible. All this has to be taken into account. "Choose your partners carefully" is probably the lesson that is most applicable.

Perhaps the more radical NGOs also need to take stock of where they are going and where they are coming from, and think about new agendas for themselves as well. Perhaps more radical NGOs could think about less radical measures that might better achieve their ends—in other words, become more strategic themselves.

The nuclear beast is still strong and fighting very hard. The more that this beast gets attacked, the more it is going to thrash. We have to be prepared for that. It is going to be dirty; it is going to be tough. The tests by India and Pakistan have dealt quite a severe blow to the process of nuclear disarmament. As we persevere, we must remember that we cannot have nuclear disarmament without the five nuclear powers and the three undeclared nuclear powers. These new ideas and new initiatives offer us new ways to engage these states and to accelerate the process of disarmament.

THE HUMAN SECURITY AGENDA
By Marina Laker*

Canada has had a long-standing disarmament and non-proliferation policy, one that has been actively and forcefully promoted for decades. In fact it has existed since the time when—as an alumnus of the Manhattan Project—Canada opted to forgo developing a nuclear weapons capability. Since then, Canada has "worked the room" as an NPT non–nuclear weapon state, striving to strengthen and promote the non-proliferation regime, often acting as brokers within key negotiations.

It is perhaps this commitment to multilateralism that distinguishes Canada from our great neighbor to the south. From promoting hemisphere-wide free trade to restoring the Euro-Atlantic partnership. From contributing to the reform of the international financial system to responding to the economic and social costs of the Asian and Russian meltdowns. And kicking at the shins of the international community to shore up solidarity in rejecting the Indian and Pakistani nuclear tests.

All these multilateral initiatives and objectives leave Canada well placed to consider the viability of new agendas and engage new coalitions that spring up. On the eve of the convening of the 1998 United Nations General Assembly, Canada was approached by the New Agenda Coalition, and we engaged early in the game rather than reject outright what some claimed was a wholly flawed and unfixable draft resolution on nuclear disarmament.

Why did Canada choose to engage? The resolution's cosponsors represented a novel and dynamic group of states that had demonstrated genuine commitments to nuclear disarmament and nuclear non-proliferation. The resolution possessed a potential to bring states in, and move them away from hard-line positions at both ends of the spectrum—positions that have plagued and frustrated the international community's discussions over the past years.

Also, the New Agenda's approach reflected the steps Canada has taken in preserving the NPT and the need to combat what Minister Axworthy enunciated in a statement before the House of Commons in May: a new nuclear real politic being used by proliferators in nuclear weapon states to justify the proliferation or retention of nuclear weapons. This latter point reflects a two-track approach that

* The views expressed are those of the author and do not necessarily reflect the position of the Government of Canada.

Canada has favored in response to the South Asian nuclear tests. Some consider the tests as only a case of regional misbehavior with a limited impact, while Canada has actively sought to sustain pressure on India and Pakistan to restrain and eventually reverse their nuclear programs.

The resolution failed to attract the widest possible support that we sought from the outset; the decision to abstain was a step accompanied by a commitment to continue to engage and discuss the ideas and approaches that were put forward in the resolution and elsewhere.

Canada has promoted many ideas supporting progress in the non-proliferation field for some time. One such recent idea was that an ad hoc committee in the Conference on Disarmament (CD) should be struck to discuss nuclear disarmament issues. The commonly made slippery-slope argument against establishing such a committee is a weak one. If states are going to hold discussions in the appropriate forum, like the CD on nuclear disarmament issues, then they must have an inclusive, transparent process—one that can only help build confidence, trust, and understanding of individual security needs and prepare a fertile ground for any possible negotiations that may appropriately be required in the future.

Slippery slopes are only places where one doesn't want to travel. As we all believe in the commitments laid out by the vast majority of NPT adherents, one would think that this would possibly be the most appropriate place for exploring and possibly preparing a fertile ground.

We do require new initiatives, new approaches, and new thinking, and it is within the broad overarching international security framework that the ideas of the Human Security Agenda find their place. In Canada's view, human security takes individual human beings and their communities, rather than states, as its point of reference. It uses the safety and well-being of individuals and their communities as the measure of security. It recognizes that the security of states is essential, but not sufficient to fully ensure an individual's safety and well-being. It considers threats from both military and nonmilitary sources: interstate wars, small-arms proliferation, human rights violations, crimes, and drugs. It regards the safety and well-being of individuals as integral to achieving global peace and security and conceptually isn't merely a work in progress.

It is very important to reiterate that Canada does in no way see human security as an alternative to state or national security. The legal framework we have erected since 1945 to reduce the risk of interstate conflict and to promote peace—the UN Charter, the Universal Declaration of Human Rights and its protocols, the International Court of Justice, and the nuclear non-proliferation regime—is the bedrock of the international order. The alliances we have joined to ensure our security, NORAD and NATO, remain the cornerstones of Canada's own defense and security policy.

This framework of treaties and institutions is necessary but not sufficient to ensure others' and ultimately our own security. National security and human security are opposite sides of the same coin. If we are to recognize that globalization affects us all, then we have to be concerned when governments ignore the desperate basic needs of their own citizens and neighbors by expending energy and resources that far exceed their means in order to develop weapons of mass destruction.

Canada must continue to work actively to promote long-standing disarmament and non-proliferation objectives. With one hand mindful of what the other hand is up to, within our limited resources and capabilities, Canada will work toward improving human security abroad while testing strategies and engaging with partners who share similar outlooks. Canada can influence its world, in its own way, and perhaps different ways as well. That may be the role required of us, and therefore we shouldn't shirk from playing it.

THE VIEW FROM BRAZIL
By Luiz F. Machado

Brazil has much at stake on issues of nuclear disarmament and proliferation. It is the eighth-largest economy in the world and has a population of about 150 million. It is a country that lives in peace with all of its ten neighbors, and has done so for more than a century. South America is probably the least armed region in the world and the focus of a dynamic process of economic integration, and we in Brazil are proud of the part we have played in achieving that.

Brazil is currently a party to all international non-proliferation agreements, including the Nuclear Non-Proliferation Treaty (NPT), and to an exemplary, legally binding, bilateral process with Argentina on the uses of nuclear energy for peaceful purposes only. Brazil is also a member of the Nuclear Suppliers Group and the Missile Technology Control Regime.

In his address during the ceremony of the deposit of the Brazilian instrument of accession to the NPT in Washington, Foreign Minister Luiz Felipe Lampreia stated, "Brazil strongly rejects the notion that nuclear weapons can bring security to any nation. On the contrary, they breed only tension and instability and constitute a major roadblock to international peace and security."

He went on, "Limiting the spread of nuclear weapons is not enough. The NPT will not have fulfilled its goal, as set out in Article VI, until all existing nuclear weapons are gone. That was certainly the understanding of the Brazilian government and Congress when they approved the accession to the treaty."

This simple truth is behind the long-standing Brazilian policy in dealing with disarmament issues and nuclear disarmament in particular. That is why non-proliferation of weapons of mass destruction continues to be a central concern. Non-proliferation implies the horizontal, vertical, and geographic dimensions of the concept. Brazil has historically stood against both the spread of nuclear weapons to non–nuclear weapon states and the continuing stockpiling of those weapons and their deployment in regions of the world that would otherwise be free of them.

Non-proliferation and disarmament are different, although mutually reinforcing, concepts. Only total and complete nuclear disarmament can put an end to nuclear proliferation. This is the very logic behind the NPT's basic bargain, by which the non-nuclear weapon states agreed to forgo those weapons and the nuclear weapon states agreed to negotiate disarmament measures aimed at the ultimate elimination of nuclear weapons.

The present situation gives reason for concern regarding the continued threat to the human species—and to all species, for that matter—posed by nuclear weapons.

The end of the Cold War did not solve the problem. On the contrary, it made even more obvious the fallacies behind the logic of nuclear deterrence and its mutually assured destruction pillar.

What does the New Agenda initiative represent for us? It is, on the one hand, an appeal for a new era in international peace and security and, on the other, the consolidation of a number of logical and pragmatic steps already taken toward that end. Brazil, defined by Secretary of State Albright as a "could have been" in terms of nuclear weapon capabilities, is very comfortable in vigorously advocating the need of banning the use of nuclear energy for nonpeaceful purposes. That is the deeply felt will of the Brazilian people, enshrined in our constitution and reiterated by our membership in all international nuclear non-proliferation agreements.

The Conference on Disarmament, as the single multilateral negotiating body in the field of disarmament, should be allowed to pursue meaningful discussions on nuclear disarmament. This can be done on a step-by-step basis. An ad hoc committee could serve as a forum where ongoing discussions on nuclear disarmament could be the subject of periodic information and clarifications by those directly engaged in them. Preparatory work on certain aspects of related matters, like problems related to timing and verification, could be envisaged, as was the case with the group of seismic experts who paved the way for a Comprehensive Test Ban Treaty verification mechanism. In short, there is no lack of serious possibilities for a gradual approach that could involve the whole international community.

Attention should also be focused on the problems posed by fissile materials and their relevance both to disarmament and to non-proliferation. Brazilian representatives have consistently voiced concerns about fissile material stockpiles. If a cutoff treaty is certainly important, the question of the treatment of existing stocks is directly relevant for such a treaty to make a genuine contribution to nuclear disarmament and not only to certain aspects of non-proliferation.

Another problem directly related to this question is the always present possibility of international smuggling of fissile materials and the terrible consequences this would entail. Here again, the only final answer to the problem is nuclear disarmament. As long as there are nuclear weapons, there will be weapon-grade fissile materials. As long as there are nonsafeguarded fissile materials in the five nuclear weapon countries and in the nuclear-capable countries not members of the NPT, there will be no guarantees that those materials will never reach the hands of terrorist entities.

The question of nuclear weapon–free zones is of particular importance to the Brazilian government. Nineteen ninety-eight was the third consecutive year that Brazil presented to the First Committee of the United Nations General Assembly an initiative on "the nuclear weapon–free Southern Hemisphere and adjacent areas." The treaties of Tlatelolco, Rarotonga, Pelindaba, and Bangkok and the Antarctic Treaty are important contributions to nuclear disarmament and non-proliferation efforts and express the views of an impressive number of countries that want to keep their regions free from nuclear weapons.

Reprinted below is the resolution sponsored by the New Agenda Coalition of nations and approved at the seventy-ninth plenary meeting of the United Nation's General Assembly on December 4. 1998.

U.N. RESOLUTION 53/77Y

YES: 114
NO: 18
ABSTAIN: 38

NO: Bulgaria, Czech Republic, Estonia, France, Hungary, India, Israel, Latvia, Lithuania, Monaco, Pakistan, Poland, Romania, Russian Fed, Slovakia, Turkey, United Kingdom, United States.

ABSTENTIONS: Albania, Algeria, Andorra, Argentina, Australia, Belgium, Bhutan, Canada, China, Croatia, Denmark, Finland, Georgia, Germany, Greece, Honduras, Iceland, Italy, Japan, Kazakhstan, Kyrgyzstan, Luxembourg, Mauritius, Marshall Islands, Micronesia, Myanmar, Netherlands, Norway, Portugal, Rep. of Korea, Rep. of Moldova, Slovenia, Spain, Former Yugoslav Republic of Macedonia, Ukraine, Uzbekistan.

The General Assembly,

Alarmed by the threat to the very survival of mankind posed by the existence of nuclear weapons,

Concerned at the prospect of the indefinite possession of nuclear weapons,

Concerned also at the continued retention of the nuclear-weapons option by those three States that are nuclear-weapons capable and that have not acceded to the Treaty on the Non-Proliferation of Nuclear Weapons,

Believing that the proposition that nuclear weapons can be retained in perpetuity and never used accidentally or by decision defies credibility, and that the only complete defence is the elimination of nuclear weapons and the assurance that they will never be produced again,

Concerned that the nuclear-weapon States have not fulfilled speedily and totally their commitment to the elimination of their nuclear weapons,

Concerned also that those three States that are nuclear-weapons capable and that have not acceded to the Treaty on the Non-Proliferation of Nuclear Weapons have failed to renounce their nuclear-weapons option,

Bearing in mind that the overwhelming majority of States entered into legally binding commitments not to receive, manufacture or otherwise acquire nuclear weapons or other nuclear explosive devices, and that these undertakings have been made in the context of the corresponding legally binding commitments by the nuclear-weapon States to the pursuit of nuclear disarmament,

Recalling the unanimous conclusion of the International Court of Justice in its 1996 advisory opinion that there exists an obligation to pursue in good faith and bring to a conclusion negotiations leading to nuclear disarmament in all its aspects under strict and effective international control,

Stressing that the international community must not enter the third millennium with the prospect that the possession of nuclear weapons will be considered legitimate for the indefinite future, and convinced that the present juncture provides a unique opportunity to proceed to prohibit and eradicate them for all time,

Recognizing that the total elimination of nuclear weapons will require measures to be taken firstly by those nuclear-weapon States that have the largest arsenals, and stressing that these States must be joined in a seamless process by those nuclear-weapon States with lesser arsenals in the near future,

Welcoming the achievements to date and the future promise of the Strategic Arms Reduction Talks process and the possibility it offers for development as a plurilateral mechanism including all the nuclear-weapon States, for the practical dismantling and destruction of nuclear armaments undertaken in pursuit of the elimination of nuclear weapons,

Believing that there are a number of practical steps that the nuclear-weapon States can and should take immediately before the actual elimination of nuclear arsenals and the development of requisite verification regimes take place, and, in this connection, noting certain recent unilateral and other steps,

Welcoming the agreement recently reached in the Conference on Disarmament on the establishment of an Ad Hoc Committee under item 1 of its agenda entitled "Cessation of the nuclear arms race and nuclear disarmament," to negotiate, on the basis of the report of the Special Coordinator and the mandate contained therein, a non-discriminatory, multilateral and internationally and effectively verifiable treaty banning the production of fissile material for nuclear weapons or other nuclear explosive devices, and considering that such a treaty must further underpin the process towards the total elimination of nuclear weapons,

Emphasizing that, for the total elimination of nuclear weapons to be achieved, effective international cooperation to prevent the proliferation of nuclear weapons is vital and must be enhanced through, inter alia, the extension of international controls over all fissile material for nuclear weapons or other nuclear explosive devices,

Emphasizing also the importance of existing nuclear-weapon-free zone treaties and of the signature and ratification of the relevant protocols to these treaties,

Noting the joint ministerial declaration of 9 June 1998 and its call for a new international agenda to achieve a nuclear-weapon-free world, through the pursuit, in parallel, of a series of mutually reinforcing measures at the bilateral, plurilateral and multilateral levels,

1. Calls upon the nuclear-weapon States to demonstrate an unequivocal commitment to the speedy and total elimination of their respective nuclear weapons and, without delay, to pursue in good faith and bring to a conclusion negotiations leading to the elimination of these weapons, thereby fulfilling their obligations under article VI of the Treaty on the Non-Proliferation of Nuclear Weapons;

2. Calls upon the United States of America and the Russian Federation to bring the Treaty on Further Reduction and Limitation of Strategic Offensive Arms (START II) into force without further delay and immediately thereafter to proceed with negotiations on START III with a view to its early conclusion; that the present juncture provides a unique opportunity to proceed to prohibit and eradicate them for all time,

3. Calls upon the nuclear-weapon States to undertake the necessary steps towards the seamless integration of all five nuclear-weapon States into the process leading to the total elimination of nuclear weapons;

4. Also calls upon the nuclear-weapon States to pursue vigorously the reduction of reliance on non-strategic nuclear weapons and negotiations on their elimination as an integral part of their overall nuclear disarmament activities;

5. Further calls upon the nuclear-weapon States, as an interim measure, to proceed to the de-alerting of their nuclear weapons and, in turn, to the removal of nuclear warheads from delivery vehicles;

6. Urges the nuclear-weapon States to examine further interim measures, including measures to enhance strategic stability and accordingly to review strategic doctrines;

7. Calls upon those three States that are nuclear-weapon capable and that have not yet acceded to the Treaty on the Non-Proliferation of Nuclear Weapons to reverse clearly and urgently the pursuit of all nuclear weapons development or deployment and to refrain from any action which could undermine regional and international peace and security and the efforts of the international community towards nuclear disarmament and the prevention of nuclear weapons proliferation;

8. Calls upon those States that have not yet done so to adhere unconditionally and without delay to the Treaty on the Non-Proliferation of Nuclear Weapons and to take all the necessary measures which flow from adherence to this instrument;

9. Also calls upon those States that have not yet done so to conclude full-scope safeguards agreements with the International Atomic Energy Agency and to conclude additional protocols to their safeguards agreements on the basis of the Model Protocol approved by the Board of Governors of the Agency on 15 May 1997;

10. Further calls upon those States that have not yet done so to sign and ratify, unconditionally and without delay, the Comprehensive Nuclear-Test-Ban Treaty and, pending the entry into force of the Treaty, to observe a moratorium on nuclear tests;

11. Calls upon those States that have not yet done so to adhere to the Convention on the Physical Protection of Nuclear Material and to work towards its further strengthening;

12. Calls upon the Conference on Disarmament to pursue its negotiations in the Ad Hoc Committee established under item 1 of its agenda entitled "Cessation of the nuclear arms race and nuclear disarmament," on the basis of the report of the Special Coordinator and the mandate contained therein, of a non-discriminatory, multilateral and internationally and effectively verifiable treaty banning the production of fissile material for nuclear weapons or other nuclear explosive devices, taking into consideration both nuclear non-proliferation and nuclear disarmament objectives, and to conclude these negotiations without delay, and, pending the entry into force of the treaty, urges States to observe a moratorium on the production of fissile materials for nuclear weapons or other nuclear explosive devices;

13. Also calls upon the Conference on Disarmament to establish an appropriate subsidiary body to deal with nuclear disarmament and, to that end, to pursue as a matter of priority its intensive consultations on appropriate methods and approaches with a view to reaching such a decision without delay;

14. Considers that an international conference on nuclear disarmament and nuclear non-proliferation, which would effectively complement efforts being undertaken in other settings, could facilitate the consolidation of a new agenda for a nuclear-weapon-free world;

15. Recalls the importance of the decisions and resolution adopted at the 1995 Review and Extension Conference of the Parties to the Treaty on the Non-Proliferation of Nuclear Weapons, and underlines the importance of implementing fully the decision on strengthening the review process for the Treaty;

16. Affirms that the development of verification arrangements will be necessary for the maintenance of a world free from nuclear weapons, and requests the International Atomic Energy Agency, together with any other relevant international organizations and bodies, to explore the elements of such a system;

17. Calls for the conclusion of an internationally legally binding instrument to effectively assure non-nuclear-weapon States parties to the Treaty on the Non-Proliferation of Nuclear Weapons against the use or threat of use of nuclear weapons;

18. Stresses that the pursuit, extension and establishment of nuclear-weapon-free zones, on the basis of arrangements freely arrived at, especially in regions of tension, such as the Middle East and South Asia, represent a significant contribution to the goal of a nuclear-weapon-free world;

19. Affirms that a nuclear-weapon-free world will ultimately require the underpinnings of a universal and multilaterally negotiated legally binding instrument or a framework encompassing a mutually reinforcing set of instruments;

20. Requests the Secretary-General, within existing resources, to compile a report on the implementation of the present resolution;

21. Decides to include in the provisional agenda of its fifty-fourth session an item entitled "Towards a nuclear-weapon-free world: the need for a new agenda," and to review the implementation of the present resolution.

NOTES

1. The text of the entire statement is available at: (http://www.peacenet.org/disarm/abolish.html).

2. Article VI of the NPT states: "Each of the Parties to the Treaty undertakes to pursue negotiations in good faith on effective measures relating to cessation of the nuclear arms race at an early date and to nuclear disarmament, and on a Treaty on general and complete disarmament under strict and effective international control."

—APPENDIXES—

The International Non-Proliferation Regime

The international non-proliferation regime has been constructed over the better part of the twentieth century and is based upon the premise that the danger posed by weapons of mass destruction grows, and their use becomes more likely, as the number of countries possessing such weapons increases. Moreover, the regime was formed out of the widely held belief that the possession of weapons of mass destruction by some states encourages the acquisition of such weapons by additional countries, further increasing the likelihood of their use.

To address these risks, the international community has developed an interlocking set of treaties, agreements, arrangements, and verification tools collectively referred to as the "non-proliferation regime." The regime includes components that address nuclear, chemical, and biological weapons, missile delivery systems, and the equipment, materials, and technologies needed to produce such weapons.

The regime's components can be placed into three main categories: treaties and agreements establishing norms and legal obligations; tools to verify compliance with obligations; and systems to control the means of producing weapons. Norms against the possession, acquisition, or proliferation of weapons of mass destruction and missile delivery systems are traditionally established through multilateral, legally binding treaties. Such treaties exist for nuclear, chemical, and biological weapons, but not for missiles. In some cases, the treaty itself establishes the norm, and in other cases, the legal document codifies a norm that has already been established. Verification of non-proliferation obligations encompassed in these treaties is typically carried out by neutral, third-party organizations with the technical assets needed to conduct both routine and special-access inspections. Such organizations exist in the nuclear and chemical areas, and one is being contemplated in the case of biological weapons. Last, members within the various regimes have established "supplier control mechanisms" that seek to limit access to sensitive technology and equipment to those countries that abide by the other parts of the regime. While these control regimes have been attacked in some quarters as overly restrictive, they have proved effective in slowing the pace of proliferation, if not stopping it completely.

NUCLEAR NON-PROLIFERATION REGIME

While the Treaty on the Non-Proliferation of Nuclear Weapons (NPT) is its center-piece, the global nuclear non-proliferation regime consists of a series of interlocking international treaties, bilateral undertakings, and multilateral inspections aimed at halting the spread of nuclear weapons. Other major elements of the regime are the International Atomic Energy Agency (IAEA) and two closely connected export control systems implemented by the key nuclear supplier countries.

NUCLEAR NON-PROLIFERATION TREATY (NPT)

The NPT, which was opened for signature in 1968 and entered into force in 1970, divides the countries of the world into two categories, "nuclear weapon states" and "non–nuclear weapon states." It defines "nuclear weapon states" as countries that detonated a nuclear explosion before January 1, 1967, namely, the United States (first detonation in 1945), the Soviet Union (1949), Great Britain (1952), France (1960), and China (1964). Russia succeeded to the Soviet Union's status as a nuclear weapon state under the treaty in 1992. The NPT treats all other countries as non–nuclear weapon states.[1]

Under the NPT:

- Non–nuclear weapon states party to the treaty pledge not to manufacture or receive nuclear explosives. (Both nuclear weapons and "peaceful nuclear explosives" are prohibited.)
- To verify that they are living up to this pledge, non-nuclear weapon states also agree to accept IAEA inspections on all nuclear activities, an arrangement known as "full-scope safeguards."
- All countries party to the treaty agree not to export nuclear equipment or material to non-nuclear weapon states except under IAEA safeguards, and nuclear-weapon states agree not to assist non-nuclear weapon states in obtaining nuclear weapons.
- All countries accepting the treaty agree to facilitate the fullest possible sharing of peaceful nuclear technology.
- All countries accepting the treaty agree to pursue negotiations in good faith to end the nuclear-arms race and to achieve nuclear disarmament under international control. (In practice, this applies to the nuclear weapon states.)
- A party may withdraw from the treaty on ninety days' notice if "extraordinary events related to the subject matter of the Treaty" have "jeopardized its supreme interests."

All five established nuclear weapon states are parties to the NPT. The United States, Russia, and Great Britain are the treaty's depositary states; China and France did not join until 1992. By mid-1999, the treaty had 181 non–nuclear weapon state parties, for a total of 186 parties.

The NPT originally entered into force for twenty-five years, with periodic reviews of the treaty occurring every five years. At the NPT Review and Extensions

Conference held in New York City in April–May 1995, the parties agreed to extend the treaty indefinitely without conditions. In addition, they approved a set of principles and objectives to guide the parties during a strengthened review process in the future (see appendix II).

Among the principal states of proliferation concern today, India, Israel, and Pakistan are not parties to the pact. Each has nuclear installations not subject to IAEA safeguards that contribute to its respective nuclear-weapons capability. Iran, Iraq, and Libya are non–nuclear weapon state parties to the treaty, but their commitment to the accord is suspect because of their demonstrated interest in acquiring nuclear arms.

North Korea became a party to the treaty in 1985 but did not agree to accept IAEA inspections of its nuclear activities until April 1992. During the interval, it may have produced and separated a quantity of plutonium sufficient for one or two nuclear weapons. North Korea has not satisfactorily accounted for this material and is not in compliance with its IAEA safeguards obligations under the treaty because of its refusal to permit an IAEA "special inspection" of two nuclear waste sites believed to contain information regarding past production of plutonium. Under an "Agreed Framework" signed with the United States in October 1994, North Korea agreed to resolve these issues at a future date; in the meantime, it has accepted restrictions on its nuclear activities that go beyond its obligations under the NPT, including a freeze on the operation and construction of a number of sensitive facilities.

INTERNATIONAL ATOMIC ENERGY AGENCY (IAEA)

The IAEA is part of the foundation of the international non-proliferation regime. Created in 1957, the Vienna-based IAEA is an international organization with 126 member countries. Its principal missions are to facilitate the use of nuclear energy for peaceful purposes and to implement a system of audits and on-site inspections, collectively known as "safeguards," to verify that nuclear facilities and materials are not being diverted for nuclear explosive purposes.[2]

In addition to monitoring all peaceful nuclear activities in non–nuclear weapon state parties to the NPT, the agency also monitors individual facilities and associated nuclear materials in non-NPT parties at the request of these states. Thus, even though India, Israel, and Pakistan are not parties to the NPT, several nuclear facilities in each of these countries are subject to IAEA monitoring, and these facilities cannot easily be used to support these nations' nuclear-weapons programs.

Until 1991, in non–nuclear weapon state parties to the NPT, the IAEA monitored only those facilities declared by the inspected country and did not seek out possible undeclared nuclear installations. After the 1991 Gulf War, however, it was learned that Iraq had secretly developed a network of undeclared nuclear facilities as part of an extensive nuclear-weapons program. This led the IAEA to announce in late 1991 that it would begin to exercise its previously unused authority to conduct "special inspections," that is, to demand access to undeclared sites where it suspected nuclear activities were being conducted. Subsequent measures were adopted under Program 93 + 2 in two installments. Part 1, implemented initially in 1996, consisted of measures that could be traced to existing legal authority. Part 2 consisted of measures whose implementation would require complementary legal authority. Part 2 measures were approved by the IAEA Board of Governors on May 15, 1997.

The agency first attempted to conduct a special inspection in North Korea in 1992, but Pyongyang refused to comply with the IAEA's request, triggering a crisis that has yet to be fully resolved. However, the IAEA's new authority has indirectly provided added access for the agency in Iran. Because an IAEA demand for special inspections carries the implied accusation that a country may be violating the NPT, Iran, anticipating that the agency might seek special inspections within its territory, has sought to avert the stigma associated with such inspections by agreeing to permit the IAEA to visit any location in Iran on request. The agency has visited undeclared sites in Iran several times but has not detected any activities in violation of Iran's NPT obligations.

COMPREHENSIVE TEST BAN TREATY (CTBT)[3]

The newest element of the regime is the CTBT, a barrier to vertical as well as horizontal proliferation. The conclusion of this treaty fulfilled a preambular commitment of NPT parties to carry through with pledges made in the 1963 Partial Test Ban Treaty "to seek to achieve the discontinuance of all test explosions of nuclear weapons for all time." Opened for signature in New York on September 24, 1996, the CTBT prohibits nuclear test explosions of any size and establishes a rigorous verification system, including seismic monitoring and on-site inspections, to detect any violations.

The CTBT was negotiated at the Geneva Conference on Disarmament (CD), where decisions normally are made by consensus. India temporarily blocked approval of the treaty in mid-August 1996; it objected to the fact that the treaty did not include provisions demanded by India prescribing a "time-bound framework" for the global elimination of nuclear weapons. India also opposed the treaty's entry-into-force provision, which, in effect, would require India's ratification to bring the pact into force. To circumvent India's veto, Australia introduced the treaty into the UN General Assembly, where decisions are made by majority rather than by consensus. The CTBT was adopted by the UN General Assembly on September 10, 1996, by a vote of 158 to 3 (the negative votes coming from India, Bhutan, and Libya).

NUCLEAR SUPPLIER CONTROL MECHANISMS

Two informal coalitions of nations that voluntarily restrict the export of equipment and materials that could be used to develop nuclear weapons form a third major element of the non-proliferation regime.

Shortly after the NPT came into force in 1970, a number of Western and Soviet-bloc nuclear-supplier states began consultations concerning the procedures and standards that would apply to nuclear exports to non–nuclear weapon states. The group, known as the NPT Exporters Committee (or the Zangger Committee, so named after its Swiss chairman), adopted a set of guidelines in August 1974, including a list of export items that would trigger the requirement for the application of IAEA safeguards in recipient states. These procedures and the "trigger list," updated in subsequent years, represent the first major agreement on uniform regulation of nuclear exports by actual and potential nuclear suppliers.

Following India's nuclear test in 1974, an overlapping group of nuclear supplier states—but in this case including France, which was not then a party to the NPT— met in London to elaborate export guidelines further. In January 1976, this London group—which became known as the Nuclear Suppliers Group (NSG)—adopted guidelines that were similar to those of the NPT Exporters Committee but also extended to transfers of technology and included agreement to "exercise restraint" in the transfer of uranium-enriched and plutonium-extraction equipment and facilities.

In April 1992, in the wake of the Gulf War, the NSG expanded its export control guidelines, which until then had covered only uniquely nuclear items, to cover sixty-five "dual-use" items as well. The group also added as a requirement for future exports that recipient states accept IAEA inspection on all of their peaceful nuclear activities. This rule, previously adopted by only some NSG members, effectively precludes nuclear commerce by NSG member states with India, Israel, and Pakistan.

In addition to agreeing to such full-scope safeguards, all nations importing regulated items from NSG member states must promise to furnish adequate physical security for transferred nuclear materials and facilities, pledge not to export nuclear materials and technologies to other nations without the permission of the original exporting nation or without a pledge from the recipient nation to abide by these same rules, and promise not to use any imports to build nuclear explosives. Similar rules—apart from the full-scope safeguards requirement—apply to exports regulated by the Zangger Committee, which continues to function, although it has been partially eclipsed by the Nuclear Suppliers Group, whose export controls have been more far reaching.

NUCLEAR-WEAPON-FREE ZONES (NWFZs)

NWFZs complement NPT arrangements because they can be geared to specific regional situations. The growing role of NWFZs as part of the non-proliferation regime was reflected in the draft review document of the 1995 NPT Review and Extension Conference: "The establishment of nuclear-weapon-free zones . . . constitutes an important disarmament measure which greatly strengthens the international non-proliferation regime in all its aspects." NWFZs have been established in Latin America (Treaty of Tlatelolco, 1967), the South Pacific (1996), and Africa (1996), and efforts have been made to establish one in Southeast Asia. In some cases, the verification procedures laid out in the NPT have been used to verify compliance with NWFZ agreements, while in others, separate, regional organizations have been established. Such regional bodies have additional confidence-building benefits.

CHEMICAL AND BIOLOGICAL WEAPONS NONPROLIFERATION REGIME

The proliferation of chemical and biological weapons is an issue of increasing concern in the last part of the twentieth century. Efforts to prevent the spread of chemical and biological weapons, however, date back to the early 1920s, after the experience with the use of chemical weapons during World War I. While largely symbolic and without verification procedures, the Geneva Protocol for the Prohibition of the Use in War of Asphyxiating, Poisonous or Other Gases, and of Bacteriological Methods of Warfare marked the first attempt by states to establish an international norm against the use of weapons of mass destruction. The treaty, however, did not restrict the ability of states to acquire or store such weapons, and it had no verification provision, greatly limiting its impact.

BIOLOGICAL AND TOXIN WEAPONS CONVENTION (BWC)

The BWC, which was opened for signature in April 1972 and entered into force in 1975, prohibits the development, production, stockpiling, acquisition, and transfer of pathogens or toxins in "quantities that have no justification for prophylactic, protective, and other peaceful purposes." Additionally, the BWC bans weapon systems and other means of delivery for biological agents. The United States, United Kingdom, and the Russian Federation are the three depositary governments for the BWC, which has 142 state parties and 18 additional signatories. Review conferences are held approximately every five years, with conferences having been held in 1980, 1986, 1991, and 1996.

When it entered into force, the BWC was unique in that it prohibited an entire class of weapons. However, the BWC does not contain enforcement or effective verification measures to ensure compliance. An attempt was made in 1991 to improve the effectiveness of the treaty by adopting a number of confidence-building measures, such as requiring declarations by states regarding past biological weapons activities. The deficiencies in the treaty, however, have remained, as highlighted by recent revelations, including violations of the convention by the former Soviet Union and persistent concerns about Iraq's past biological weapons activities. These cases, as well as the doubling in number of countries suspected of pursuing a BW capability since the BWC entered into force, have led to doubts about the convention's utility. Efforts are now under way to negotiate a legally binding verification protocol to the convention.

CHEMICAL WEAPONS CONVENTION (CWC)

Efforts on creating a chemical weapons treaty were initiated in the early 1970s, soon after the conclusion of the Biological and Toxin Weapons Convention. However, due to difficulties in negotiating compliance and verification issues, little progress was made until 1986, when the Soviet Union agreed to systematic inspections at chemical weapons storage and production facilities, the destruction of production facilities, and declarations and routine inspections at commercial industry sites. In 1987, the Soviet Union not only accepted the principle of mandatory short-notice challenge inspections but also insisted that this procedure apply to all facilities or locations. The use of chemical weapons during the Iran-Iraq war drew international attention to the lack of effective means for preventing the acquisition and use of such weapons and provided an important impetus for completing the Chemical Weapons Convention.

Entered into force on April 29, 1997, the Chemical Weapons Convention prohibits the development, production, acquisition, stockpiling, retention, transfer, and use of chemical weapons. The treaty also bans engaging in any military preparation for the use of CW and assisting any other states engaging in treaty-banned activities. The CWC also requires state parties to destroy any chemical weapons and chemical weapons production facilities under its ownership, possession, or control—all within ten years after the entry into force of the convention. Currently there are 126 state parties to the CWC.

In order to build confidence that state parties are in compliance with the treaty, the CWC establishes transparency through a verification regime subjecting all declared chemical weapons and production facilities and certain commercial chemical industrial facilities to systematic inspections. The convention, categorizing chemicals into three "schedules" depending on their applicability for CW programs and for commercial purposes, applies varying degrees of control to these chemicals and their production facilities. Facilities producing chemicals listed in any of the three schedules in quantities in excess of allotted amounts must be declared and are subject to inspections. The CWC also contains provisions for challenge inspections of any declared or nondeclared facility.

THE AUSTRALIA GROUP

The Australia Group (AG) is an informal arrangement among thirty states designed to impede CBW proliferation by harmonizing national export controls on equipment and materials that could be used in chemical and/or biological weapons programs. These restrictions apply to items such as CW precursor chemicals, BW pathogens, and CBW dual-use equipment. In addition, participant nations exchange information on programs of concern and consider other measures to address CBW proliferation and use.

The group was formed in 1984 in the wake of the extensive CW use during the Iran-Iraq war. Initially, the AG focused on imposing export controls on dual-use chemicals. Since its inception, the list of eight chemical precursors subject to control has expanded to fifty-four. Many of the chemicals used in the production of chemical weapons also have legitimate applications, making control a complicated matter that must balance security concerns with peaceful commerce. In the late 1980s, the AG's list of controlled items was expanded beyond chemical precursors to include CW- related equipment and technology. Beginning in 1990, members of the AG agreed to impose restrictions on certain biological toxins and pathogens, and the group has also established export controls on specific microorganisms, toxins, and equipment with potential applications in a BW program.

The AG has periodically used warning mechanisms to educate chemical-related enterprises in their own countries to the risk posed by CBW proliferation. The group has issued an informal "warning list" of dual-use precursors and bulk chemicals, and of CW-related equipment. Members develop and share the warning lists with their chemical industries and ask industry to report on any suspicious transactions. The AG has also used a similar approach to warn industry, the scientific community, and other relevant groups of the risk of inadvertently aiding BW proliferation.

THE MISSILE TECHNOLOGY CONTROL REGIME

The centerpiece of international efforts to prevent the proliferation of missiles is the Missile Technology Control Regime (MTCR). The regime, which now has twenty-nine members and a number of adherents, was announced by the G-7 countries on April 16, 1987. Originally, the MTCR sought to control the proliferation of missiles capable of carrying a nuclear warhead—systems capable of carrying a payload of 500 kilograms over a distance of 300 kilometers. The regime was modified in 1993, however, to control all unmanned delivery systems capable of carrying weapons of mass destruction.

The MTCR is a supplier control mechanism that prohibits the transfer by member states of key components and associated production materials, technology, and equipment needed in the production of missiles, defined by the regime as ballistic missiles, space launch vehicles, and sounding rockets. In addition, the regime defines unmanned aerial vehicles to include cruise missiles, drones, and remotely piloted vehicles.

Originally, the regime required all new members to eliminate any missile or missile development programs that exceeded the limits of the regime. This restriction did not apply to the originating seven countries. More recently, however, countries with active space launch programs with potential military applications (e.g., Brazil) have been permitted to enter the regime in the hopes of controlling the possible transfer of missile-related equipment to other states. The regime's terms state that it is not "designed to impede national space programs . . . as long as such programs could not contribute to delivery systems for weapons of mass destruction." The regime's members are expected to take special precautions in such transfers, however, since the technology used in space launch vehicles (SLVs) is virtually identical to those used in ballistic missiles.

The regime has been successful in complicating the missile acquisition programs of several countries and has even led to the termination of some missile development programs. Countries such as North Korea, Iran, Pakistan, and India, however, have been able to develop increasingly capable missiles systems despite the existence of the regime.

NOTES

1. In this book, Israel, India, and Pakistan are described as de facto, non-NPT or "self-declared" nuclear-weapon states. In May 1998, India and Pakistan each conducted nuclear-weapon tests and declared themselves "nuclear powers." As a result, this book refers to the original five NPT-recognized nuclear weapon states as the de jure or "established" nuclear weapon states. The NPT and the non-proliferation regime have no legal category and no provision for additional nuclear weapon states. Until a better term emerges, non-NPT or "self-declared" nuclear weapon states may be acceptable as descriptive terminology.

2. "Full-scope safeguards" were developed pursuant to the NPT and provide for IAEA inspections and monitoring of all nuclear materials, and the facilities that contain those materials, within the jurisdiction of the state in question. The goal of IAEA inspections and monitoring under the NPT is to verify that nuclear materials are not being diverted by the state in question for any uses relating to nuclear weapons or explosives. A state may declare and exempt nuclear materials from IAEA inspection for narrow military purposes, such as fueling naval nuclear reactors. To date, no non–nuclear weapon state parties to the NPT have built nuclear submarines and obtained this exemption for naval nuclear propulsion. Since the IAEA monitors only activities connected with the production or use of nuclear materials, it does not have under its original charter (or even under the NPT) a basis for searching for and investigating nuclear weapons-related activities, such as fabricating or testing the non-nuclear components of nuclear weapons, unless nuclear materials are present in these activities.

3. The CTBT's entry-into-force provision requires the ratification of forty-four nations that possess either nuclear power or research reactors—a group that includes both the five established nuclear-weapon states and the de facto nuclear-weapon states (India, Israel, and Pakistan). If the treaty still has not entered into force by September 1999, three years after it was opened for signature, the nations that have ratified it may convene a conference to discuss ways to accelerate entry into force. As of October 1997, 148 nations (including the five established nuclear-weapon states and Israel) had signed the treaty. However, India and Pakistan, whose ratification of the treaty was seen as essential, had not signed.

Principles and Objectives for Nuclear Non-Proliferation and Disarmament

Adopted by the 1995 NPT Review
and Extensions Conference
New York, May 12, 1995

Reaffirming the preamble and articles of the Treaty on the Non-Proliferation of Nuclear Weapons,

Welcoming the end of the cold war, the ensuing easing of international tension and the strengthening of trust between States,

Desiring a set of principles and objectives in accordance with which nuclear non-proliferation, nuclear disarmament and international cooperation in the peaceful uses of nuclear energy should be vigorously pursued and progress, achievements and shortcomings evaluated periodically within the review process provided for in article VIII (3) of the Treaty, the enhancement and strengthening of which is welcomed,

Reiterating the ultimate goals of the complete elimination of nuclear weapons and a treaty on general and complete disarmament under strict and effective international control,

The Conference affirms the need to continue to move with determination towards the full realization and effective implementation of the provisions of the Treaty, and accordingly adopts the following principles and objectives:

Universality

1. Universal adherence to the Treaty on the Non-Proliferation of Nuclear Weapons is an urgent priority. All States not yet party to the Treaty are called upon to accede to the Treaty at the earliest date, particularly those States that operate unsafeguarded nuclear facilities. Every effort should be made by all States parties to achieve this objective.

Non-proliferation

2. The proliferation of nuclear weapons would seriously increase the danger of nuclear war. The Treaty on the Non-Proliferation of Nuclear Weapons has a vital role to play in preventing the proliferation of nuclear weapons. Every

effort should be made to implement the Treaty in all its aspects to prevent the proliferation of nuclear weapons and other nuclear explosive devices, without hampering the peaceful uses of nuclear energy by States parties to the Treaty.

Nuclear disarmament

3. Nuclear disarmament is substantially facilitated by the easing of international tension and the strengthening of trust between States which have prevailed following the end of the cold war. The undertakings with regard to nuclear disarmament as set out in the Treaty on the Non-Proliferation of Nuclear Weapons should thus be fulfilled with determination. In this regard, the nuclear-weapon States reaffirm their commitment, as stated in article VI, to pursue in good faith negotiations on effective measures relating to nuclear disarmament.

4. The achievement of the following measures is important in the full realization and effective implementation of article VI, including the programme of action as reflected below:

(a) The completion by the Conference on Disarmament of the negotiations on a universal and internationally and effectively verifiable Comprehensive Nuclear-Test-Ban Treaty no later than 1996. Pending the entry into force of a Comprehensive Test-Ban Treaty, the nuclear-weapon States should exercise utmost restraint;

(b) The immediate commencement and early conclusion of negotiations on a non-discriminatory and universally applicable convention banning the production of fissile material for nuclear weapons or other nuclear explosive devices, in accordance with the statement of the Special Coordinator of the Conference on Disarmament and the mandate contained therein;

(c) The determined pursuit by the nuclear-weapon States of systematic and progressive efforts to reduce nuclear weapons globally, with the ultimate goals of eliminating those weapons, and by all States of general and complete disarmament under strict and effective international control.

Nuclear-weapon-free zones

5. The conviction that the establishment of internationally recognized nuclear-weapon-free zones, on the basis of arrangements freely arrived at among the States of the region concerned, enhances global and regional peace and security is reaffirmed.

6. The development of nuclear-weapon-free zones, especially in regions of tension, such as in the Middle East, as well as the establishment of zones free of all weapons of mass destruction should be encouraged as a matter of priority, taking into account the specific characteristics of each region. The establishment of additional nuclear-weapon-free zones by the time of the Review Conference in the year 2000 would be welcome.

7. The cooperation of all the nuclear-weapon States and their respect and support for the relevant protocols is necessary for the maximum effectiveness of such nuclear-weapon-free zones and the relevant protocols.

Security assurances

8. Noting United Nations Security Council resolution 984 (1995), which was adopted unanimously on 11 April 1995, as well as the declarations by the nuclear-weapon States concerning both negative and positive security assurances, further steps should be considered to assure non-nuclear-weapon States party to the Treaty against the use or threat of use of nuclear weapons. These steps could take the form of an internationally legally binding instrument.

Safeguards

9. The International Atomic Energy Agency (IAEA) is the competent authority responsible to verify and assure, in accordance with the statute of the IAEA and the Agency's safeguards system, compliance with its safeguards agreements with States parties undertaken in fulfillment of their obligations under article III (1) of the Treaty, with a view to preventing diversion of nuclear energy from peaceful uses to nuclear weapons or other nuclear explosive devices. Nothing should be done to undermine the authority of the IAEA in this regard. States parties that have concerns regarding non-compliance with the safeguards agreements of the Treaty by the States parties should direct such concerns, along with supporting evidence and information, to the IAEA to consider, investigate, draw conclusions and decide on necessary actions in accordance with its mandate.

10. All States parties required by article III of the Treaty to sign and bring into force comprehensive safeguards agreements and which have not yet done so should do so without delay.

11. IAEA safeguards should be regularly assessed and evaluated. Decisions adopted by its Board of Governors aimed at further strengthening the effectiveness of IAEA safeguards should be supported and implemented and the IAEA's capability to detect undeclared nuclear activities should be increased. Also States not party to the Treaty on the Non-Proliferation of Nuclear Weapons should be urged to enter into comprehensive safeguards agreements with the IAEA.

12. New supply arrangements for the transfer of source or special fissionable material or equipment or material especially designed or prepared for the processing, use or production of special fissionable material to non-nuclear-weapon States should require, as a necessary precondition, acceptance of IAEA full-scope safeguards and internationally legally binding commitments not to acquire nuclear weapons or other nuclear explosive devices.

13. Nuclear fissile material transferred from military use to peaceful nuclear activities should, as soon as practicable, be placed under IAEA safeguards in the framework of the voluntary safeguards agreements in place with the nuclear-weapon States. Safeguards should be universally applied once the complete elimination of nuclear weapons has been achieved.

Peaceful uses of nuclear energy

14. Particular importance should be attached to ensuring the exercise of the inalienable right of all the parties to the Treaty to develop research, production and use of nuclear energy for peaceful purposes without discrimination and in conformity with articles I, II as well as III of the Treaty.

15. Undertakings to facilitate participation in the fullest possible exchange of equipment, materials and scientific and technological information for the peaceful uses of nuclear energy should be fully implemented.

16. In all activities designed to promote the peaceful uses of nuclear energy, preferential treatment should be given to the non-nuclear-weapon States party to the Treaty, taking the needs of developing countries particularly into account.

17. Transparency in nuclear-related export controls should be promoted within the framework of dialogue and cooperation among all interested States party to the Treaty.

18. All States should, through rigorous national measures and international cooperation, maintain the highest practicable levels of nuclear safety, including in waste management, and observe standards and guidelines in nuclear materials accounting, physical protection and transport of nuclear materials.

19. Every effort should be made to ensure that the IAEA has the financial and human resources necessary in order to meet effectively its responsibilities in the areas of technical cooperation, safeguards and nuclear safety. The IAEA should also be encouraged to intensify its efforts aimed at finding ways and means for funding technical assistance through predictable and assured resources.

20. Attacks or threats of attack on nuclear facilities devoted to peaceful purposes jeopardize nuclear safety and raise serious concerns regarding the application of international law on the use of force in such cases, which could warrant appropriate action in accordance with the provisions of the Charter of the United Nations.

The Conference requests that the President of the Conference bring this decision, the Decision on Strengthening the Review Process for the Treaty and the Decision on the Extension of the Treaty to the attention of the heads of State or Government of all States and seek their full cooperation on these documents and in the furtherance of the goals of the Treaty.

Membership in the Regime

Country	NPT[a]	CWC[b]	BWC[c]	CTBT[d]	MTCR
Afghanistan	†	S	†		
Albania	†	†	†	S	
Algeria	†	†		S#	
Antigua and Barbuda	†			S	
Andorra	†			S	
Angola	†			S	
Argentina	†	†	†	S#R	†
Armenia	†	†	†	S	
Australia	†	†	†	S#R	†
Austria	†	†	†	S#R	†
Azerbaijan	†	S		SR	
Bahamas, The	†	S	†		
Bahrain	†	†	†	S	
Bangladesh	†	†	†	S#	
Barbados			†		
Belarus	†	†	†	S	
Belgium	†	†	†	S#	†
Belize	†		†		
Benin	†	†	†	S	
Bhutan	†	S	†		
Bolivia	†	†	†	S	
Bosnia & Herzegovina	†	†	†	S	
Botswana	†	S	†		
Brazil	†	S	†	S#R	†
Brunei	†	S	†	S	
Bulgaria	†	†	†	S#	
Burkina Faso	†	†	†	S	
Burundi	†	†	S	S	
Cambodia	†	S	†	S	
Cameroon	†	†			
Canada	†	†	†	S#R	
Cape Verde	†	S	†	S	
Central African Republic	†	S	S		
Chad	†	S		S	

Country	NPT[a]	CWC[b]	BWC[c]	CTBT[d]	MTCR
Chile	†	†	†	S#	
China	†	†	†	S#	
Colombia	†	S	†	S#	
Comoros	†	S		S	
Congo, Republic of (Brazzaville)	†			S	
Congo, Democratic Republic of (Kinshasa)	†	S	†	S#	
Cook Islands		†		S	
Costa Rica	†	†	†	S	
Côte d'Ivoire	†	†	S	S	
Croatia	†	†	†	S	
Cuba		†	†		
Cyprus	†	†	†	S	
Czech Republic		†	†	SR	
Denmark	†	†	†	SR	†
Djibouti	†	S		S	
Dominica	†	S	†		
Dominican Republic	†	S	†	S	
Ecuador	†	†	†	S	
Egypt	†		S	S#	
El Salvador	†	†	†	SR	
Equatorial Guinea	†	†	†	S	
Eritrea	†				
Estonia	†	S	†	S	
Ethiopia	†	†	†	S	
Fiji	†	†	†	SR	
Finland	†	†	†	S#R	†
Former Yugoslav Republic of Macedonia	†	†	†	S	
France	†	†	†	S#R	†
Gabon	†	S	S	S	
Gambia, The	†	†	†		
Georgia	†	†	†	S	
Germany, Federal Republic of	†	†	†	S#R	†
Ghana	†	†	†	S	
Greece	†	†	†	SR	†
Grenada	†	S	†	SR	
Guatemala	†	S	†		
Guinea	†	†		S	
Guinea-Bissau	†	S	†	S	
Guyana	†	†	S		
Haiti	†	S	S	S	
Holy See	†	†		S	
Honduras	†	S	†	S	
Hungary, Rep of	†	†	†	S#	†
Iceland	†	†	†	S	†
India		†	†	#	

Country	NPT[a]	CWC[b]	BWC[c]	CTBT[d]	MTCR
Indonesia	†	†	†	S#	
Iran	†	†	†	S#	
Iraq	†		†		
Ireland	†	†	†	S	†
Israel		S		S#	
Italy	†	†	†	S#R	†
Jamaica	†	S	†	S	
Japan	†	†	†	S#R	†
Jordan	†	†	†	SR	
Kazakhstan	†	S		S	
Kenya	†	†	†	S	
Kiribati	†				
Korea, Democratic People's Republic of	†		†	#	
Korea, Republic of	†	†	†	S#	
Kuwait	†	†	†	S	
Kyrgyzstan	†	S	†[e]	S	
Laos	†	†	†	S	
Latvia	†	†	†	S	
Lebanon	†		†		
Lesotho	†	†	†	S	
Liberia	†	S	S	S	
Libya	†		†		
Liechtenstein	†	S	†	S	
Lithuania	†	†	†	S	
Luxembourg	†	†	†	SR	†
Madagascar	†	S	S	S	
Malawi	†	†	S	S	
Malaysia	†	S	†	S	
Maldive Islands	†	†	†	S	
Mali	†	†	S	S	
Malta	†	†	†	S	
Marshall Islands	†	S		S	
Mauritania	†	†		S	
Mauritius	†	†	†		
Mexico	†	†	†	S#	
Micronesia	†	S		SR	
Moldova	†	†		S	
Monaco	†	†		SR	
Mongolia	†	†	†	SR	
Morocco	†	†	S	S	
Mozambique	†			S	
Myanmar (Burma)	†		S	S	
Namibia	†	†		S	
Nauru	†	S			
Nepal	†	†	S	S	
Netherlands	†	†	†	S#R	†
New Zealand	†	†	†	SR	†
Nicaragua	†	S	†	S	

Country	NPT[a]	CWC[b]	BWC[c]	CTBT[d]	MTCR
Niger	†	†	†	S	
Nigeria	†	†	†		
Norway	†	†	†	S#	†
Oman	†	†	†		
Pakistan		†	†	#	
Palau	†				
Panama	†	†	†	SR	
Papua New Guinea	†	†	†	S	
Paraguay	†	†	†	S	
Peru	†	†	†	S#R	
Philippines	†	†	†	S	
Poland	†	†	†	S#R	
Portugal	†	†	†	S	
Qatar	†	†	†	SR	
Romania	†	†	†	S#	
Russia	†[f]	†	†	S#	†
Rwanda	†	S	†		
St. Kitts and Nevis	†	S	†		
St. Lucia	†	†	†	S	
St. Vincent & the Grenadines	†	S			
Samoa		S		S	
San Marino	†	S	†	S	
Sao Tome & Principe	†		†	S	
Saudi Arabia	†	†	†		
Senegal	†	†	†	S	
Seychelles	†	†	†	S	
Sierra Leone	†	S	†		
Singapore	†	†	†	S	
Slovakia	†	†	†	S#R	
Slovenia	†	†	†	S	
Solomon Islands	†		†	S	
Somalia	†		S		
South Africa	†	†	†	S#R	†
Spain	†	†	†	S#R	†
Sri Lanka	†	†	†	S	
Sudan	†	†			
Suriname	†	†	†	S	
Swaziland	†	†	†	S	
Sweden	†	†	†	S#R	†
Switzerland	†	†	†	S#	†
Syrian Arab Republic	†		S		
Taiwan[g]	†		†	S	
Tajikistan	†	†		SR	
Tanzania	†	†	S		
Thailand	†	S	†	S	
Togo	†	†	†	S	
Tonga	†		†		
Trinidad & Tobago	†	†			

Country	NPT[a]	CWC[b]	BWC[c]	CTBT[d]	MTCR
Tunisia	†	†	†	S	
Turkey	†	†	†	S#	†
Tuvalu	†				
Turkmenistan	†	†	†	SR	
Uganda	†	S	†	S	
Ukraine	†	†	†	S#	
United Arab Emirates	†	S	S	S	
United Kingdom	†	†	†	S#R	†
United States	†	†	†	S#	†
Uruguay	†	†	†	S	
Uzbekistan	†	†	†	SR	
Vanuatu	†		†	S	
Venezuela	†	†	†	S	
Vietnam, Socialist Republic of	†	†	†	S#	
Western Samoa	†				
Yemen	†	S	†	S	
Yugoslavia, Socialist Federal Republic of			†		
Zaire		S	†		
Zambia	†	S		S	
Zimbabwe	†	†	†		

† — Participant of the enacted treaty

S — Signed

R — Ratified

— One of the forty-four states that must deposit ratification of treaty for it to take effect.

a— As of December 1999

b— As of 24 May 1999

c— As of 17 February 1999

d— As of 1 June 1999

e— Formerly part of the Soviet Union that signed and ratified the convention on behalf of Kyrgyzstan. Date of accession is unknown, but Confidence Building Measures Data Declaration submitted to the UN in 1993.

f— Russia has given notice that it would continue to exercise the rights and fulfill the obligations of the former Soviet Union arising from the NPT.

g— Effective January 1, 1979, the United States recognized the government of the People's Republic of China as the sole government of China. The authorities on Taiwan state they will continue to abide by the provisions of the convention, and the United States regards them as bound by its obligations.

Nuclear Status 1999

NUCLEAR-WEAPON STATES

China, France, Russia, United Kingdom, United States

Each of these five states originally declared its nuclear-weapons program and was recognized under the 1968 Nuclear Non-Proliferation Treaty (NPT) as a nuclear-weapon state because it had tested a nuclear weapon prior to January 1, 1967. Estimated total nuclear warhead stockpiles: United States, 12,070; Russia, 22,500; United Kingdom, 260; France, 450; China, 400.

When the Soviet Union collapsed in late 1991, nuclear weapons remained on the territory of many of the new independent states. Strategic nuclear weapons remained in three besides Russia: Belarus, Kazakhstan, and Ukraine. Russia was recognized as the Soviet Union's sole nuclear-weapon-state successor. All tactical nuclear weapons were withdrawn to Russia by June 1992. Russia assumed control over all Soviet nuclear weapons, and all strategic nuclear weapons were withdrawn to Russia by November 1996—completing an unprecedented denuclearization process (see renunciations below).

NON-NPT NUCLEAR-WEAPON STATES

India, Israel, Pakistan

Both India and Pakistan conducted nuclear explosives tests in May 1998 and declared themselves nuclear-weapon states. Neither is an NPT member, and neither is recognized by the NPT or other international treaties as a nuclear-weapon state. Neither is believed to have deployed nuclear weapons as of June 1998, but India is considered to be able to assemble sixty to seventy weapons, and Pakistan about fifteen weapons, on short notice. Israel, which also is not an NPT member, has not declared its nuclear weapon capability but is believed to have an operational arsenal of over one hundred weapons.

HIGH-RISK STATES

Iran, Iraq, Libya, North Korea

All are suspected of seeking nuclear weapons but are currently subject to international controls and technological constraints. Although these states are party to the NPT and have denied seeking nuclear weapons, their non-proliferation commitments are still considered suspect. North Korea is closest to having nuclear weapons; it agreed to freeze and ultimately dismantle its nuclear-weapons program under the October 1994 U.S.–North Korean Agreed Framework; it may have separated enough weapon-grade material for a nuclear device. Iran is eight to ten years from nuclear weapons—but could accelerate its program if nuclear

HIGH-RISK STATES *continued*

assets leaked from the former Soviet Union. Iraq's extensive nuclear program was dismantled by UN inspectors, but clandestine procurement efforts and nuclear-weapons-related research probably continue. Libya has an extremely limited nuclear infrastructure.

RENUNCIATIONS

Algeria, Argentina, Belarus, Brazil, Kazakhstan, Romania, South Africa, Ukraine

South Africa dismantled its arsenal of six nuclear weapons in the early 1990s and signed the NPT in 1991; the IAEA has verified complete dismantlement of all nuclear devices. Belarus, Kazakhstan, and Ukraine fulfilled earlier commitments to non–nuclear weapon status and cooperated with Russia's removal of all strategic and tactical nuclear weapons located on their territory after the Soviet Union collapsed. The three joined the NPT as non-nuclear-weapon states and opened all of their nuclear facilities to IAEA inspections by the end of 1996. Argentina and Brazil each brought into force the Treaty of Tlatelolco and agreed to implement a system of comprehensive IAEA and bilateral inspections; Argentina acceded to the NPT in February 1995. Algeria acceded to the NPT in January 1995. Romania, under the Ceausescu regime, apparently pursued a nuclear-weapons-development program that included experimental plutonium extraction not subject to IAEA monitoring; after Ceausescu's overthrow in 1989, the Iliescu government terminated the program.

ABSTAINING COUNTRIES

Australia, Belgium, Bulgaria, Canada, the Czech Republic, Denmark, Finland, Germany, Hungary, Italy, Japan, Mexico, the Netherlands, Norway, Slovakia, South Korea, Spain, Sweden, Switzerland, and Taiwan

All are countries with a significant industrial base and at least one commercial-scale nuclear facility. Several had seriously explored a nuclear-weapons option in the 1960s of 1970s, but all have signed the NPT as non–nuclear weapon states, have accepted comprehensive IAEA inspections, and are believed to be in compliance with their NPT obligations.

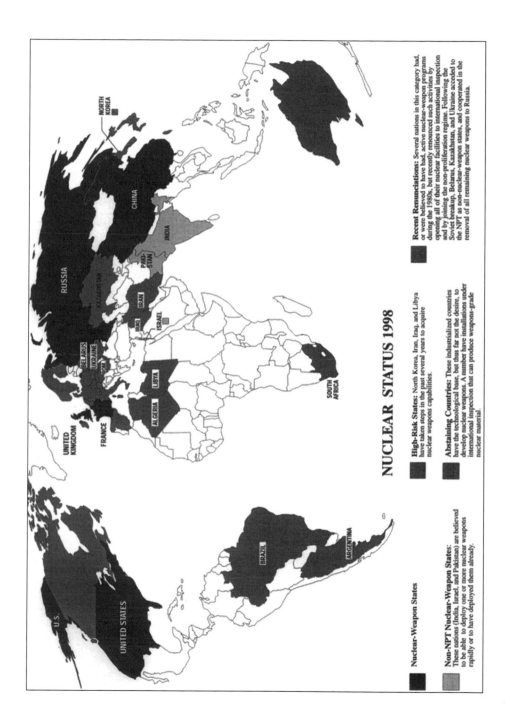

NUCLEAR STATUS 1998

High-Risk States: North Korea, Iran, Iraq, and Libya have taken steps in the past several years to acquire nuclear weapons capabilities.

Abstaining Countries: These industrialized countries have the technological base, but thus far not the desire, to develop nuclear weapons. A number have installations under international inspection that can produce weapons-grade nuclear material.

Recent Renunciations: Several nations in this category had, or were believed to have had, active nuclear-weapon programs during the 1980s, but recently renounced such activities by opening all of their nuclear facilities to international inspection and by joining the non-proliferation regime. Following the Soviet breakup, Belarus, Kazakhstan, and Ukraine acceded to the NPT as non-nuclear-weapon states, and cooperated in the removal of all remaining nuclear weapons to Russia.

Nuclear-Weapon States

Non-NPT Nuclear-Weapon States: These nations (India, Israel, and Pakistan) are believed to be able to deploy one or more nuclear weapons rapidly or to have deployed them already.

Estimated Nuclear Stockpiles 1990–2000

Year	United States	USSR Russia	United Kingdom	France	China
1990	21,000	38,000	300	504	432
1991	19,500	35,000	300	538	434
1992	18,200	33,500	300	538	434
1993	16,750	32,000	300	524	434
1994	15,380	30,000	250	512	400
1995	14,000	28,000	300	500	400
1996	12,900	26,000	300	500	400
1997	12,425	24,000	260	450	400
1998	11,425	22,000	260	450	400
1999	10,925	20,000	185	450	400
2000	10,500	20,000	185	450	400

Source: Natural Resources Defense Council. Includes strategic and tactical nuclear weapons in the active and reserve stockpiles, but does not include weapons awaiting dismantlement.

Examples of Biological Warfare Agents[a]

BW Agent (causative organism)	Incubation Period[b] (days)	Symptoms/ Clinical Manifestations[c]	Vaccine Available?	Direct Person-to-Person Aerosol Transmission?	Weaponized U.S.[d] FSU Iraq		
Bacterial Agents							
Anthrax (*Bacillus anthracis*)	2–43[e]	Fever, malaise, and fatigue, which may be followed by an improvement in symptoms for 2–3 days. Alternatively, initial symptoms may progress directly to severe respiratory distress. Death normally follows within 24–36 hours of initiation of symptoms. 80–90% fatality rate if untreated.	Yes	No	X	X	X
Brucellosis (*Brucella suis*)		Fever, chills, malaise. Symptoms may last for weeks or months. Fatalities in less than 5% of untreated patients.	No	No	X	X	
Glanders (*Burkholderia mallei*)		Fever, sweats, muscle pain, headache, chest pain, and generalized papular/pustular eruptions. Almost always fatal without treatment.	No	No		X	

a. The Non-Proliferation Project would like to thank Dr. Thomas Inglesby of the Johns Hopkins Center for Civilian Biodefense studies for reviewing this table.

b. Incubation periods apply to inhalation of the causative organism.

c. Symptoms/clinical manifestations apply to inhalation of the causative organism.

d. The United States' offensive BW program was unilaterally terminated by executive order in 1969. All offensive biological research and production were discontinued, and pathogen and biological weapon stockpiles were destroyed.

e. Military textbooks often cite an incubation period of 1–5 days. However, the 1979 accidental aerosolized release of anthrax spores from a military microbiology facility in Sverdlovsk, Russia, resulted in cases from 2 to 43 days following exposure.

BW Agent (causative organism)	Incubation Period (days)	Symptoms/ Clinical Manifestations	Vaccine Available?	Direct Person-to-Person Aerosol Transmission?	Weaponized U.S. FSU Iraq		
Bacterial Agents							
Tularemia (*Francisella tularensis*)		Fever, exhaustion, and weight loss. 35% fatality if untreated.	Yes[f]	No	X	X	
(Pneumonic) Plague (*Yersinia pestis*)	2–3	Pneumonia with malaise, high fever, chills, headache, muscle pain, and productive cough with bloody sputum. Progresses rapidly, resulting in shortness of breath, stridor, bluish discoloration of skin and mucous membranes. Untreated pneumonic plague is usually fatal.	No[g]	High			X
Viral Agents							
Smallpox (*Variola major*)	7–17	Initial symptoms include fever, malaise, vomiting, headache, and backache. Rash and lesions develop in 2–3 days on face, hands, and forearms, followed by the lower extremities and then centrally. Fatalities in 20–40% of untreated patients.	Yes[h]	High			X
Venezuelan equine encephalitis (*VEE*)	2–6	Initial symptoms include general malaise, severe headache, and fever. Full recovery usually occurs within 1–2 weeks. Fatalities in less than 1% of untreated patients.	Yes[i]	Low	X	X	

f. Investigational new drug.

g. Vaccine is available but has been shown to be ineffective against aerosol challenge.

h. Vaccine is available in limited quantities. Initiative in progress to augment supplies.

i. Investigational new drug.

BW Agent (causative organism)	Incubation Period (days)	Symptoms/ Clinical Manifestations[1]	Vaccine Available?	Direct Person-to-Person Aerosol Transmission?	Weaponized U.S.	FSU	Iraq
Viral Agents							
Viral hemorrhagic fevers (RNA viruses from several families, incl. Filiviridae •Ebola •Marburg Arenaviridae •Lassa •Junin •Machupo Flaviviridae •Yellow fever Bunyaviridae •Congo •Crimean Hemorrhagic Fever •Rift Valley Fever)	4–21	Fever, muscle aches, and exhaustion. Can be complicated by easy bleeding, hypotension, flushing of the face and chest, and edema.	No[j]	Unclear[k]		X[l]	
Rickettsial Agents							
Q fever *(Coxiella burnetti)*	10–40	Fever, chills, headache, excessive sweating, malaise, fatigue, loss of appetite, weight loss.	Yes[m]	Rare	X	X	
Typhus *(Rickettsia prowazekii)*	14	Severe headache, sustained high fever, depression, delirium, and eruption of red rashes on the skin. Fatalities in 30% of untreated patients.	Yes[n]	No		X	

j. Licensed vaccine available for yellow fever. A vaccine for Argentine hemorrhagic fever is available as an investigational new drug. This vaccine may provide cross protection against Bolivian hemorrhagic fever.

k. It is unclear how easily filoviruses can be transmitted from human to human. Transmission clearly occurs via direct contact with infected blood, secretions, organs, or semen.

l. According to Alibek, the Soviet program weaponized the Marburg virus.

m. Investigational new drug.

n. Vaccine production in the United States has been discontinued.

BW Agent (causative organism)	Incubation Period (days)	Symptoms/ Clinical Manifestations	Vaccine Available?	Direct Person to Person Aerosol Transmission?	Weaponized U.S. FSU Iraq

Viral Agents

BW Agent (causative organism)	Incubation Period (days)	Symptoms/ Clinical Manifestations	Vaccine Available?	Direct Person to Person Aerosol Transmission?	U.S.	FSU	Iraq
Aflatoxin (Aspergillus flavus and Aspergillus parasiticus)	Years to decades	Powerful liver carcinogen. Aflatoxicosis in humans has been reported following ingestion of contaminated food. Short-term effects include vomiting, abdominal pain, pulmonary edema, gastrointestinal hemorrhage, convulsions, coma, and death. The only documented health effect from low-level exposure is an increased prevalence of liver cancer years to decades after exposure.	No	No			X
Botulinum toxin (Clostridium botulinum)	1–2	Ptosis, generalized weakness, dizziness, dry mouth, blurred vision, and difficulty in speaking and swallowing. Progression to muscle paralysis and respiratory failure.	Yes°	No	X		X
Ricin (castor beans)	18–24 hours	Weakness, fever, cough, and pulmonary edema. Progression to severe respiratory distress and death within 36–72 hours.	No	No			
Staphylococcal enterotoxin b (Staphylococcus aureus)	18–24 hours	Sudden onset of fever, chills, headache, muscle pain, and nonproductive cough. Fever may last for 2–5 days. Cough may persist for 4 weeks.	No	No	X		

°· Investigational new drug.

Sources: David R. Franz, Peter B. Jahrling et al., "Clinical Recognition and Managementof Patients Exposed to Biological Warfare Agents," Journal of the American Medical Association (JAMA) 278, no. 5 (August 6, 1997) 399–411; Col. Edward Eitzen, Maj. Julie Pavlin et al., eds., Medical Management of Biological Casuaties Handbook, found at http://www.nbcmed.org/SiteContent/MedRef/OnlineRef/Field-Manuals/medmaHandbook.htm.

Mitretek Systems, *Background on Biological Warfare,* located at http://www.mitretek.-org/mission/envene/biological/bio_back.html.

Presidential Advisory Committee on Gulf War Veterans' Illnesses: Final Report (December 1996), located at http://ww.pbs.org/wgbh/pages/frontline/shows/syndrome/analysis/biowarfare.html.

George W. Christopher, Theodore J. Cieslak et al., "Biological Warfare: A Historical Perspective," *Journal of the American Medical Association* (JAMA), 278, no. 5 (August 6, 1997): 412–17.

Kenneth Alibek, statement before the Joint Economic Committee, Terrorism and Intelligence Operations: *Hearing before the Joint Economic Committee,* 105th Cong., 2d Sess., May 20, 1998, located at http://www.house.gov/jec/hearings/intell,alibek.htm.

Organization for the Prohibition of Chemical Weapons, *Toxins: Potential Chemical Weapons from Living Organisms,* located at http://www.opcw.nl/chemhaz/toxins.htm.

Thomas V. Inglesby, Donald A. Henderson, John G. Bartlett et al., "Anthrax as a Biological Weapon; Medical and Public Health Management," *Journal of the American Medical Association,* 281, no. 18 (May 12, 1999) 1735–45.

Frederick R. Sidell, William C. Patrick III, Thomas R. Dashiell, *Jane's Chem-Bio Handbook* (London: Jane's Information Group, 1998).

Examples of Chemical Warfare Agents

Agent Type	Agent Identification and Common Name	Mechanism	Time for Effect	Symptoms
Nerve agents	GA, tabun GB, sarin GD, soman GF, cyclohexyl sarin VX	These agents effectively prevent the transmission of nerve signals by inhibiting the enzyme cholinesterase. This enzyme normally breaks down acetylcholine, the neurotransmitter released by nerves to stimulate smooth and skeletal muscles, the central nervous system, and most exocrine glands. The result of nerve agent inhibition of cholinesterase leads to accumulation of acetylcholine, causing continued over-stimulation of target organs and clinical symptoms such as muscle paralysis.	**Vapor:** Within seconds to several minutes after exposure. **Liquid:** Within minutes to an hour after exposure. Commonly, there is an asymptomatic period of one to thirty minutes, which is followed by a sudden onset of symptoms.	**Vapor:** *Small exposure:* contraction of pupils, dim vision, headache, runny nose, shortness of breath. *Large exposure:* sudden loss of consciousness, severe breathing difficulty or cessation of respiration, convulsions, muscular twitching, weakness or paralysis, copious secretions. **Liquid on skin:** *Small to moderate exposure:* localized sweating, muscle twitching at site of exposure, vomiting, nausea, diarrhea. *Large exposure:* severe breathing difficulty or cessation of breathing, sudden loss of consciousness, convulsions, muscle twitching, weakness or paralysis, copious secretions.

Agent Type	Agent Identification and Common Name	Mechanism	Time for Effect	Symptoms
Vesicants	H, HD mustard L, lewisite CX, phosgene oxime	Following absorption, the structure of mustard changes. In this form, it is extremely reactive to water and binds with intra- and extracellular enzymes and proteins. Lewisite causes an increase in capillary permeability. The exact mechanisms of mustard, lewisite, and phosgene oxime are not known.	**Mustard:** Binds irreversibly to tissue within several minutes after contact. Clinical signs and symptoms may appear as early as two hours after a high-dose exposure or extend to twenty-four hours after a low-dose vapor exposure. Exposure does not cause immediate pain. **Lewisite:** Immediate pain or irritation. Lesions develop within hours. **Phosgene oxime:** Immediate burning and irritation.	**Mustard:** Skin, eyes, and airways most commonly affected. Appearance of redness and blisters on skin, irritation, conjunctivitis and corneal opacity and damage in the eyes, irritation of nares, sinus and pharynx and increasingly severe productive cough if the lower airways are affected. **Lewisite:** Skin, eyes, and airways affected by direct contact. Redness and blister formation occur more rapidly than following exposure to mustard. Eye exposure causes pain and twitching of the eyelid. Edema of the conjunctiva and lids follow, and eyes may be swollen shut within an hour. Contact with airways leads to similar signs and symptoms to mustard. Increased permeability of capillaries resulting in low intravascular volume and shock. May lead to hepatic or renal necrosis with vomiting and diarrhea. **Phosgene oxime:** Does not cause blisters. Elongated, wheal-like lesions on skin. Damage to eyes similar to that caused by Lewisite. Causes pulmonary edema.

Agent Type	Agent Identification and Common Name	Mechanism	Time for Effect	Symptoms
Cyanide	AC, hydrocyanic acid CK, cyanogen chloride	Cyanide ion combines with iron in a component of the mitochondrial cytochrome oxidase complex. This complex is necessary for cellular respiration, an energy-providing process using oxygen. If respiration is prevented, then cells cannot utilize oxygen and cell death occurs.	Death occurs six to eight minutes after inhalation.	**Cyanide**: *Small exposure:* No effects. *Moderate exposure:* Dizziness, nausea, feeling of weakness. *Large exposure:* Central nervous system and heart are most susceptible to cyanide. 15 seconds after inhalation of a highly concentrated vapor, there is a period of rapid breathing which is followed in 15–30 seconds by convulsions. Respiratory activity stops 2–3 minutes later, followed by cessation of cardiac activity. **Cyanogen Chloride**: *Small exposure:* Irritation, nausea, feeling of weakness. *Large exposure:* Similar symptoms as those following large exposure to cyanide.

Sources: Frederick R. Sidell, William C. Patrick III, Thomas R. Dashiell, *Jane's Chem-Bio Handbook* (London: Jane's Information Group, 1998).

United States Army Medical Research Institute of Chemical Defense, *Medical Management of Chemical Casualties Handbook*, April 1995, located at http://chemdef.apgea.army.mil/ChemCasu/titlepg. htm.

Mitretek Systems, *Background on Chemical Warfare*, located at http://ww.mitretek.org/mission/envene/-chemical/chem_back.html.

Organization for the Prohibition of Chemical Weapons, *Chemical Warfare Agents: An Overview of Chemicals Defined as Chemical Weapons*, located at http://www.opcw.nl/chemhaz/cwagents.htm.

Acronyms

ABM	Antiballistic Missile
ACRS	Arms Control Regional Security Group
ASEAN	Association of South East Asian Nations
BW	Biological Weapons
BWC	Biological and Toxin Weapons Convention
CBW	Chemical and Biological Weapons
CD	United Nations Conference on Disarmament
CFE	Conventional Forces in Europe
CTBT	Cooperative Test Ban Treaty
CW	Chemical Weapons
CWC	Chemical Weapons Convention
DOD	U.S. Department of Defense
DOE	U.S. Department of Energy
FMCT	Fissile Material Cut-Off Treaty
GA	General Assembly
GDR	Global Depository Receipts
HEU	Highly Enriched Uranium
IAEA	International Atomic Energy Agency
ICBM	Intercontinental Ballistic Missile
IDB	Islamic Development Bank
IFI(s)	International Financial Institution(s)
IMF	International Monetary Fund
INF	Intermediate Nuclear Forces
IPP	Initiatives for Proliferation Prevention
IRBM	Intermediate-Range Ballistic Missile
ISTC	International Science and Technology Center
LEU	Low-Enriched Uranium
MIRV	Multiple Independently Targeted Re-entry Vehicle

MOD	Ministry of Defense
MOX	Mixed Oxide Fuel
MPC&A	Materials Protection, Control, and Accounting
MRBM	Medium-Range Ballistic Missile
MTCR	Missile Technology Control Regime
NAC	New Agenda Coalition
NAS	National Academy of Sciences
NCA	National Command Authority
NCI	Nuclear Cities Initiative
NGO	Nongovernmental Organization
NMD	National Missile Defense
NPT	Nuclear Non-Proliferation Treaty
NSG	Nuclear Suppliers Group
NWS	Nuclear-Weapon State
OPIC	Overseas Private Investment Corporation
SALT	Strategic Arms Limitation Treaty
SLBM	Submarine-Launched Ballistic Missile
SLV	Space Launch Vehicle
SSBN	Strategic Nuclear Submarine
START	Strategic Arms Reduction Treaty
TLE	Treaty-Limited Equipment
TMD	Theater Missile Defense
UNESCO	United Nations Educational, Scientific, and Cultural Organization
UNGA	United Nations General Assembly
UNSCOM	United Nations Special Commission on Iraq
USAID	U.S. Agency for International Development
USEC	United States Enrichment Corporation
WMD	Weapons of Mass Destruction

ABOUT THE CONTRIBUTORS

David Albright is president of the Institute for Science and International Security.

Alexei Arbatov is a member of the State Duma of the Russian Federation, elected by the federal list of Russian main democratic party "YABLOKO." On the Defense Committee he is responsible for the elaboration of the defense budget and processing of arms control treaties.

Robert Bell is the special assistant to the president for national security affairs and counselor to the assistant to the president for national security affairs.

Samuel R. Berger is assistant to the president of the United States for national security affairs.

Bruce Blair is a senior fellow in the Foreign Policy Studies Program at the Brookings Institution.

Matthew Bunn is assistant director of the Science, Technology and Public Policy Program in the Belfer Center for Science and International Affairs at Harvard University's John F. Kennedy School of Government.

Richard Butler is the former executive chairman of the United Nations Special Commission on Iraq (UNSCOM).

Michael Carriere is a junior fellow at the Carnegie Endowment for International Peace.

Jayantha Dhanapala is undersecretary-general for disarmament affairs at the United Nations. He served as president of the 1995 Review and Extension Conference for the Non-Proliferation Treaty.

Benjamin Frankel is the editor of *Security Studies*.

Robert Gallucci is dean of Georgetown University's School of Foreign Service, and the Department of State's special envoy for ballistic missile and WMD proliferation.

Rose Gottemoeller is assistant secretary of energy for nonproliferation and national security at the U.S. Department of Energy.

Ambassador Thomas Graham Jr. is the president of the Lawyers Alliance for World Security. He served as the president's special representative for arms control, nonproliferation, and disarmament from 1994 to 1997.

Camille Grand is currently a lecturer in strategic studies at the Ecole spéciale militaire de St Cyr-Coëtquidan (French Army College) and in international politics at the *Institut d'études politiques de Paris*. Grand is an analyst on international security and disarmament based in Paris.

Khidhir Hamza is a senior fellow at the Institute for Science and International Security and is the former head of the Iraqi Nuclear Weaponization Program.

Elisa Harris is the director for non-proliferation and export controls, National Security Council.

Bruce Jentleson is a senior fellow at the United States Institute of Peace.

Neil Joeck is a political analyst in the Directorate for Nonproliferation, Arms Control, and International Security at the Lawrence Livermore National Laboratory.

Michael Krepon is the president of the Henry L. Stimson Center.

Marina Laker is a nuclear officer with the Department of Foreign Affairs and International Trade, Canada.

Ariel Levite is the head of Israel's Bureau of International Security and Arms Control.

Patricia Lewis is the director of the United Nations Institute for Disarmament Research.

Ken Luongo is the executive director of the Russian American Nuclear Security Advisory Council.

Darach MacFhionnbhairr is the head of disarmament and non-proliferation at the Department of Foreign Affairs of Ireland.

Luiz F. Machado is the political counselor at the Embassy of Brazil, Washington D.C.

Jessica Mathews is the president of Carnegie Endowment for International Peace.

Viktor Mizin is head of the Office for UN Peacekeeping and Sanctions at the Ministry of Foreign Affairs of the Russian Federation.

Stephen V. Mladineo is a senior program manager at Pacific Northwest National Laboratory responsible for nuclear arms control and nonproliferation programs.

Daniel Morrow was a senior associate at the Carnegie Endowment for International Peace during 1997–99. He has been on the staff of the World Bank in various positions since 1979.

Harald Müller is the program director for the Peace Research Institute Frankfurt, Nonproliferation and Disarmament Program.

Herb Okun is a member of the United Nations International Narcotics Control Board and a Lecturer at the Yale Law School. He was formerly U.S. Ambassador to the United Nations and Germany.

Alexander A. Pikayev is a scholar in residence at the Carnegie Endowment for International Peace, Moscow Center.

Bill Richardson is the United States secretary of energy.

Brad Roberts is with the Institute for Defense Analyses.

Lev Ryabev is the first deputy minister of atomic energy of the Russian Federation.

Robbie Sabel is the deputy director general of the department of Arms Control and Disarmament at Israel's Ministry of Foreign Affairs.

Richard Speier is an independent consultant in the Washington, D.C., area, specializing in nuclear and missile non-proliferation and counter-proliferation.

Jonathan B. Tucker is with the Chemical and Biological Weapons Non-Proliferation Project, Center for Nonproliferation Studies, Monterey Institute of International Studies.

Sha Zukang is director general of the Arms Control and Disarmament Division of the Ministry of Foreign Affairs, People's Republic of China.

ABOUT THE EDITOR

Joseph Cirincione has been a senior associate and director of the Carnegie Non-Proliferation Project since March 1998. He directs all aspects of the project's work, including research, publications, the Proliferation Roundtable seminar series, and the Carnegie International Non-Proliferation conferences. He is a frequent commentator on proliferation issues and is widely quoted in major publications, broadcasts, and journals.

Mr. Cirincione served for nine years (1985–1994) as a national security specialist in the U.S. House of Representatives, including six years as a member of the professional staff of the Armed Services Committee and as deputy staff director of the government Operations Subcommittee on Legislation and National Security. He had oversight responsibilities for programs on missile defense, NATO, and nuclear force posture, among other issues. From 1994 to 1998, he was a senior associate at the Henry L. Stimson Center in Washington, D.C., specializing in nuclear policy issues. Before 1985, he was associate director of the Central American Project at the Carnegie Endowment for International Peace, a special assistant to the associate director of the U.S. Information Agency, and an analyst at the Center for Strategic and International Studies.

He previously edited *Central America and the Western Alliance*, was the assistant editor of *Central America: Anatomy of Conflict*, and is the author of numerous articles and reports on national security and threat reduction issues. He is a member of the Council on Foreign Relations, the International Institute for Strategic and International Studies, the editorial board of *The Non-Proliferation Review*, and the advisory panel for the Georgetown University Masters of Science in Foreign Service Program.

Mr. Cirincione is an honors graduate of Boston College and holds a Masters of Science degree with highest honors from the Georgetown University School of Foreign Service.

INDEX